PERSONA Q Side: P4
SHADOW OF THE LABYRINTH

4

CREATED BY: **ATLUS**   MANGA BY: **MIZUNOMOTO**

PERSONA Q Side: P4
SHADOW OF THE LABYRINTH

CHARACTERS & STORY

OUR HERO

A high school second-year who recently transferred to Yasogami High School. He forms a special investigation team to solve the series of murders that has been occurring in the city.

YUKIKO AMAGI

A second-year at Yasogami High School. Her parents own the famous Amagi Inn. When she's not doing schoolwork, she helps with the family business.

CHIE SATONAKA

A second-year at Yasogami High School. Born and raised in Inaba, she is best friends with Yukiko. She loves steak and kung-fu.

YOSUKE HANAMURA

Second-year classmate of our hero, Chie, and Yukiko. Lightens the mood with his bright personality.

NAOTO SHIROGANE

A first-year in high school, and the fifth in the long line of Shirogane detectives. Came to Inaba at the police's request to help with the murder investigation.

RISE KUJIKAWA

A first-year at Yasogami High School. She is a popular idol across the country, but she suddenly transferred to Yasogami High School.

KANJI TATSUMI

An infamous problem child who is rumored to have single-handedly beaten up an entire gang when he was in middle school. He's a rare hardcore lone wolf. He's one year below our story's hero.

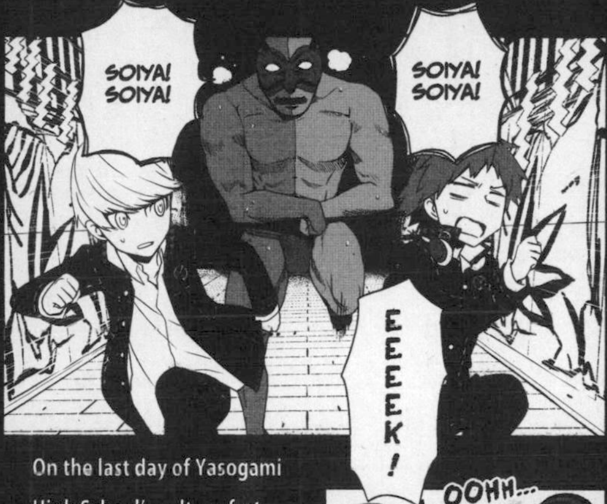
SOIYA! SOIYA!
SOIYA! SOIYA!
EEEEK!

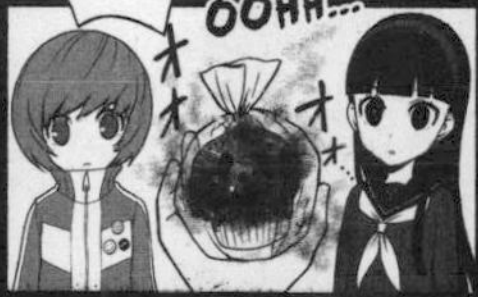
OOHH...

On the last day of Yasogami High School's culture fest, our friends from P4 got lost in another world. In the deepest depths of a labyrinth called "You in Wonderland," they were saved from disaster by the students of Gekkokan Academy, who had become lost in that world just as they had. The two groups decided to cooperate to try to find some way back to their own world...

While searching the fourth labyrinth, the Inaba Pride Exhibit, an individual F.O.E. locks on to each member and attacks. Facing enemies they can't hope to defeat with normal methods, the leaders decide to try a strategy hitherto off-limits. But just what is "Mystery Food X Combo"?!

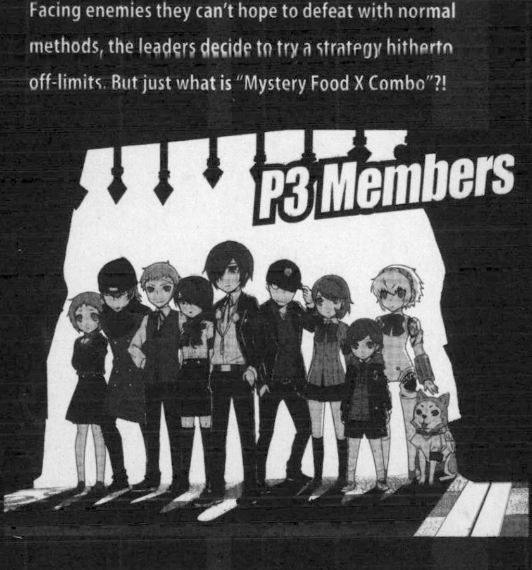
P3 Members

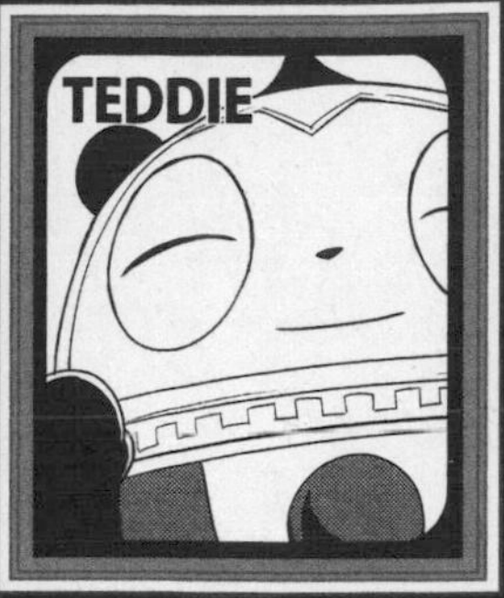
TEDDIE

A mysterious being who lives in the world inside the TV. He appears to be a costumed character, but on the inside, he is actually...

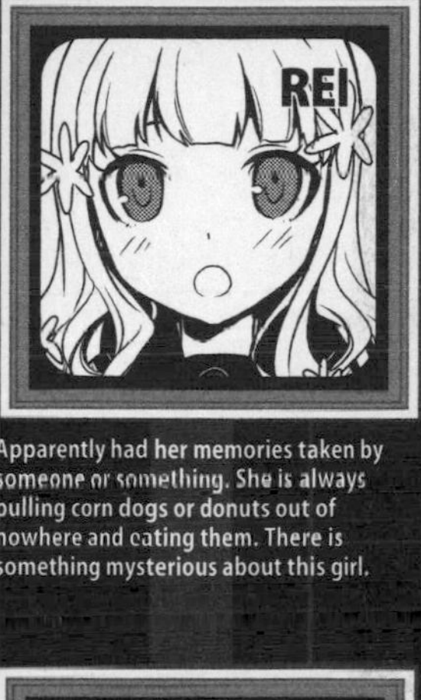
REI

Apparently had her memories taken by someone or something. She is always pulling corn dogs or donuts out of nowhere and eating them. There is something mysterious about this girl.

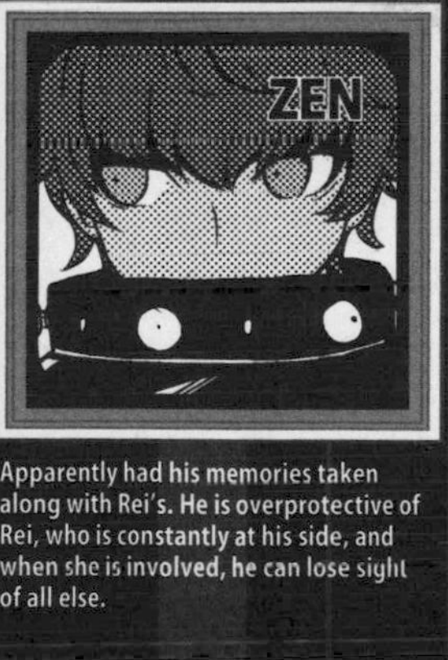
ZEN

Apparently had his memories taken along with Rei's. He is overprotective of Rei, who is constantly at his side, and when she is involved, he can lose sight of all else.

CONTENTS

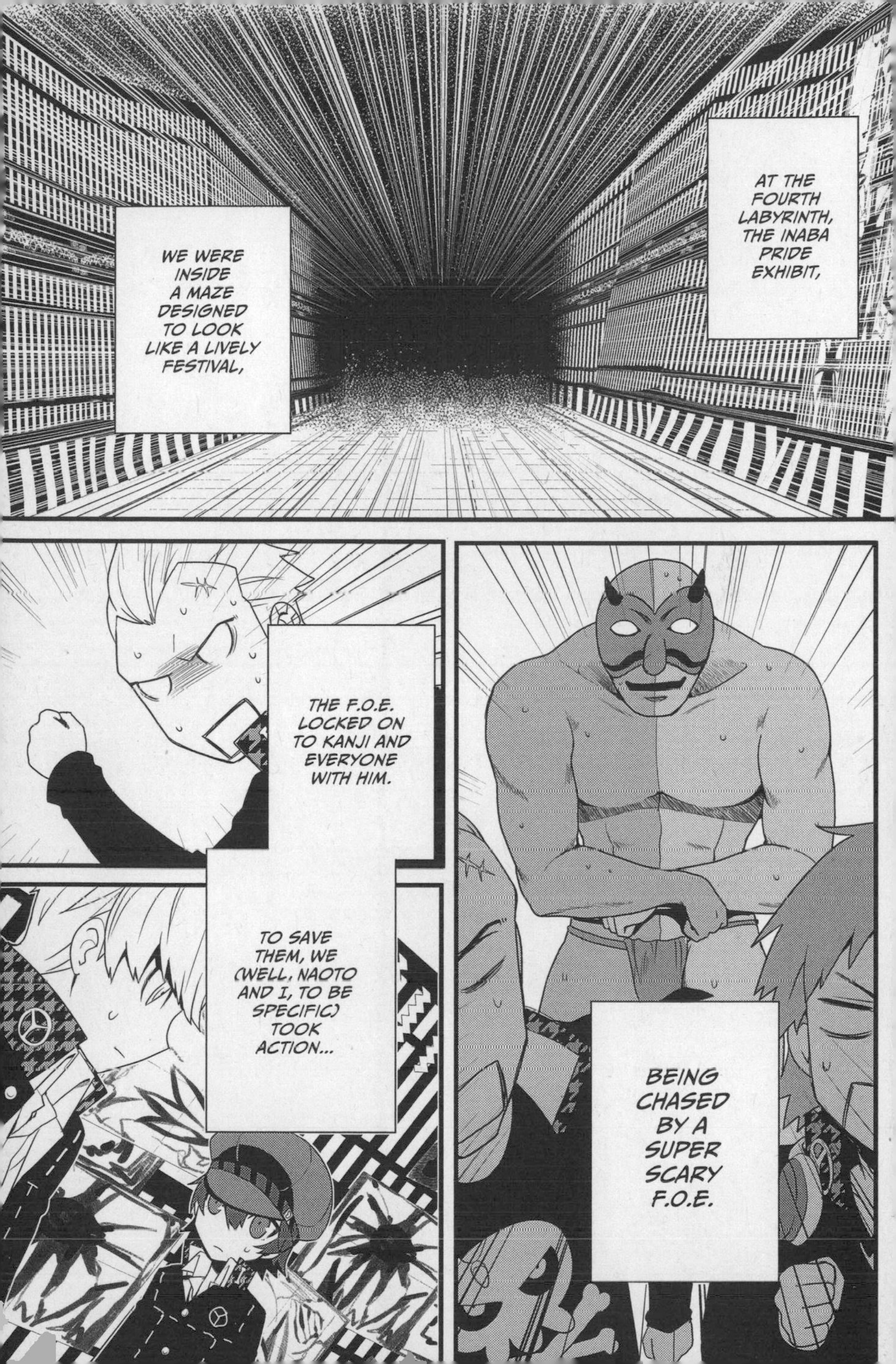
AT THE FOURTH LABYRINTH, THE INABA PRIDE EXHIBIT,
WE WERE INSIDE A MAZE DESIGNED TO LOOK LIKE A LIVELY FESTIVAL,
BEING CHASED BY A SUPER SCARY F.O.E.
THE F.O.E. LOCKED ON TO KANJI AND EVERYONE WITH HIM.
TO SAVE THEM, WE (WELL, NAOTO AND I, TO BE SPECIFIC) TOOK ACTION...

Labyrinth 19: Hazardous Material

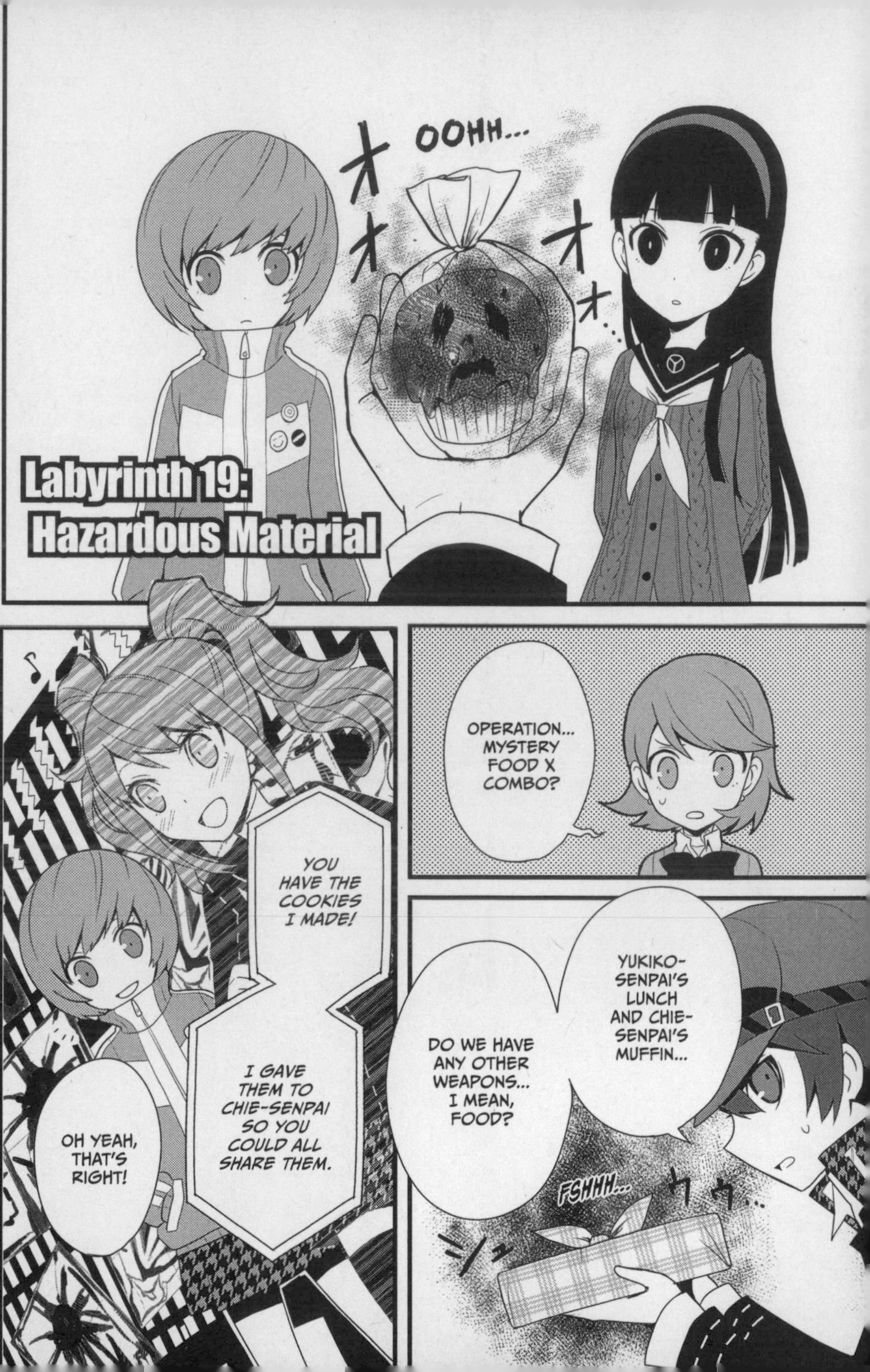
OOHH...
OPERATION... MYSTERY FOOD X COMBO?
YUKIKO-SENPAI'S LUNCH AND CHIE-SENPAI'S MUFFIN...
DO WE HAVE ANY OTHER WEAPONS... I MEAN, FOOD?
FSHHH...
YOU HAVE THE COOKIES I MADE!
I GAVE THEM TO CHIE-SENPAI SO YOU COULD ALL SHARE THEM.
OH YEAH, THAT'S RIGHT!

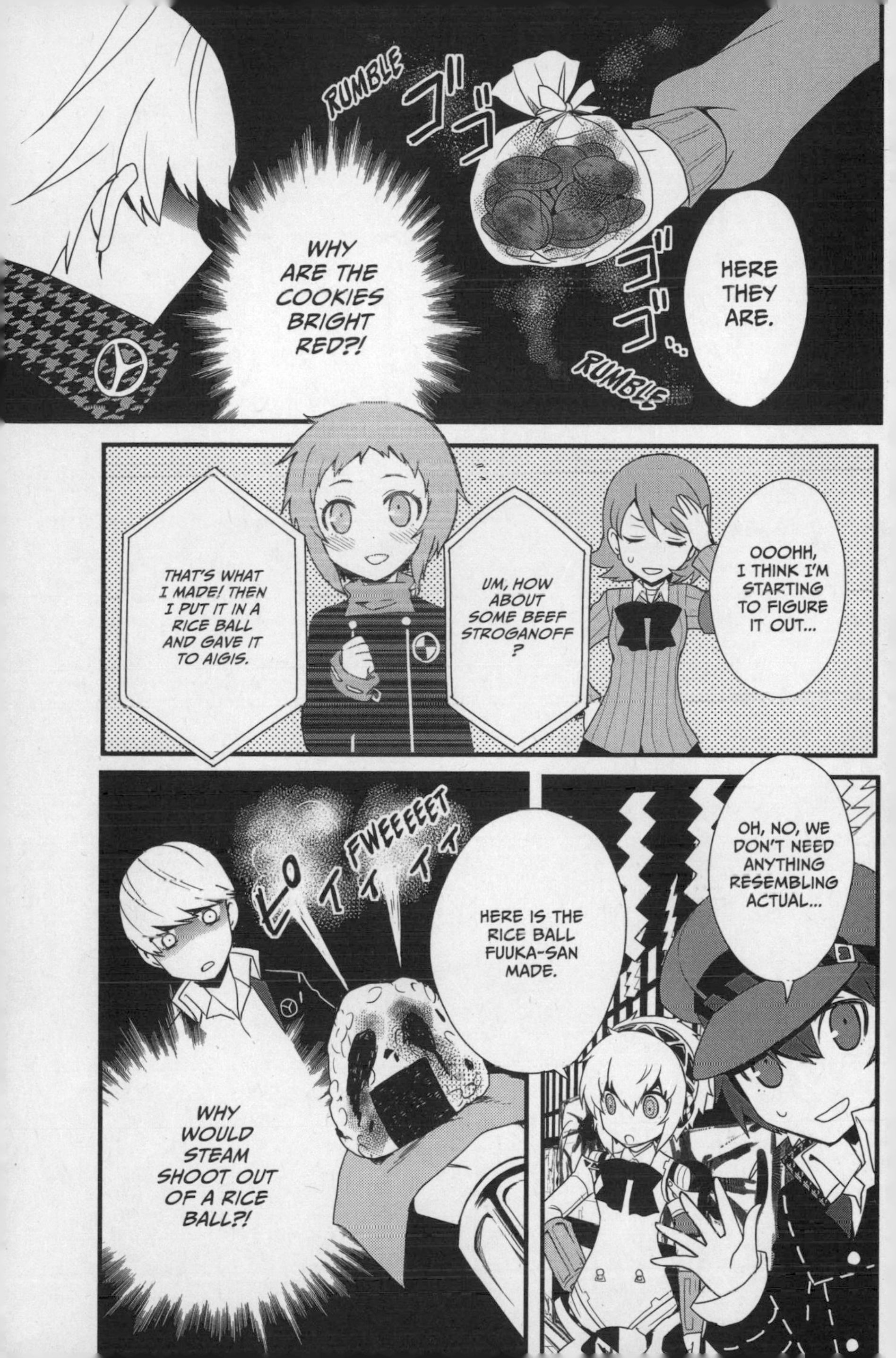
RUMBLE
ゴゴ
HERE THEY ARE.
ゴゴゴ...
RUMBLE
WHY ARE THE COOKIES BRIGHT RED?!
OOOHH, I THINK I'M STARTING TO FIGURE IT OUT...
UM, HOW ABOUT SOME BEEF STROGANOFF?
THAT'S WHAT I MADE! THEN I PUT IT IN A RICE BALL AND GAVE IT TO AIGIS.
OH, NO, WE DON'T NEED ANYTHING RESEMBLING ACTUAL...
HERE IS THE RICE BALL FUUKA-SAN MADE.
ピイイイ
FWEEEEEET
WHY WOULD STEAM SHOOT OUT OF A RICE BALL?!

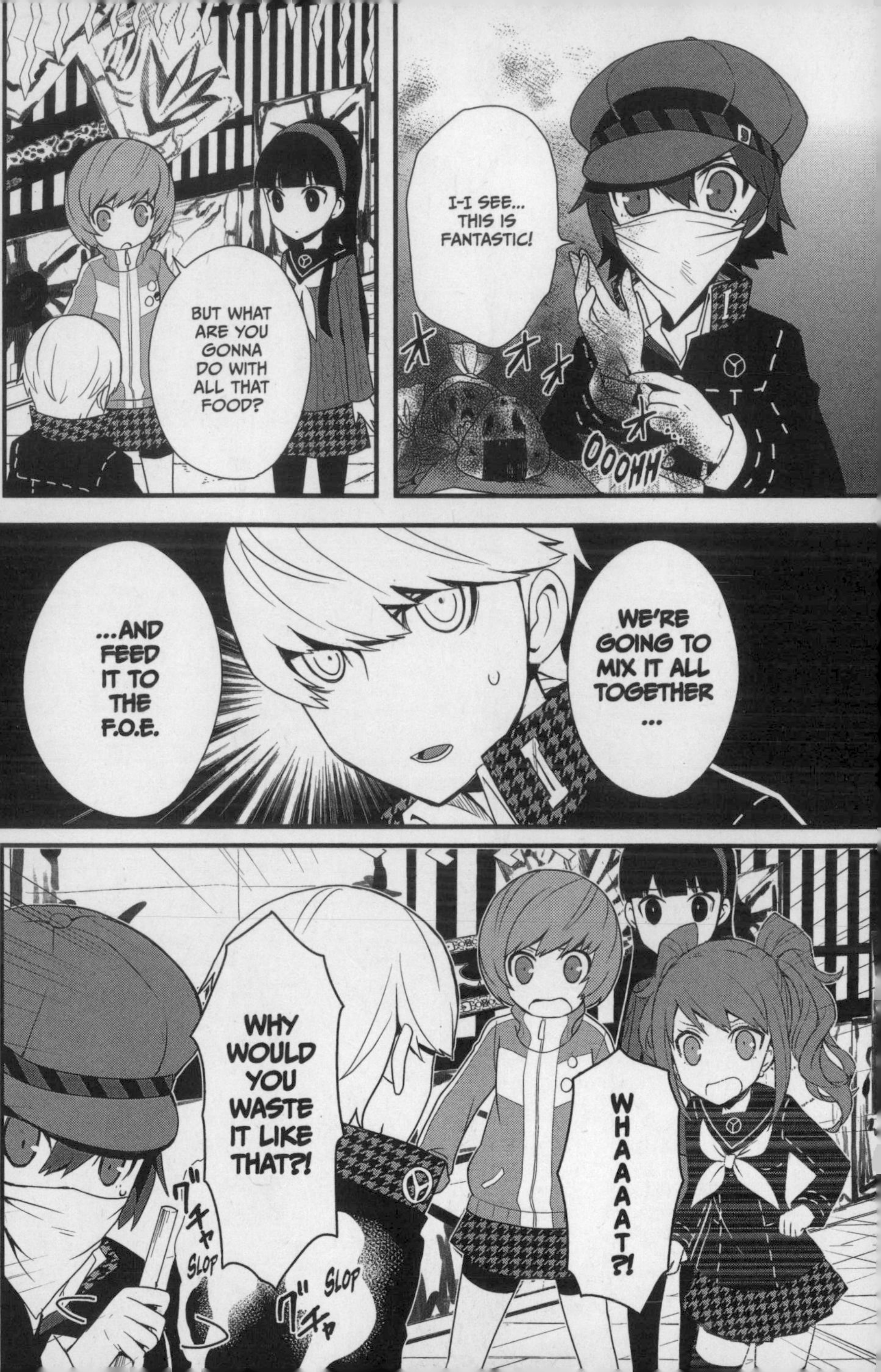
I-I SEE... THIS IS FANTASTIC!
OOOHH
BUT WHAT ARE YOU GONNA DO WITH ALL THAT FOOD?
WE'RE GOING TO MIX IT ALL TOGETHER ...
...AND FEED IT TO THE F.O.E.
WHAAAAT?!
WHY WOULD YOU WASTE IT LIKE THAT?!
SLOP
SLOP

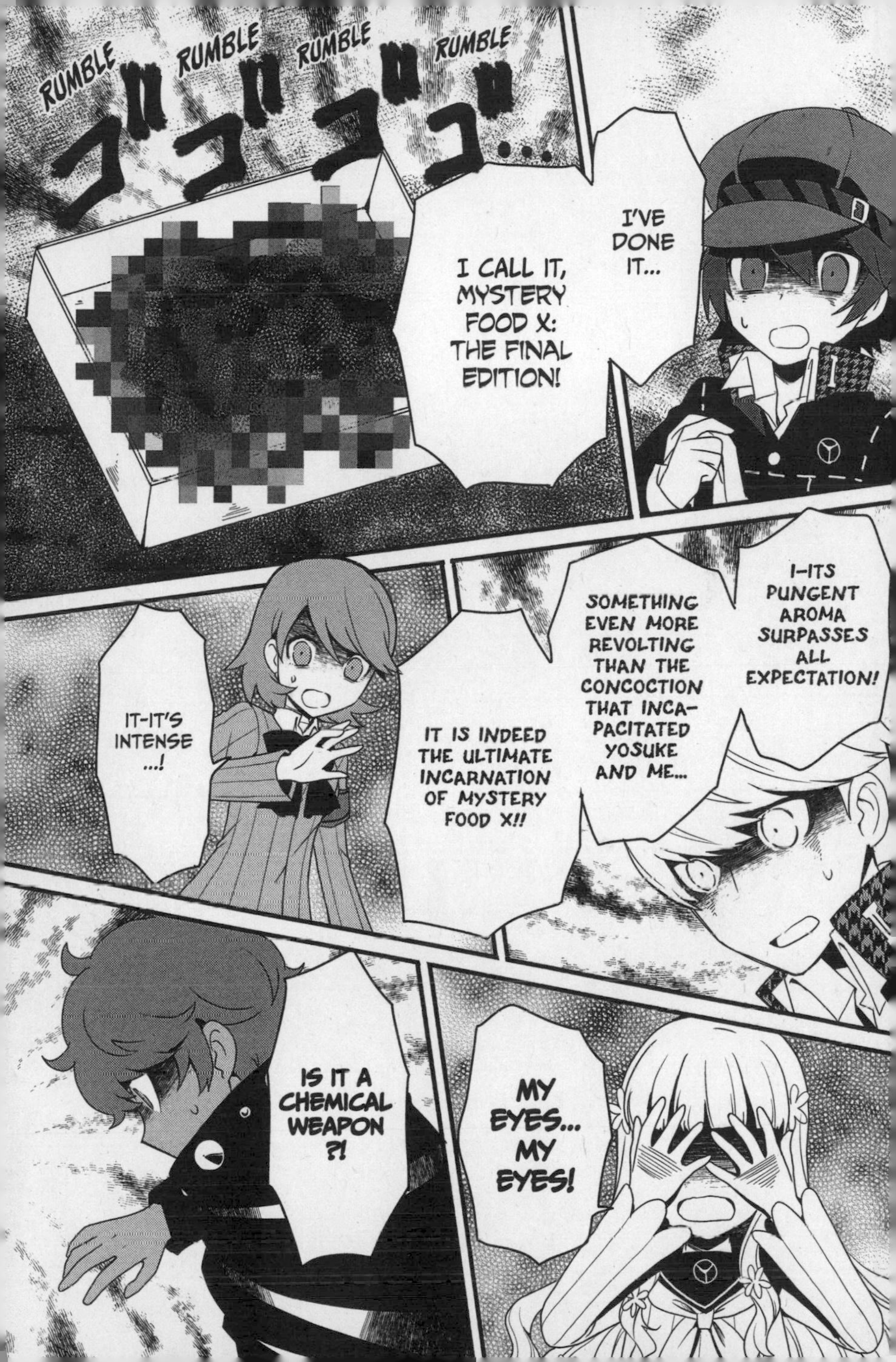
I'VE DONE IT...
I CALL IT, MYSTERY FOOD X: THE FINAL EDITION!
RUMBLE RUMBLE RUMBLE RUMBLE
ゴゴゴゴ…
I-ITS PUNGENT AROMA SURPASSES ALL EXPECTATION!
SOMETHING EVEN MORE REVOLTING THAN THE CONCOCTION THAT INCA-PACITATED YOSUKE AND ME...
IT IS INDEED THE ULTIMATE INCARNATION OF MYSTERY FOOD X!!
IT-IT'S INTENSE ...!
MY EYES... MY EYES!
IS IT A CHEMICAL WEAPON ?!

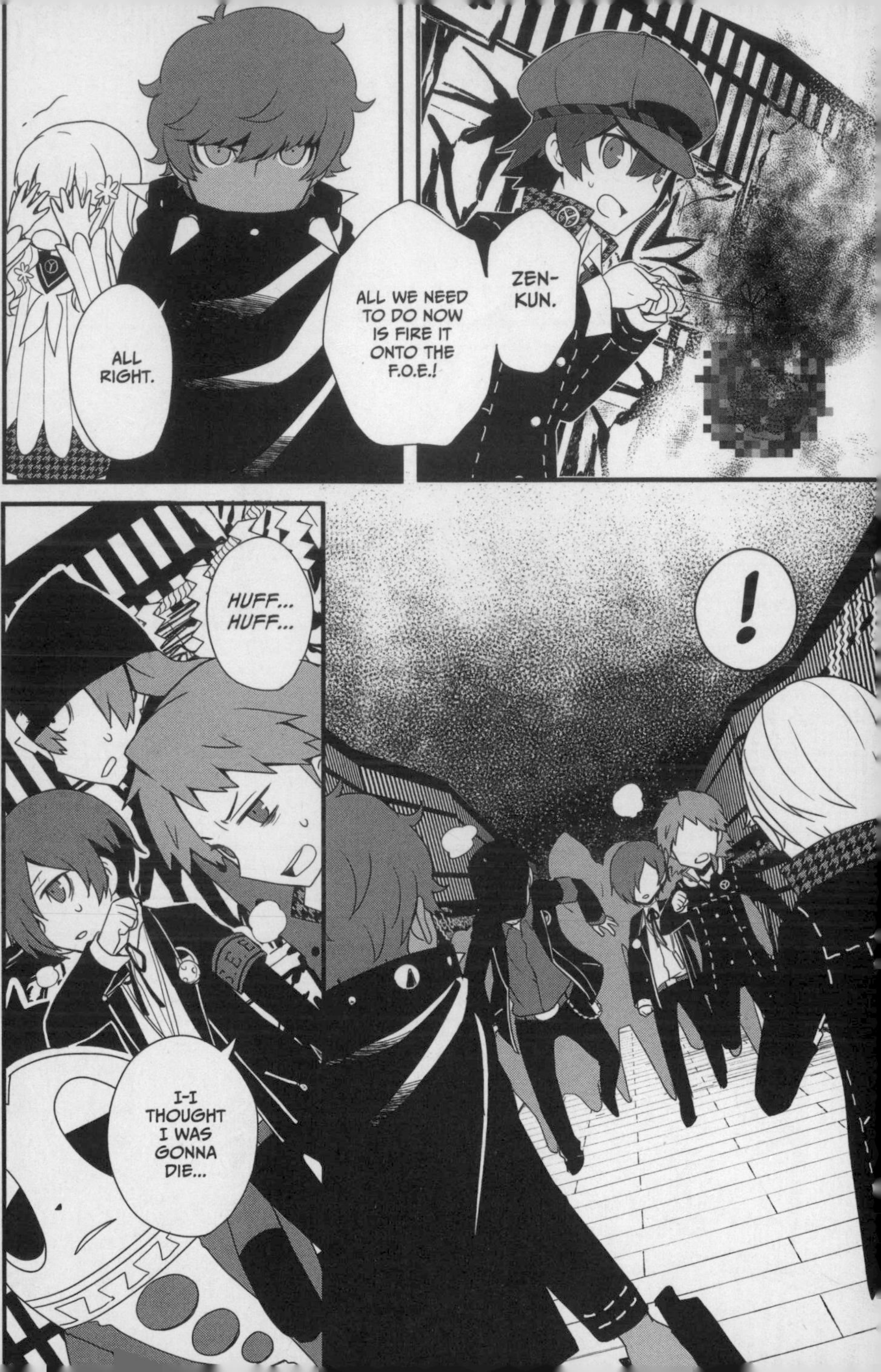
ZEN-KUN.
ALL WE NEED TO DO NOW IS FIRE IT ONTO THE F.O.E.!
ALL RIGHT.
!
HUFF... HUFF...
I-I THOUGHT I WAS GONNA DIE...

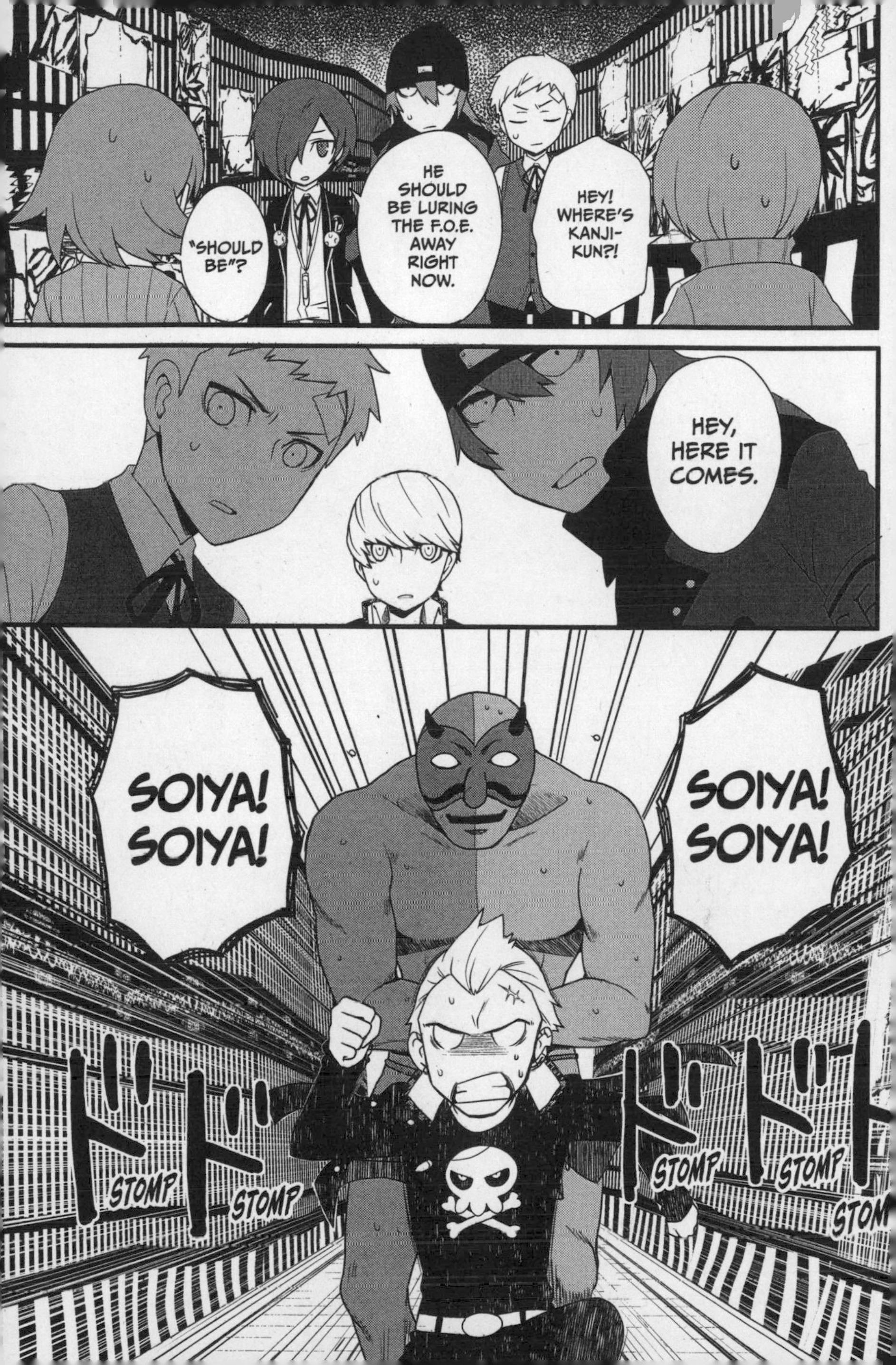
HEY! WHERE'S KANJI-KUN?!
HE SHOULD BE LURING THE F.O.E. AWAY RIGHT NOW.
"SHOULD BE"?
HEY, HERE IT COMES.
SOIYA! SOIYA!
SOIYA! SOIYA!
ドドド
STOMP STOMP STOM
ドド
STOMP STOMP

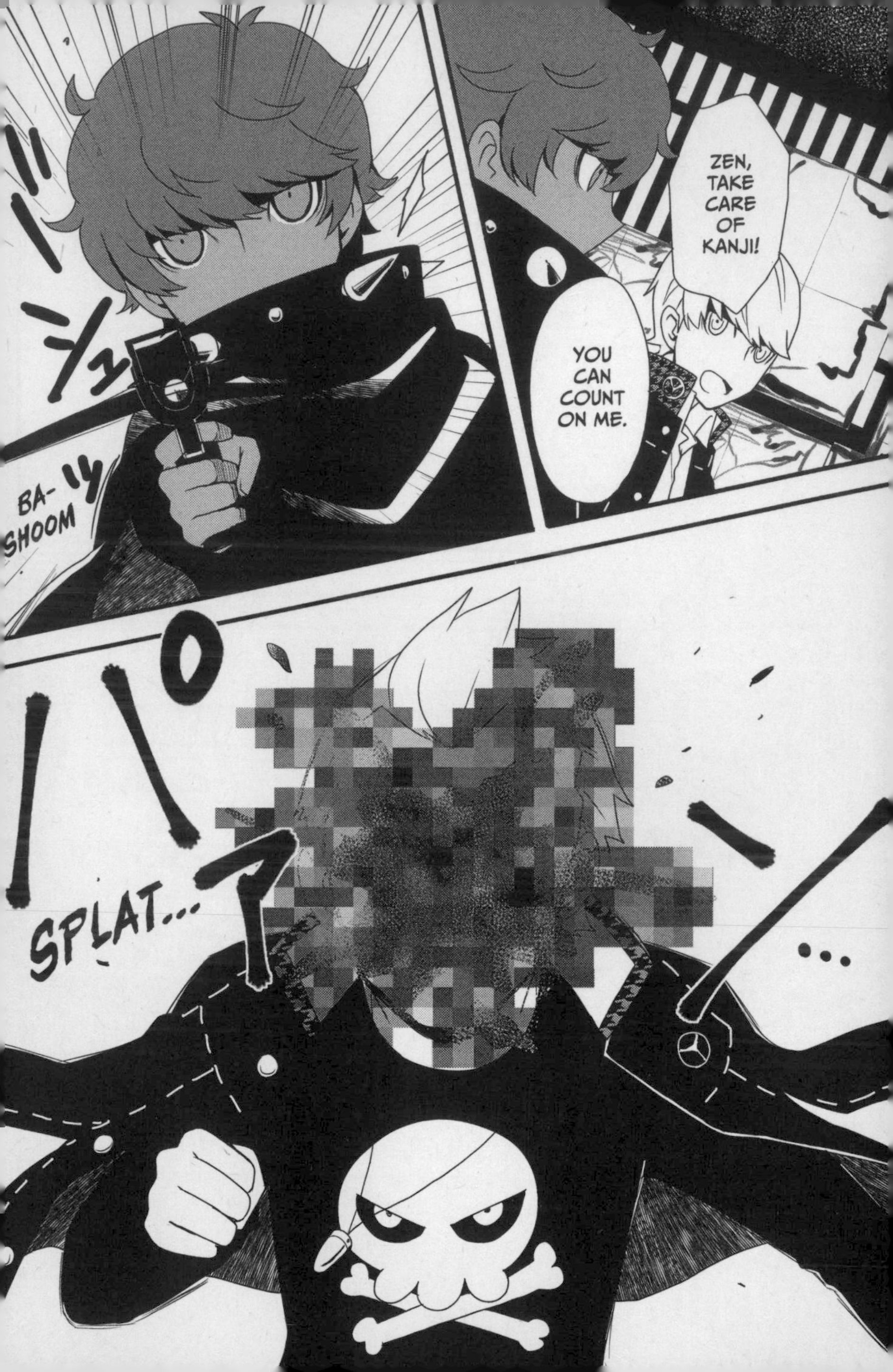
ZEN, TAKE CARE OF KANJI!
YOU CAN COUNT ON ME.
BA-SHOOM
...
SPLAT...

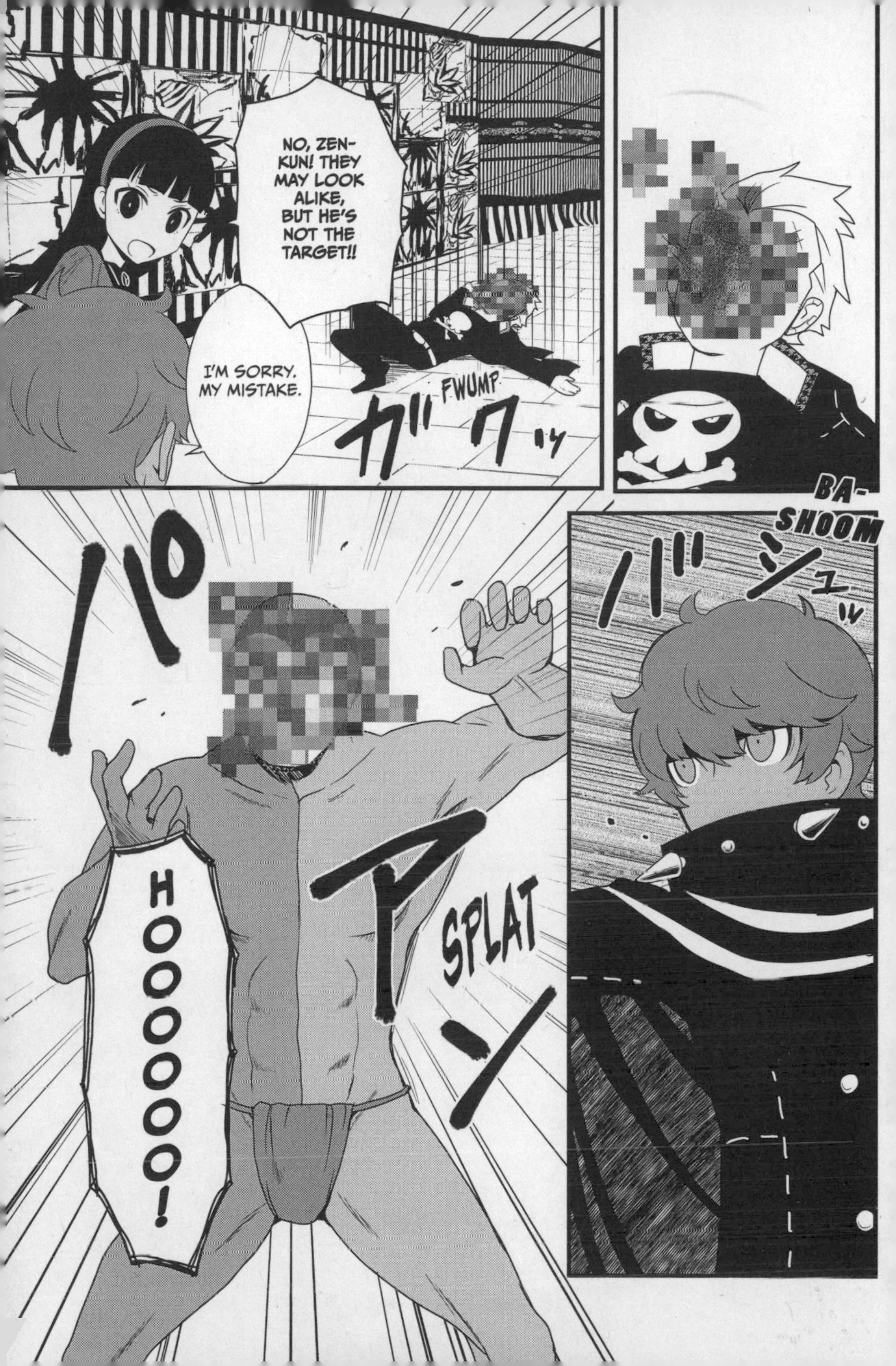

NO, ZEN-KUN! THEY MAY LOOK ALIKE, BUT HE'S NOT THE TARGET!!
I'M SORRY. MY MISTAKE.
FWUMP
ガクッ
BA-SHOOM
バシュッ
パァーン
SPLAT
HOOOOOOO!

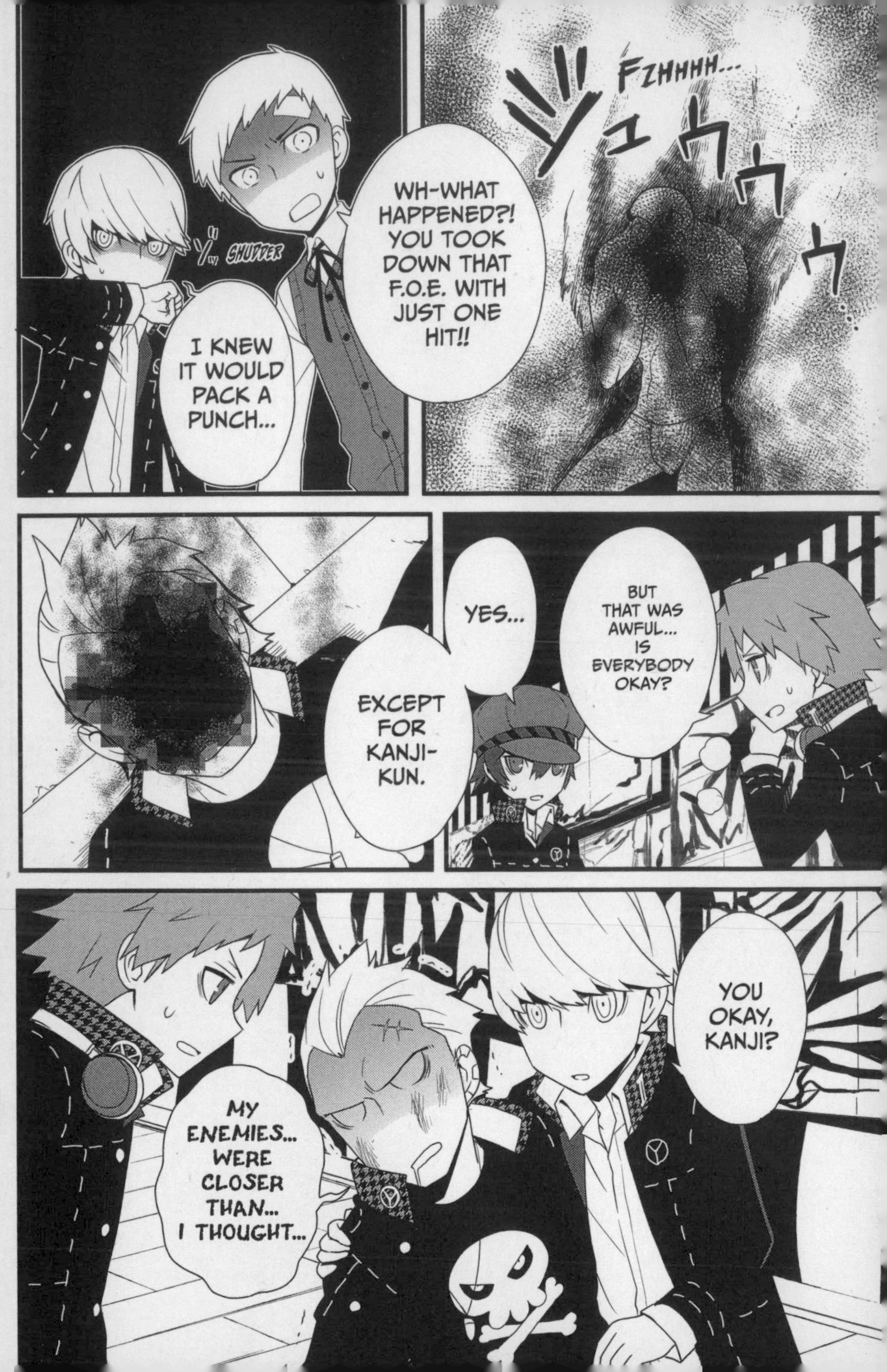
FZHHHH...
WH-WHAT HAPPENED?! YOU TOOK DOWN THAT F.O.E. WITH JUST ONE HIT!!
SHUDDER
I KNEW IT WOULD PACK A PUNCH...
BUT THAT WAS AWFUL... IS EVERYBODY OKAY?
YES...
EXCEPT FOR KANJI-KUN.
YOU OKAY, KANJI?
MY ENEMIES... WERE CLOSER THAN... I THOUGHT...

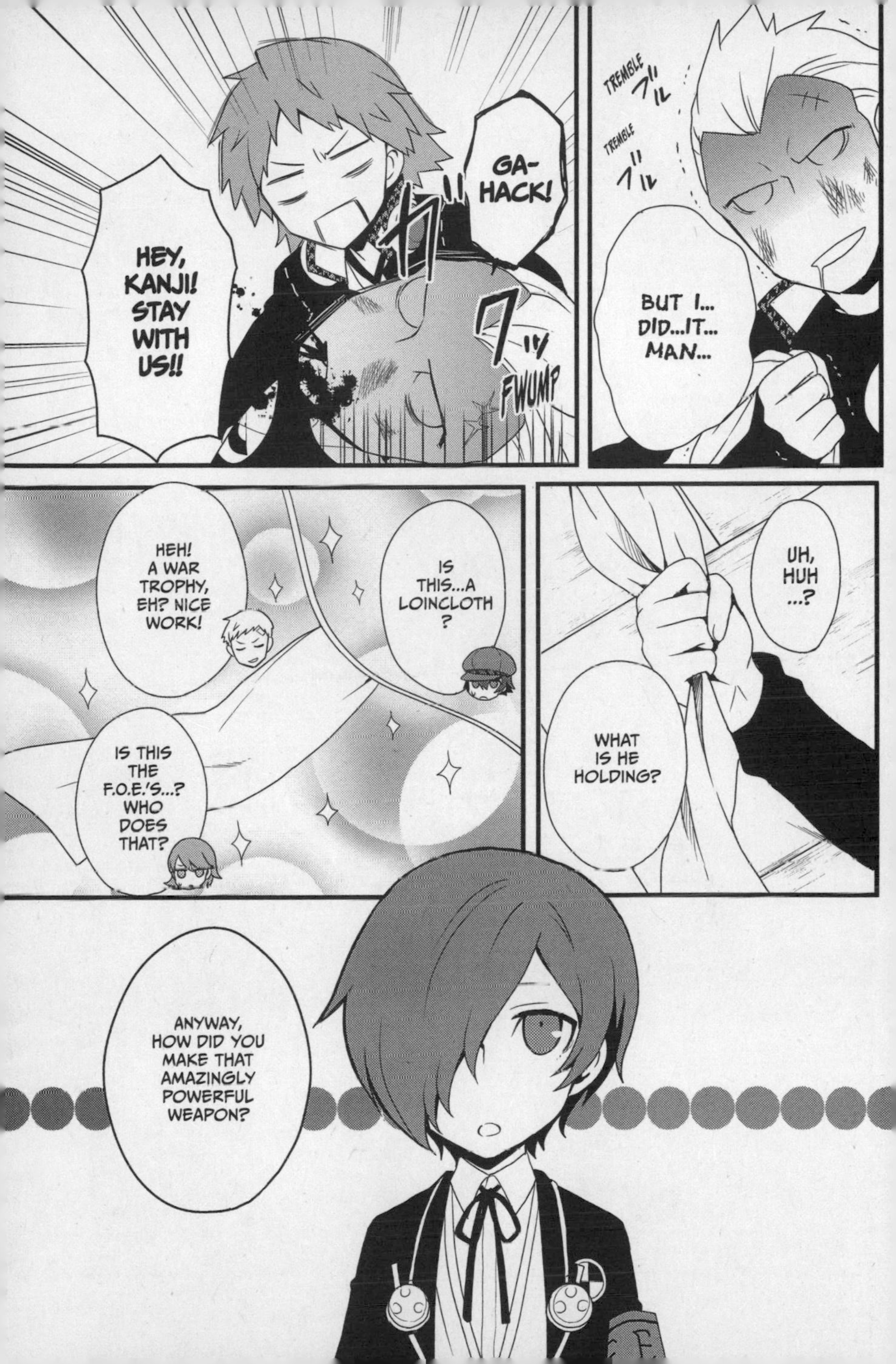

TREMBLE
ブル
TREMBLE
ブル
BUT I... DID...IT... MAN...
GA-HACK!
HEY, KANJI! STAY WITH US!!
FWUMP
UH, HUH ...?
WHAT IS HE HOLDING?
IS THIS...A LOINCLOTH ?
HEH! A WAR TROPHY, EH? NICE WORK!
IS THIS THE F.O.E.'S...? WHO DOES THAT?
ANYWAY, HOW DID YOU MAKE THAT AMAZINGLY POWERFUL WEAPON?

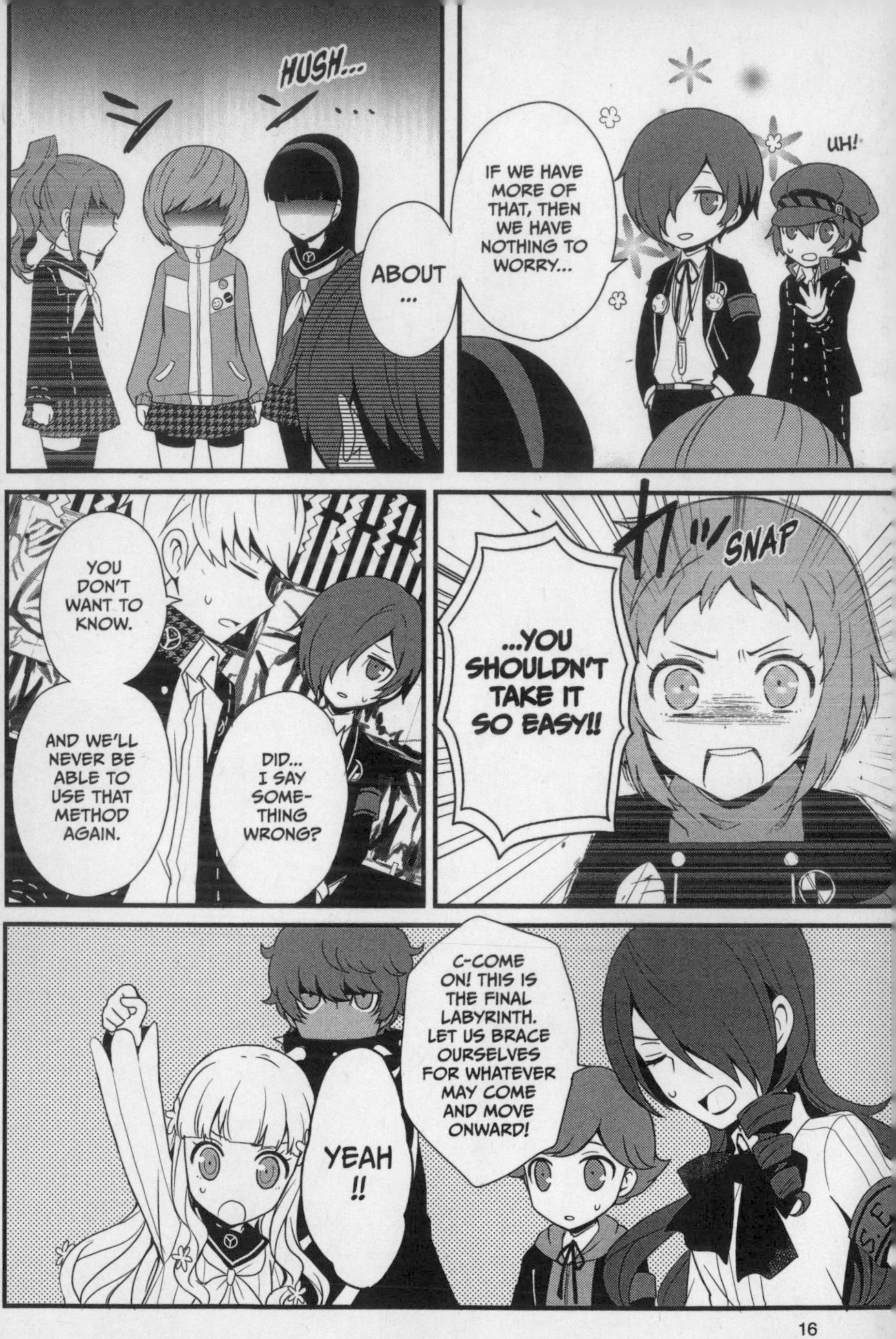
IF WE HAVE MORE OF THAT, THEN WE HAVE NOTHING TO WORRY...
UH!
HUSH...
...
ABOUT ...
SNAP
...YOU SHOULDN'T TAKE IT SO EASY!!
YOU DON'T WANT TO KNOW.
DID... I SAY SOME-THING WRONG?
AND WE'LL NEVER BE ABLE TO USE THAT METHOD AGAIN.
C-COME ON! THIS IS THE FINAL LABYRINTH. LET US BRACE OURSELVES FOR WHATEVER MAY COME AND MOVE ONWARD!
YEAH !!

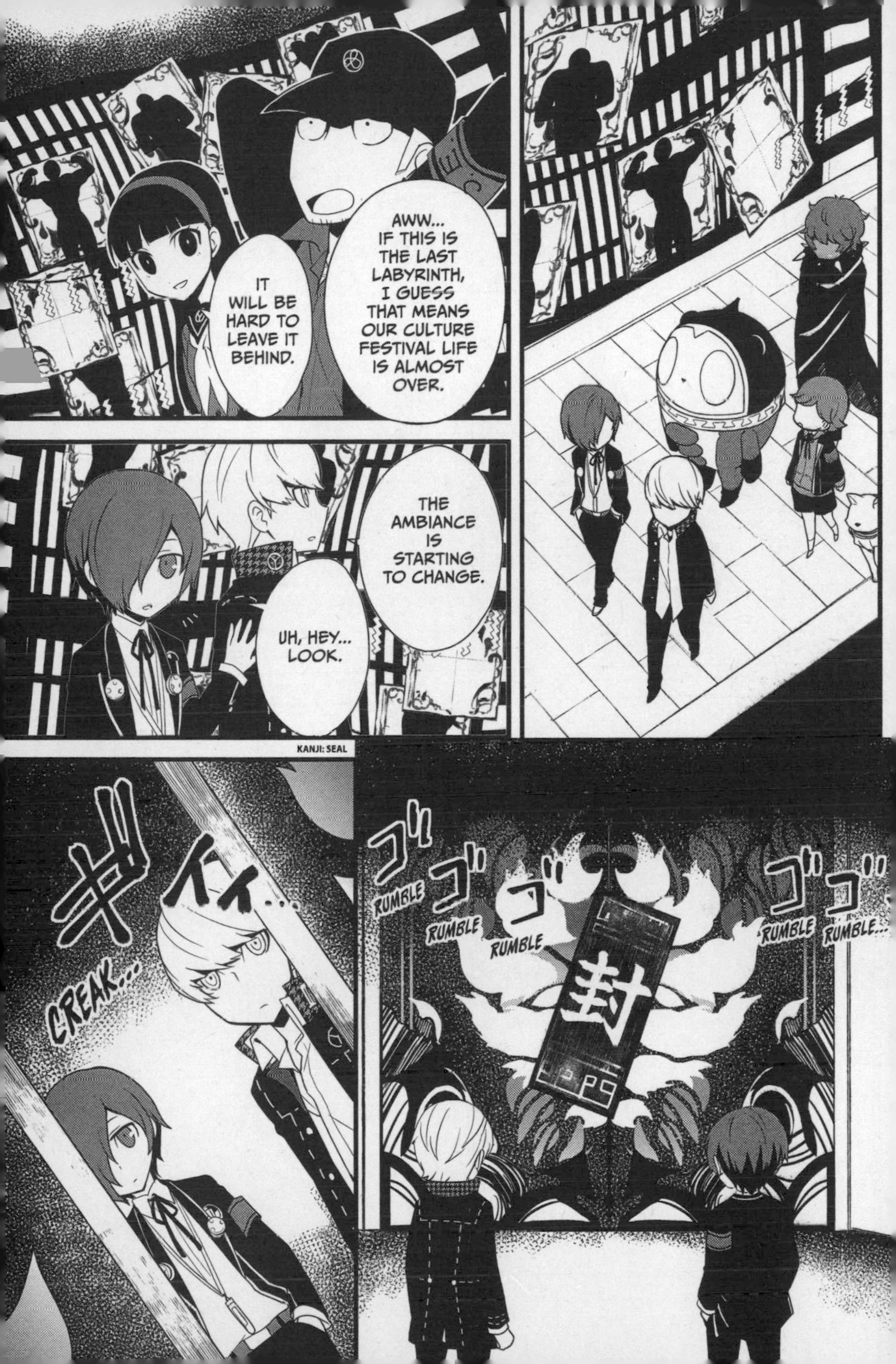
AWW... IF THIS IS THE LAST LABYRINTH, I GUESS THAT MEANS OUR CULTURE FESTIVAL LIFE IS ALMOST OVER.
IT WILL BE HARD TO LEAVE IT BEHIND.
THE AMBIANCE IS STARTING TO CHANGE.
UH, HEY... LOOK.
KANJI: SEAL
ゴゴ
RUMBLE RUMBLE
封
RUMBLE RUMBLE
ゴゴ
RUMBLE RUMBLE...
ギイイ...
CREAK...

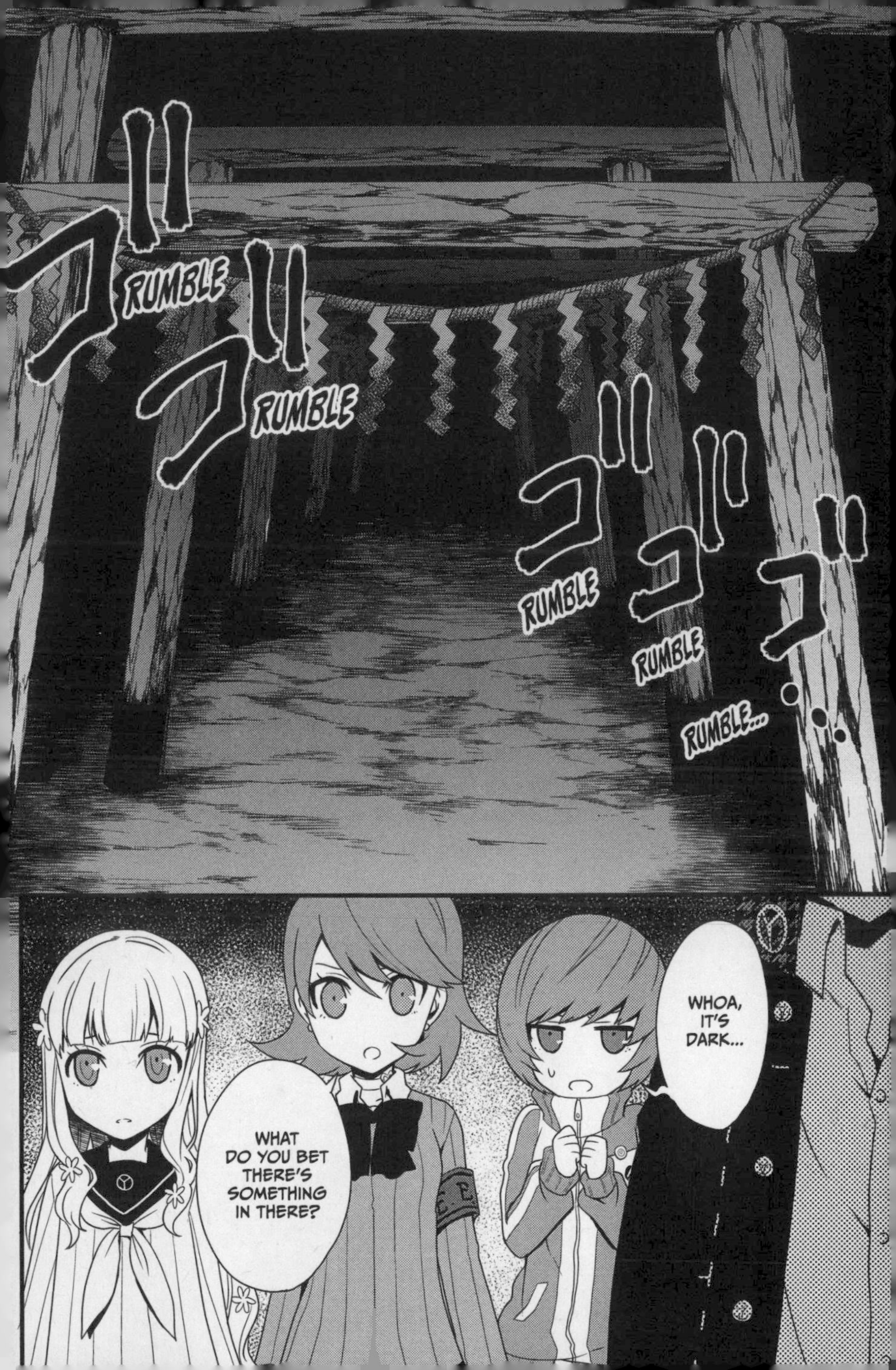
ゴゴ
RUMBLE
RUMBLE
ゴゴゴ
RUMBLE
RUMBLE
RUMBLE...
WHOA, IT'S DARK...
WHAT DO YOU BET THERE'S SOMETHING IN THERE?

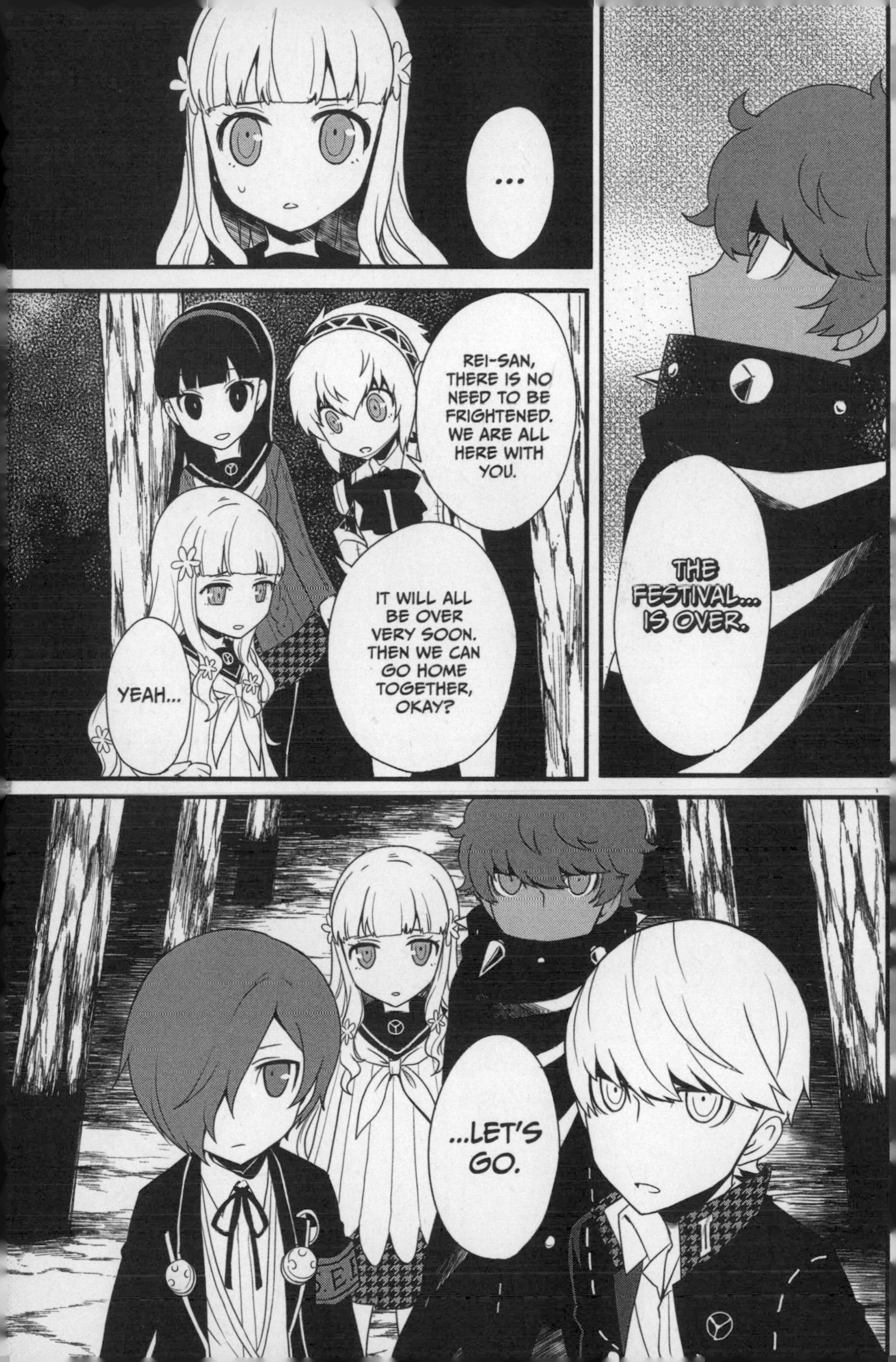
THE FESTIVAL... IS OVER.
...
REI-SAN, THERE IS NO NEED TO BE FRIGHTENED. WE ARE ALL HERE WITH YOU.
IT WILL ALL BE OVER VERY SOON. THEN WE CAN GO HOME TOGETHER, OKAY?
YEAH...
...LET'S GO.

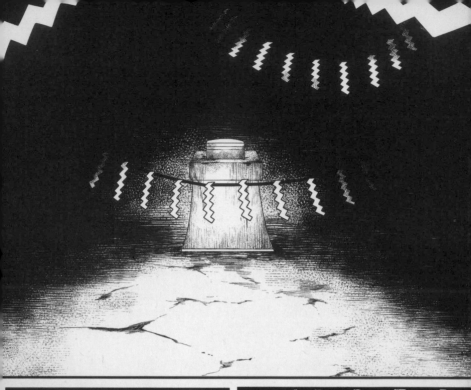

THE TREASURE BOX WITH SOMETHING RELATED TO REI.

ISN'T THERE A GUARDIAN?

THAT'S...

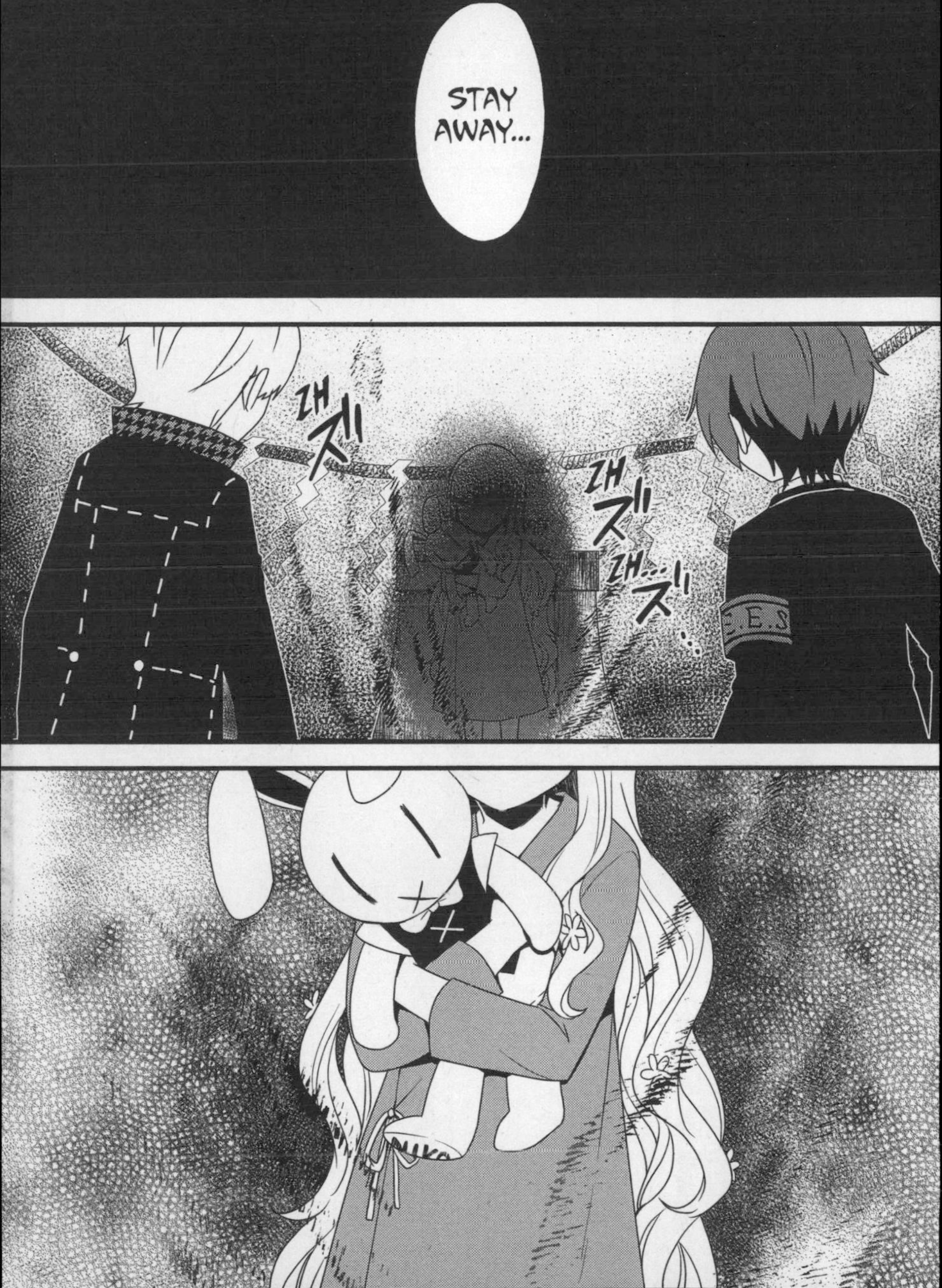
STAY AWAY...
ZH
ZH...
ZH

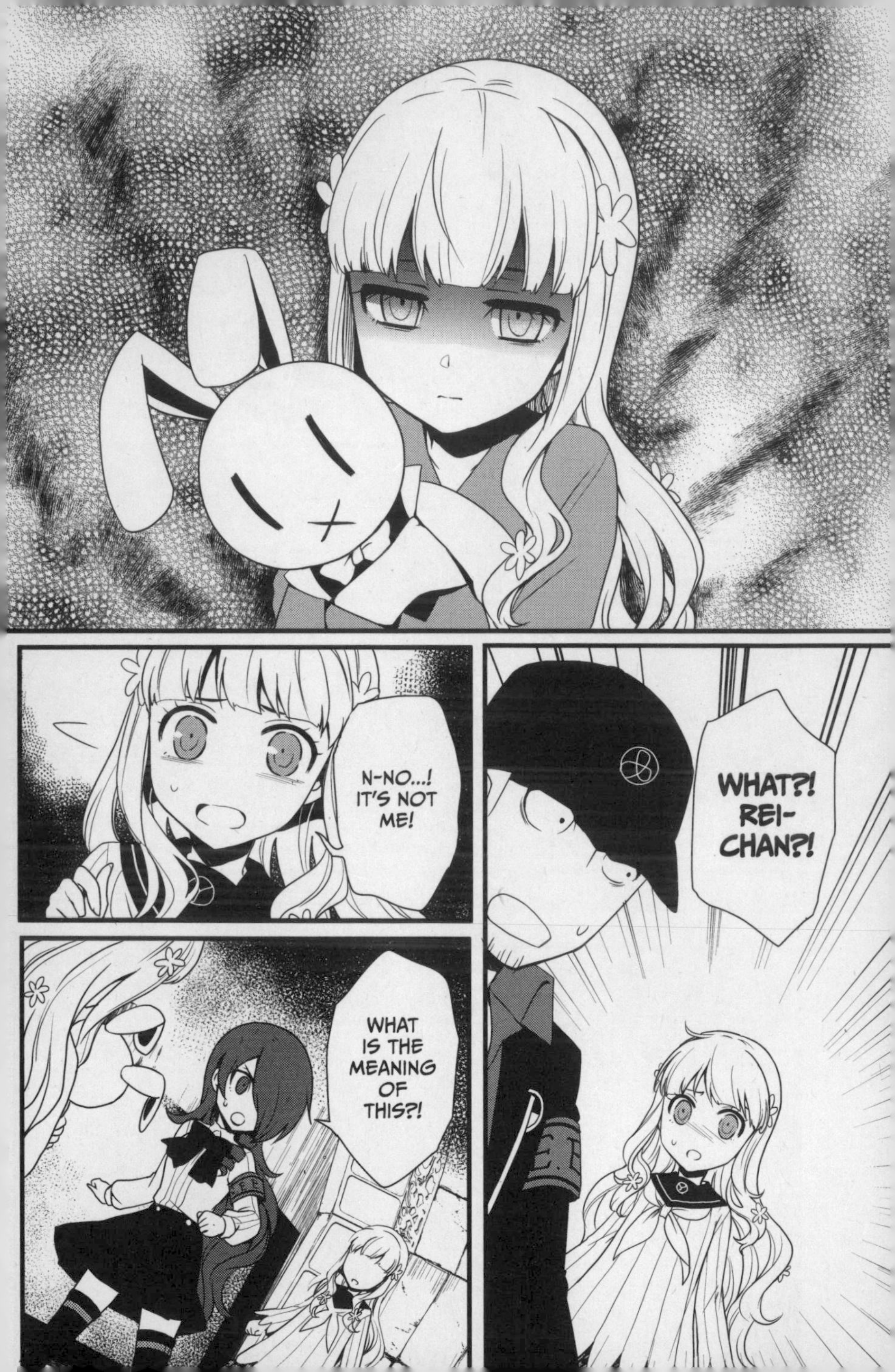
WHAT?! REI-CHAN?!
N-NO...! IT'S NOT ME!
WHAT IS THE MEANING OF THIS?!

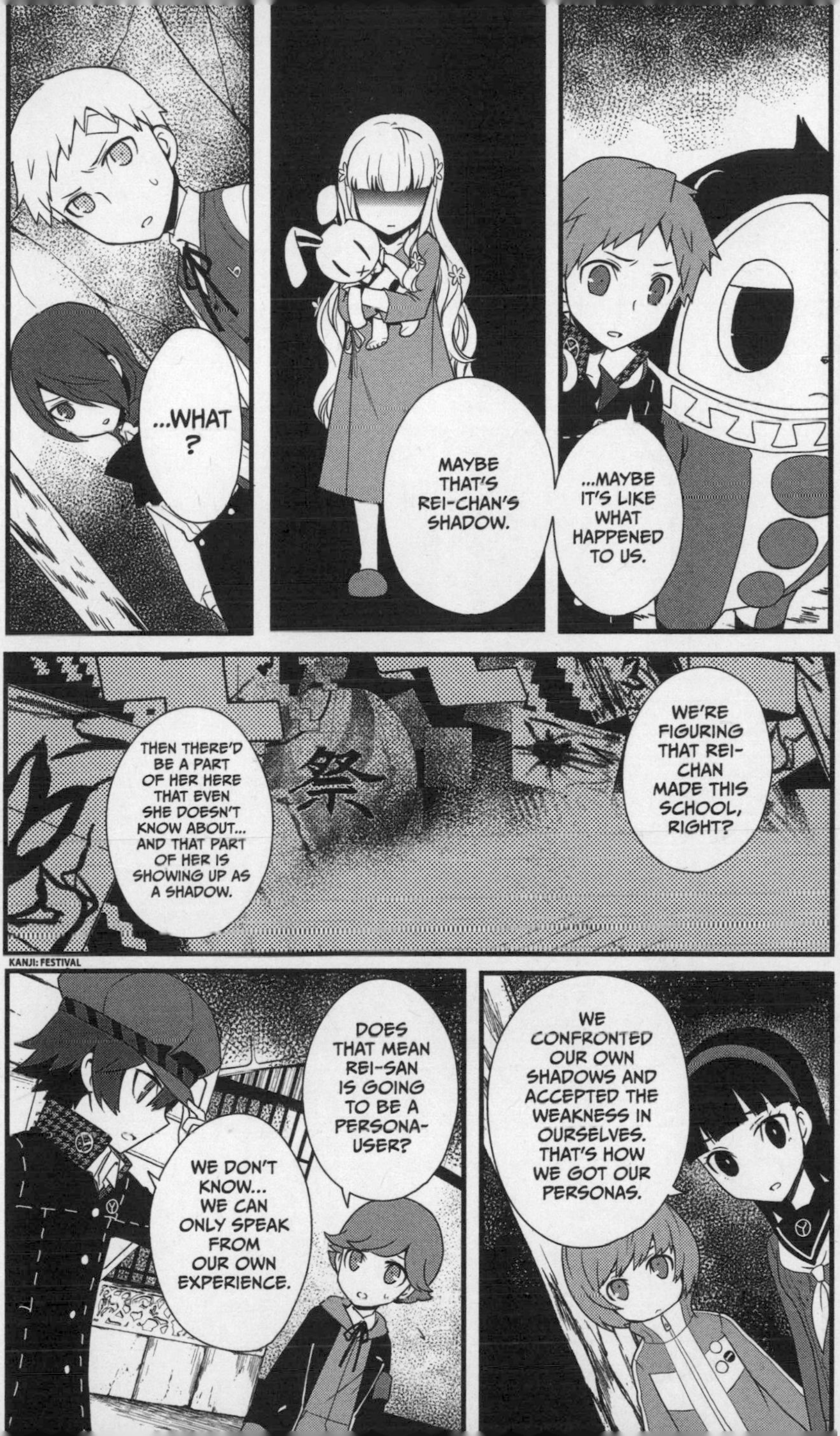
...MAYBE IT'S LIKE WHAT HAPPENED TO US.
MAYBE THAT'S REI-CHAN'S SHADOW.
...WHAT?
WE'RE FIGURING THAT REI-CHAN MADE THIS SCHOOL, RIGHT?
祭
THEN THERE'D BE A PART OF HER HERE THAT EVEN SHE DOESN'T KNOW ABOUT... AND THAT PART OF HER IS SHOWING UP AS A SHADOW.
WE CONFRONTED OUR OWN SHADOWS AND ACCEPTED THE WEAKNESS IN OURSELVES. THAT'S HOW WE GOT OUR PERSONAS.
DOES THAT MEAN REI-SAN IS GOING TO BE A PERSONA-USER?
WE DON'T KNOW... WE CAN ONLY SPEAK FROM OUR OWN EXPERIENCE.
KANJI: FESTIVAL

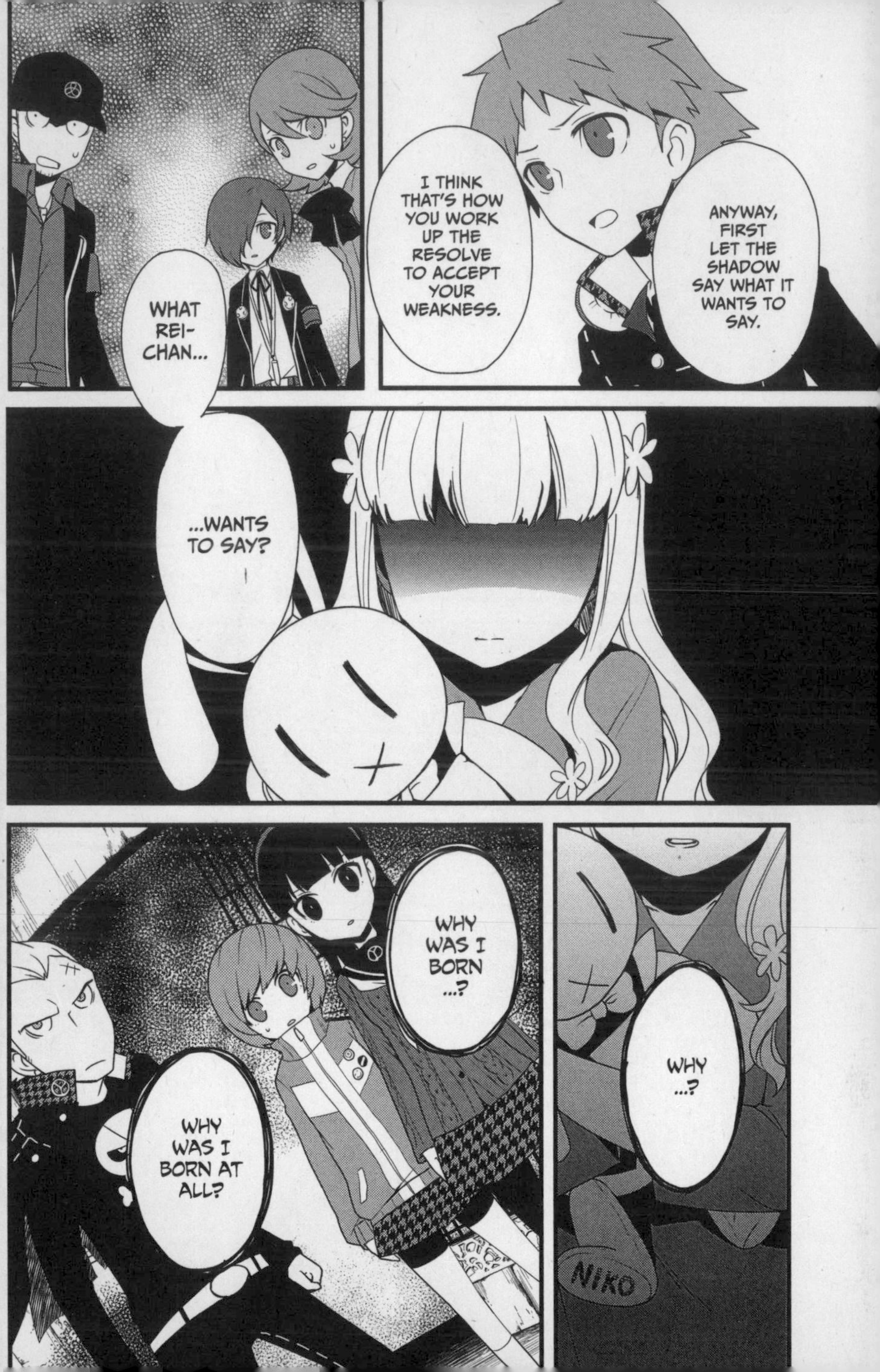
ANYWAY, FIRST LET THE SHADOW SAY WHAT IT WANTS TO SAY.
I THINK THAT'S HOW YOU WORK UP THE RESOLVE TO ACCEPT YOUR WEAKNESS.
WHAT REI-CHAN...
...WANTS TO SAY?
WHY ...?
NIKO
WHY WAS I BORN ...?
WHY WAS I BORN AT ALL?

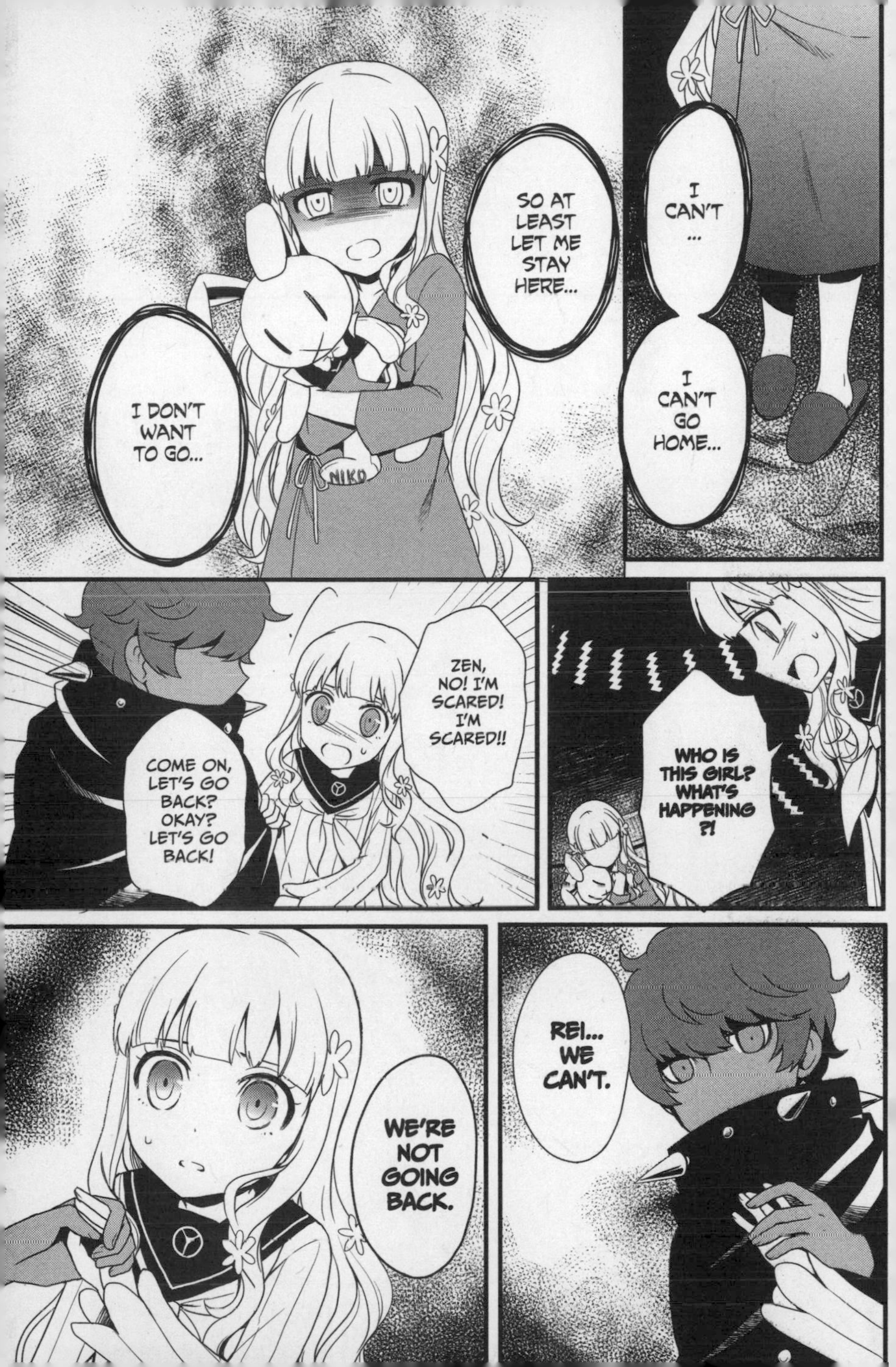
I CAN'T ...
I CAN'T GO HOME...
SO AT LEAST LET ME STAY HERE...
I DON'T WANT TO GO...
NIKO
WHO IS THIS GIRL? WHAT'S HAPPENING?!
ZEN, NO! I'M SCARED! I'M SCARED!!
COME ON, LET'S GO BACK? OKAY? LET'S GO BACK!
REI... WE CAN'T.
WE'RE NOT GOING BACK.

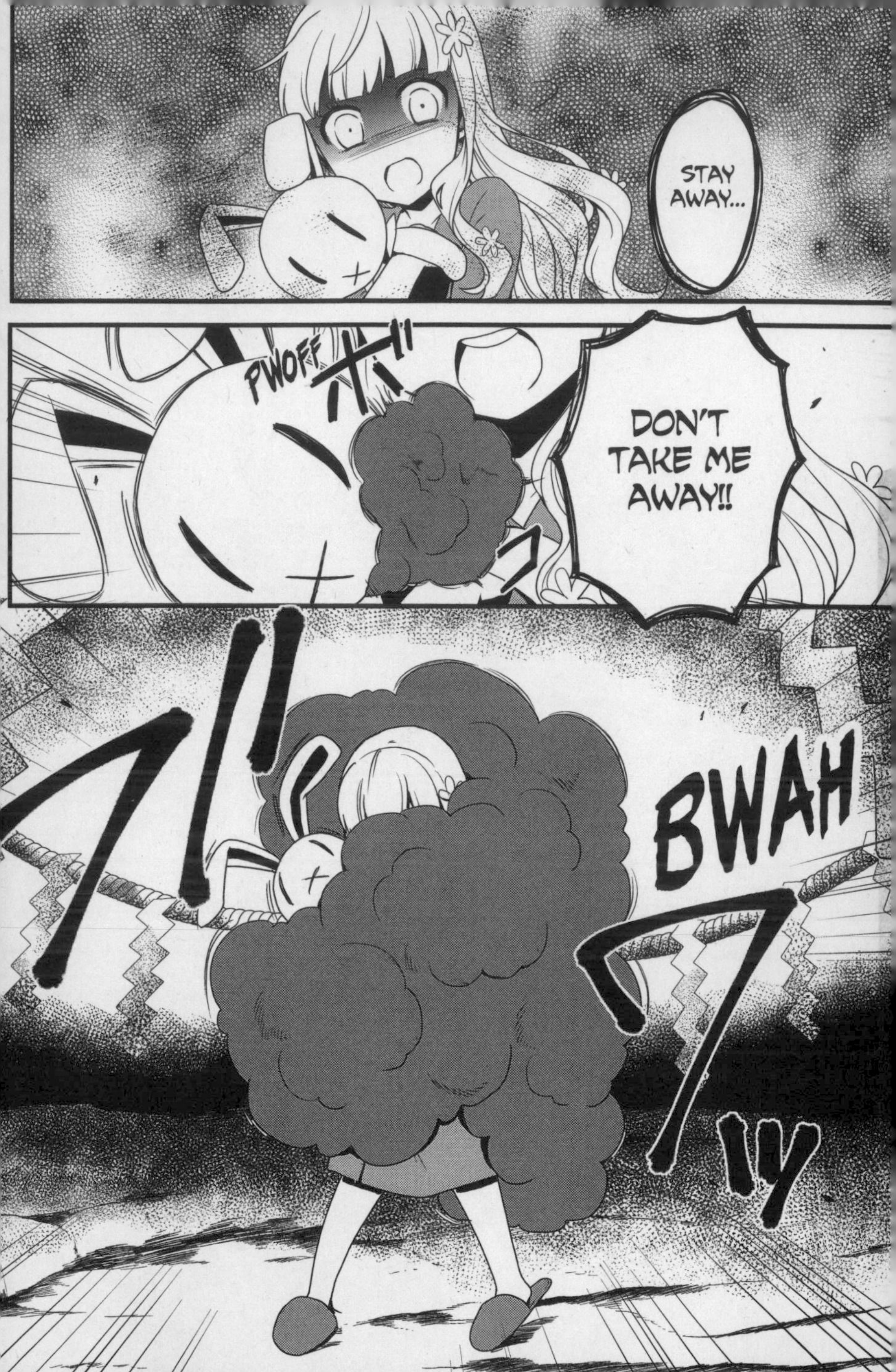
STAY AWAY...
DON'T TAKE ME AWAY!!
PWOFF
BWAH

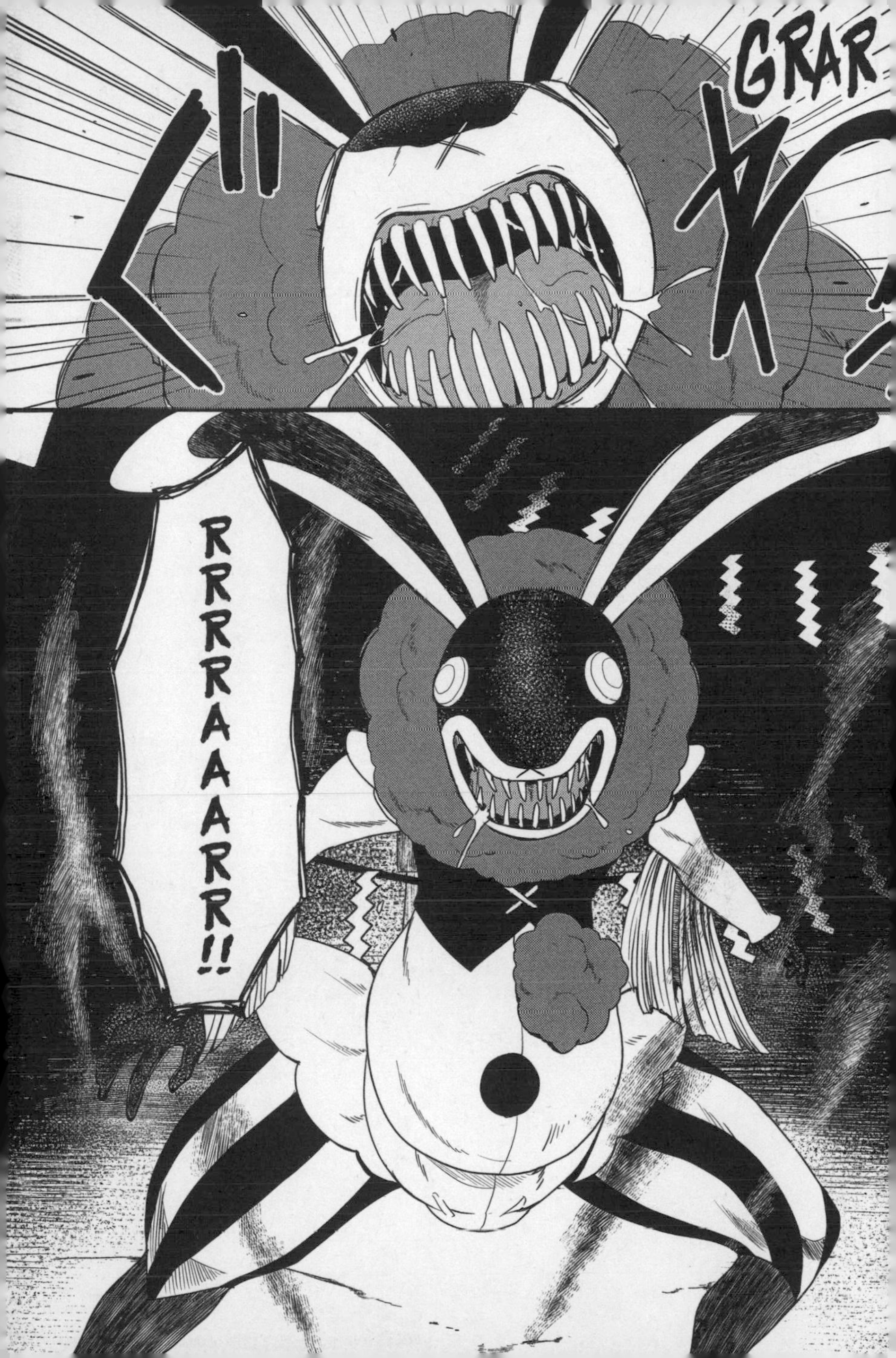
GRAR
RRRRAAARR!!

PERSONA Q Side: P4
SHADOW OF THE LABYRINTH

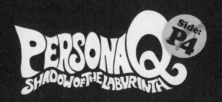

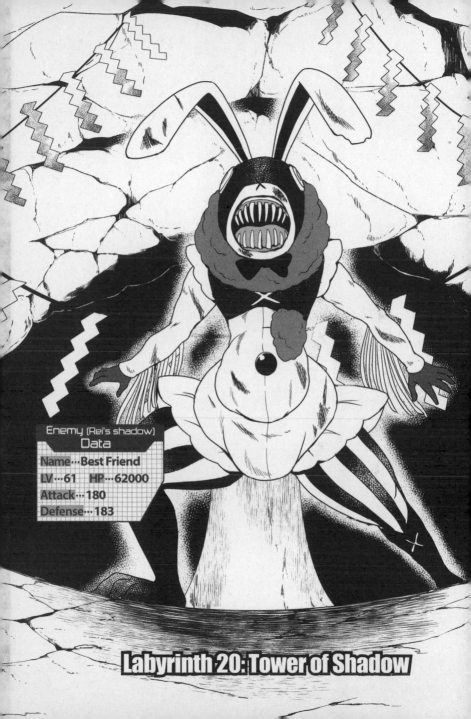

Enemy (Rei's shadow)
Data

Name···Best Friend
LV···61   HP···62000
Attack···180
Defense···183

Labyrinth 20: Tower of Shadow

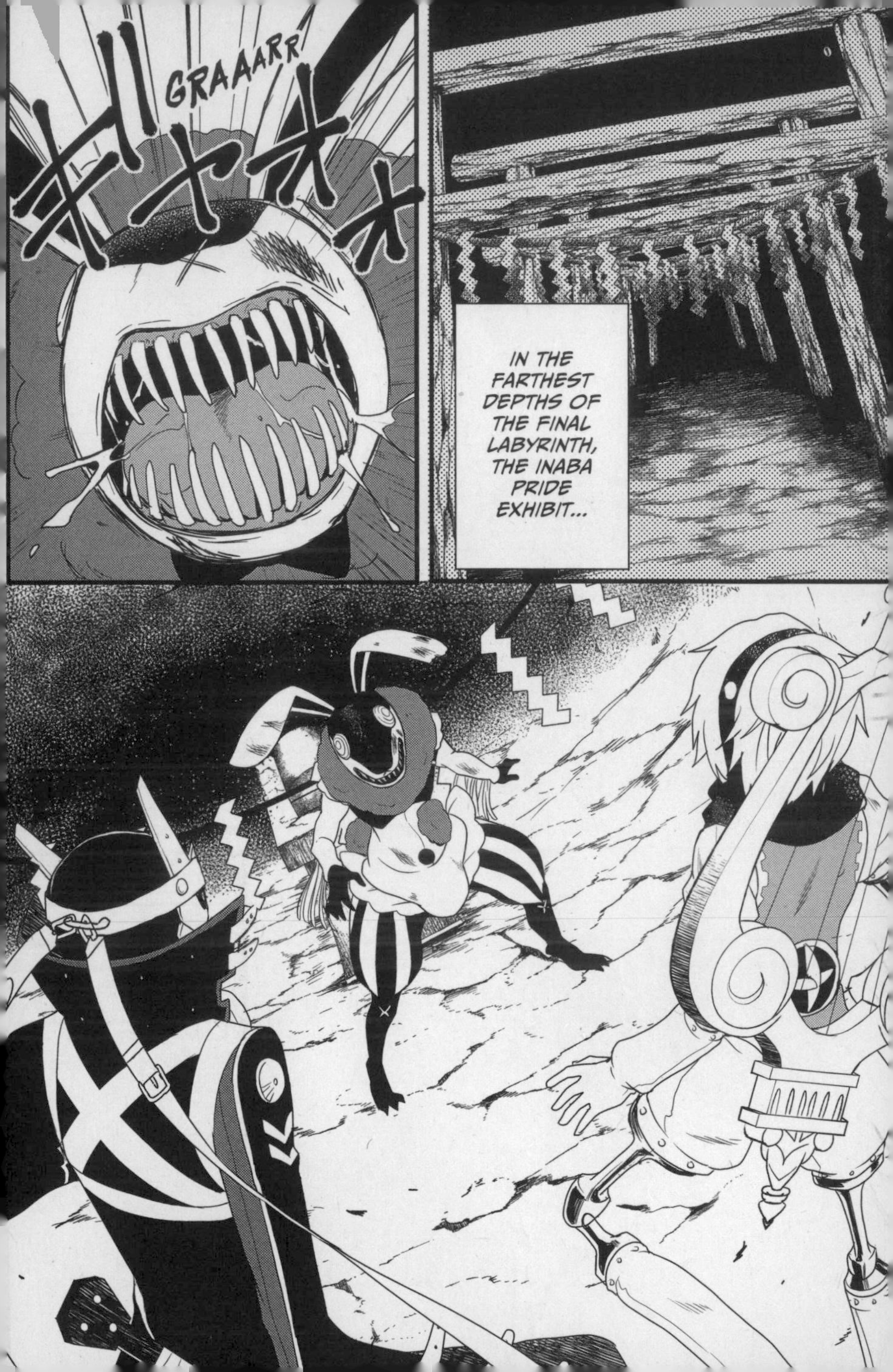
IN THE FARTHEST DEPTHS OF THE FINAL LABYRINTH, THE INABA PRIDE EXHIBIT...
GRAAARR

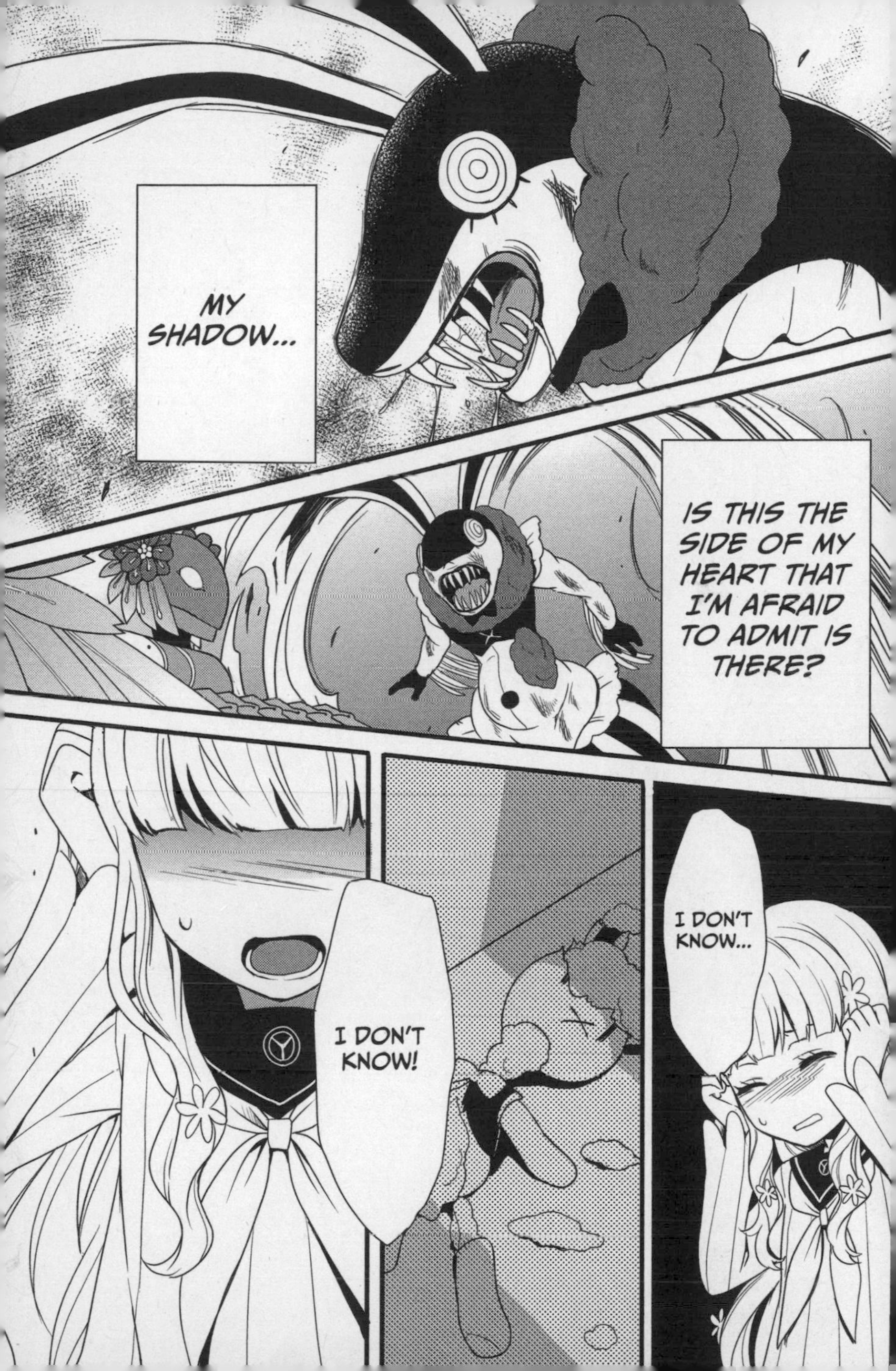
MY SHADOW...
IS THIS THE SIDE OF MY HEART THAT I'M AFRAID TO ADMIT IS THERE?
I DON'T KNOW...
I DON'T KNOW!

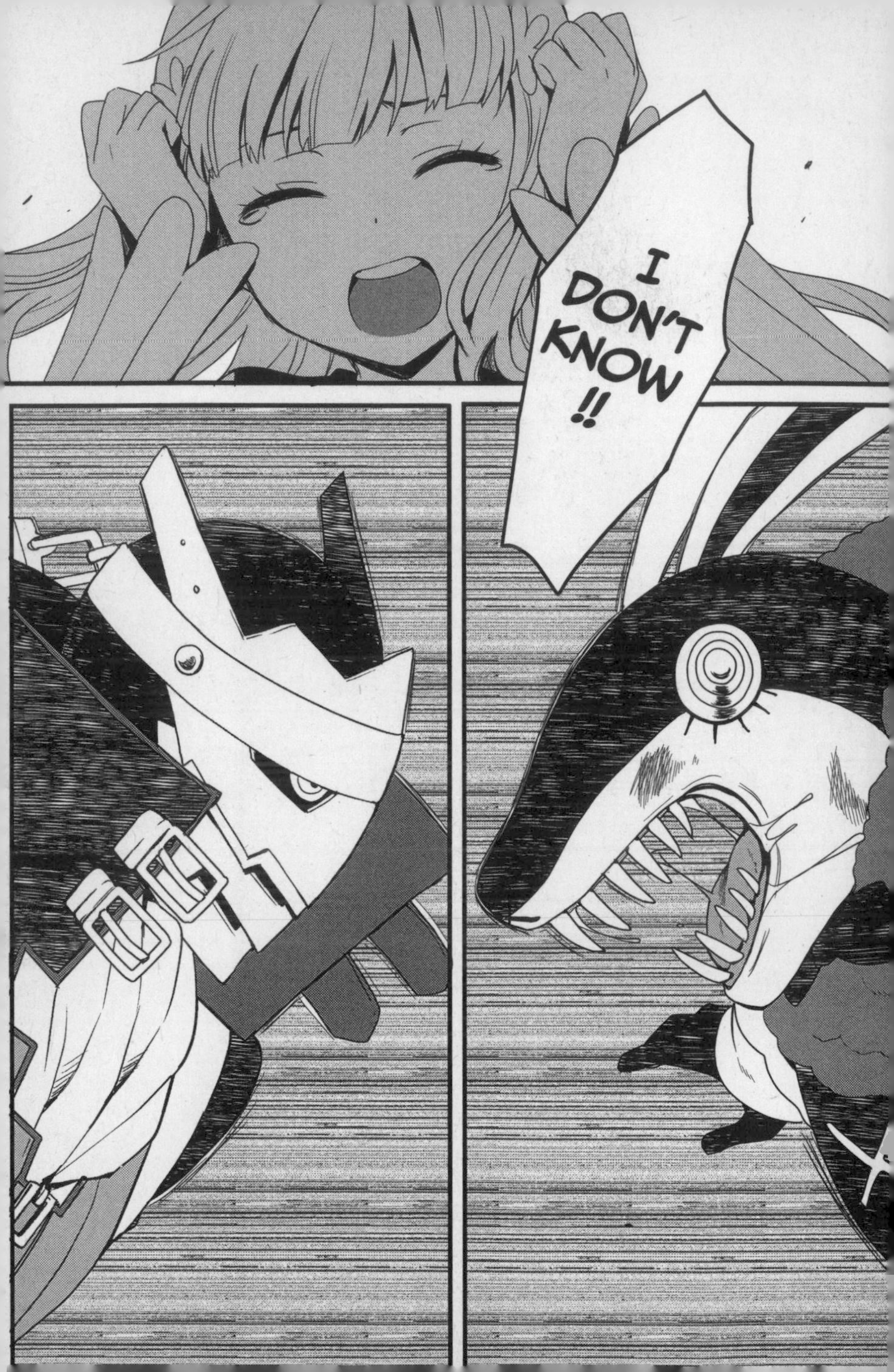
I DON'T KNOW!!

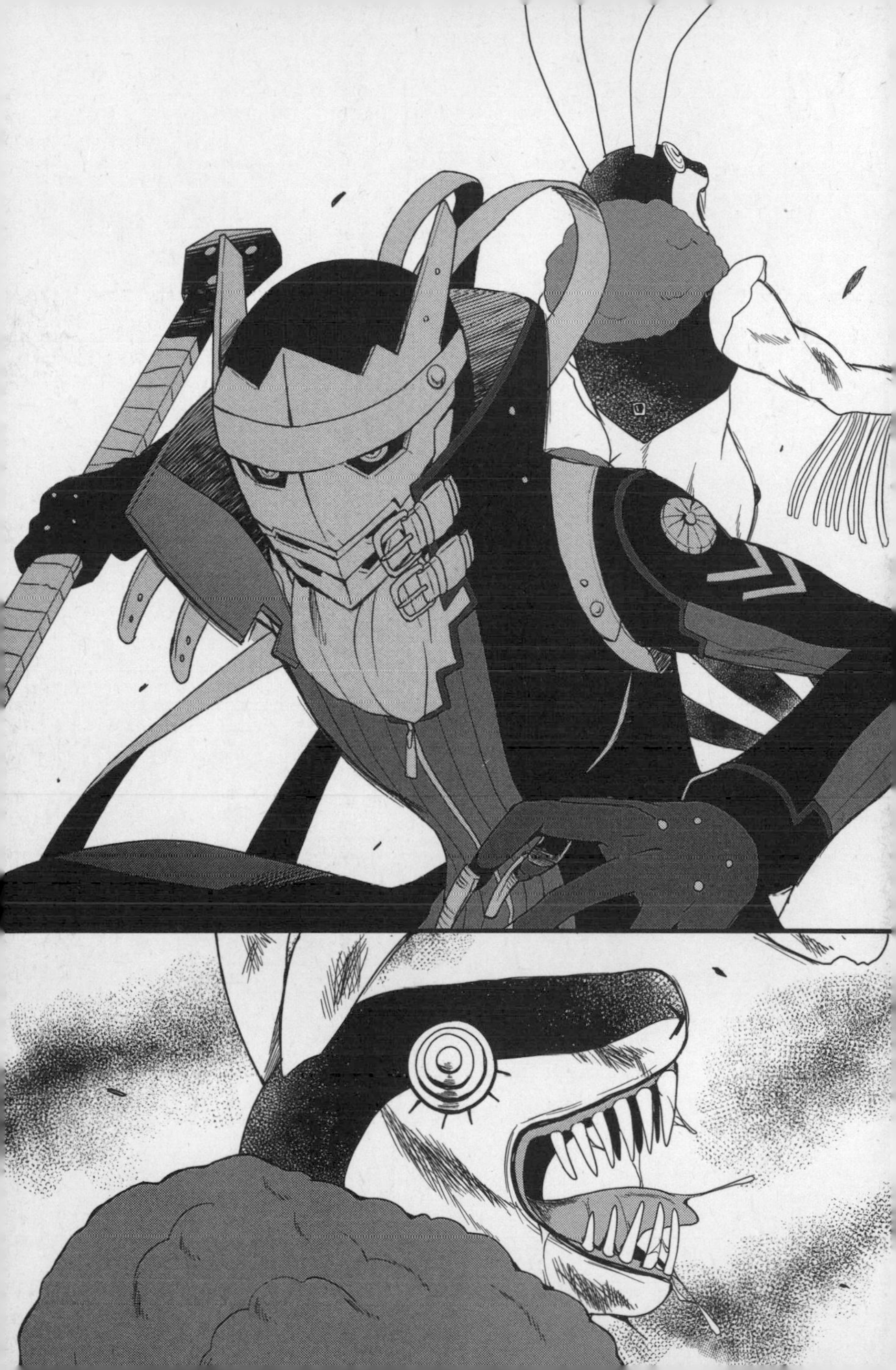

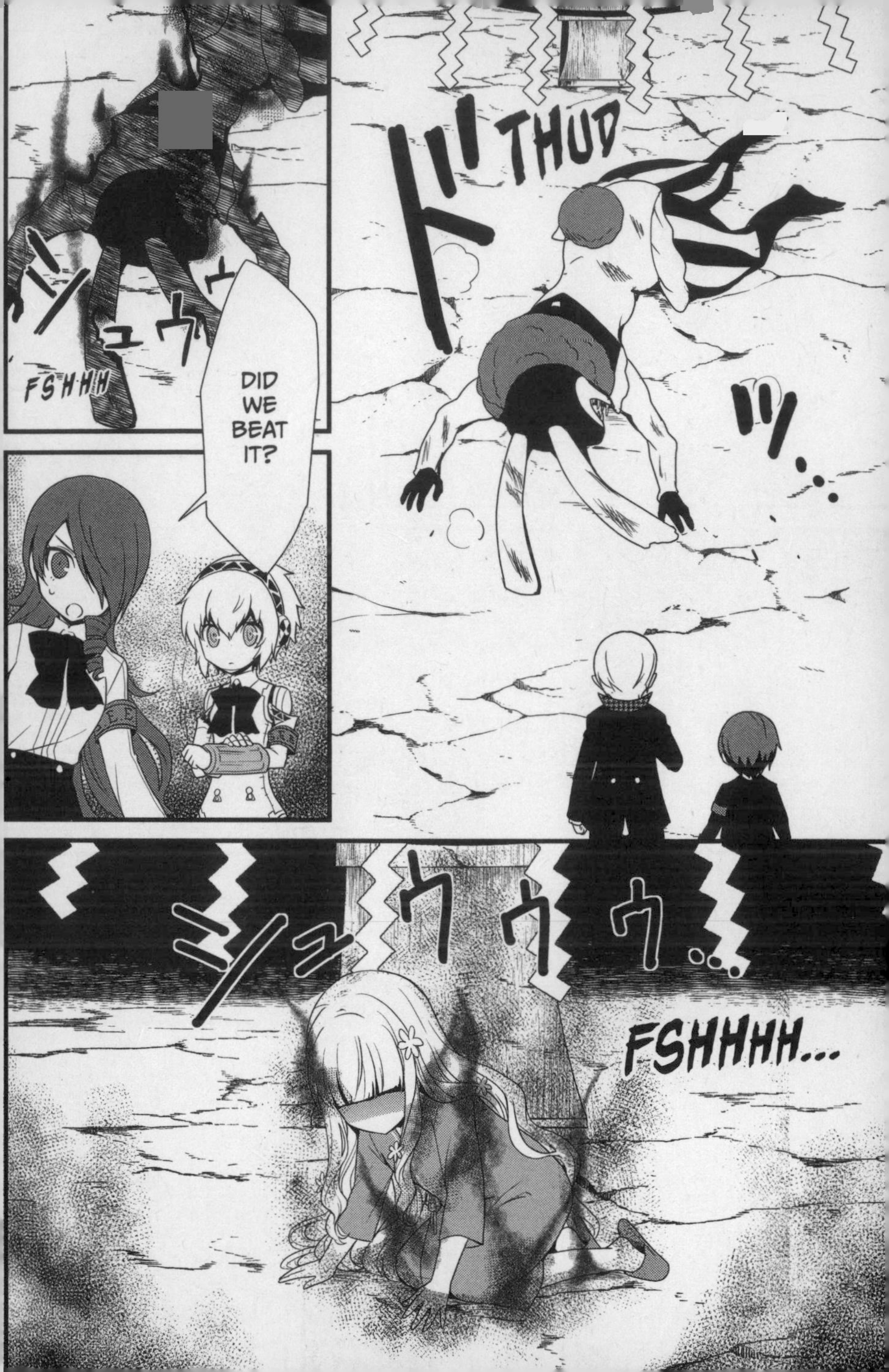
ドッ
THUD
ッ...
シュウゥ
FSHHH
DID WE BEAT IT?
シュウウウ...
FSHHHH...

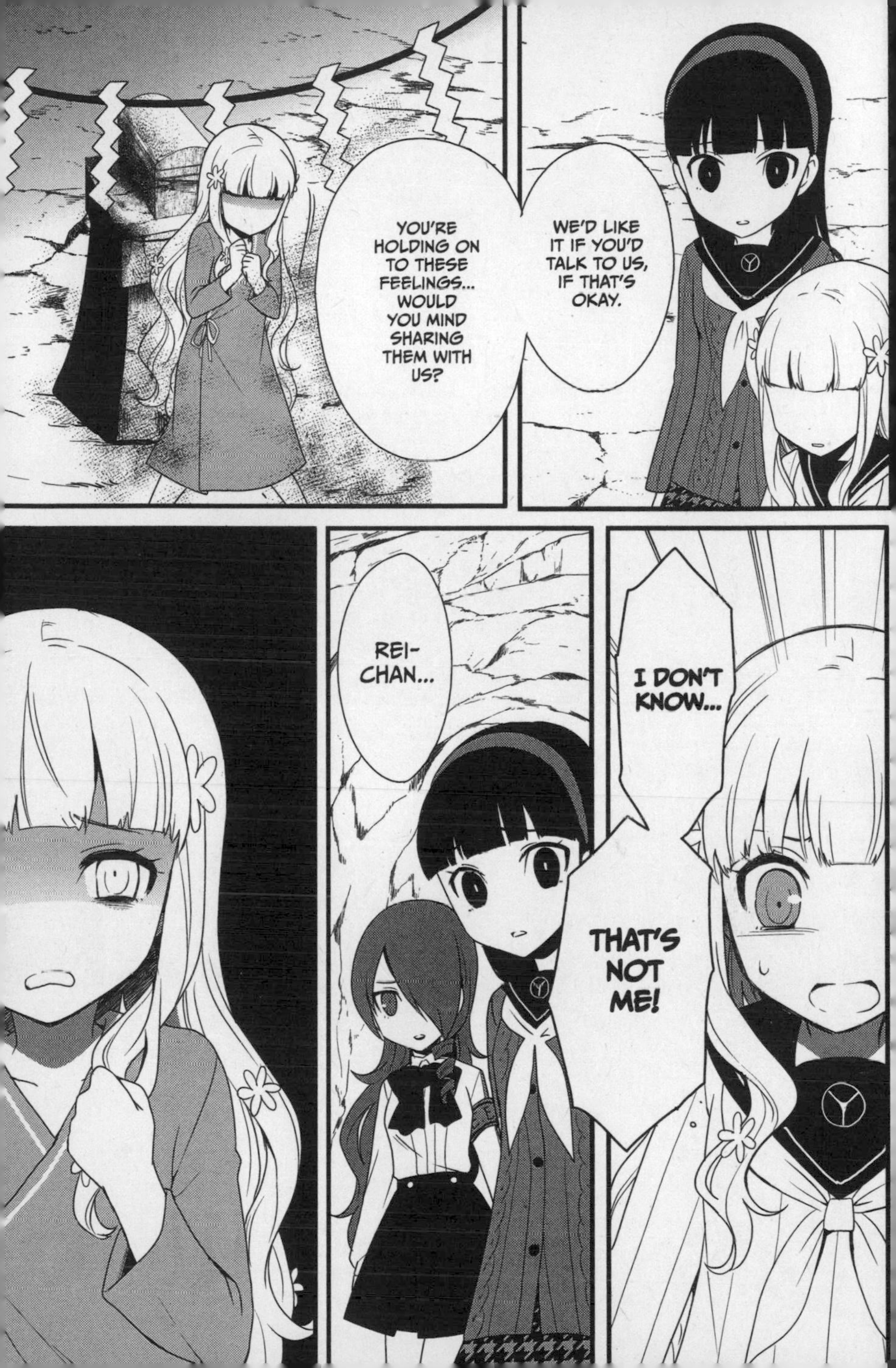
WE'D LIKE IT IF YOU'D TALK TO US, IF THAT'S OKAY.
YOU'RE HOLDING ON TO THESE FEELINGS... WOULD YOU MIND SHARING THEM WITH US?
I DON'T KNOW...
THAT'S NOT ME!
REI-CHAN...

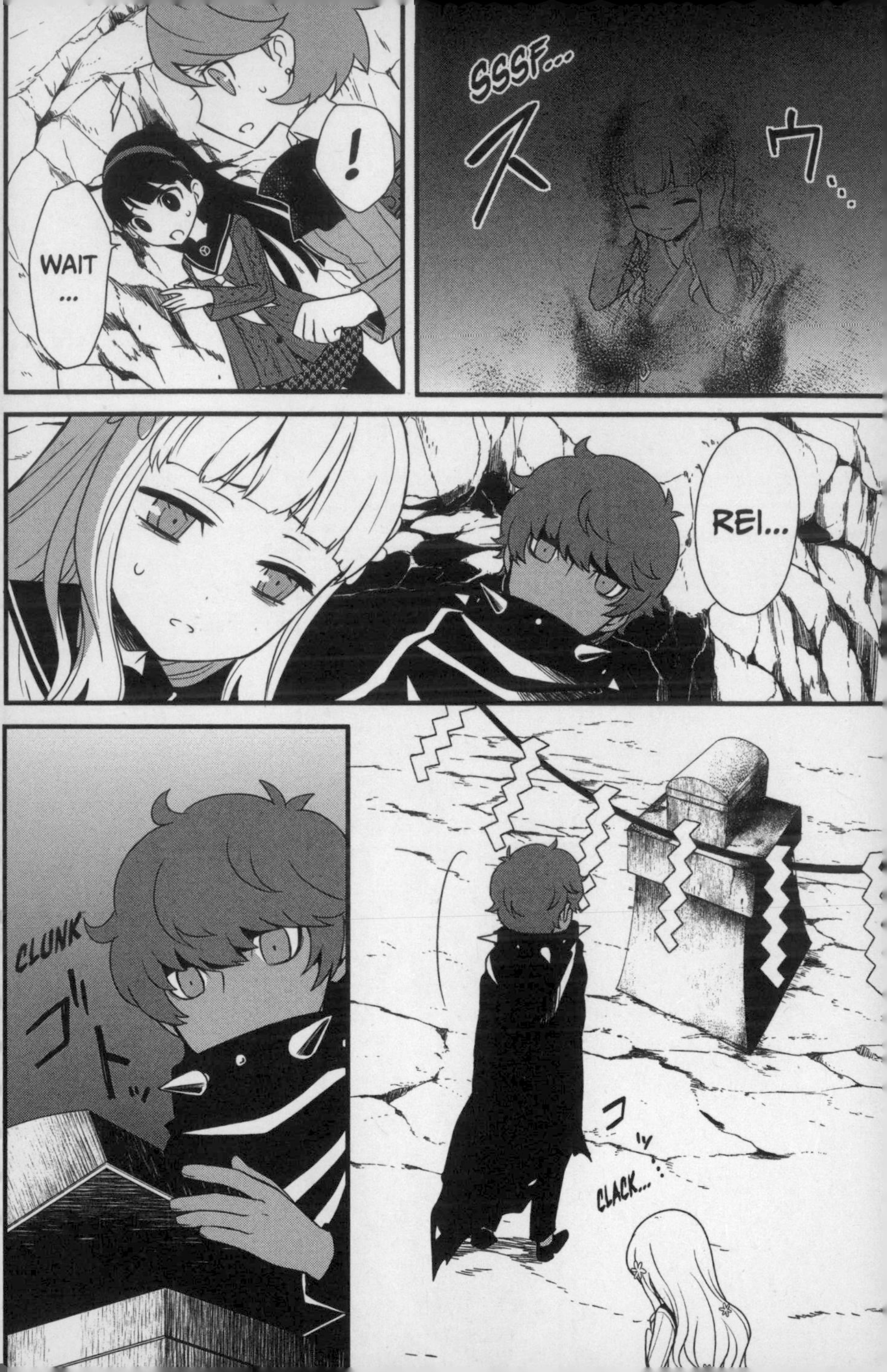
SSSF...
スウ...
!
WAIT ...
REI...
コッ
CLACK...
CLUNK
ゴトッ

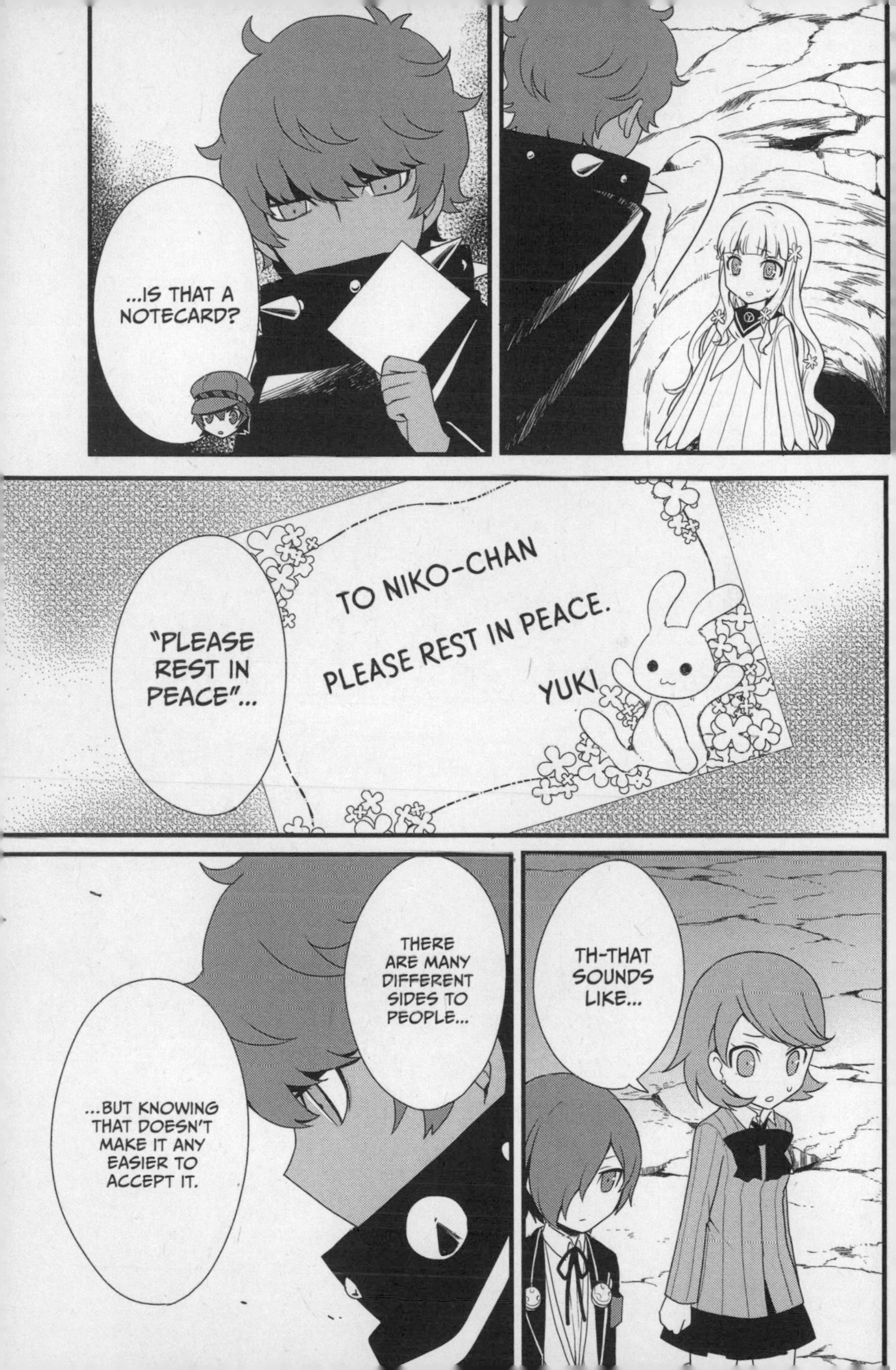
...IS THAT A NOTECARD?
TO NIKO-CHAN
PLEASE REST IN PEACE.
YUKI
"PLEASE REST IN PEACE"...
TH-THAT SOUNDS LIKE...
THERE ARE MANY DIFFERENT SIDES TO PEOPLE...
...BUT KNOWING THAT DOESN'T MAKE IT ANY EASIER TO ACCEPT IT.

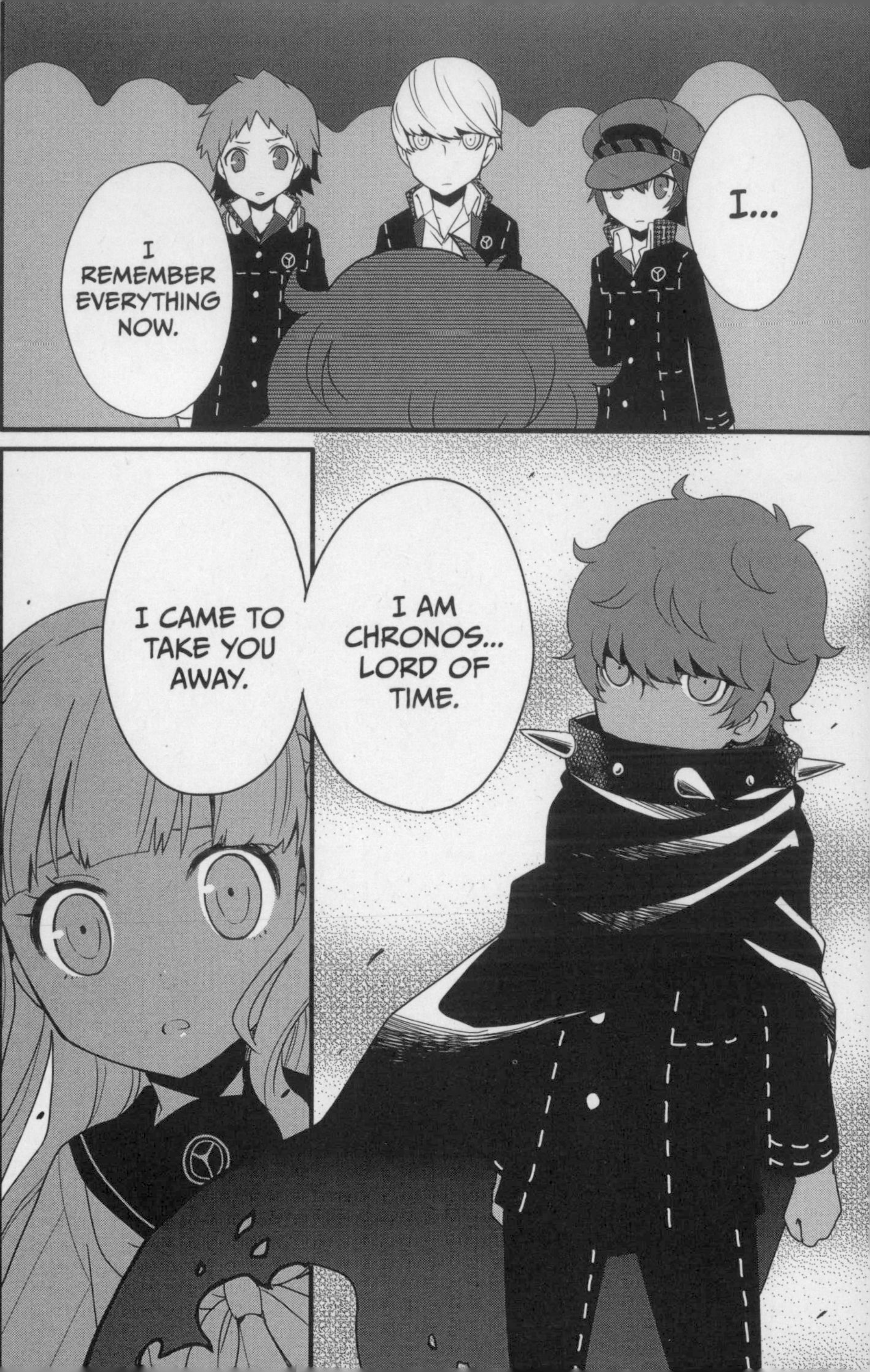
I...
I REMEMBER EVERYTHING NOW.
I AM CHRONOS... LORD OF TIME.
I CAME TO TAKE YOU AWAY.

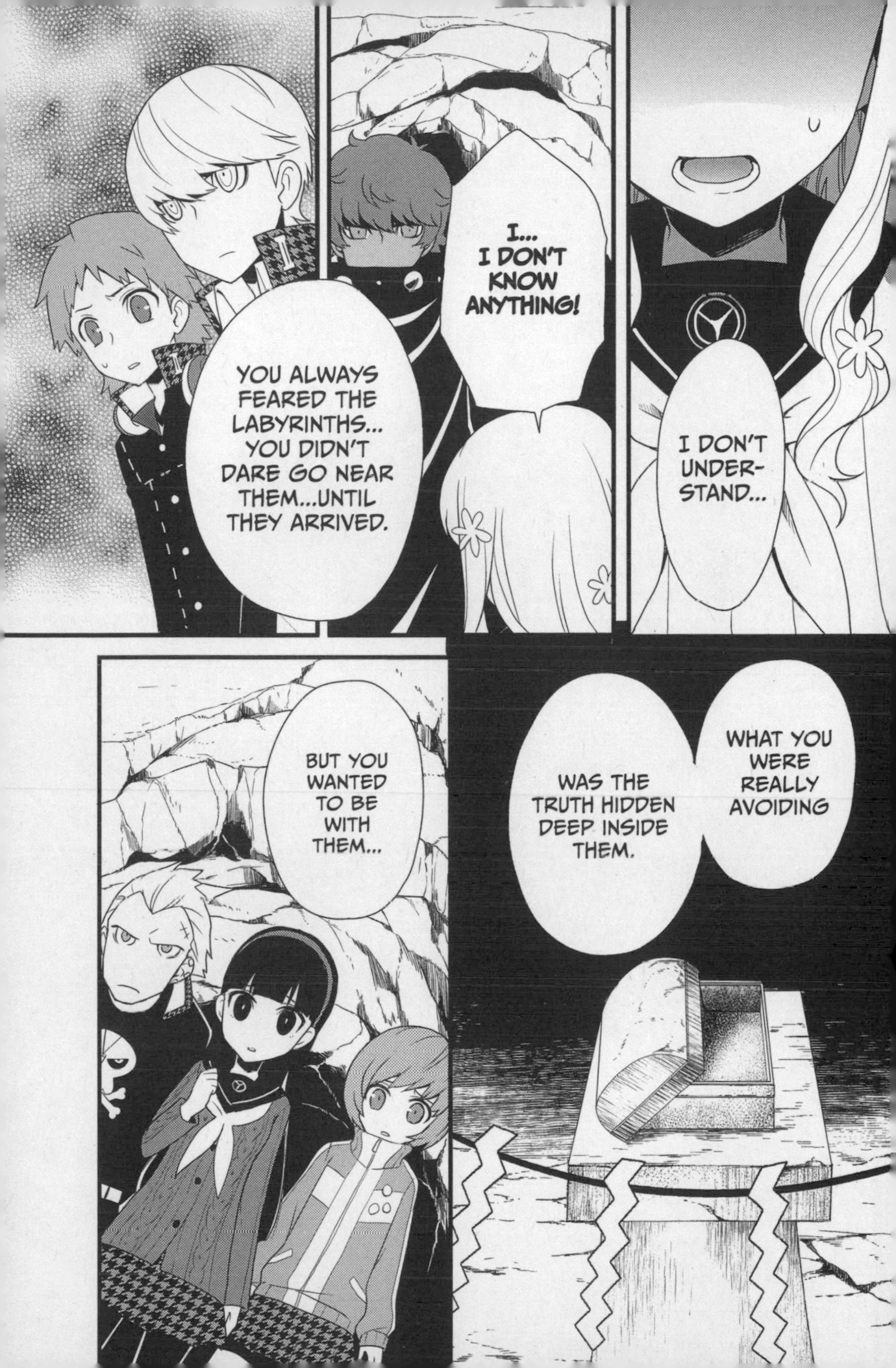
I DON'T UNDER-STAND...
I... I DON'T KNOW ANYTHING!
YOU ALWAYS FEARED THE LABYRINTHS... YOU DIDN'T DARE GO NEAR THEM...UNTIL THEY ARRIVED.
WHAT YOU WERE REALLY AVOIDING
WAS THE TRUTH HIDDEN DEEP INSIDE THEM.
BUT YOU WANTED TO BE WITH THEM...

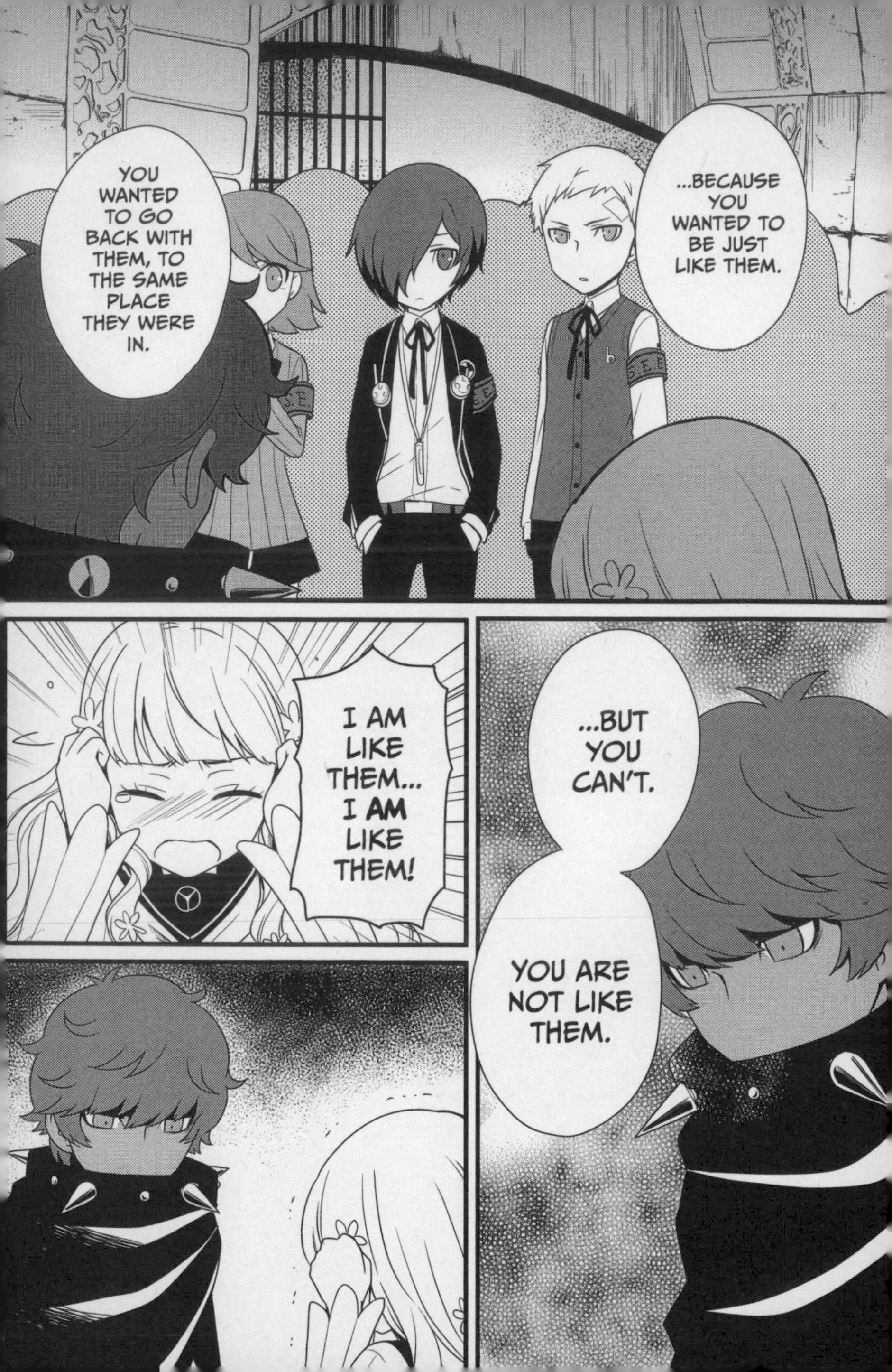
...BECAUSE YOU WANTED TO BE JUST LIKE THEM.
YOU WANTED TO GO BACK WITH THEM, TO THE SAME PLACE THEY WERE IN.
...BUT YOU CAN'T.
YOU ARE NOT LIKE THEM.
I AM LIKE THEM... I AM LIKE THEM!

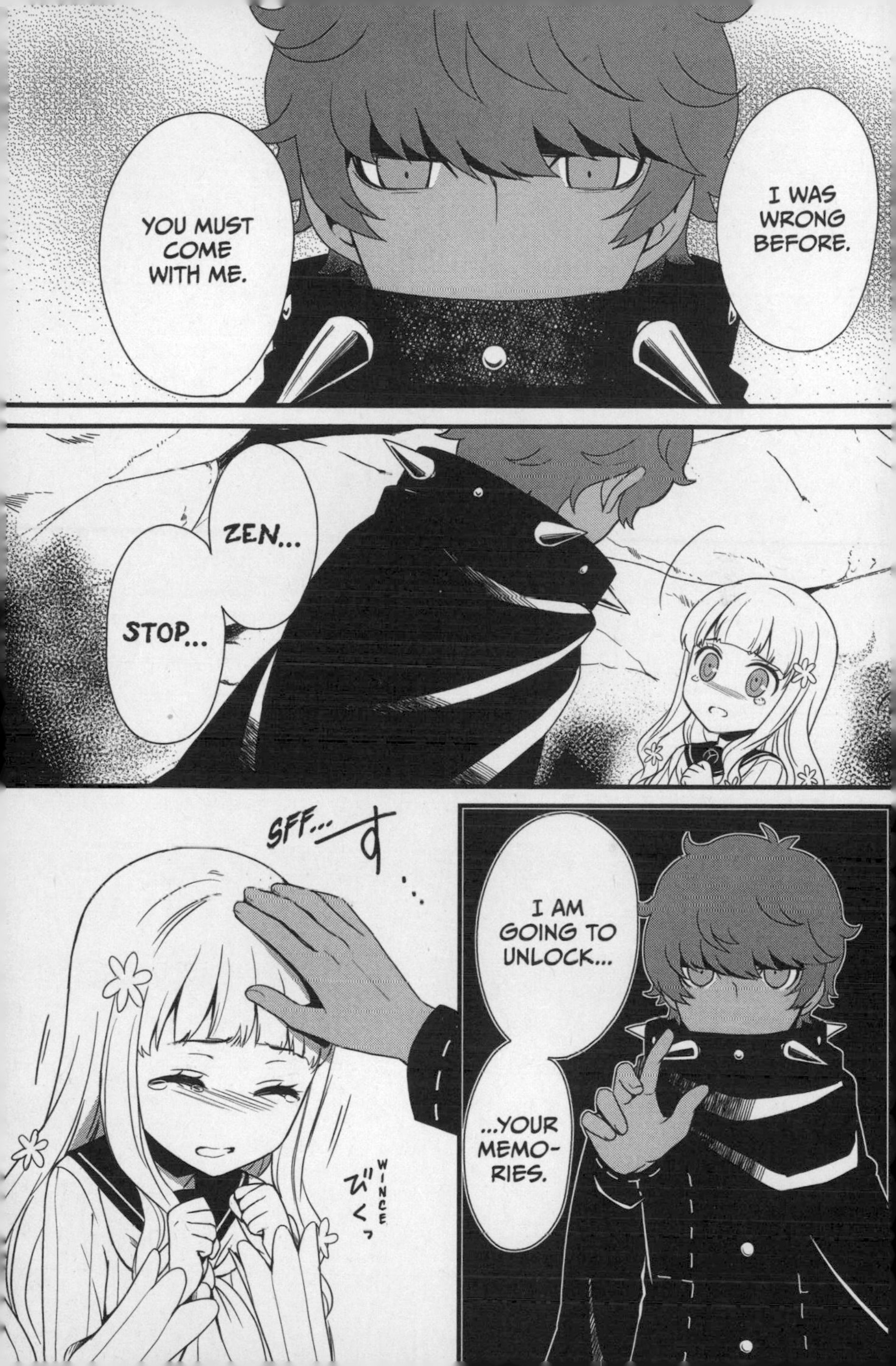
I WAS WRONG BEFORE.
YOU MUST COME WITH ME.
ZEN...
STOP...
I AM GOING TO UNLOCK...
...YOUR MEMO-RIES.
SFF... す
WINCE びくっ

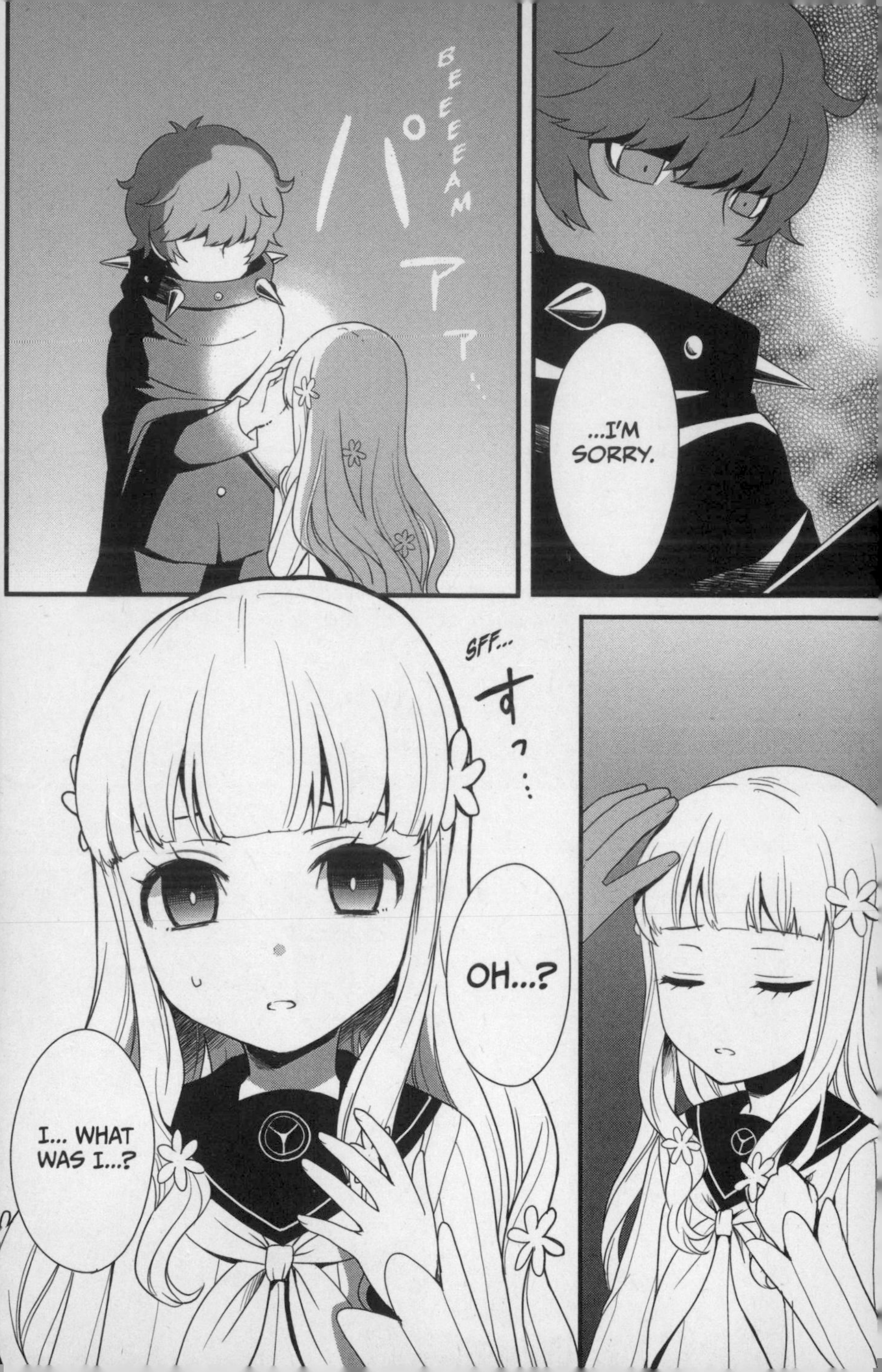
...I'M SORRY.
BEEEEEAM
パアア…
SFF...
すっ…
OH...?
I... WHAT WAS I...?

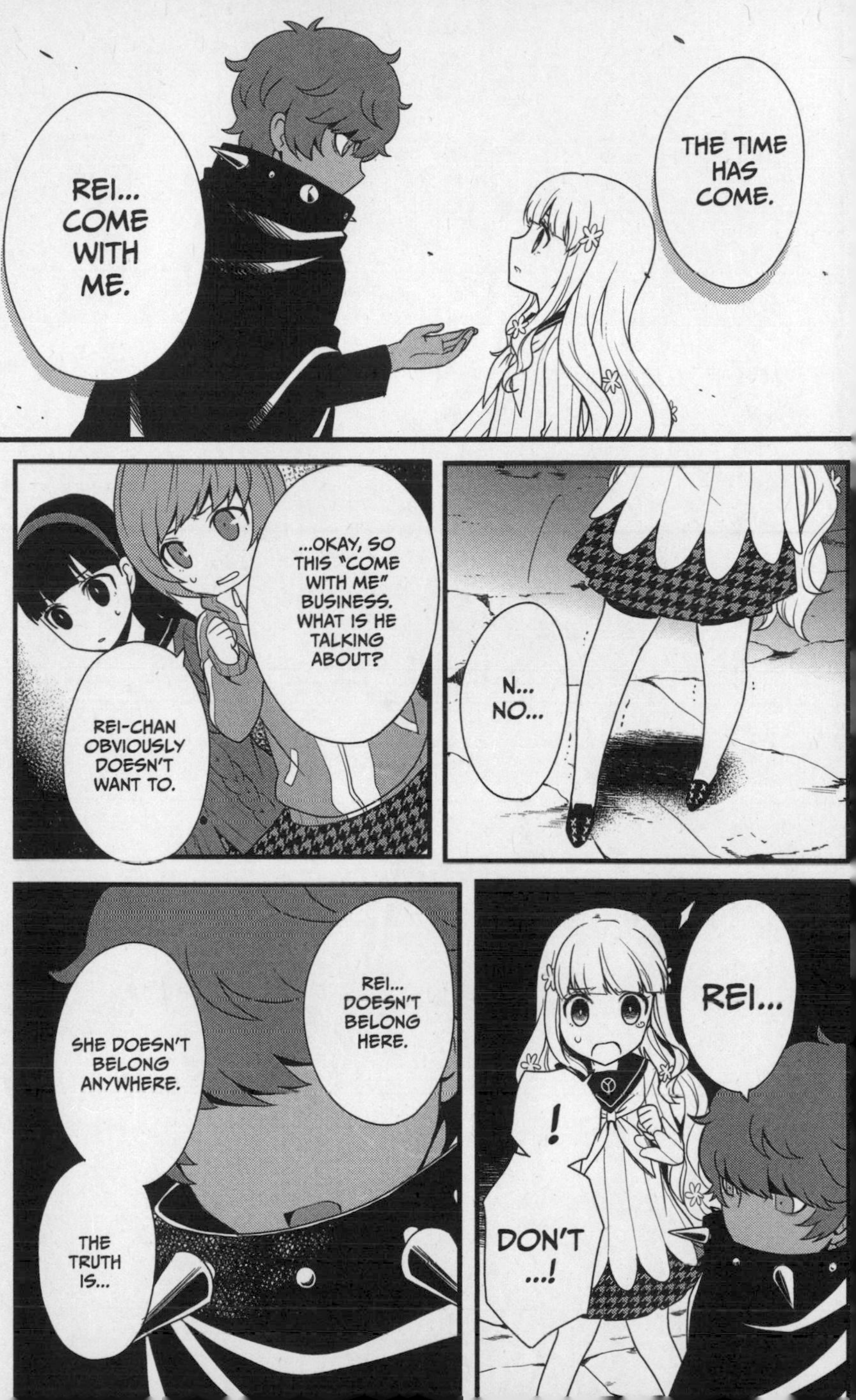
THE TIME HAS COME.
REI... COME WITH ME.
N... NO...
...OKAY, SO THIS "COME WITH ME" BUSINESS. WHAT IS HE TALKING ABOUT?
REI-CHAN OBVIOUSLY DOESN'T WANT TO.
REI...
!
DON'T ...!
REI... DOESN'T BELONG HERE.
SHE DOESN'T BELONG ANYWHERE.
THE TRUTH IS...

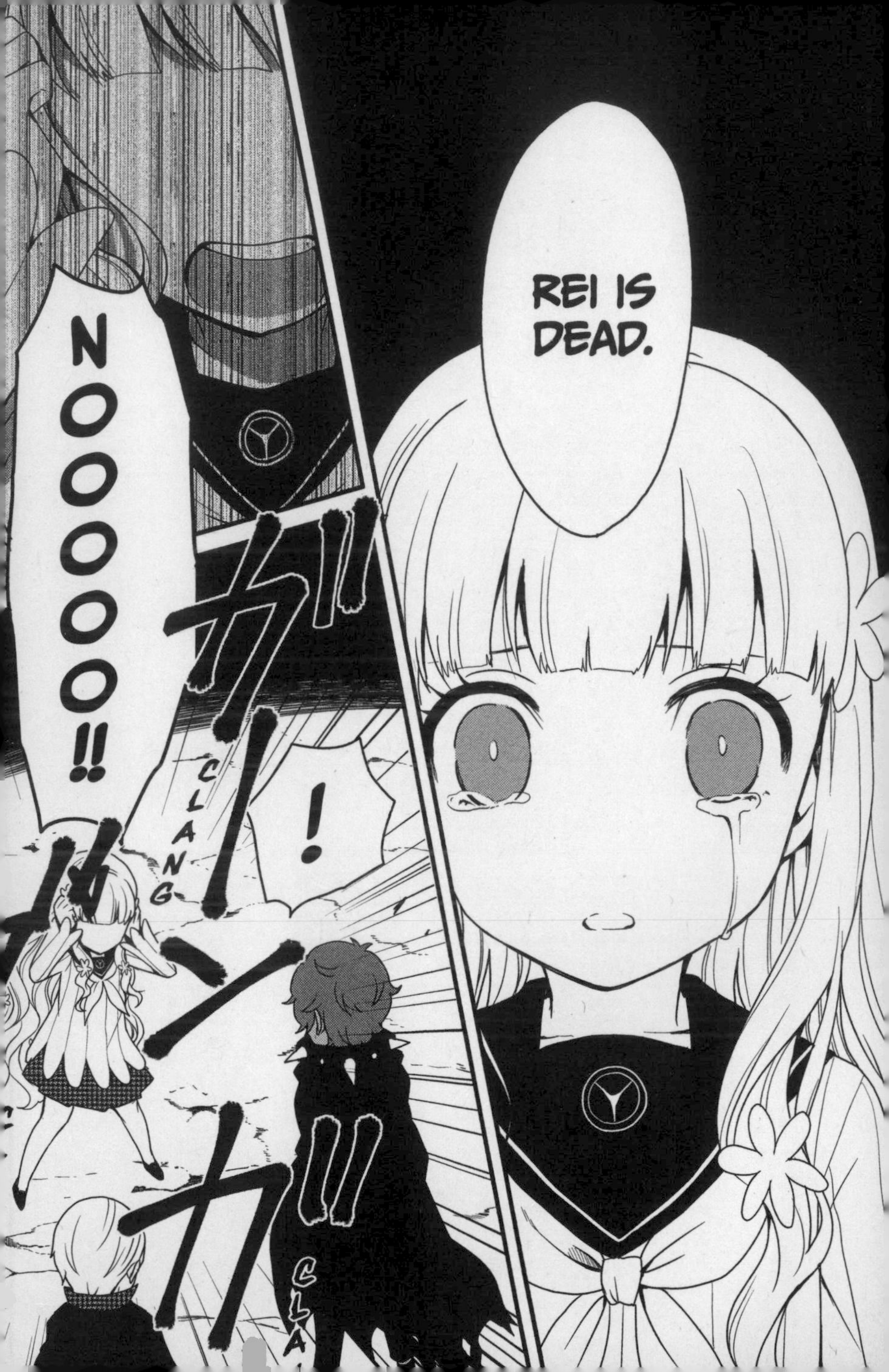
REI IS DEAD.
NOOOOOO!!
CLANG
!
CLA

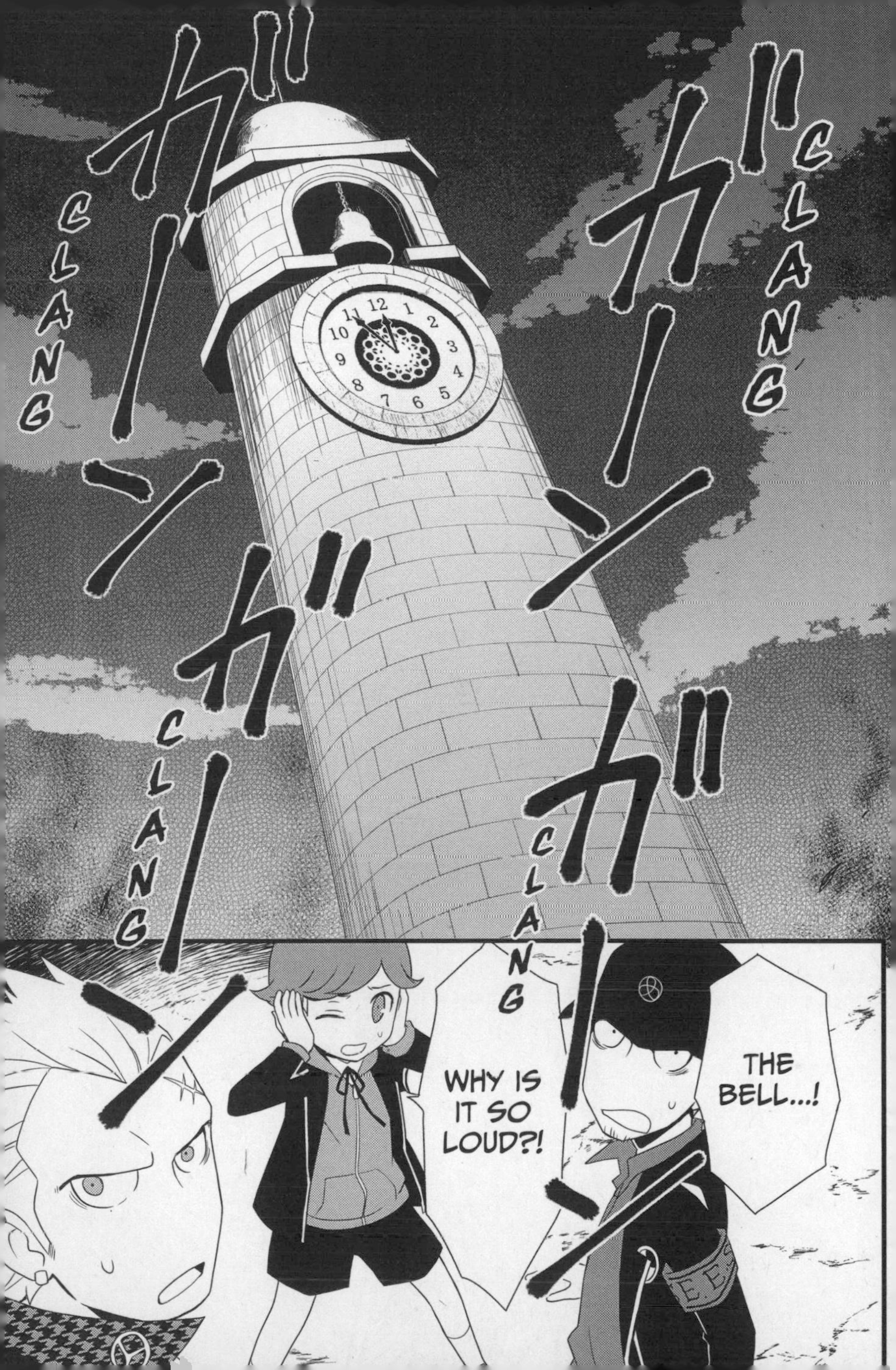
ドカーン
CLANG
ガーン
CLANG
ガー
CLANG
ガー
CLANG
THE BELL...!
WHY IS IT SO LOUD?!

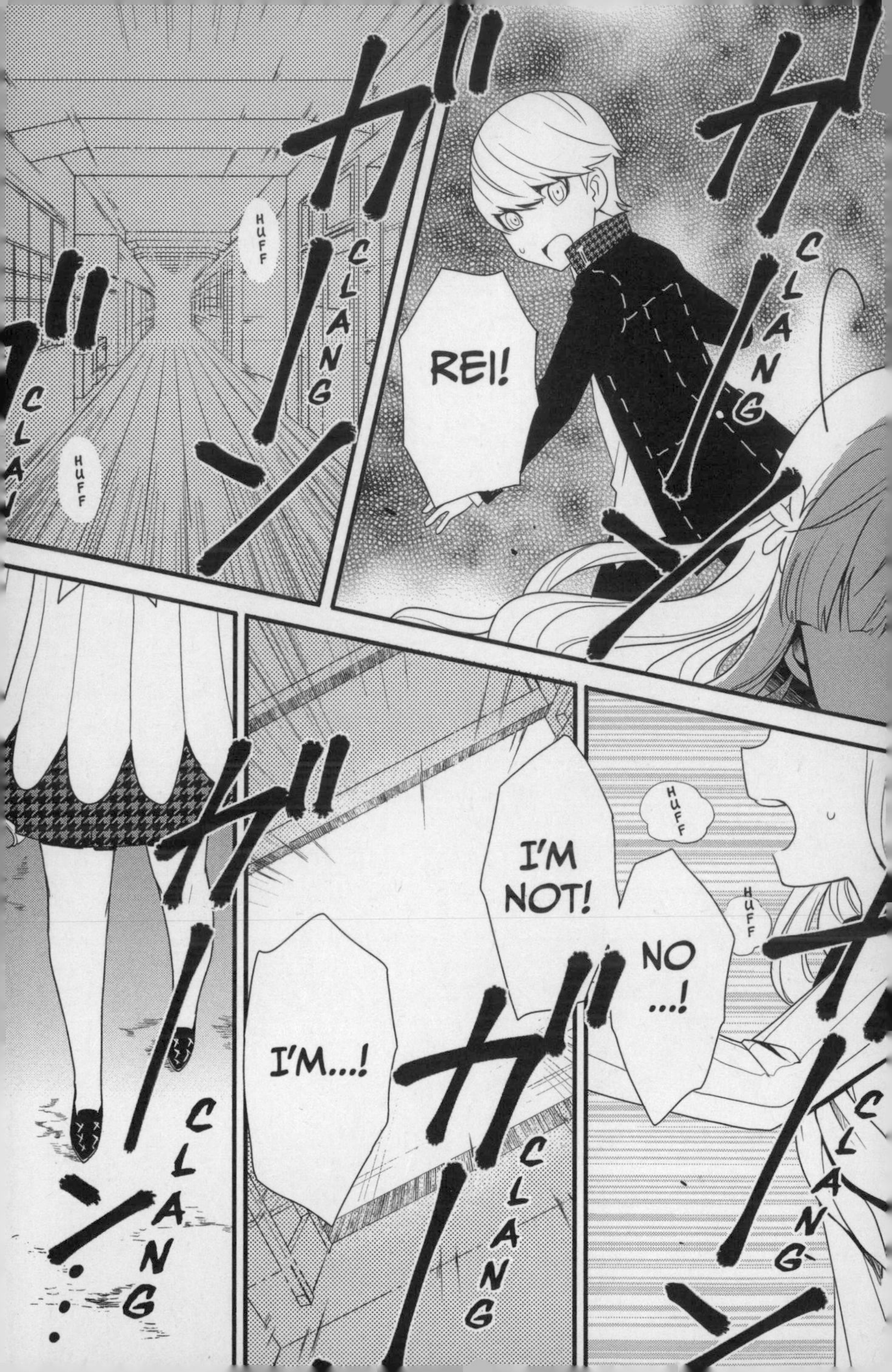
CLANG
REI!
CLANG
HUFF HUFF
HUFF HUFF
HUFF
I'M NOT!
NO ...!
HUFF
CLANG
I'M...!
CLANG
CLANG

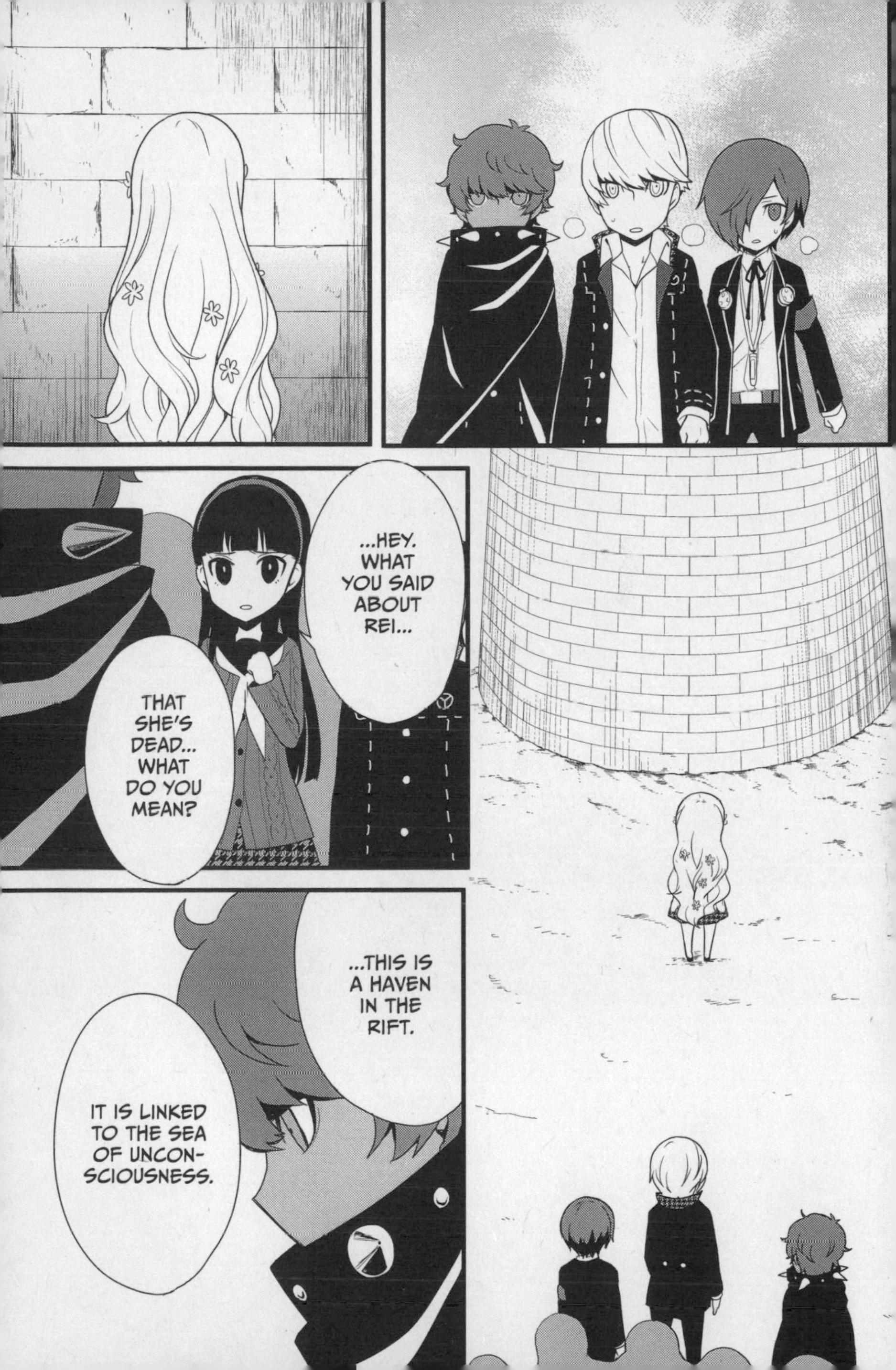
...HEY. WHAT YOU SAID ABOUT REI...
THAT SHE'S DEAD... WHAT DO YOU MEAN?
...THIS IS A HAVEN IN THE RIFT.
IT IS LINKED TO THE SEA OF UNCON-SCIOUSNESS.

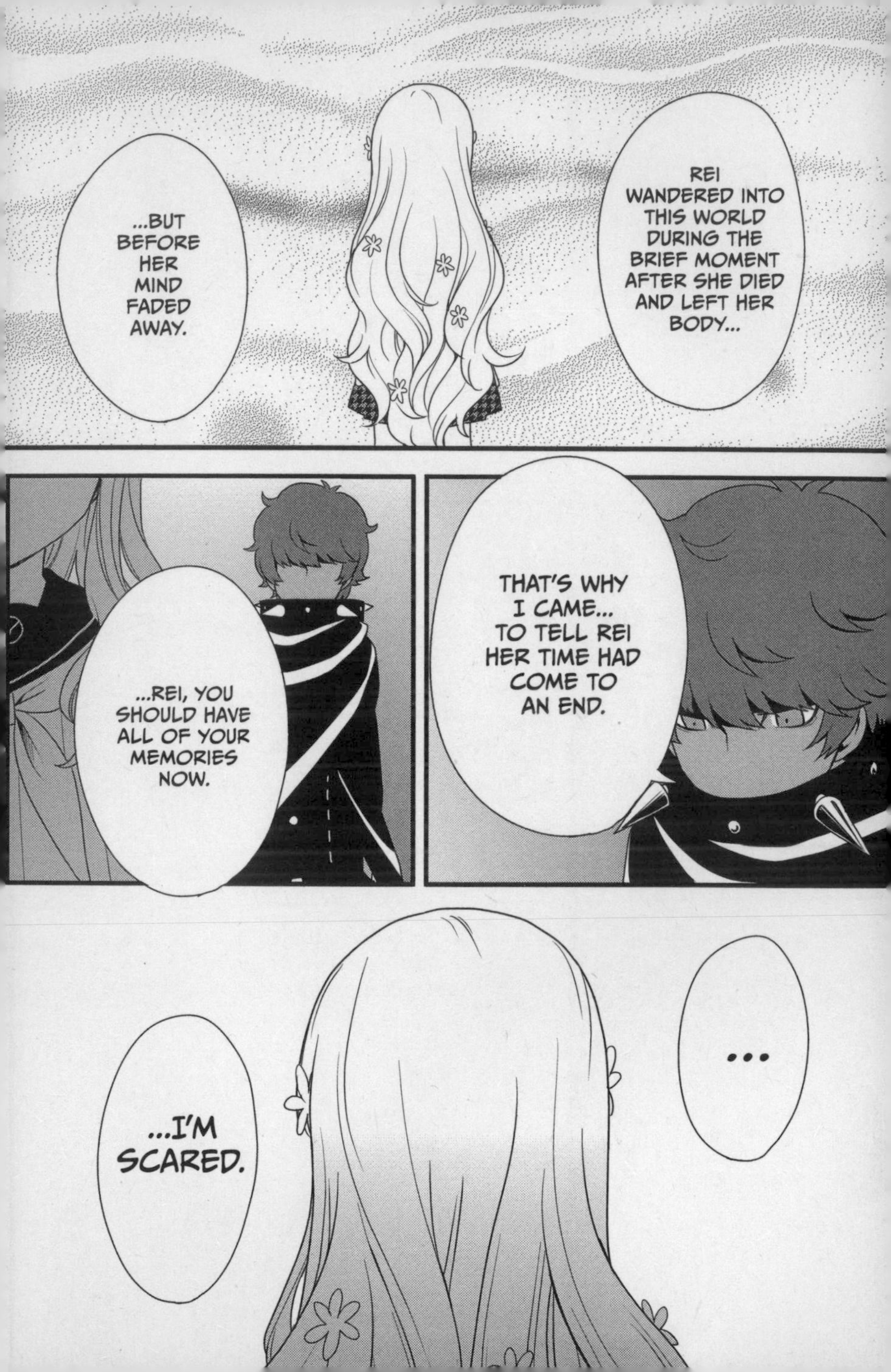
REI WANDERED INTO THIS WORLD DURING THE BRIEF MOMENT AFTER SHE DIED AND LEFT HER BODY...
...BUT BEFORE HER MIND FADED AWAY.
THAT'S WHY I CAME... TO TELL REI HER TIME HAD COME TO AN END.
...REI, YOU SHOULD HAVE ALL OF YOUR MEMORIES NOW.
...
...I'M SCARED.

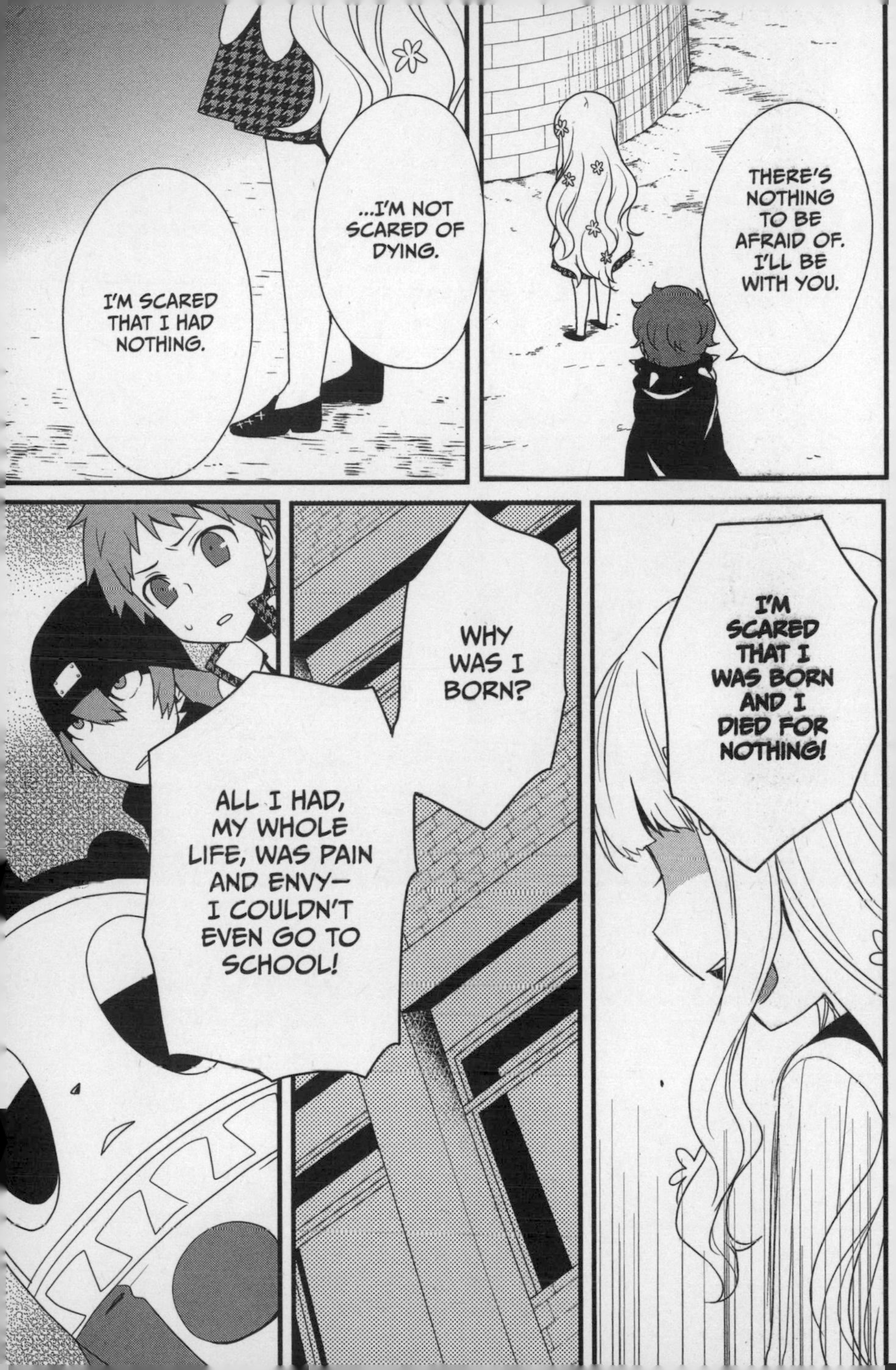
THERE'S NOTHING TO BE AFRAID OF. I'LL BE WITH YOU.
...I'M NOT SCARED OF DYING.
I'M SCARED THAT I HAD NOTHING.
I'M SCARED THAT I WAS BORN AND I DIED FOR NOTHING!
WHY WAS I BORN?
ALL I HAD, MY WHOLE LIFE, WAS PAIN AND ENVY— I COULDN'T EVEN GO TO SCHOOL!

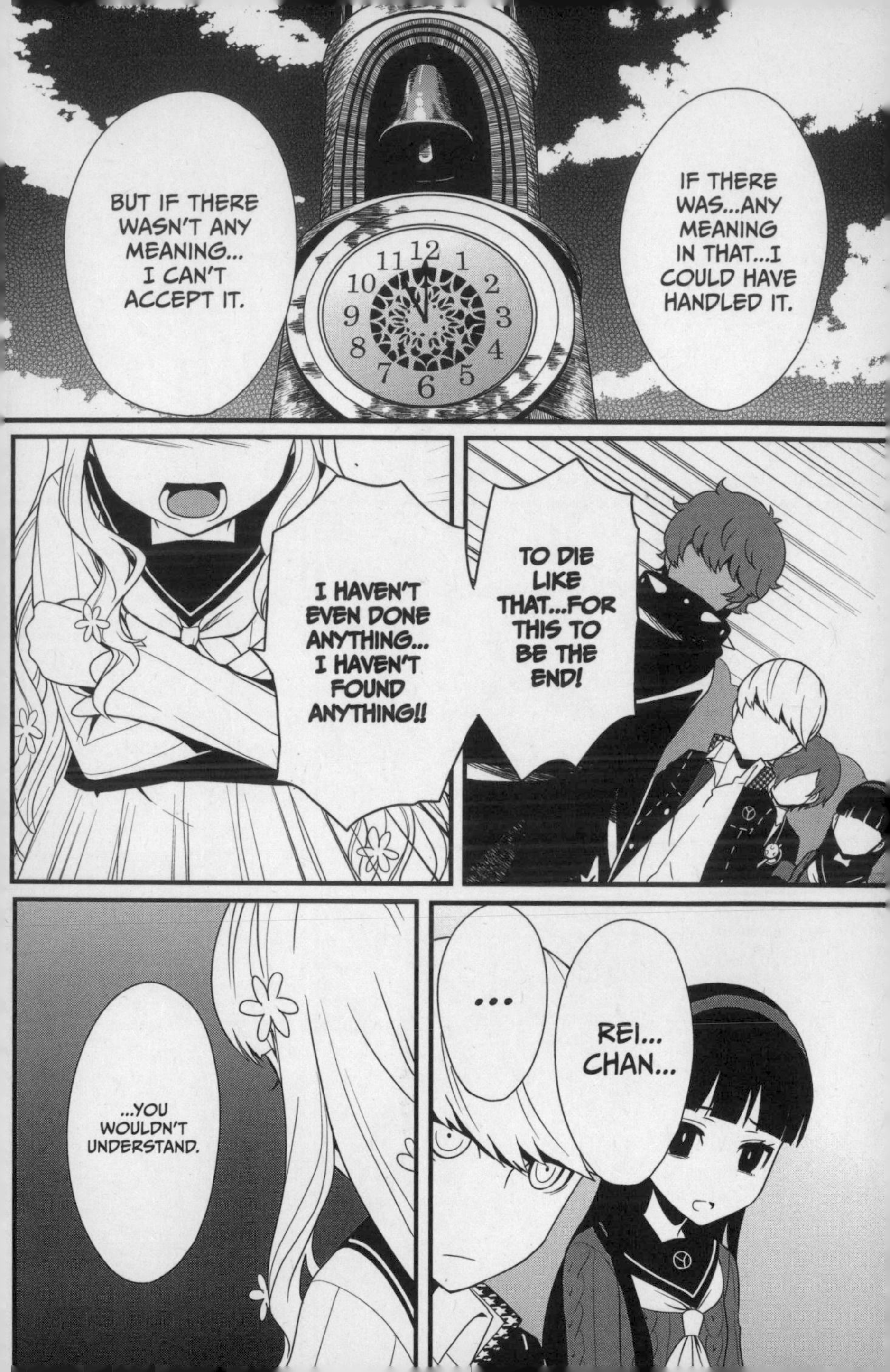

IF THERE WAS...ANY MEANING IN THAT...I COULD HAVE HANDLED IT.
BUT IF THERE WASN'T ANY MEANING... I CAN'T ACCEPT IT.
TO DIE LIKE THAT...FOR THIS TO BE THE END!
I HAVEN'T EVEN DONE ANYTHING... I HAVEN'T FOUND ANYTHING!!
REI... CHAN...
...
...YOU WOULDN'T UNDERSTAND.

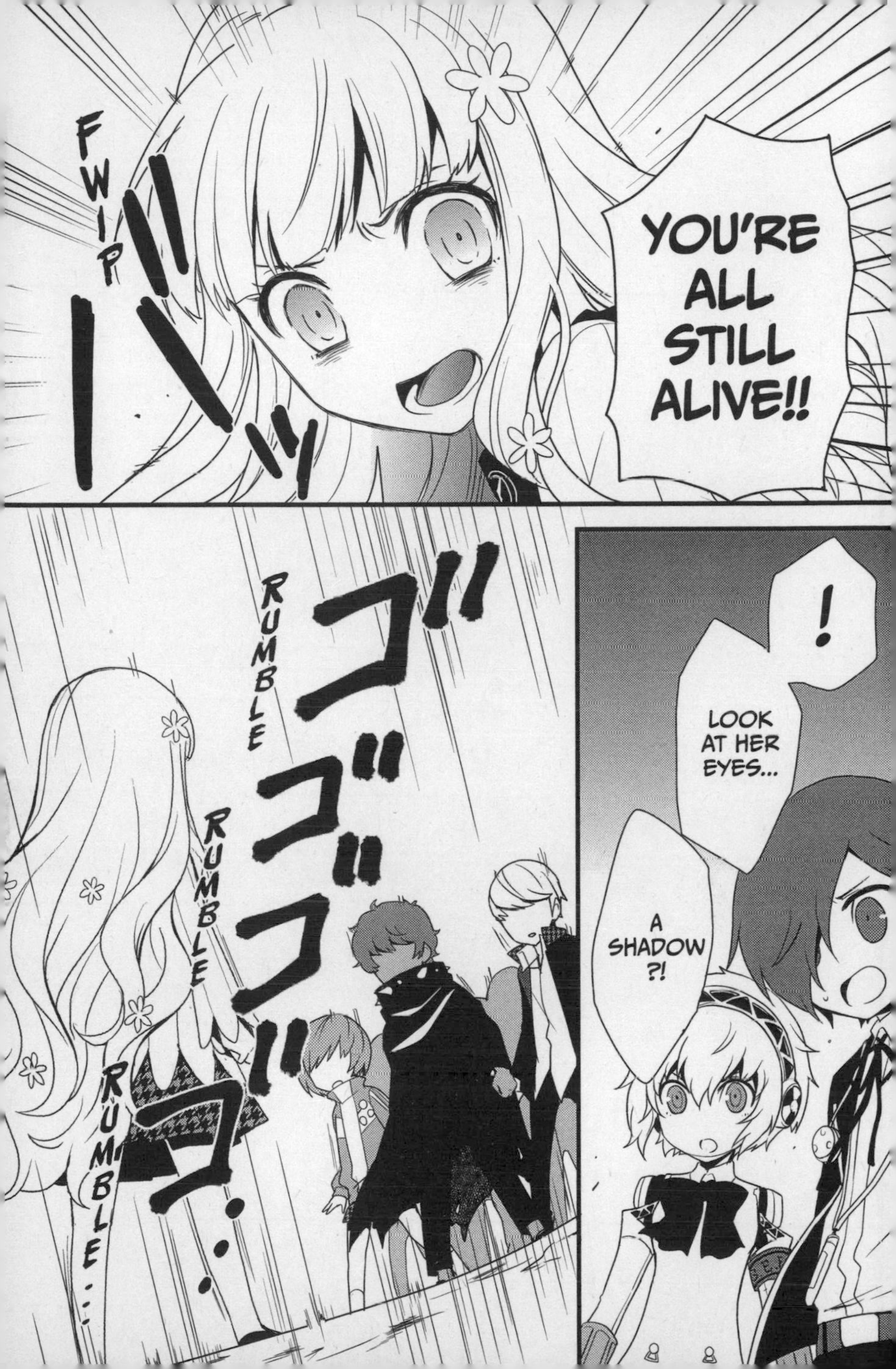
YOU'RE ALL STILL ALIVE!!
FWIP
!
LOOK AT HER EYES...
A SHADOW?!
RUMBLE
RUMBLE
RUMBLE
RUMBLE...

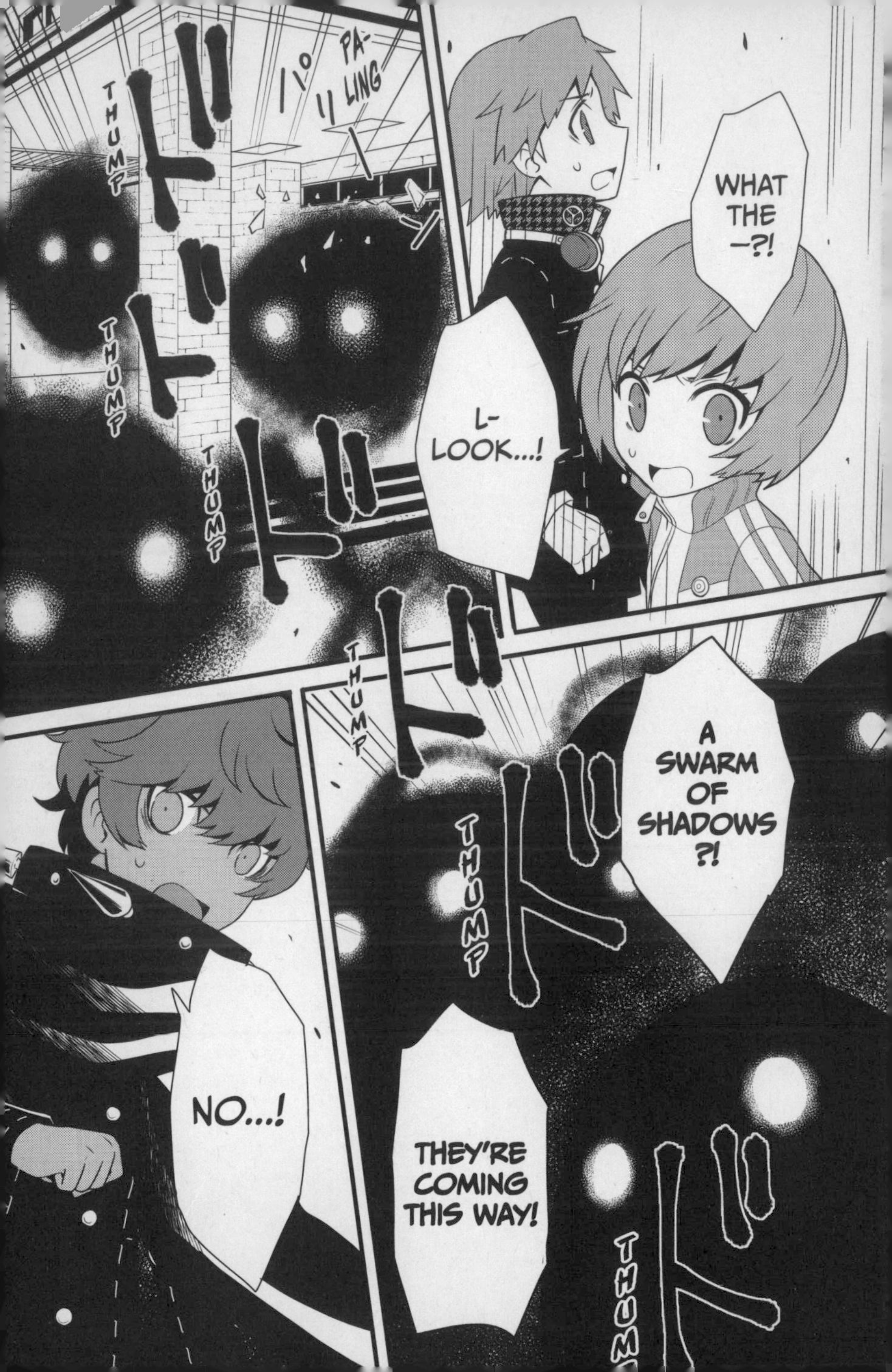
WHAT THE —?!
L-LOOK...!
PA-LING
THUMP
THUMP
THUMP
THUMP
A SWARM OF SHADOWS ?!
THUMP
THEY'RE COMING THIS WAY!
THUM
NO...!

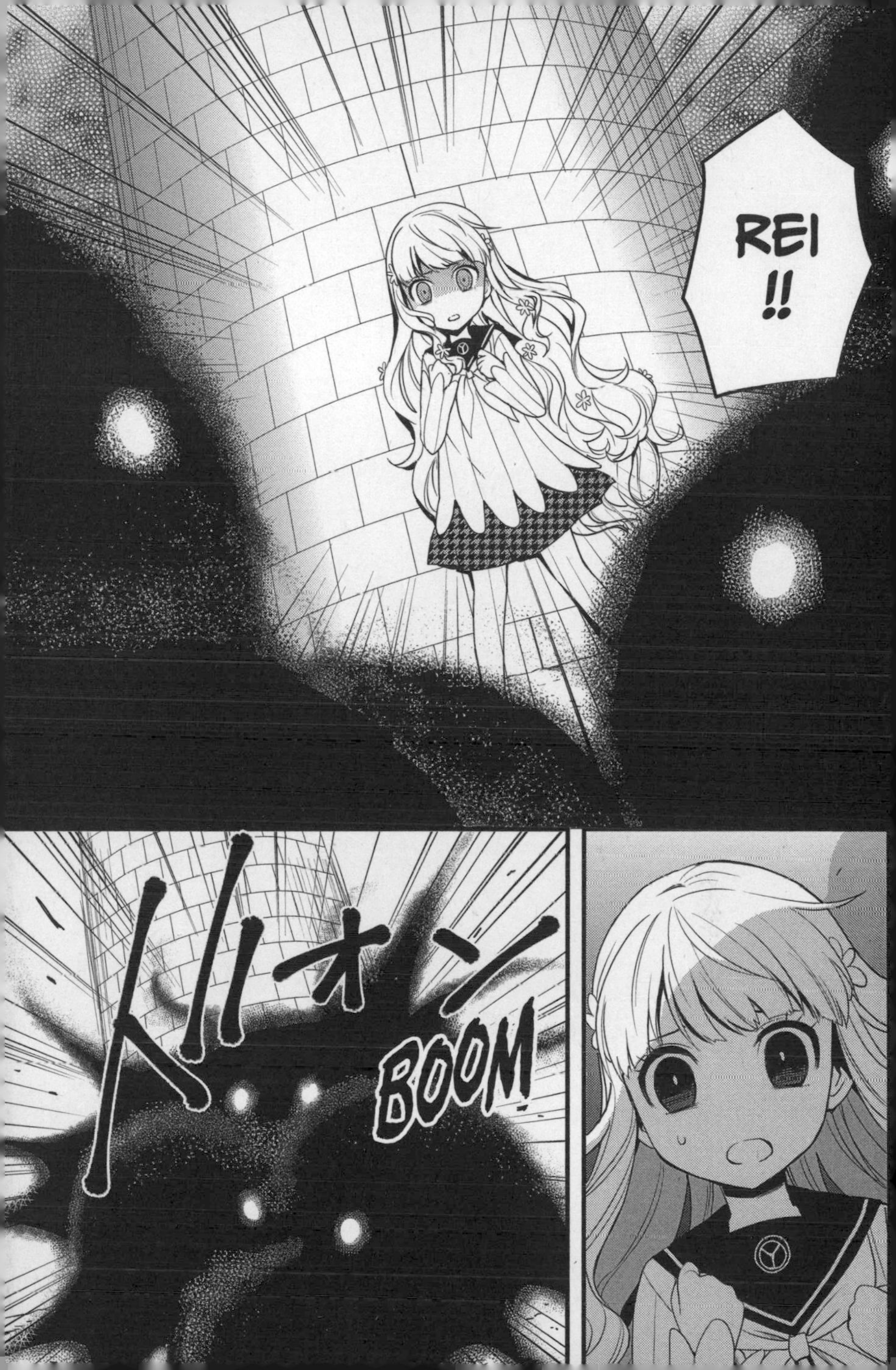
REI !!
ドオーン
BOOM

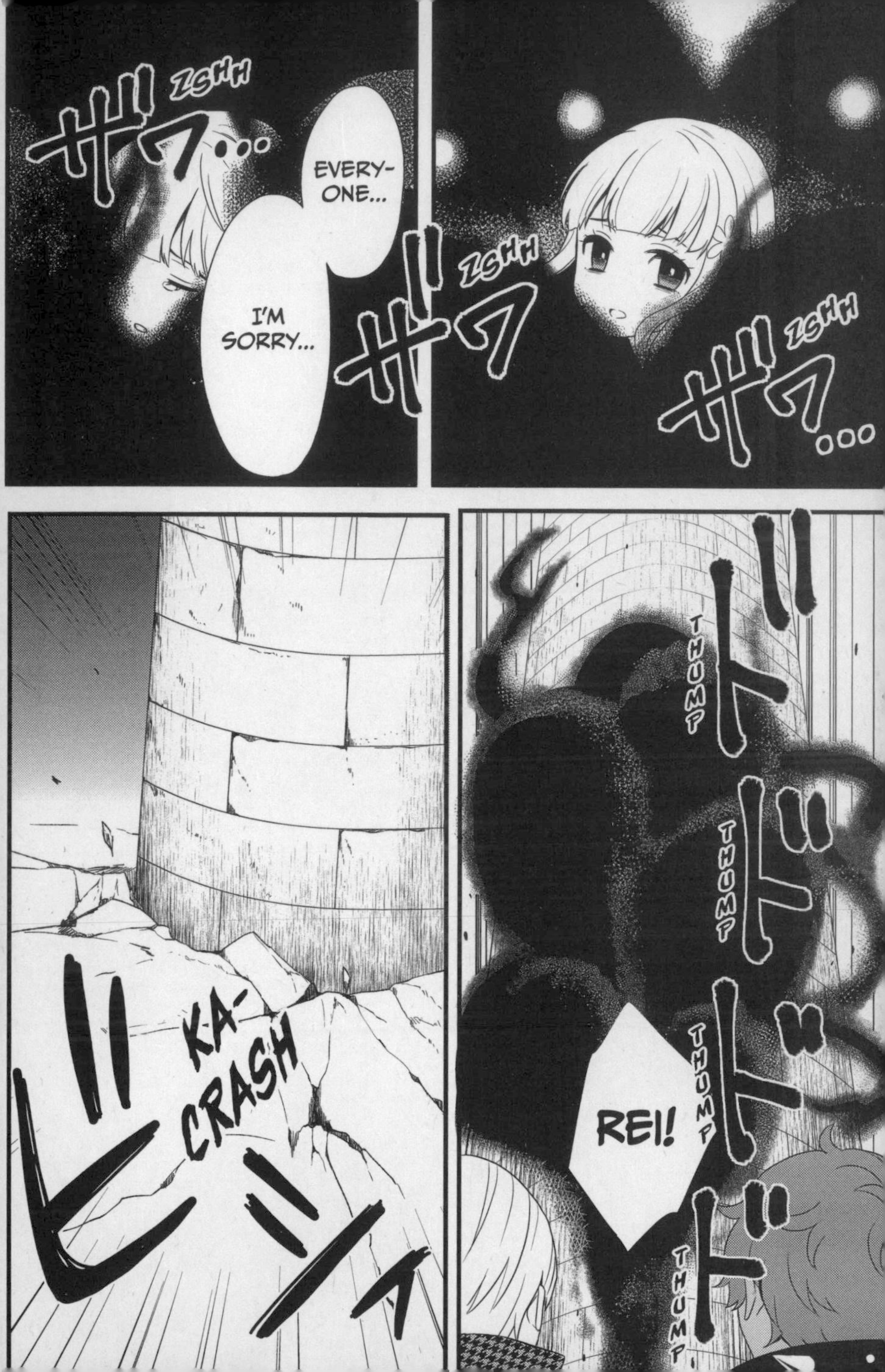
ザワ
ZSHH
ザワ…
ZSHH
ザワ…
ZSHH
EVERY-ONE...
I'M SORRY...
ドドドド
THUMP
THUMP
THUMP
REI!
THUMP
KA-CRASH
ビシッ

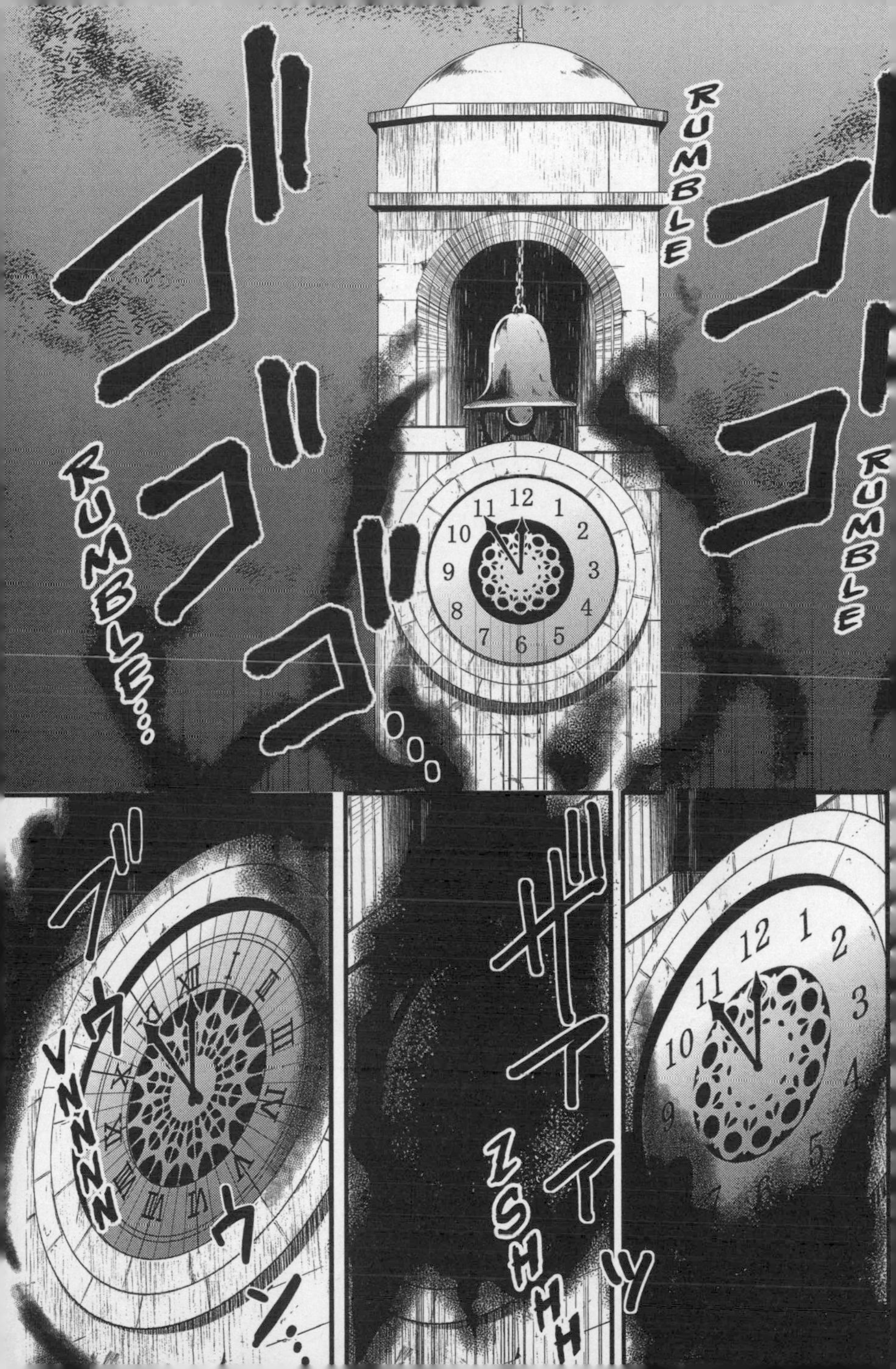
RUMBLE
RUMBLE
RUMBLE...
ZSHHH
VNNNN

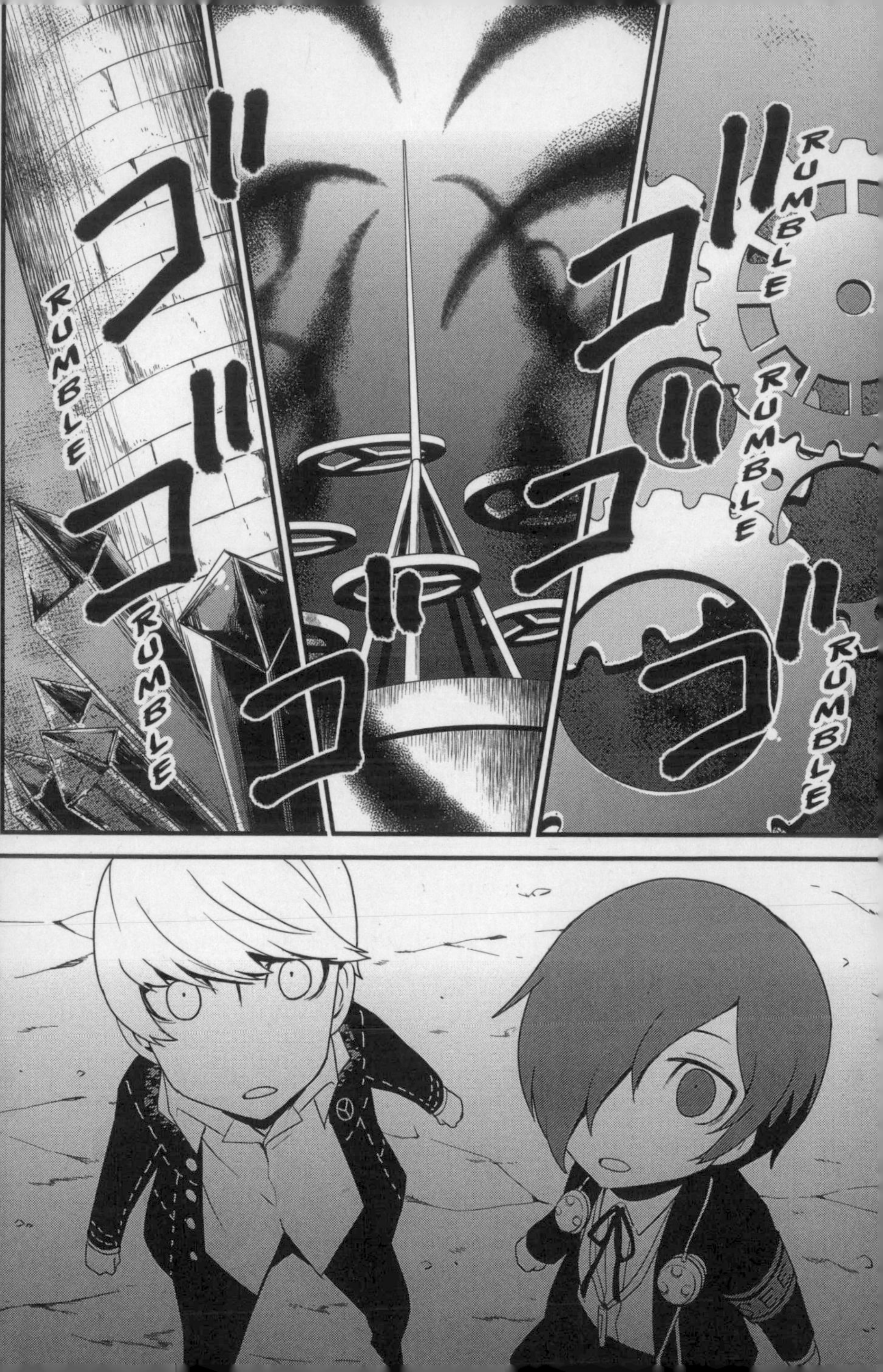
RUMBLE
RUMBLE
RUMBLE
RUMBLE
RUMBLE

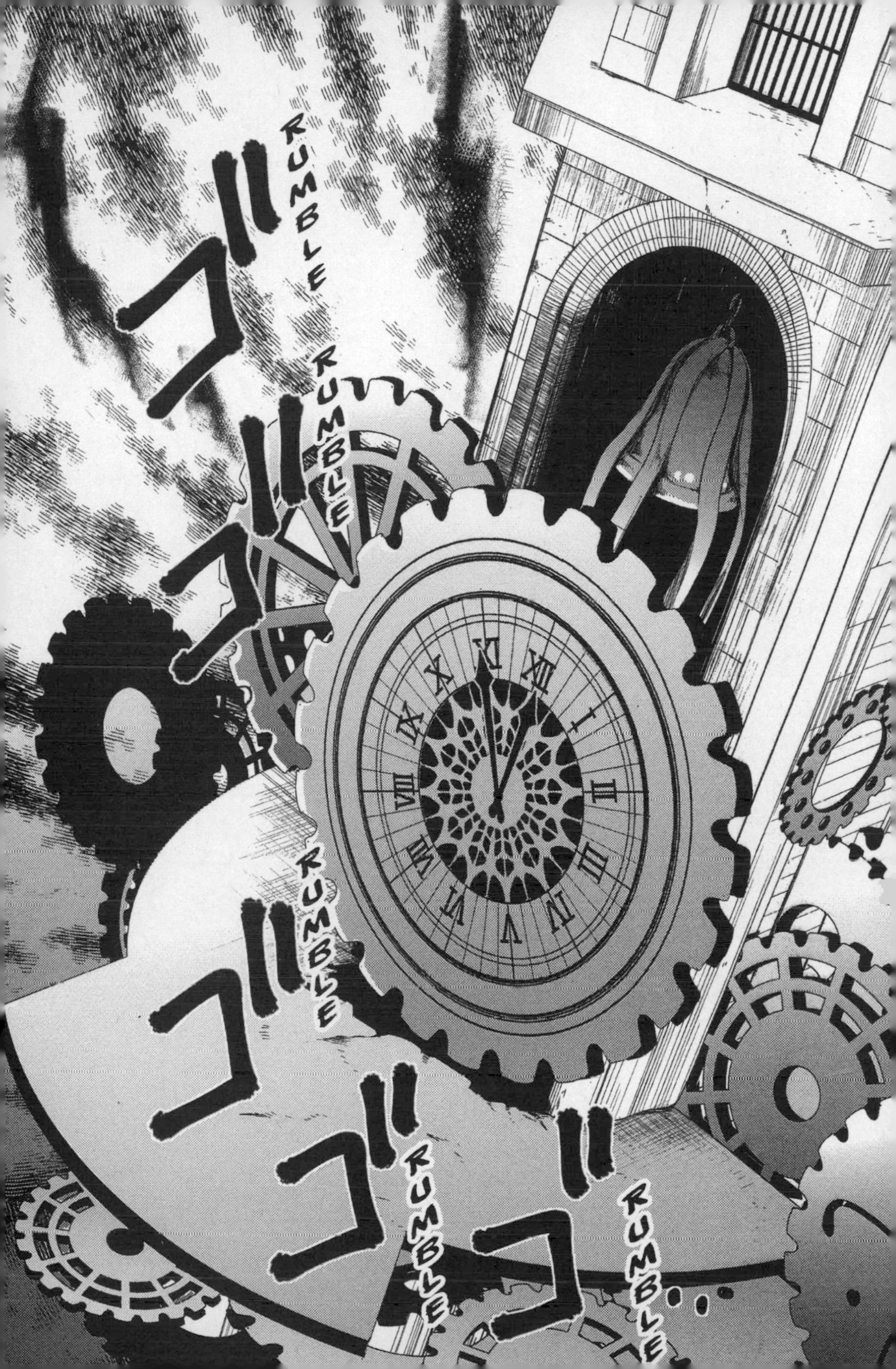
ゴゴゴ
RUMBLE
RUMBLE
ゴゴゴ…
RUMBLE
RUMBLE
RUMBLE
RUMBLE

PERSONA Q
SHADOW OF THE LABYRINTH
Side: P4

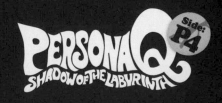

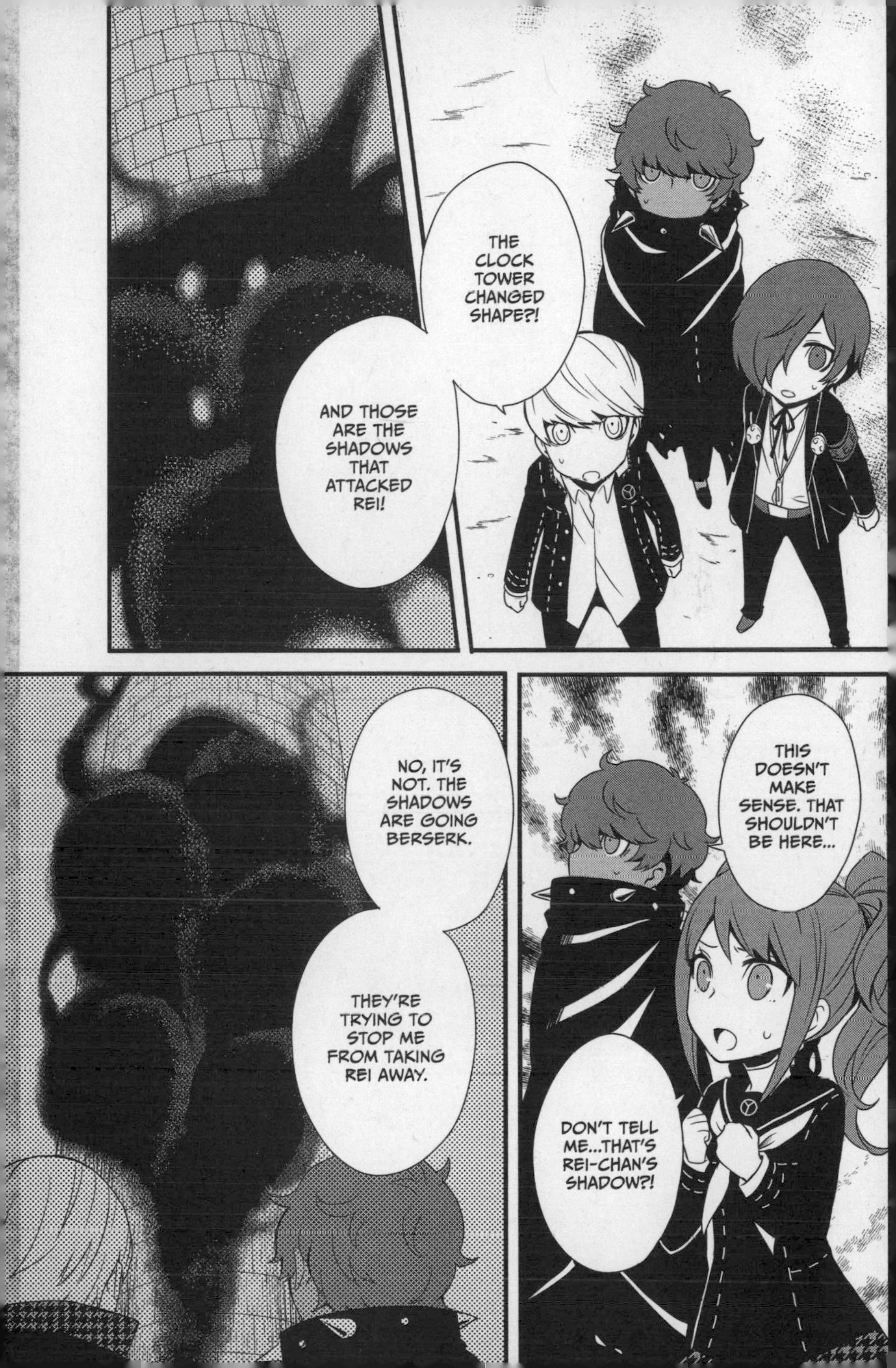
THE CLOCK TOWER CHANGED SHAPE?!
AND THOSE ARE THE SHADOWS THAT ATTACKED REI!
THIS DOESN'T MAKE SENSE. THAT SHOULDN'T BE HERE...
DON'T TELL ME...THAT'S REI-CHAN'S SHADOW?!
NO, IT'S NOT. THE SHADOWS ARE GOING BERSERK.
THEY'RE TRYING TO STOP ME FROM TAKING REI AWAY.

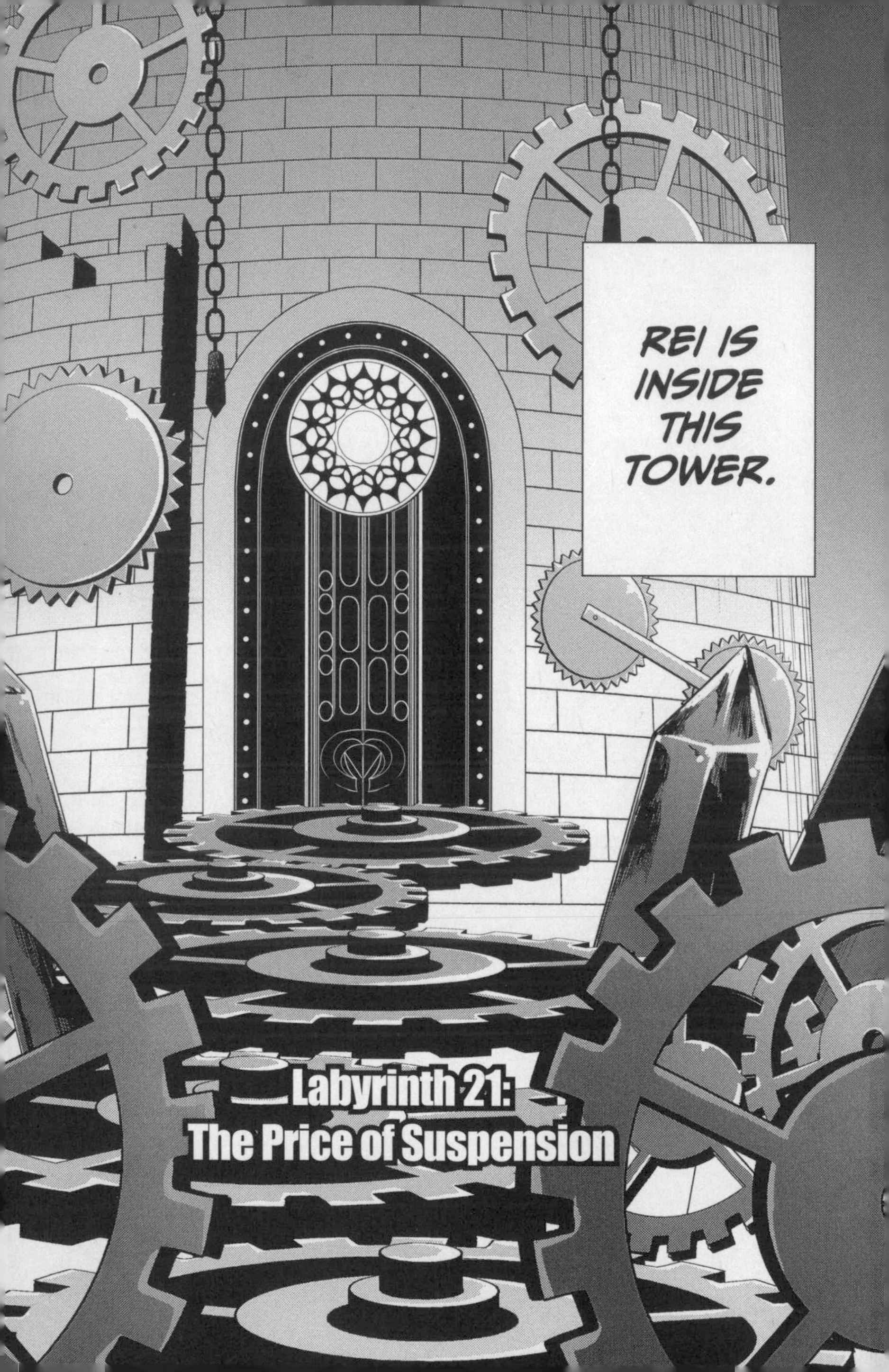
REI IS INSIDE THIS TOWER.
Labyrinth 21:
The Price of Suspension

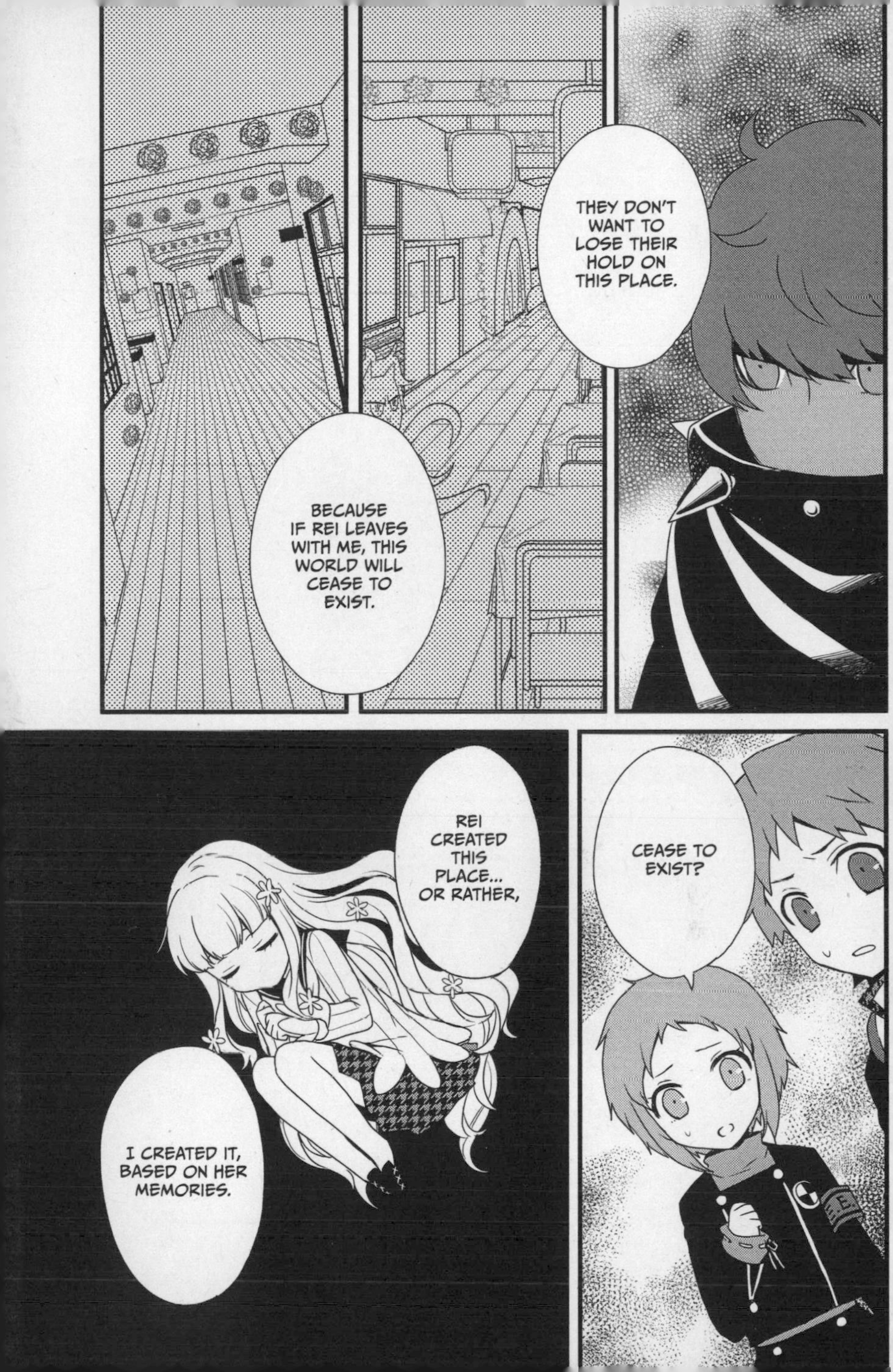
THEY DON'T WANT TO LOSE THEIR HOLD ON THIS PLACE.
BECAUSE IF REI LEAVES WITH ME, THIS WORLD WILL CEASE TO EXIST.
CEASE TO EXIST?
REI CREATED THIS PLACE... OR RATHER,
I CREATED IT, BASED ON HER MEMORIES.

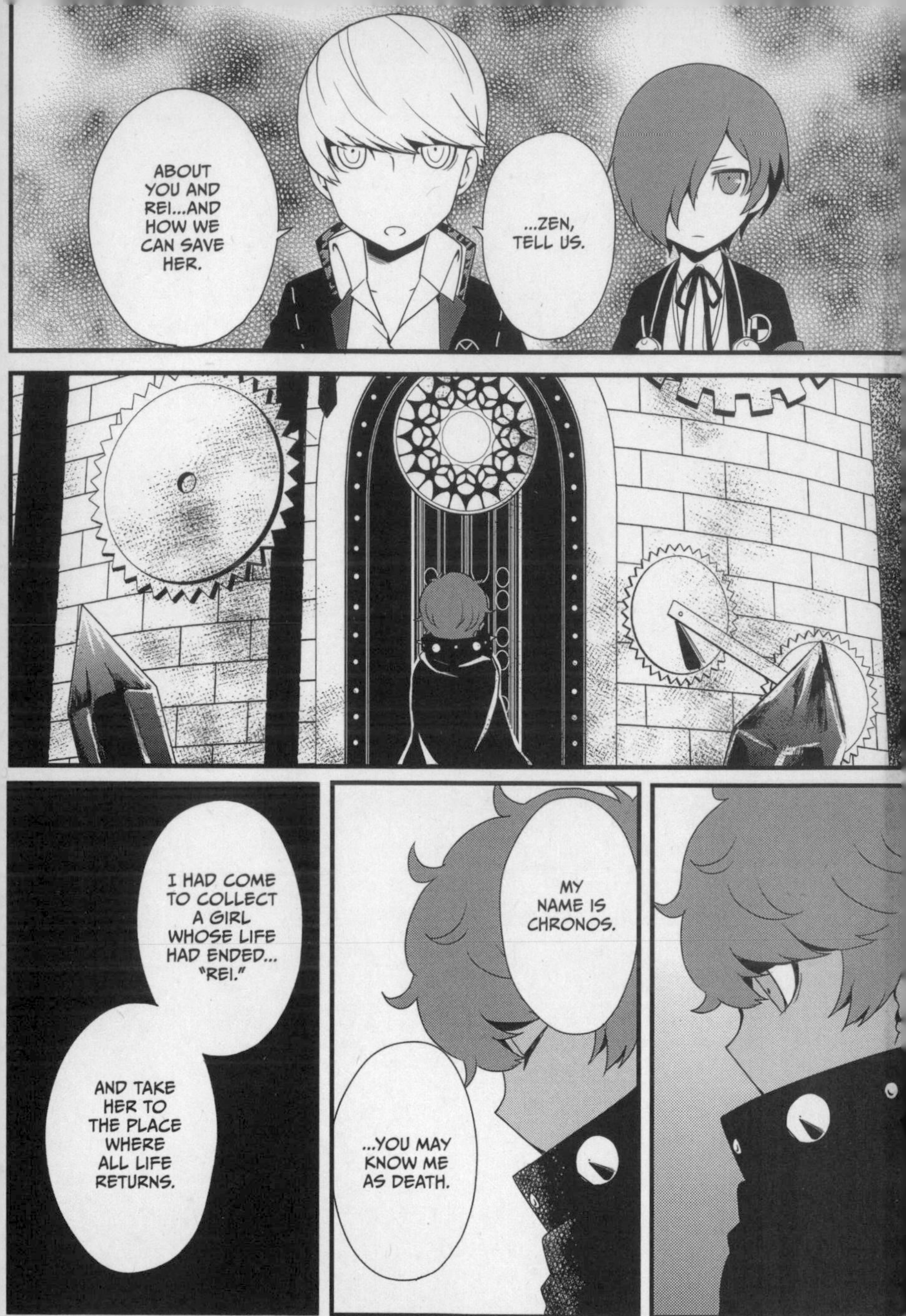
...ZEN, TELL US.
ABOUT YOU AND REI...AND HOW WE CAN SAVE HER.
MY NAME IS CHRONOS.
...YOU MAY KNOW ME AS DEATH.
I HAD COME TO COLLECT A GIRL WHOSE LIFE HAD ENDED... "REI."
AND TAKE HER TO THE PLACE WHERE ALL LIFE RETURNS.

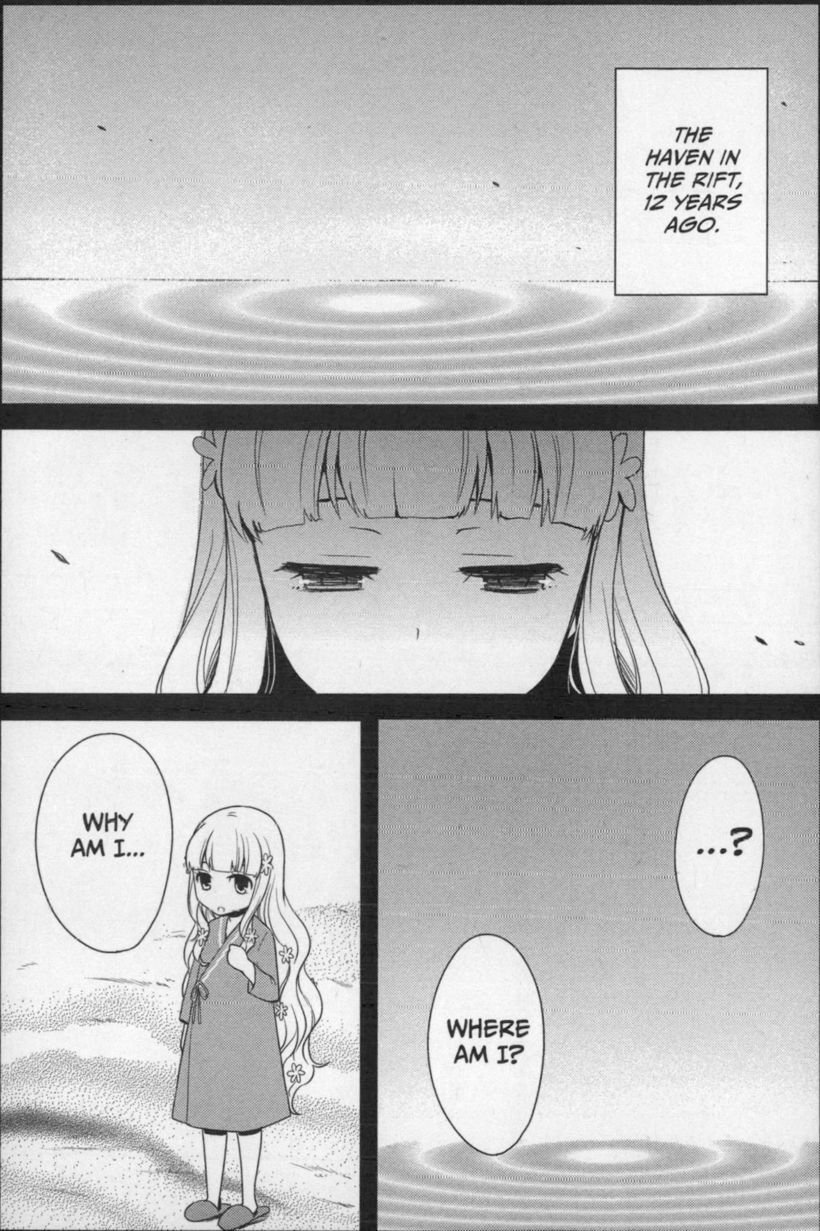
THE HAVEN IN THE RIFT, 12 YEARS AGO.
...?
WHERE AM I?
WHY AM I...

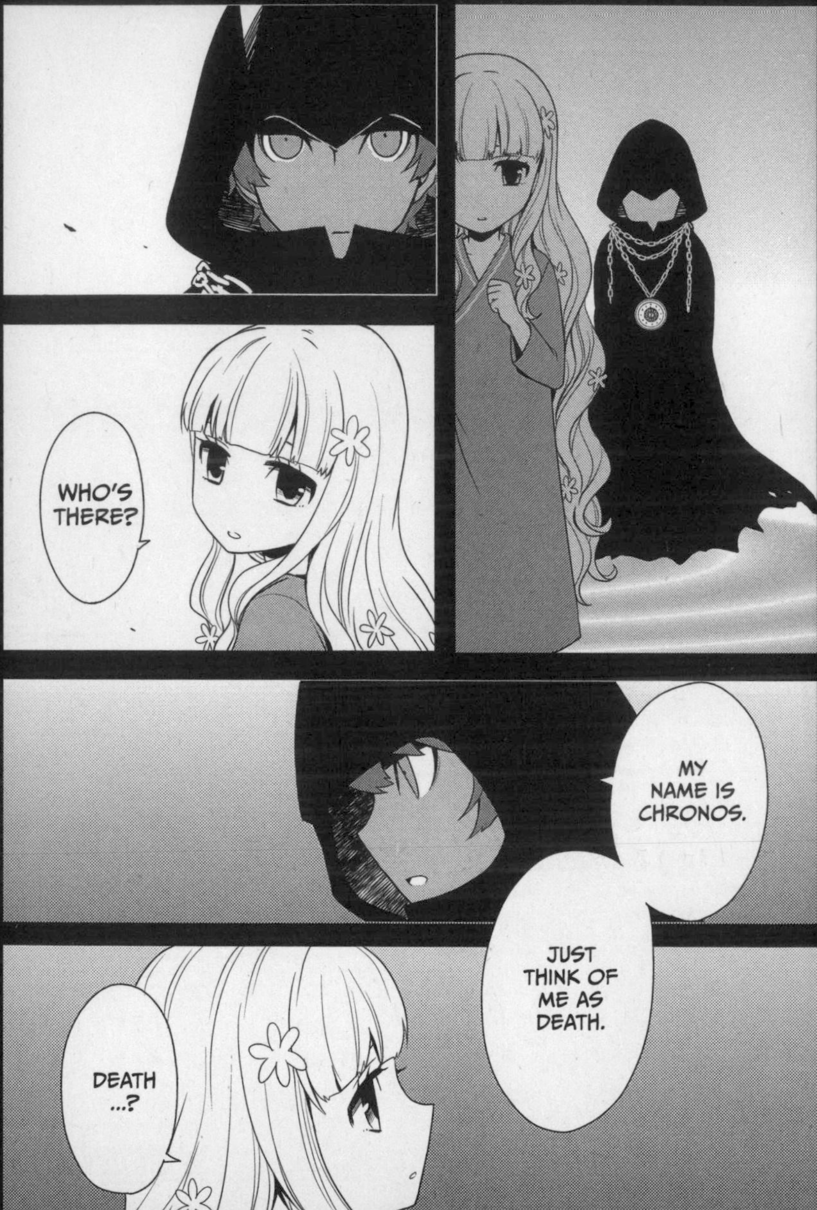
WHO'S THERE?
MY NAME IS CHRONOS.
JUST THINK OF ME AS DEATH.
DEATH ...?

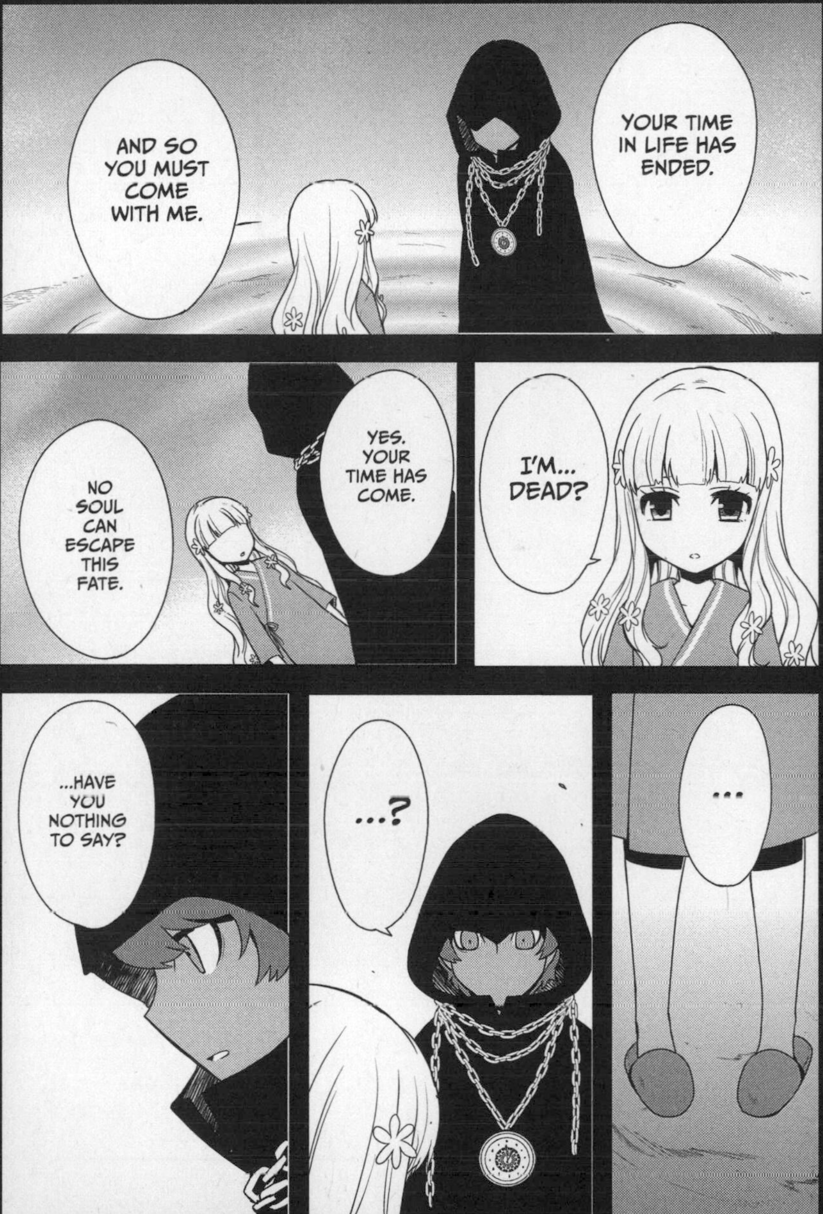
YOUR TIME IN LIFE HAS ENDED.
AND SO YOU MUST COME WITH ME.
I'M... DEAD?
YES. YOUR TIME HAS COME.
NO SOUL CAN ESCAPE THIS FATE.
...
...?
...HAVE YOU NOTHING TO SAY?

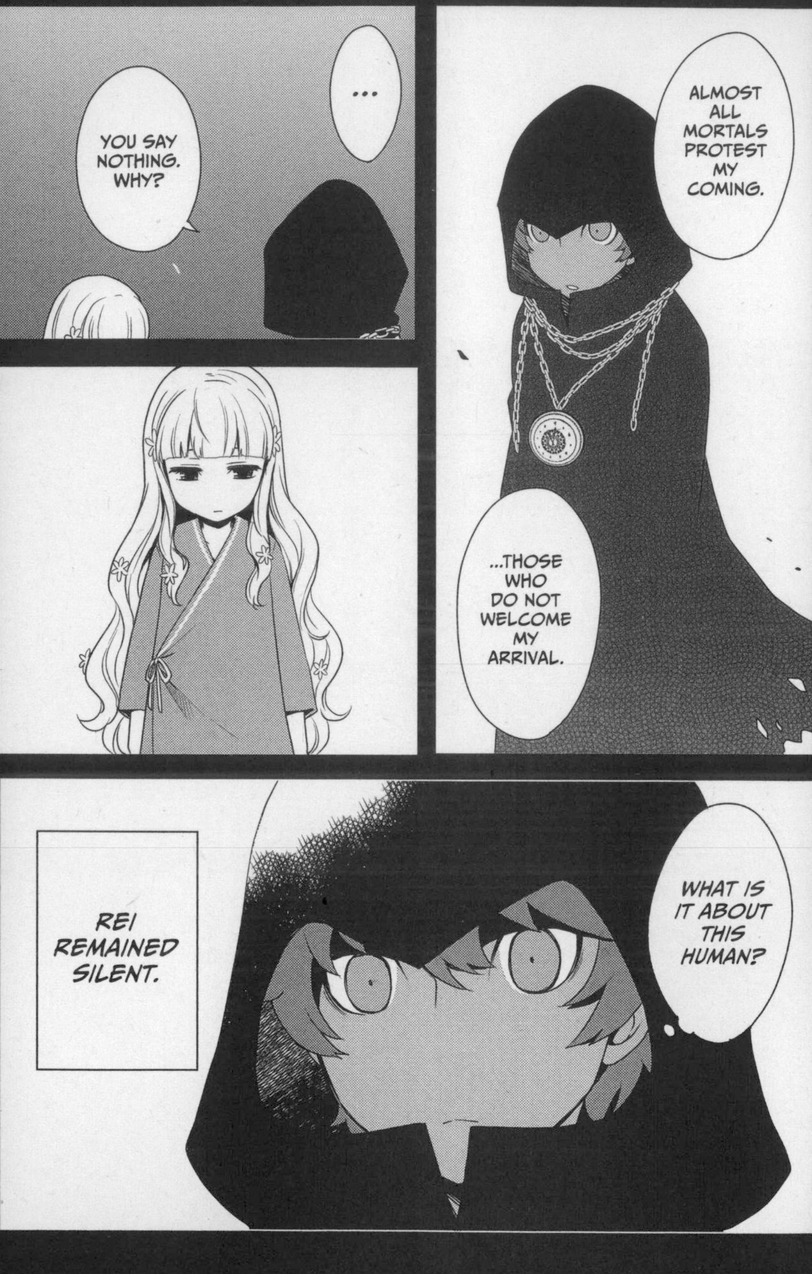
ALMOST ALL MORTALS PROTEST MY COMING.
...THOSE WHO DO NOT WELCOME MY ARRIVAL.
...
YOU SAY NOTHING. WHY?
WHAT IS IT ABOUT THIS HUMAN?
REI REMAINED SILENT.

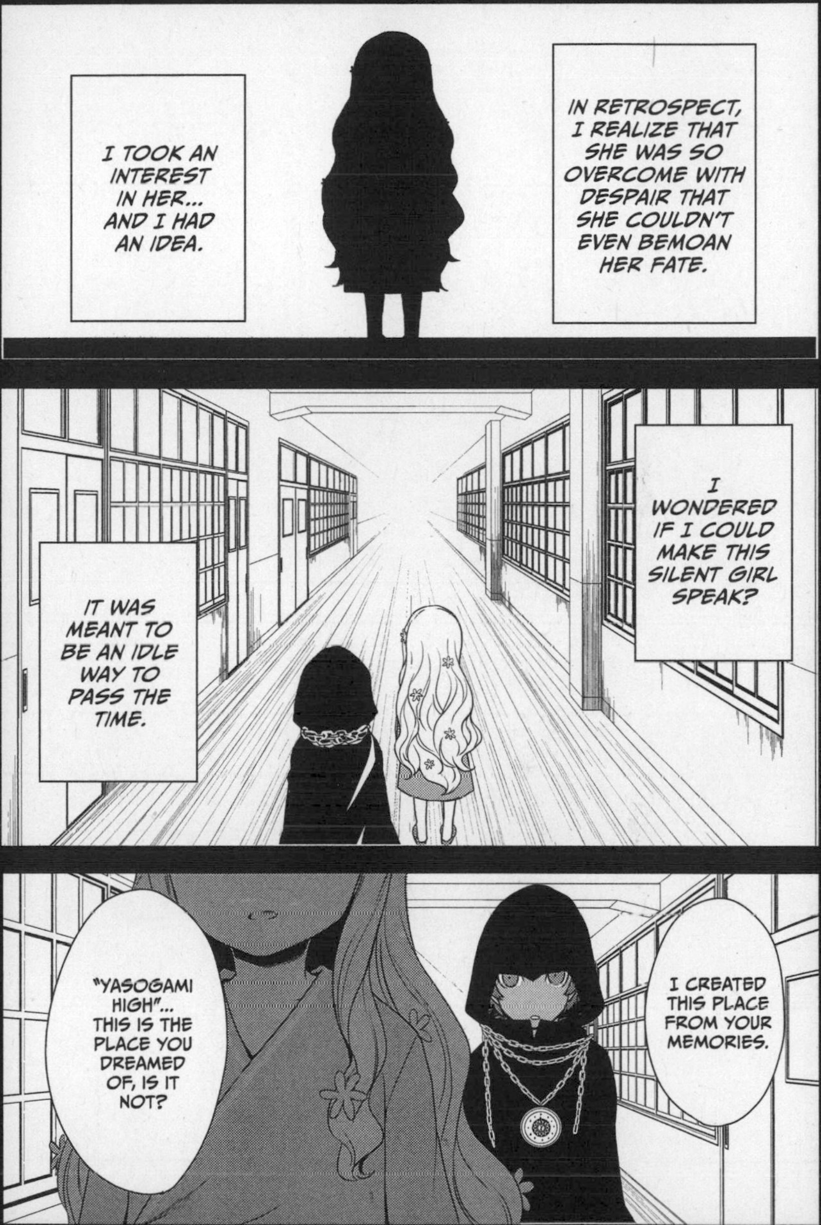
IN RETROSPECT, I REALIZE THAT SHE WAS SO OVERCOME WITH DESPAIR THAT SHE COULDN'T EVEN BEMOAN HER FATE.
I TOOK AN INTEREST IN HER... AND I HAD AN IDEA.
I WONDERED IF I COULD MAKE THIS SILENT GIRL SPEAK?
IT WAS MEANT TO BE AN IDLE WAY TO PASS THE TIME.
I CREATED THIS PLACE FROM YOUR MEMORIES.
"YASOGAMI HIGH"... THIS IS THE PLACE YOU DREAMED OF, IS IT NOT?

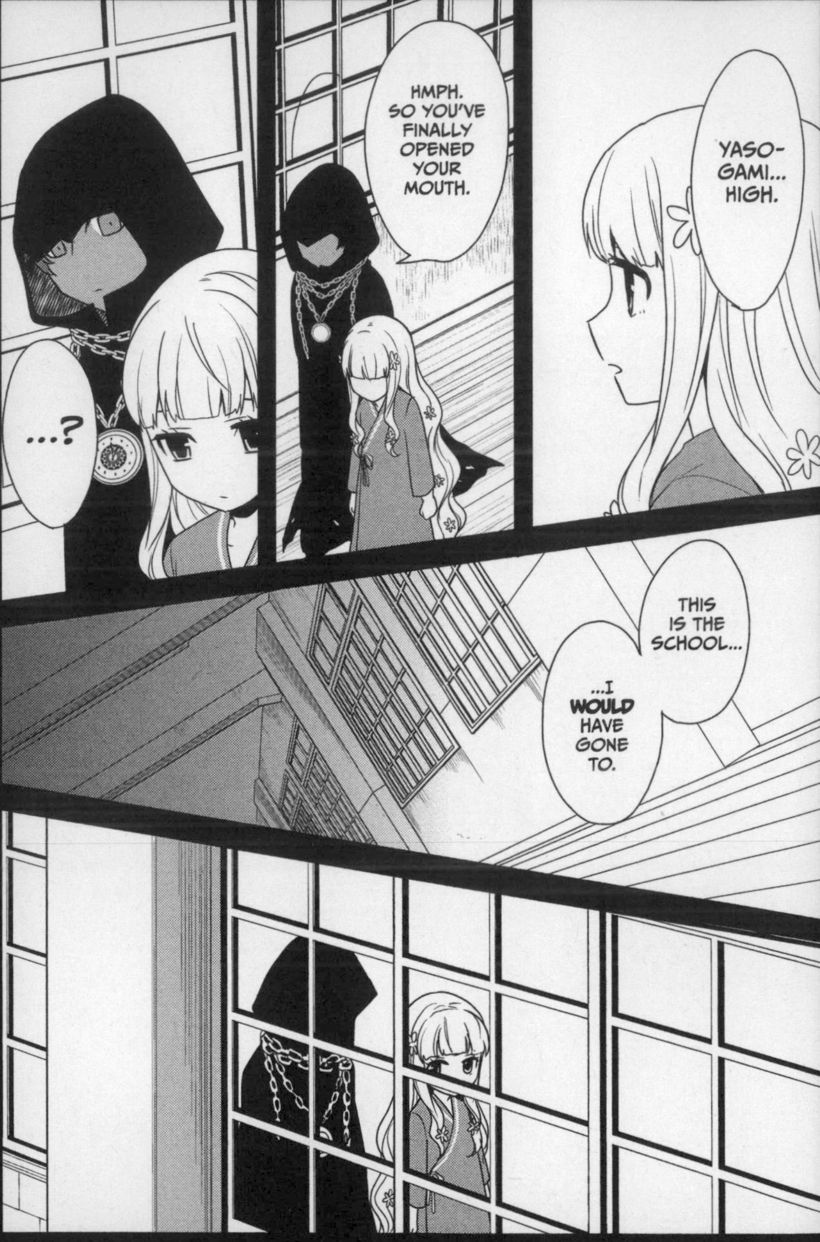
YASO-GAMI... HIGH.
HMPH. SO YOU'VE FINALLY OPENED YOUR MOUTH.
...?
THIS IS THE SCHOOL...
...I **WOULD** HAVE GONE TO.

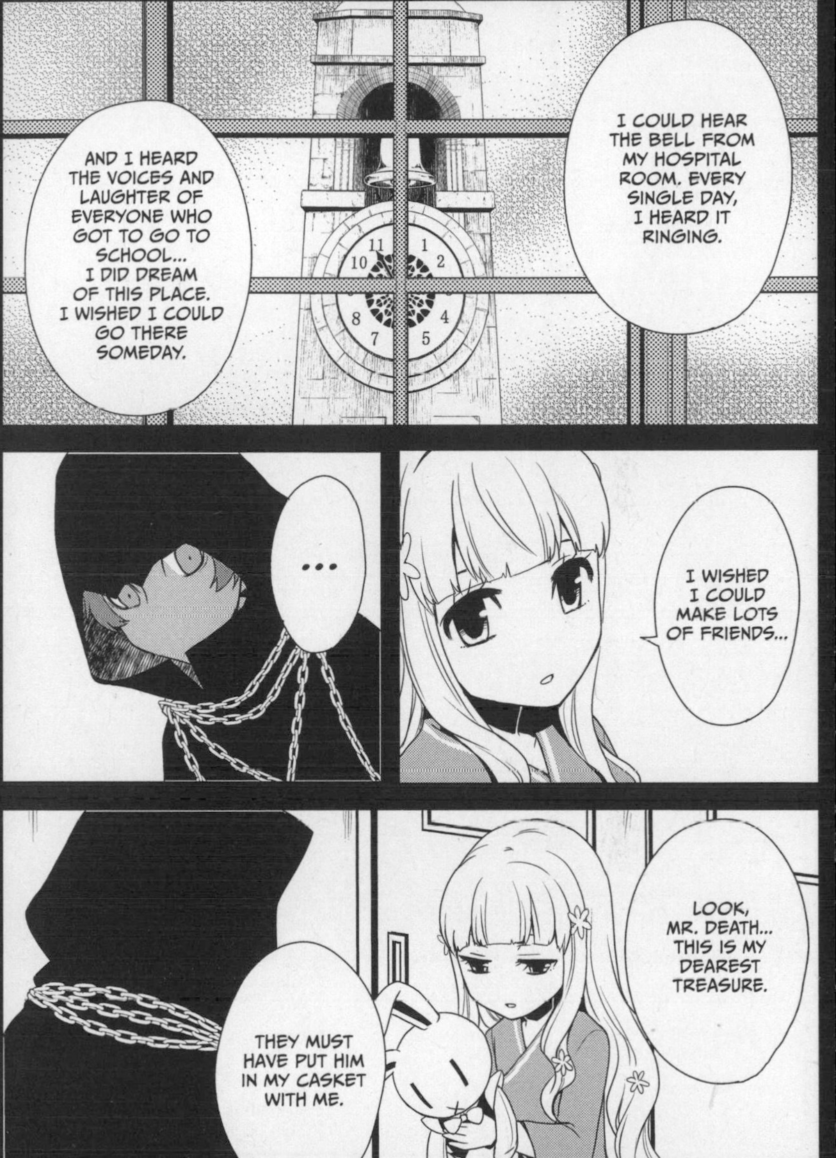
I COULD HEAR THE BELL FROM MY HOSPITAL ROOM. EVERY SINGLE DAY, I HEARD IT RINGING.
AND I HEARD THE VOICES AND LAUGHTER OF EVERYONE WHO GOT TO GO TO SCHOOL... I DID DREAM OF THIS PLACE. I WISHED I COULD GO THERE SOMEDAY.
I WISHED I COULD MAKE LOTS OF FRIENDS...
...
LOOK, MR. DEATH... THIS IS MY DEAREST TREASURE.
THEY MUST HAVE PUT HIM IN MY CASKET WITH ME.

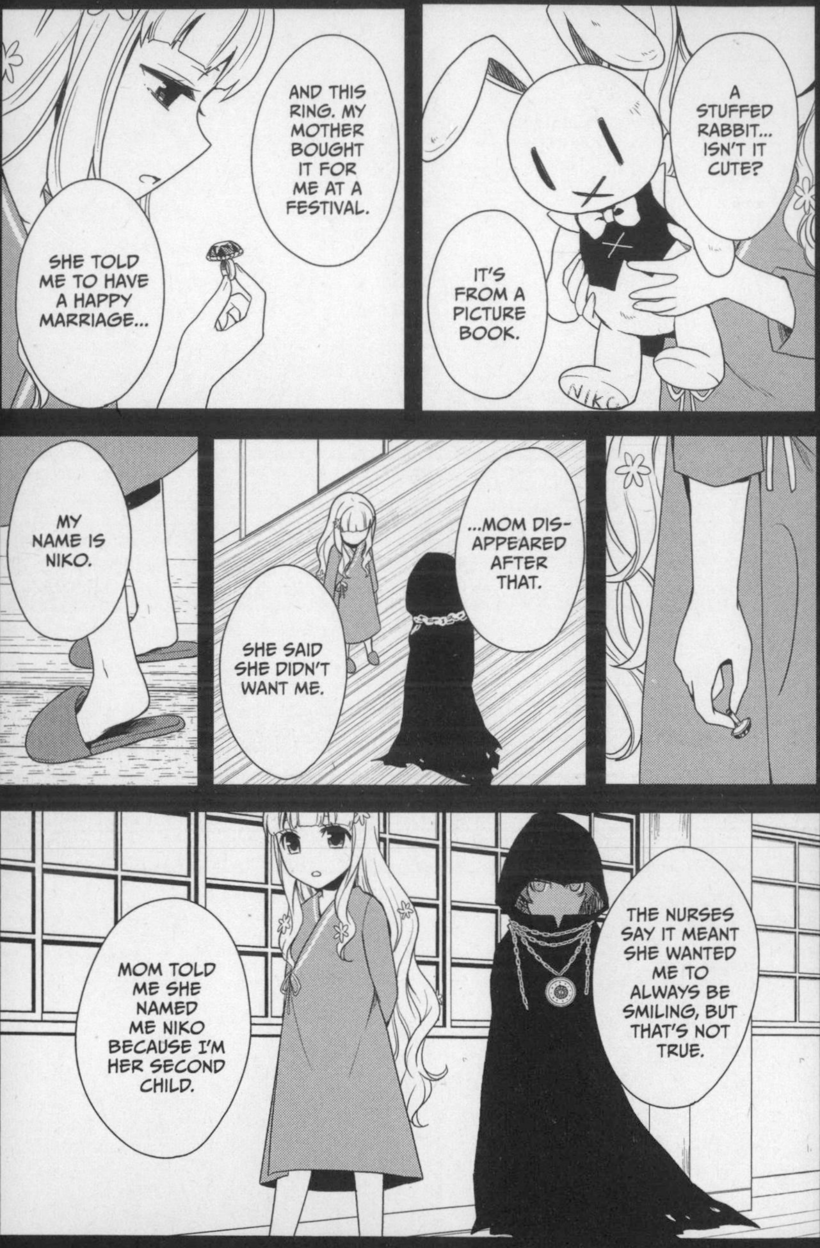
A STUFFED RABBIT... ISN'T IT CUTE?
IT'S FROM A PICTURE BOOK.
NIKO
AND THIS RING. MY MOTHER BOUGHT IT FOR ME AT A FESTIVAL.
SHE TOLD ME TO HAVE A HAPPY MARRIAGE...
...MOM DIS-APPEARED AFTER THAT.
SHE SAID SHE DIDN'T WANT ME.
MY NAME IS NIKO.
THE NURSES SAY IT MEANT SHE WANTED ME TO ALWAYS BE SMILING, BUT THAT'S NOT TRUE.
MOM TOLD ME SHE NAMED ME NIKO BECAUSE I'M HER SECOND CHILD.

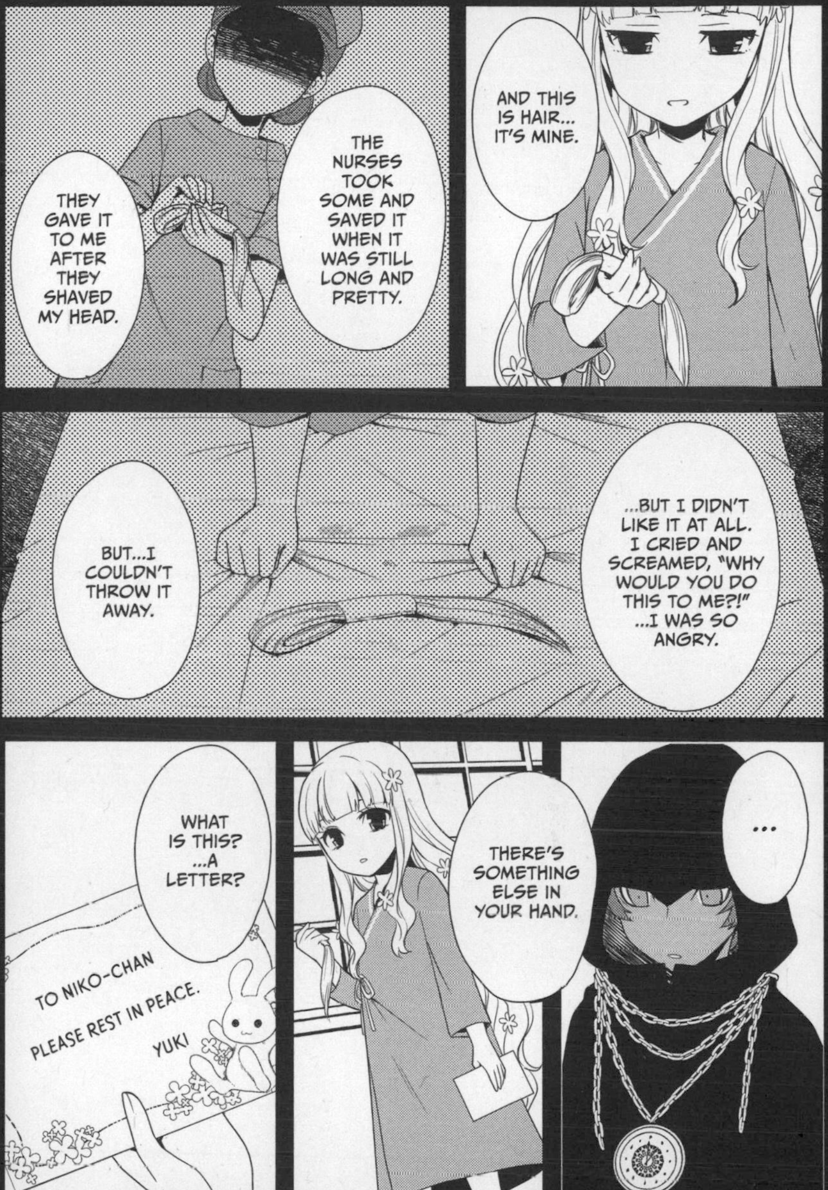
AND THIS IS HAIR... IT'S MINE.
THE NURSES TOOK SOME AND SAVED IT WHEN IT WAS STILL LONG AND PRETTY.
THEY GAVE IT TO ME AFTER THEY SHAVED MY HEAD.
...BUT I DIDN'T LIKE IT AT ALL. I CRIED AND SCREAMED, "WHY WOULD YOU DO THIS TO ME?!" ...I WAS SO ANGRY.
BUT...I COULDN'T THROW IT AWAY.
...
THERE'S SOMETHING ELSE IN YOUR HAND.
WHAT IS THIS? ...A LETTER?
TO NIKO-CHAN
PLEASE REST IN PEACE.
YUKI

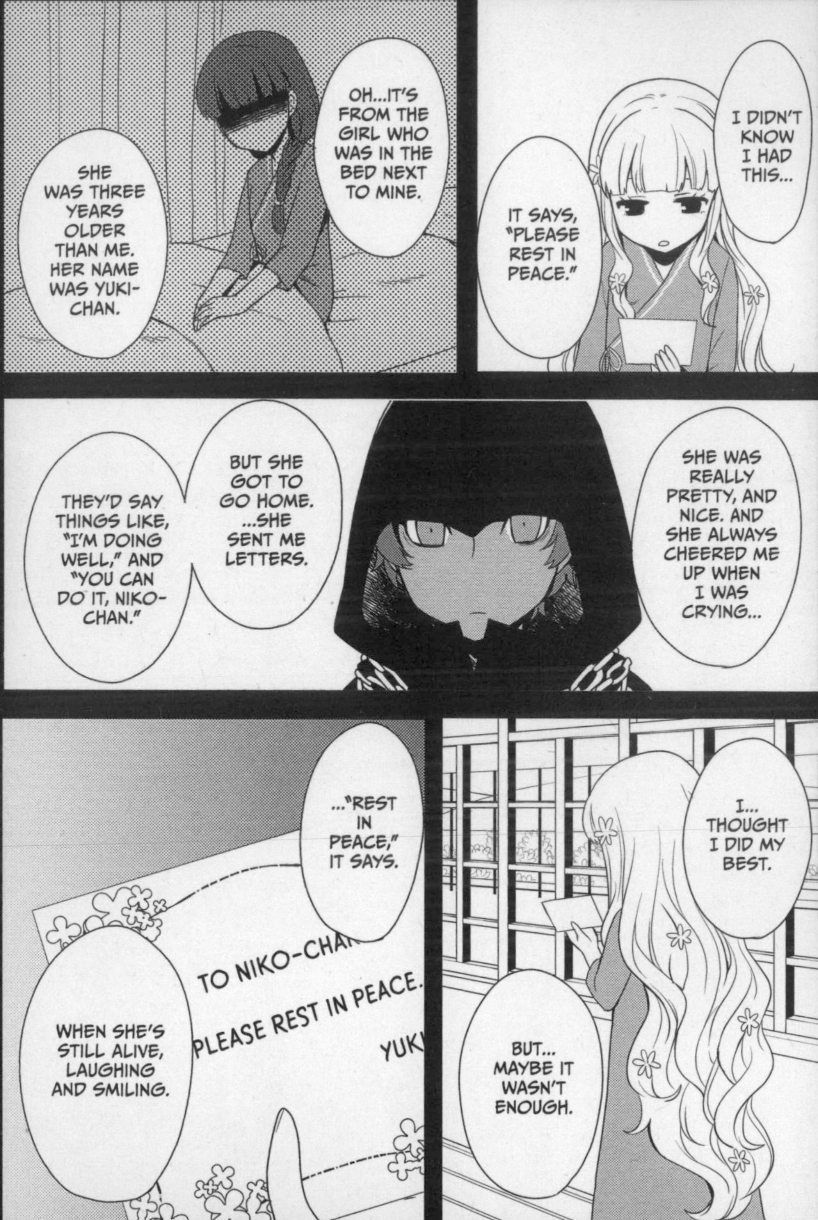
I DIDN'T KNOW I HAD THIS...
IT SAYS, "PLEASE REST IN PEACE."
OH...IT'S FROM THE GIRL WHO WAS IN THE BED NEXT TO MINE.
SHE WAS THREE YEARS OLDER THAN ME. HER NAME WAS YUKI-CHAN.
SHE WAS REALLY PRETTY, AND NICE. AND SHE ALWAYS CHEERED ME UP WHEN I WAS CRYING...
BUT SHE GOT TO GO HOME. ...SHE SENT ME LETTERS.
THEY'D SAY THINGS LIKE, "I'M DOING WELL," AND "YOU CAN DO IT, NIKO-CHAN."
I... THOUGHT I DID MY BEST.
BUT... MAYBE IT WASN'T ENOUGH.
..."REST IN PEACE," IT SAYS.
TO NIKO-CHA
PLEASE REST IN PEACE.
YUK
WHEN SHE'S STILL ALIVE, LAUGHING AND SMILING.

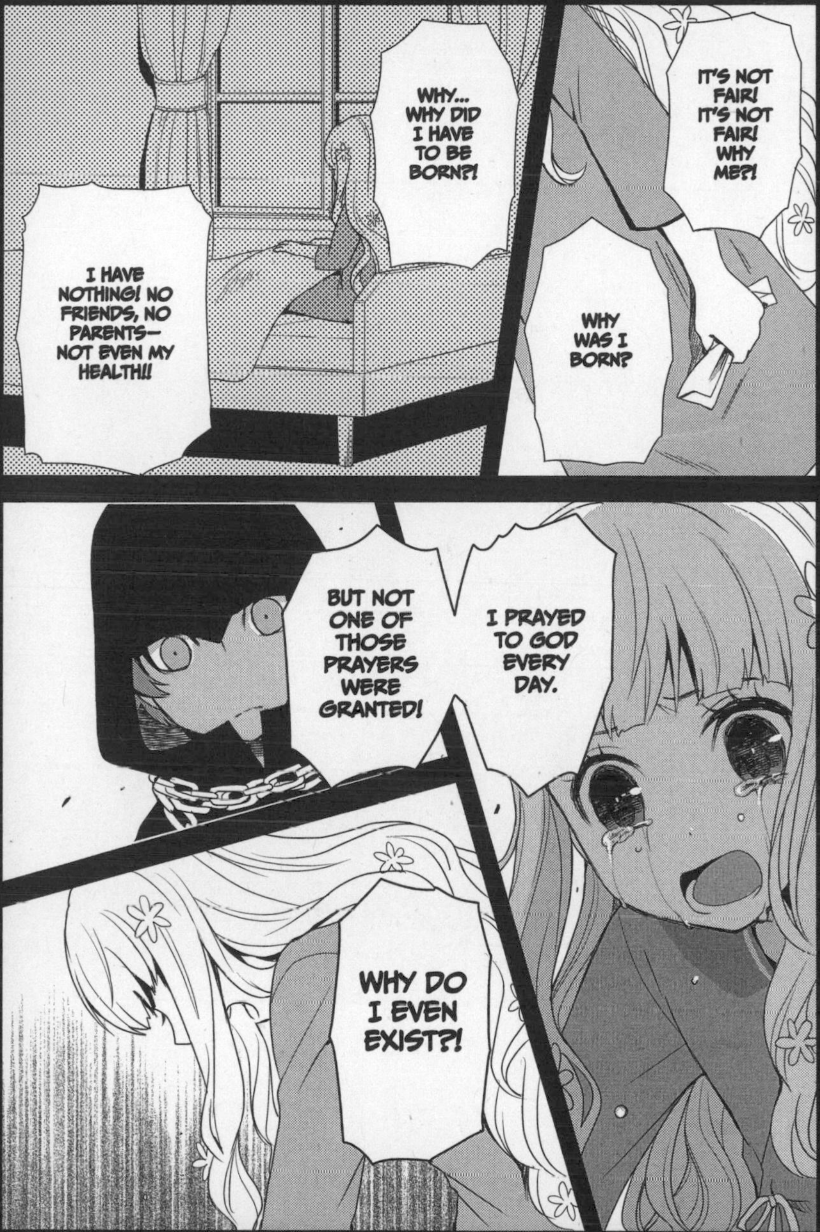
IT'S NOT FAIR! IT'S NOT FAIR! WHY ME?!
WHY WAS I BORN?
WHY... WHY DID I HAVE TO BE BORN?!
I HAVE NOTHING! NO FRIENDS, NO PARENTS— NOT EVEN MY HEALTH!!
I PRAYED TO GOD EVERY DAY.
BUT NOT ONE OF THOSE PRAYERS WERE GRANTED!
WHY DO I EVEN EXIST?!

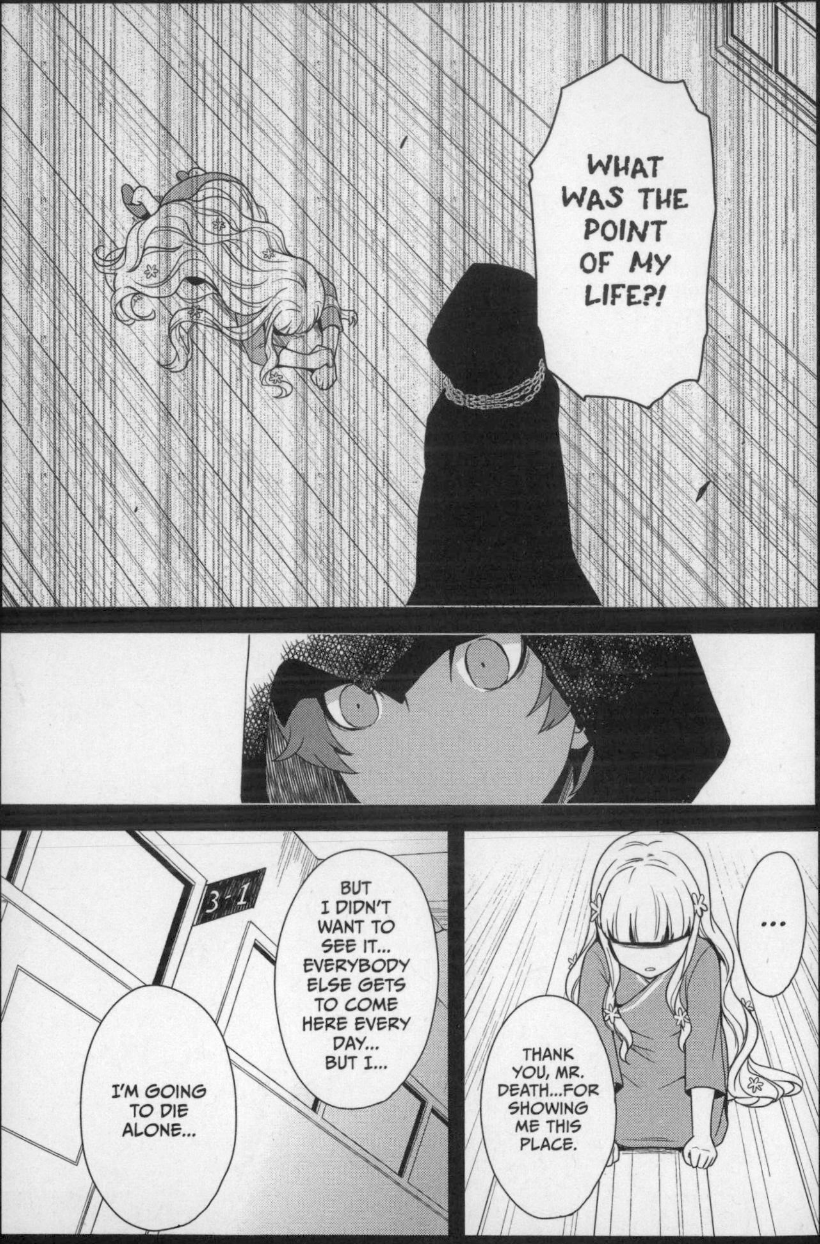
WHAT WAS THE POINT OF MY LIFE?!
...
THANK YOU, MR. DEATH...FOR SHOWING ME THIS PLACE.
3-1
BUT I DIDN'T WANT TO SEE IT... EVERYBODY ELSE GETS TO COME HERE EVERY DAY... BUT I...
I'M GOING TO DIE ALONE...

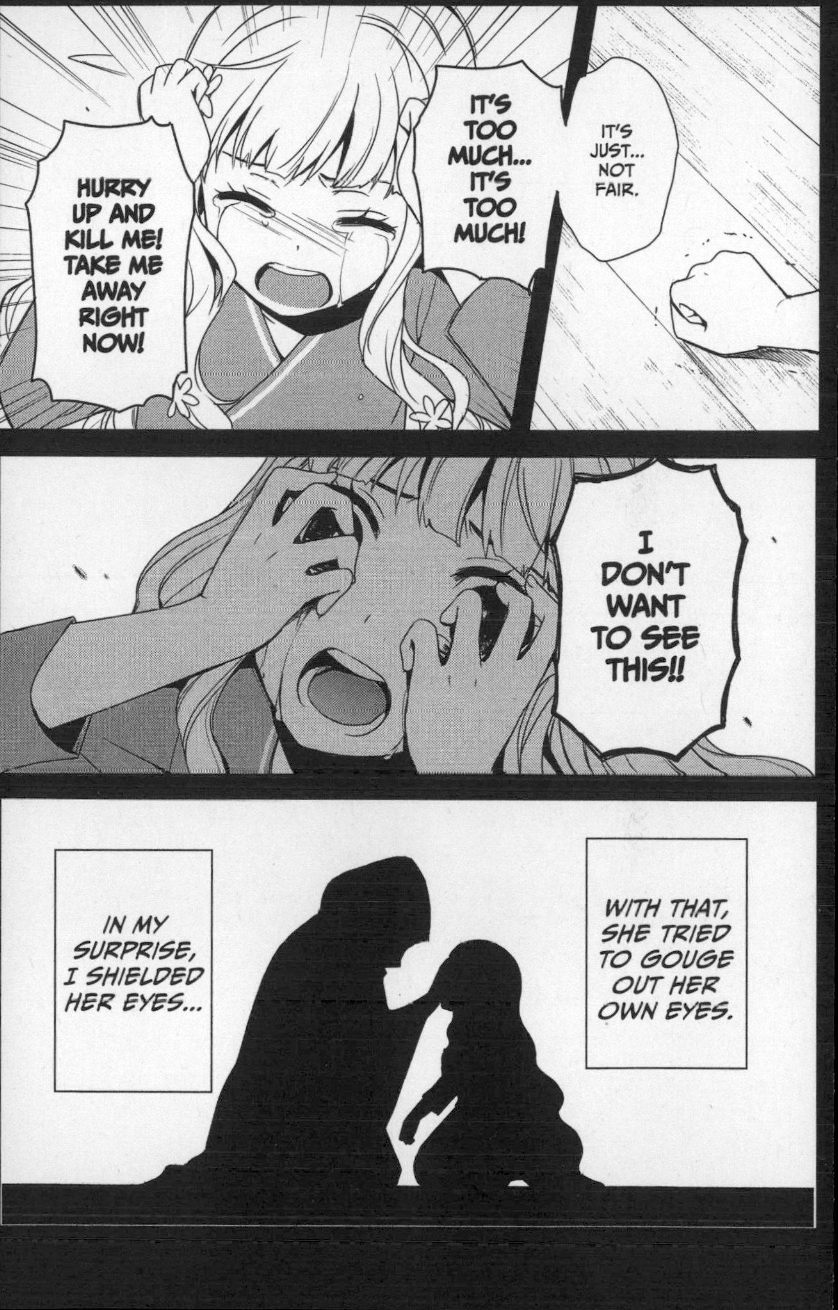
IT'S JUST... NOT FAIR.
IT'S TOO MUCH... IT'S TOO MUCH!
HURRY UP AND KILL ME! TAKE ME AWAY RIGHT NOW!
I DON'T WANT TO SEE THIS!!
WITH THAT, SHE TRIED TO GOUGE OUT HER OWN EYES.
IN MY SURPRISE, I SHIELDED HER EYES...

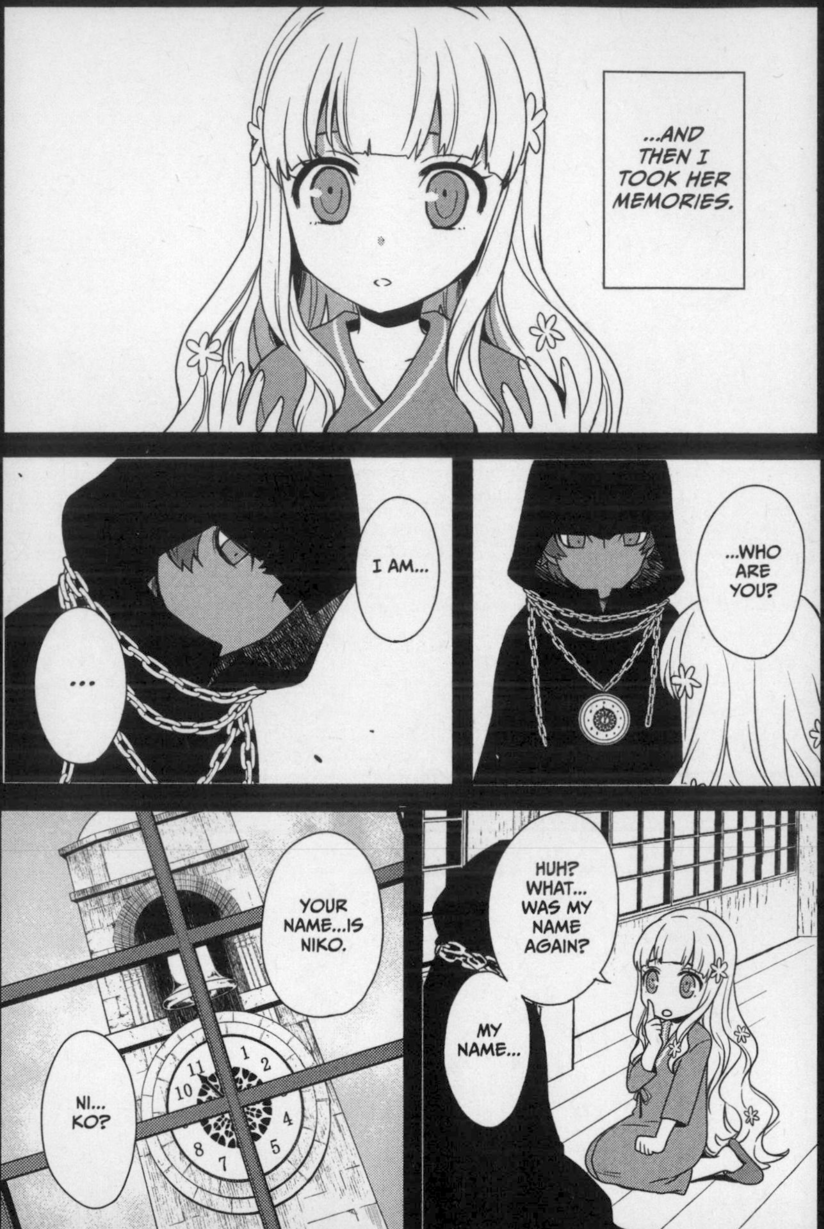
...AND THEN I TOOK HER MEMORIES.
...WHO ARE YOU?
I AM...
...
HUH? WHAT... WAS MY NAME AGAIN?
MY NAME...
YOUR NAME...IS NIKO.
NI... KO?

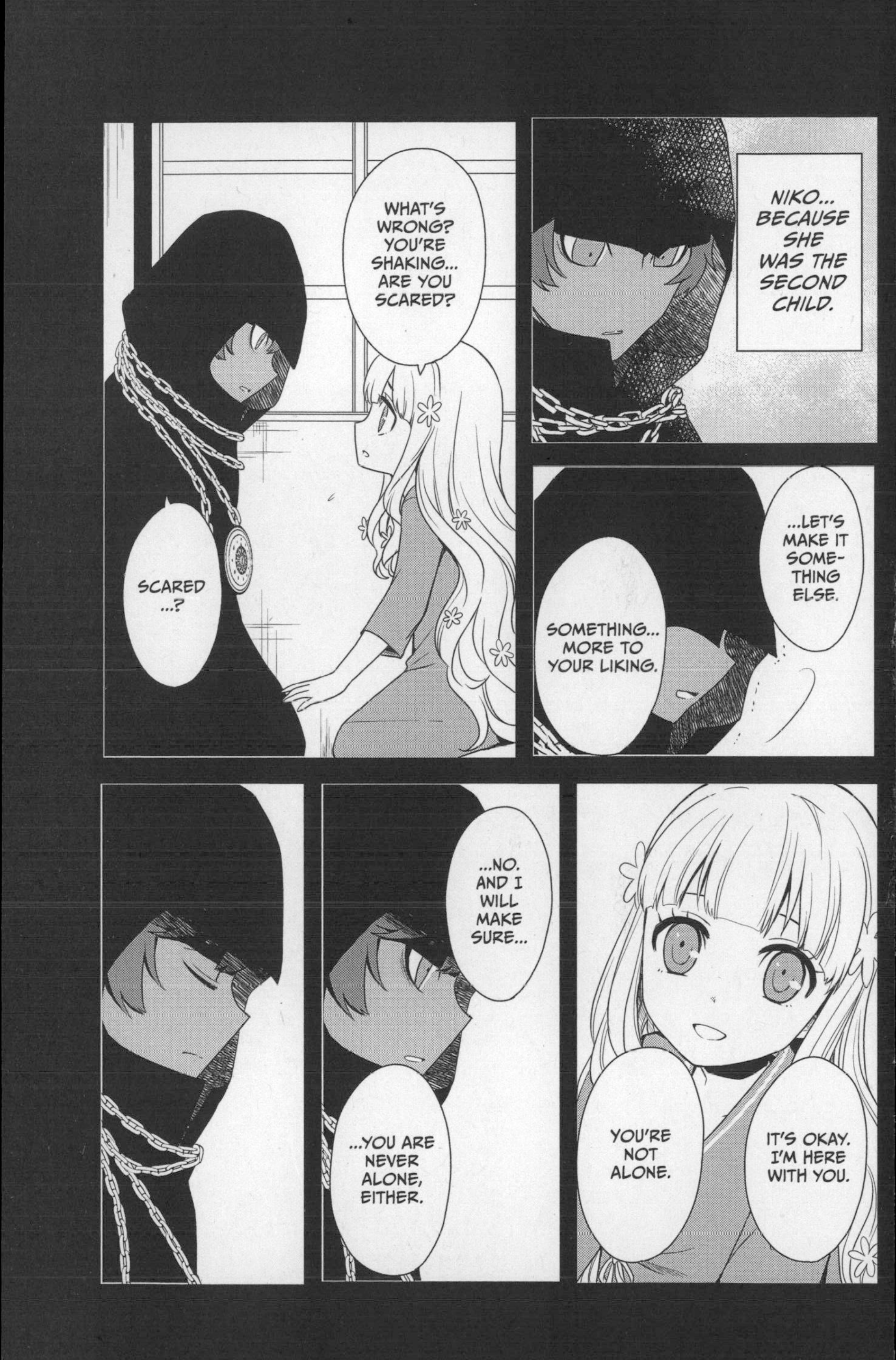
NIKO... BECAUSE SHE WAS THE SECOND CHILD.
...LET'S MAKE IT SOME-THING ELSE.
SOMETHING... MORE TO YOUR LIKING.
WHAT'S WRONG? YOU'RE SHAKING... ARE YOU SCARED?
SCARED ...?
IT'S OKAY. I'M HERE WITH YOU.
YOU'RE NOT ALONE.
...NO. AND I WILL MAKE SURE...
...YOU ARE NEVER ALONE, EITHER.

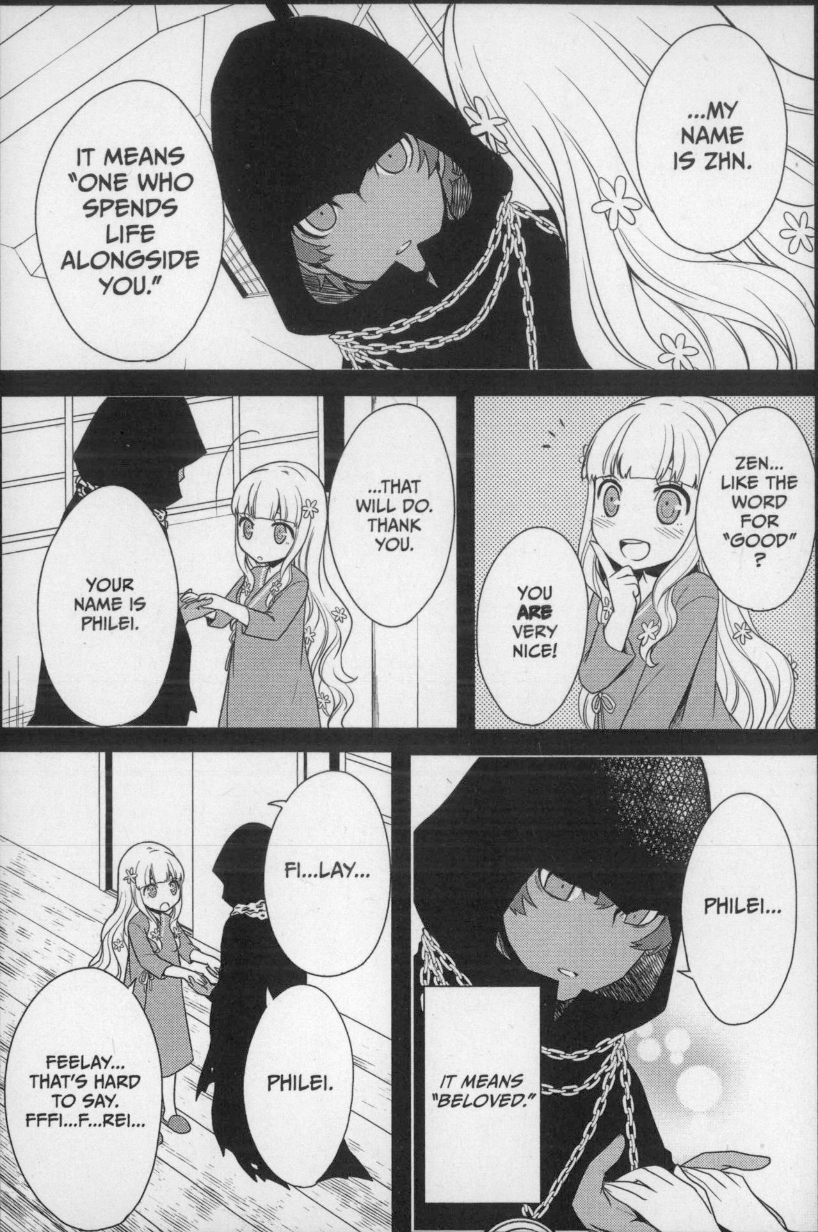
...MY NAME IS ZHN.
IT MEANS "ONE WHO SPENDS LIFE ALONGSIDE YOU."
ZEN... LIKE THE WORD FOR "GOOD"?
YOU **ARE** VERY NICE!
...THAT WILL DO. THANK YOU.
YOUR NAME IS PHILEI.
PHILEI...
IT MEANS "BELOVED."
FI...LAY...
PHILEI.
FEELAY... THAT'S HARD TO SAY. FFFI...F...REI...

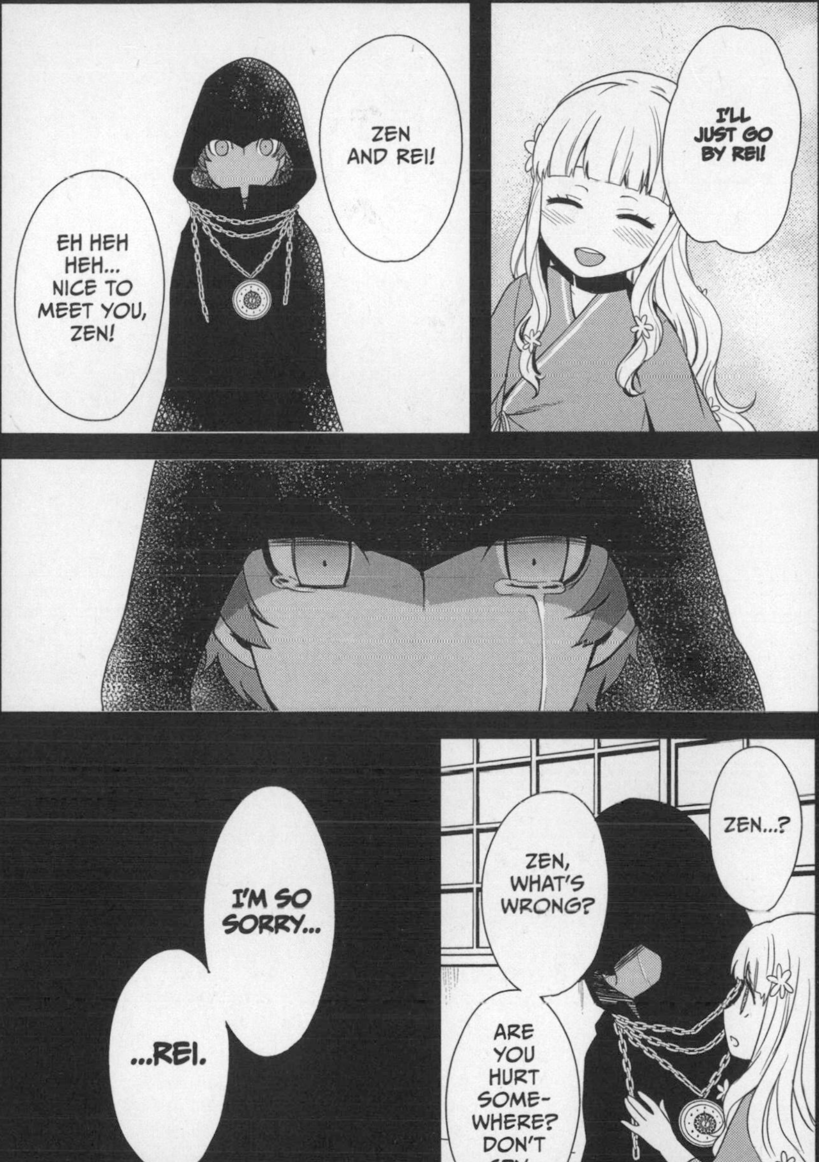
I'LL JUST GO BY REI!
ZEN AND REI!
EH HEH HEH... NICE TO MEET YOU, ZEN!
ZEN...?
ZEN, WHAT'S WRONG?
ARE YOU HURT SOME-WHERE? DON'T CRY...
I'M SO SORRY...
...REI.

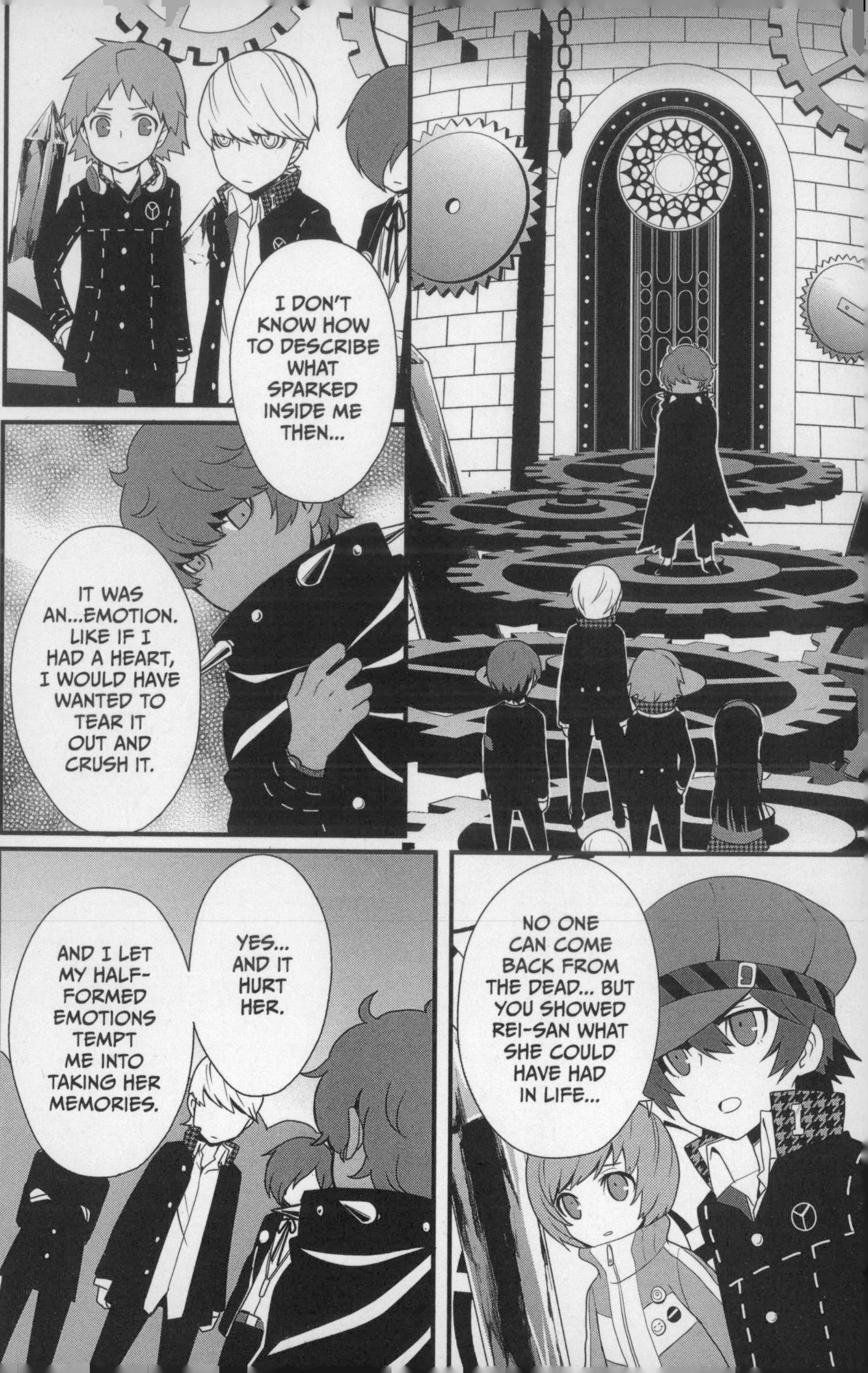
I DON'T KNOW HOW TO DESCRIBE WHAT SPARKED INSIDE ME THEN...
IT WAS AN...EMOTION. LIKE IF I HAD A HEART, I WOULD HAVE WANTED TO TEAR IT OUT AND CRUSH IT.
NO ONE CAN COME BACK FROM THE DEAD... BUT YOU SHOWED REI-SAN WHAT SHE COULD HAVE HAD IN LIFE...
YES... AND IT HURT HER.
AND I LET MY HALF-FORMED EMOTIONS TEMPT ME INTO TAKING HER MEMORIES.

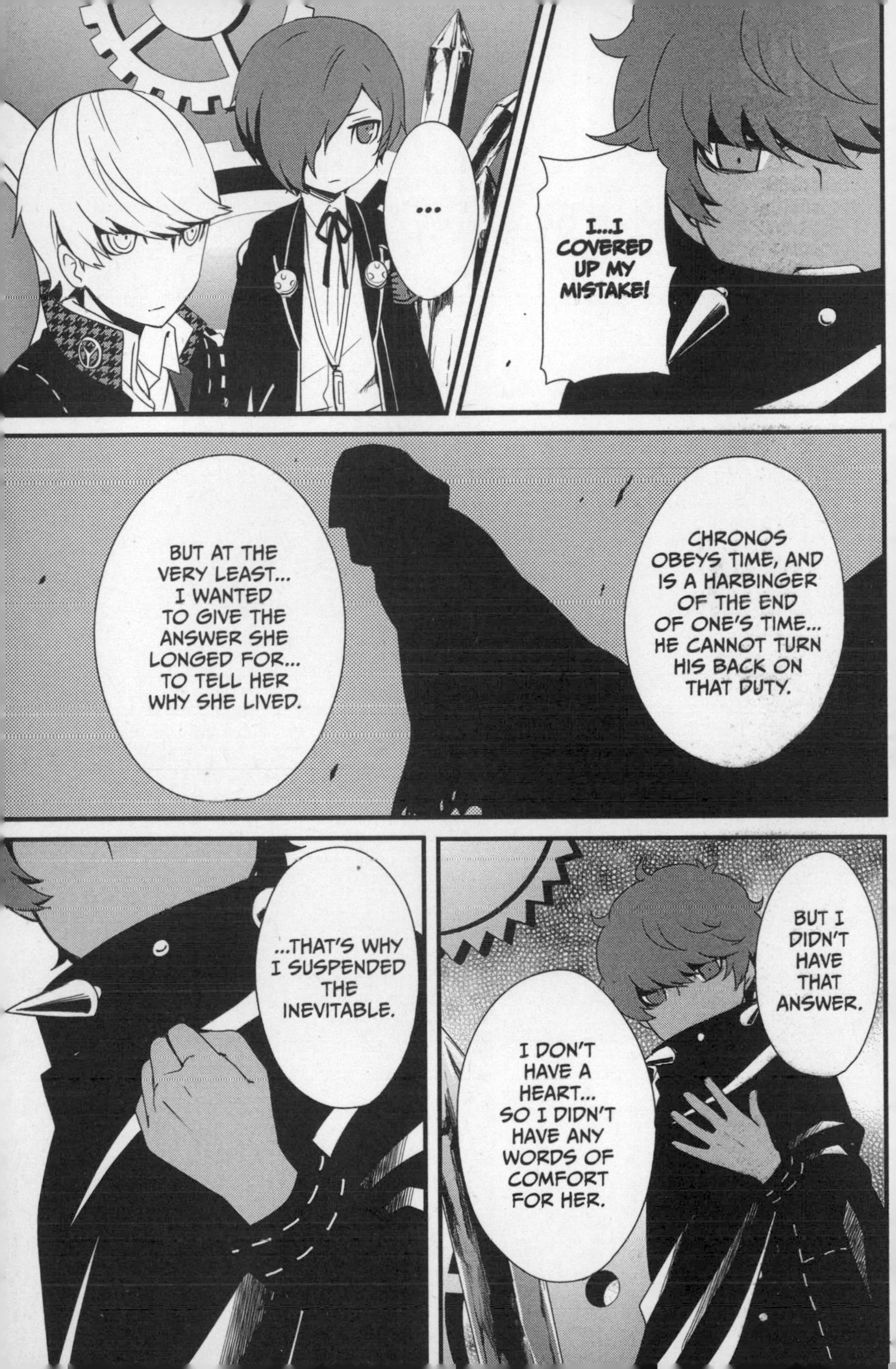
I...I COVERED UP MY MISTAKE!
...
CHRONOS OBEYS TIME, AND IS A HARBINGER OF THE END OF ONE'S TIME... HE CANNOT TURN HIS BACK ON THAT DUTY.
BUT AT THE VERY LEAST... I WANTED TO GIVE THE ANSWER SHE LONGED FOR... TO TELL HER WHY SHE LIVED.
BUT I DIDN'T HAVE THAT ANSWER.
I DON'T HAVE A HEART... SO I DIDN'T HAVE ANY WORDS OF COMFORT FOR HER.
...THAT'S WHY I SUSPENDED THE INEVITABLE.

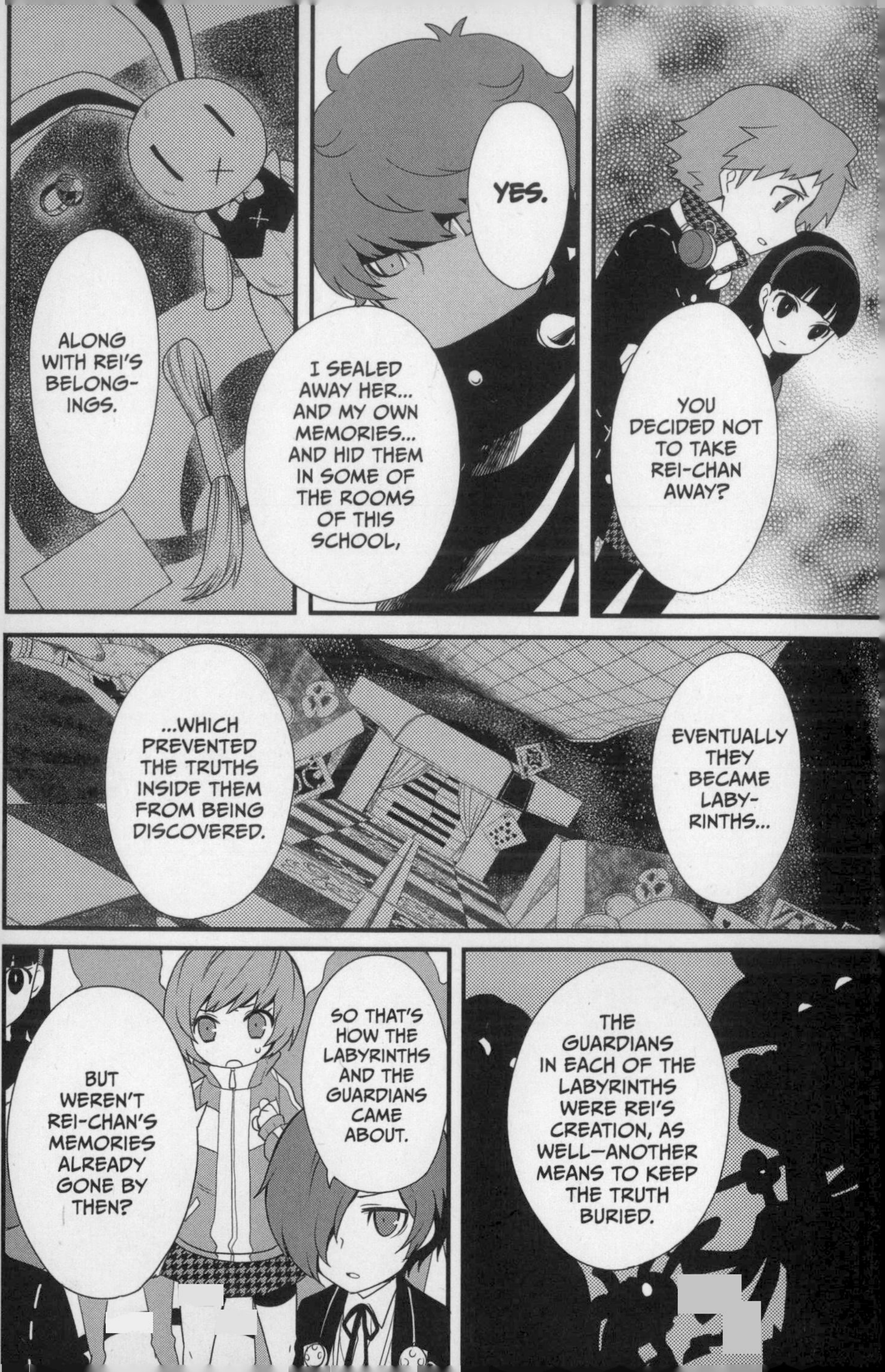
YOU DECIDED NOT TO TAKE REI-CHAN AWAY?
YES.
I SEALED AWAY HER... AND MY OWN MEMORIES... AND HID THEM IN SOME OF THE ROOMS OF THIS SCHOOL,
ALONG WITH REI'S BELONG-INGS.
EVENTUALLY THEY BECAME LABY-RINTHS...
...WHICH PREVENTED THE TRUTHS INSIDE THEM FROM BEING DISCOVERED.
THE GUARDIANS IN EACH OF THE LABYRINTHS WERE REI'S CREATION, AS WELL—ANOTHER MEANS TO KEEP THE TRUTH BURIED.
SO THAT'S HOW THE LABYRINTHS AND THE GUARDIANS CAME ABOUT.
BUT WEREN'T REI-CHAN'S MEMORIES ALREADY GONE BY THEN?

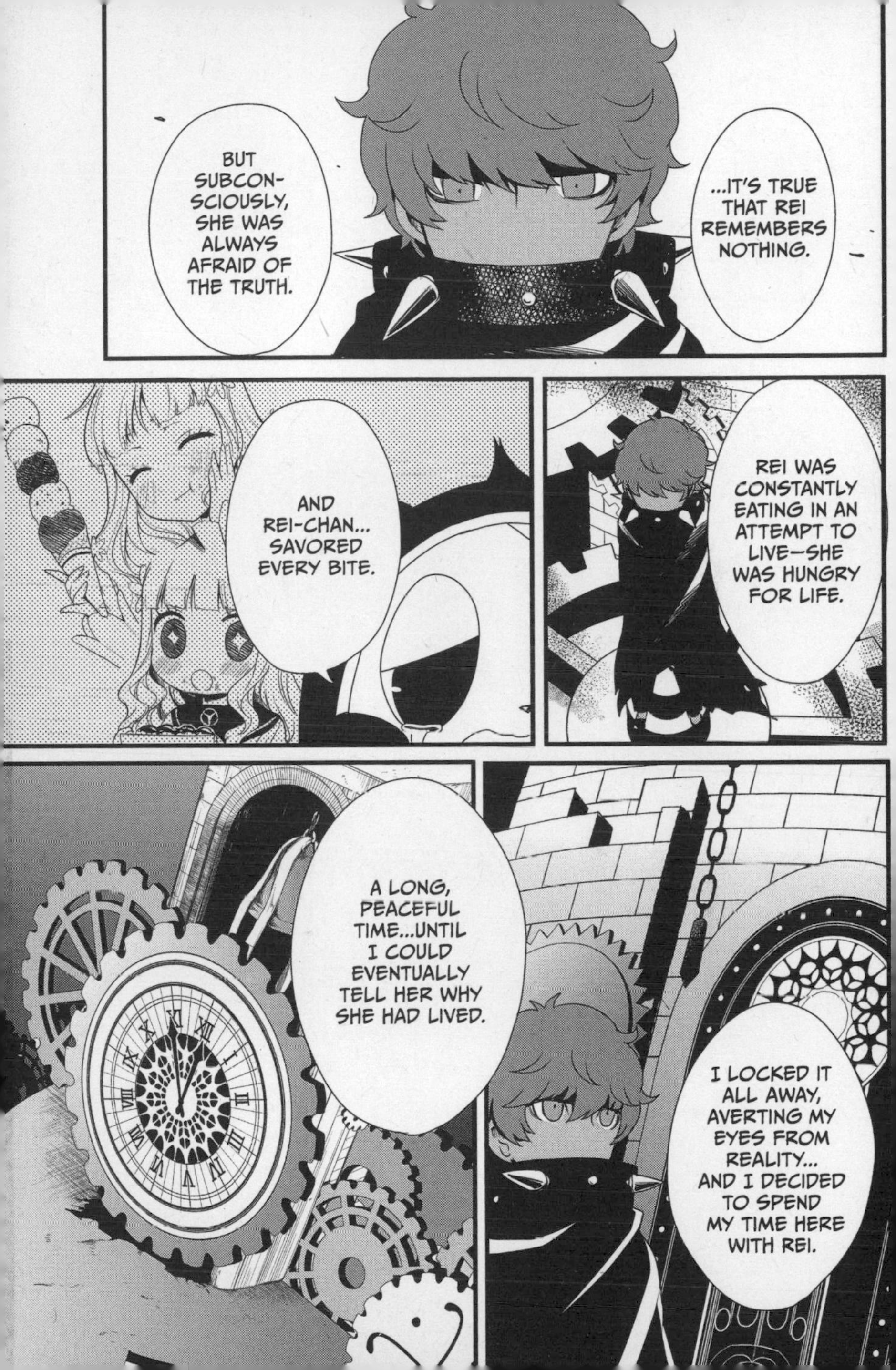
...IT'S TRUE THAT REI REMEMBERS NOTHING.
BUT SUBCON-SCIOUSLY, SHE WAS ALWAYS AFRAID OF THE TRUTH.
REI WAS CONSTANTLY EATING IN AN ATTEMPT TO LIVE—SHE WAS HUNGRY FOR LIFE.
AND REI-CHAN... SAVORED EVERY BITE.
I LOCKED IT ALL AWAY, AVERTING MY EYES FROM REALITY... AND I DECIDED TO SPEND MY TIME HERE WITH REI.
A LONG, PEACEFUL TIME...UNTIL I COULD EVENTUALLY TELL HER WHY SHE HAD LIVED.

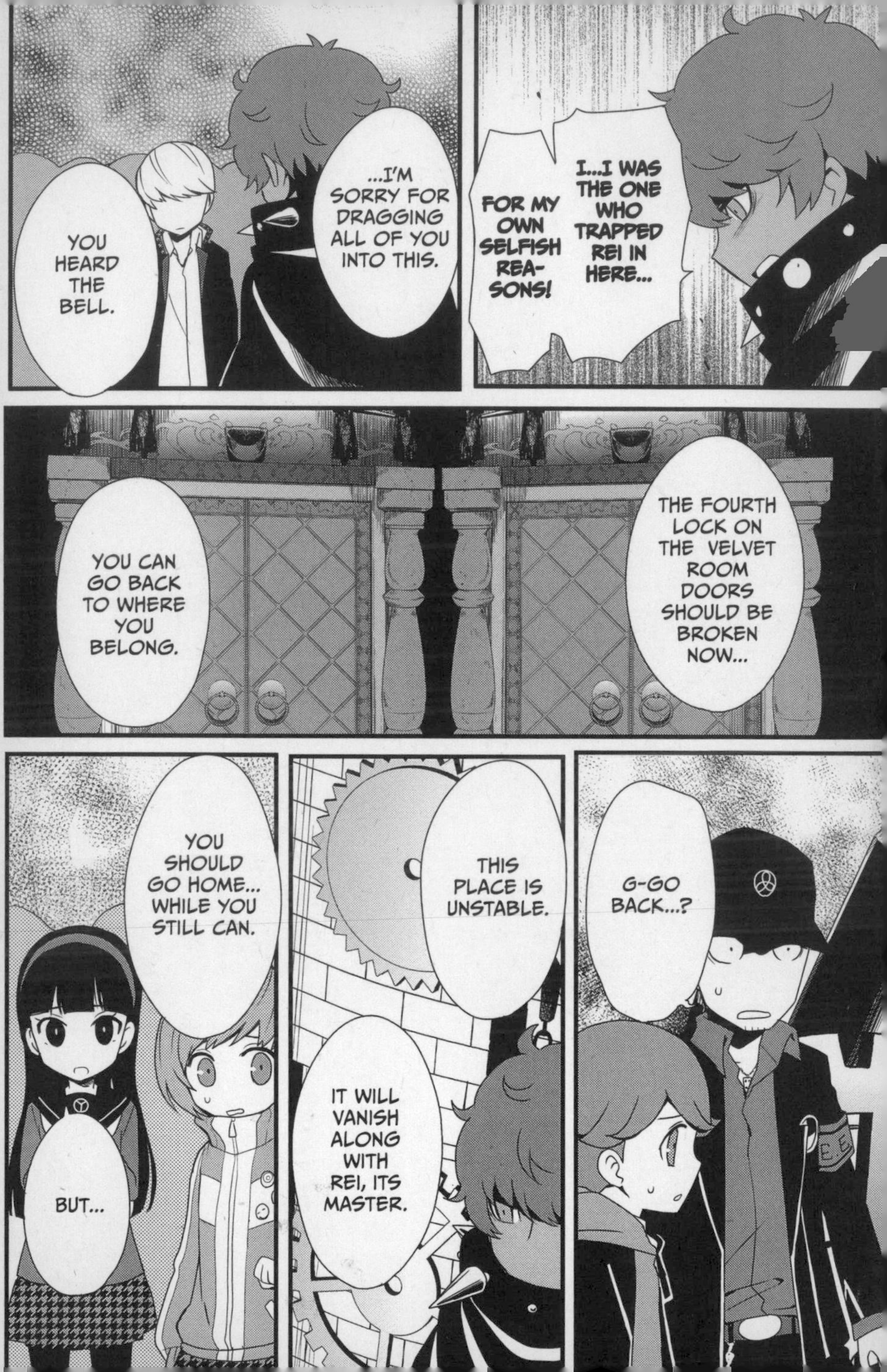
I...I WAS THE ONE WHO TRAPPED REI IN HERE...
FOR MY OWN SELFISH REA-SONS!
...I'M SORRY FOR DRAGGING ALL OF YOU INTO THIS.
YOU HEARD THE BELL.
THE FOURTH LOCK ON THE VELVET ROOM DOORS SHOULD BE BROKEN NOW...
YOU CAN GO BACK TO WHERE YOU BELONG.
G-GO BACK...?
THIS PLACE IS UNSTABLE.
IT WILL VANISH ALONG WITH REI, ITS MASTER.
YOU SHOULD GO HOME... WHILE YOU STILL CAN.
BUT...

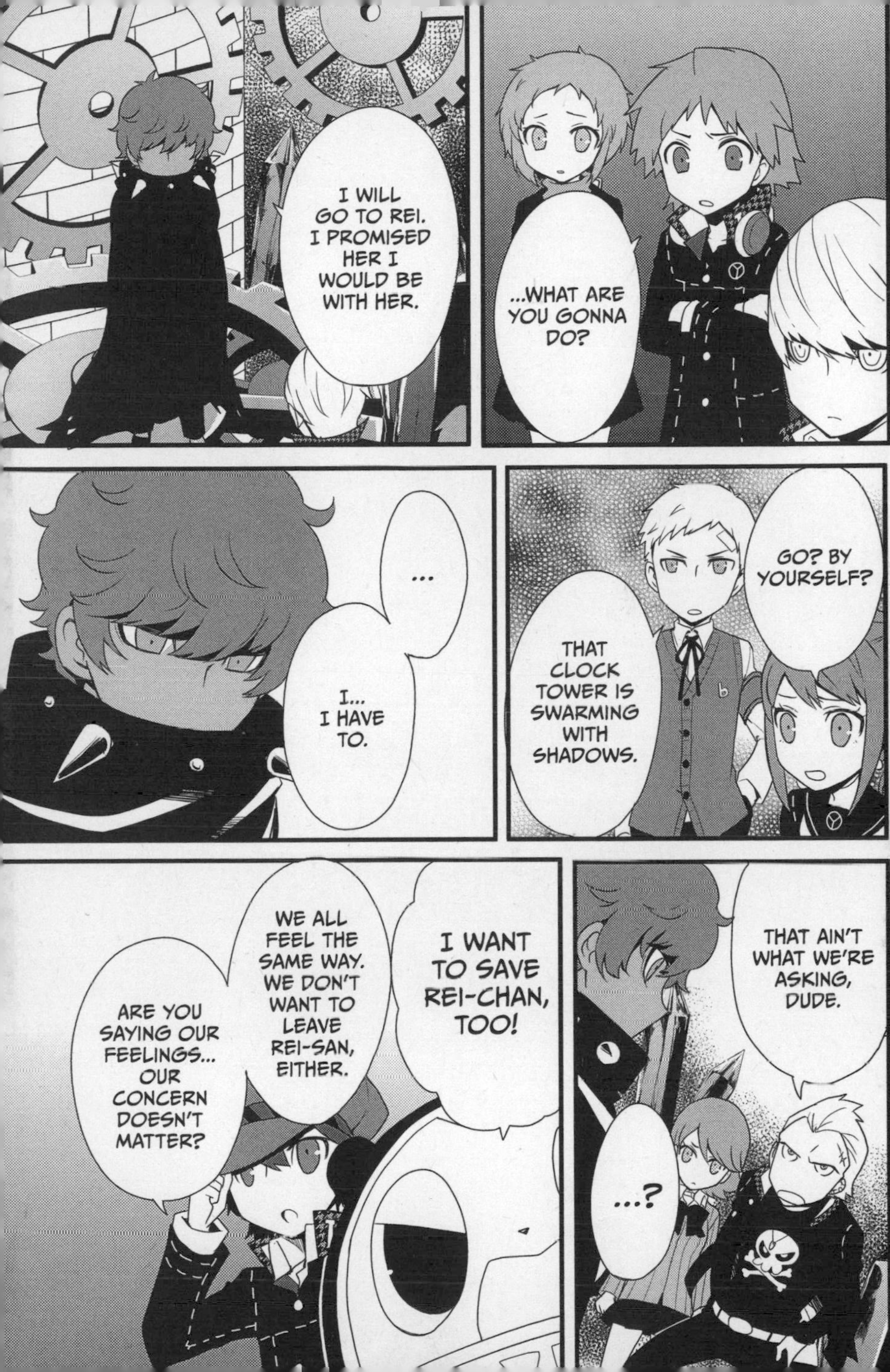
...WHAT ARE YOU GONNA DO?
I WILL GO TO REI. I PROMISED HER I WOULD BE WITH HER.
GO? BY YOURSELF?
THAT CLOCK TOWER IS SWARMING WITH SHADOWS.
...
I... I HAVE TO.
THAT AIN'T WHAT WE'RE ASKING, DUDE.
...?
I WANT TO SAVE REI-CHAN, TOO!
WE ALL FEEL THE SAME WAY. WE DON'T WANT TO LEAVE REI-SAN, EITHER.
ARE YOU SAYING OUR FEELINGS... OUR CONCERN DOESN'T MATTER?

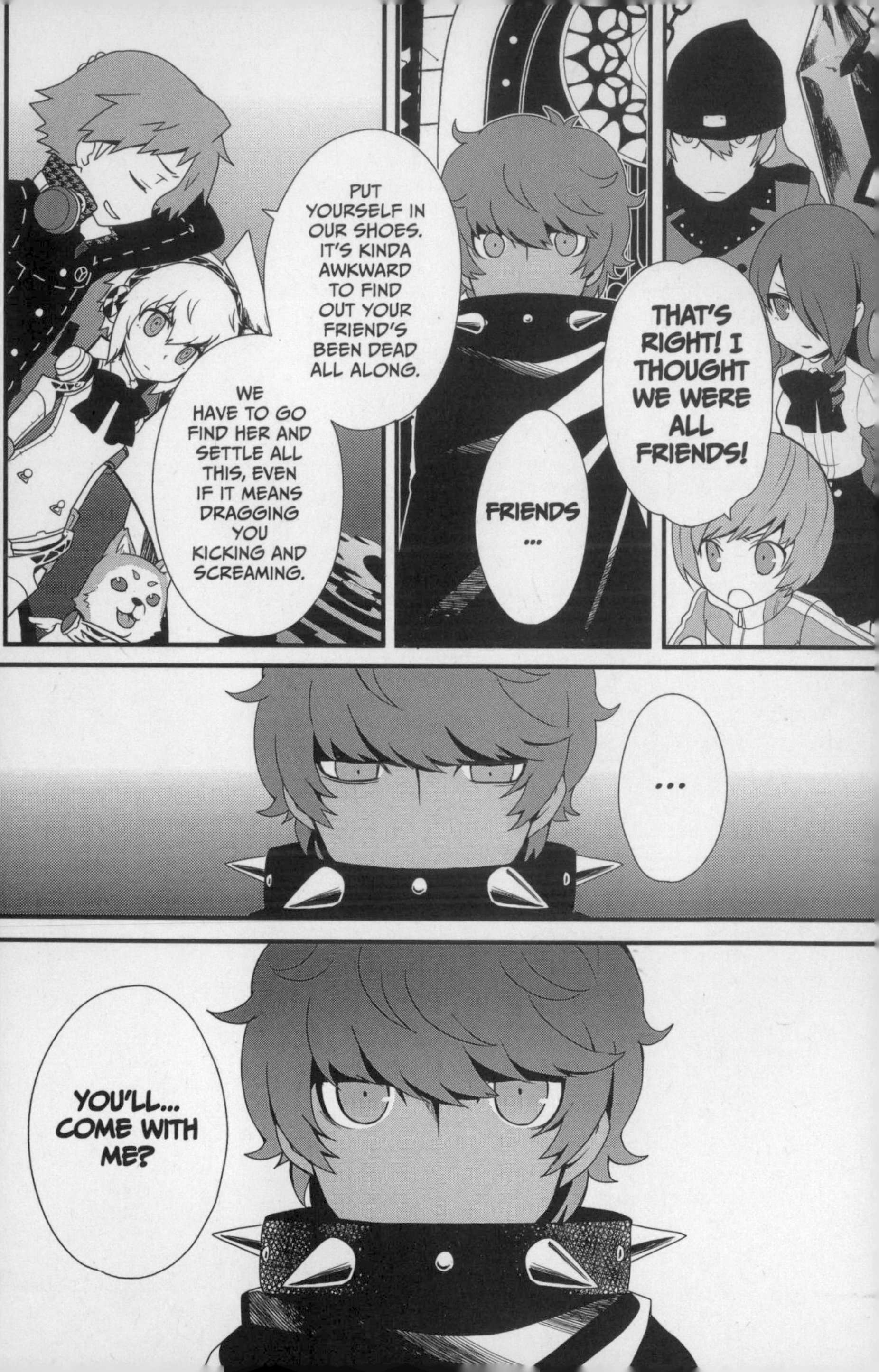
THAT'S RIGHT! I THOUGHT WE WERE ALL FRIENDS!
FRIENDS ...
PUT YOURSELF IN OUR SHOES. IT'S KINDA AWKWARD TO FIND OUT YOUR FRIEND'S BEEN DEAD ALL ALONG.
WE HAVE TO GO FIND HER AND SETTLE ALL THIS, EVEN IF IT MEANS DRAGGING YOU KICKING AND SCREAMING.
...
YOU'LL... COME WITH ME?

YOU HAVE TO ASK?

THANK YOU.

I'M SORRY... NO.

PERSONA Q Side: P4
SHADOW OF THE LABYRINTH

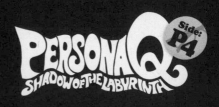

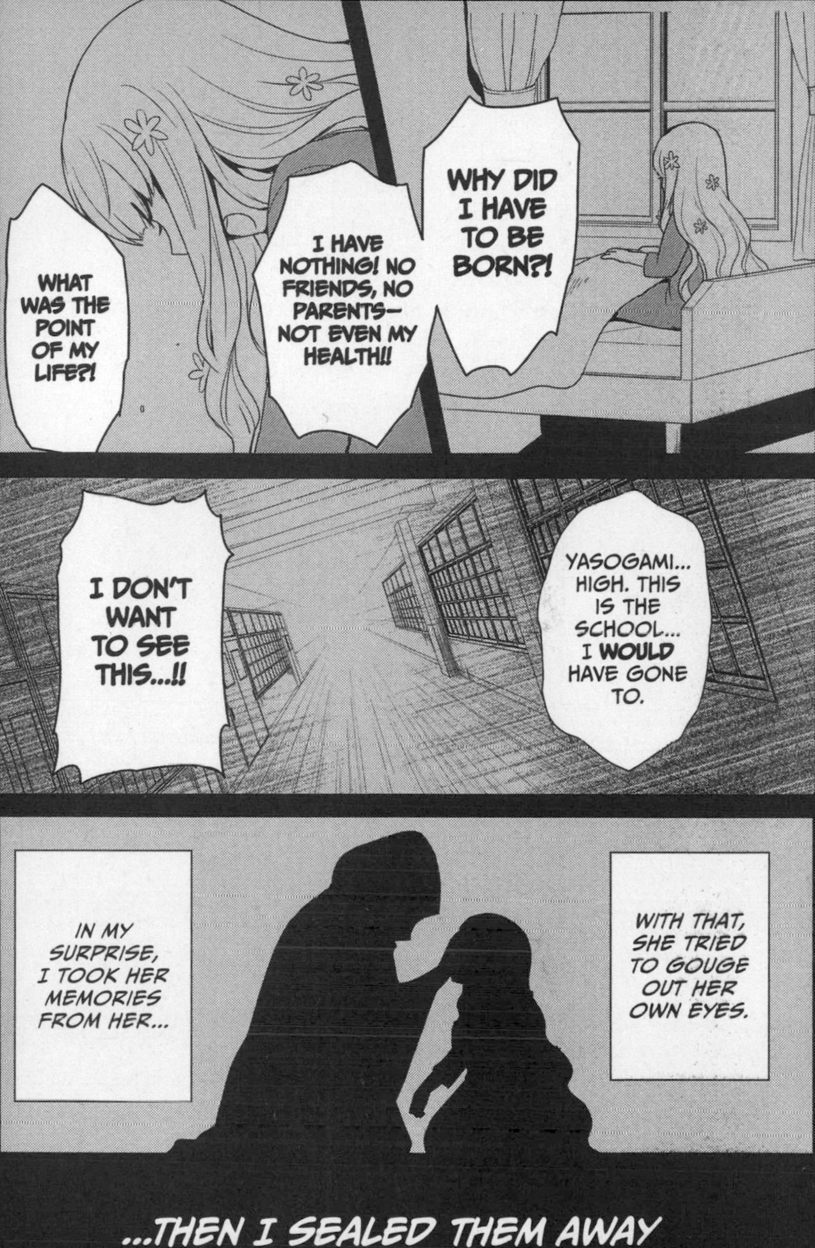
WHY DID I HAVE TO BE BORN?!
I HAVE NOTHING! NO FRIENDS, NO PARENTS— NOT EVEN MY HEALTH!!
WHAT WAS THE POINT OF MY LIFE?!
YASOGAMI... HIGH. THIS IS THE SCHOOL... I WOULD HAVE GONE TO.
I DON'T WANT TO SEE THIS...!!
WITH THAT, SHE TRIED TO GOUGE OUT HER OWN EYES.
IN MY SURPRISE, I TOOK HER MEMORIES FROM HER...
...THEN I SEALED THEM AWAY

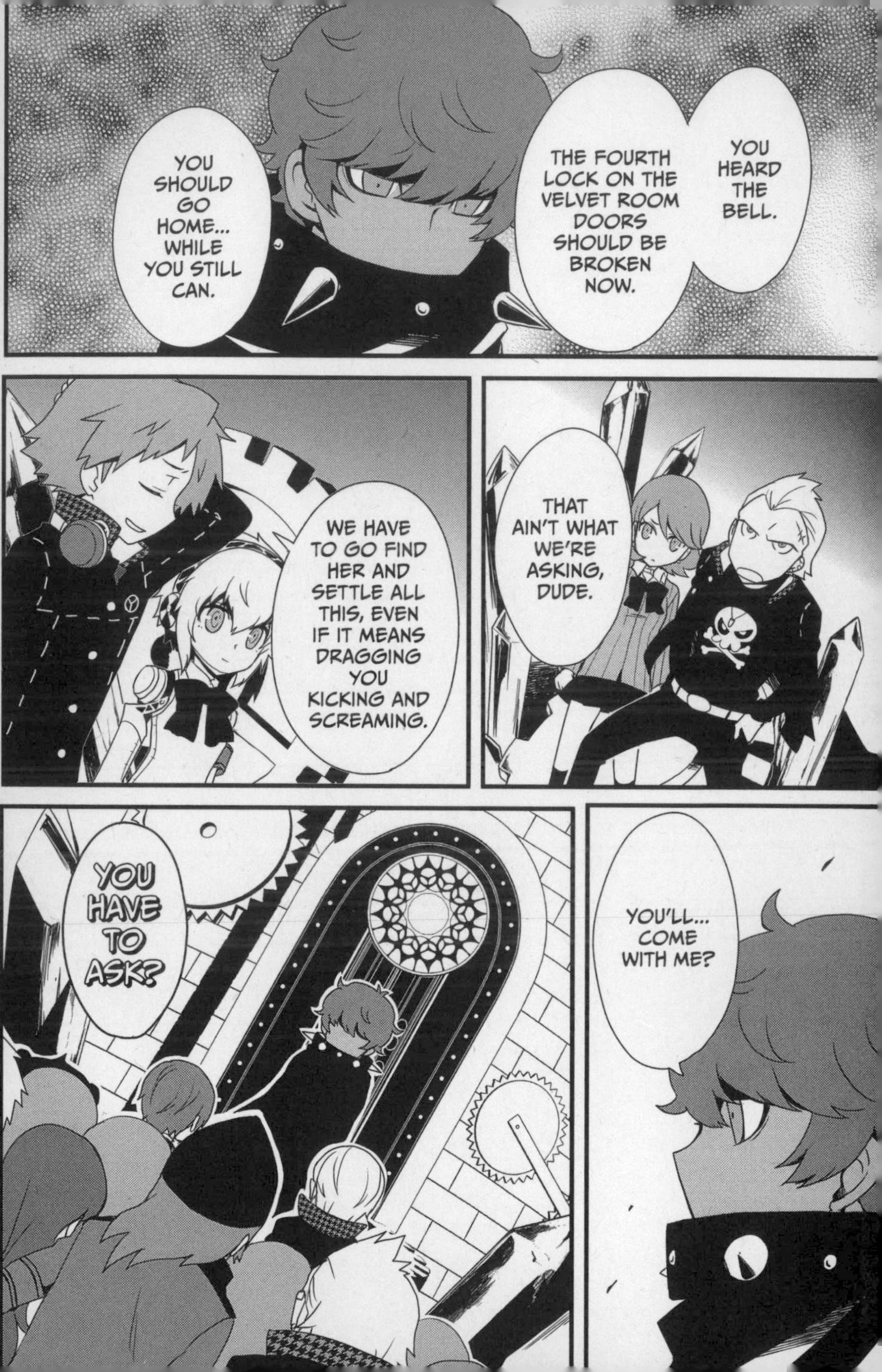
YOU HEARD THE BELL.
THE FOURTH LOCK ON THE VELVET ROOM DOORS SHOULD BE BROKEN NOW.
YOU SHOULD GO HOME... WHILE YOU STILL CAN.
THAT AIN'T WHAT WE'RE ASKING, DUDE.
WE HAVE TO GO FIND HER AND SETTLE ALL THIS, EVEN IF IT MEANS DRAGGING YOU KICKING AND SCREAMING.
YOU'LL... COME WITH ME?
YOU HAVE TO ASK?

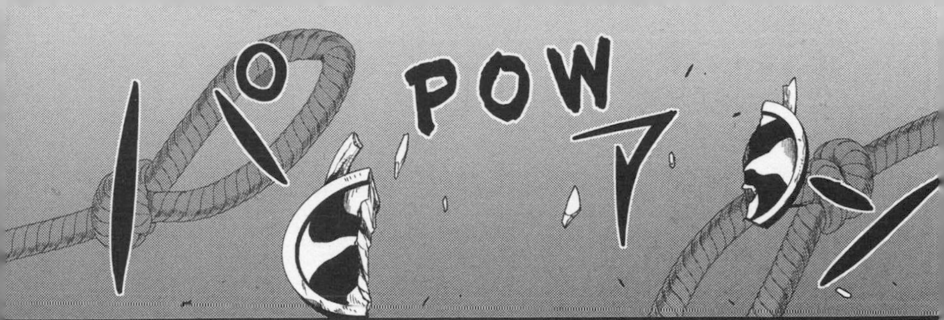
POW

Labyrinth 22: The God of the Clock Device

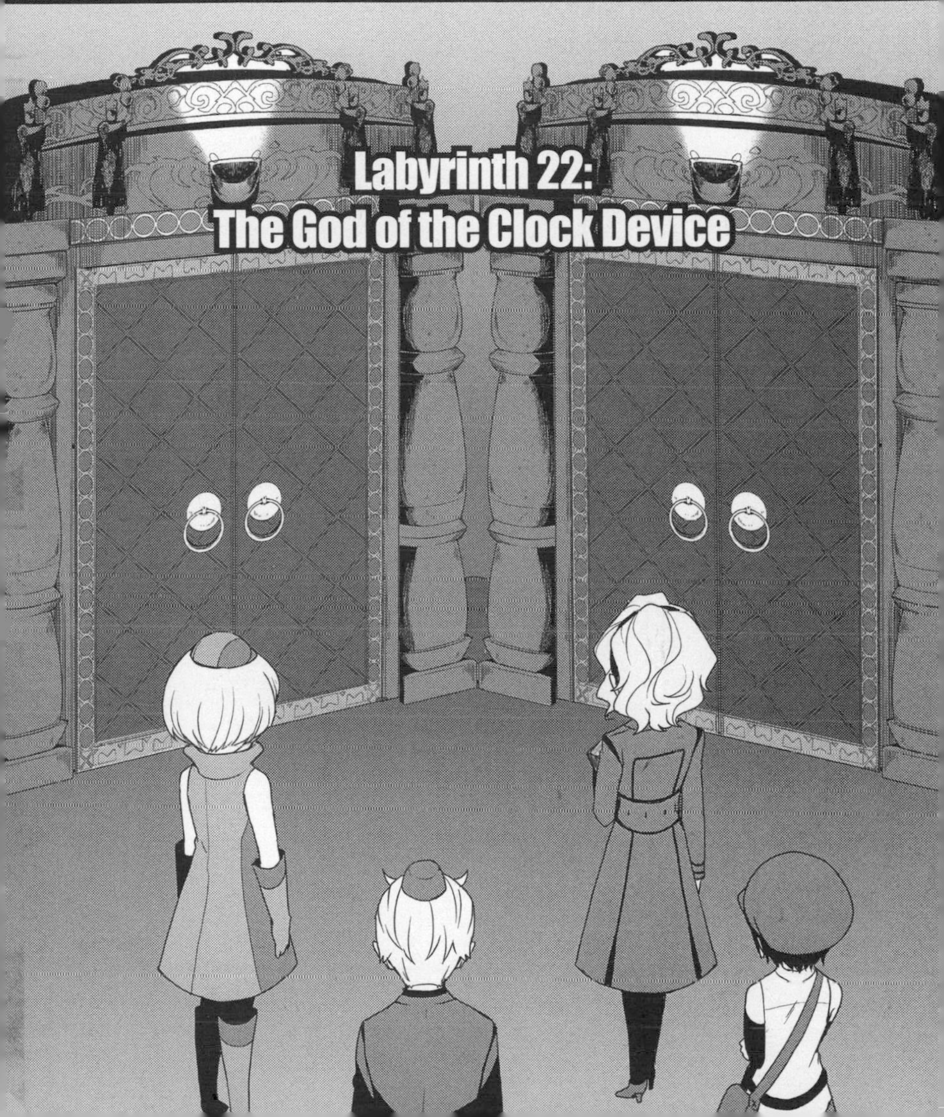

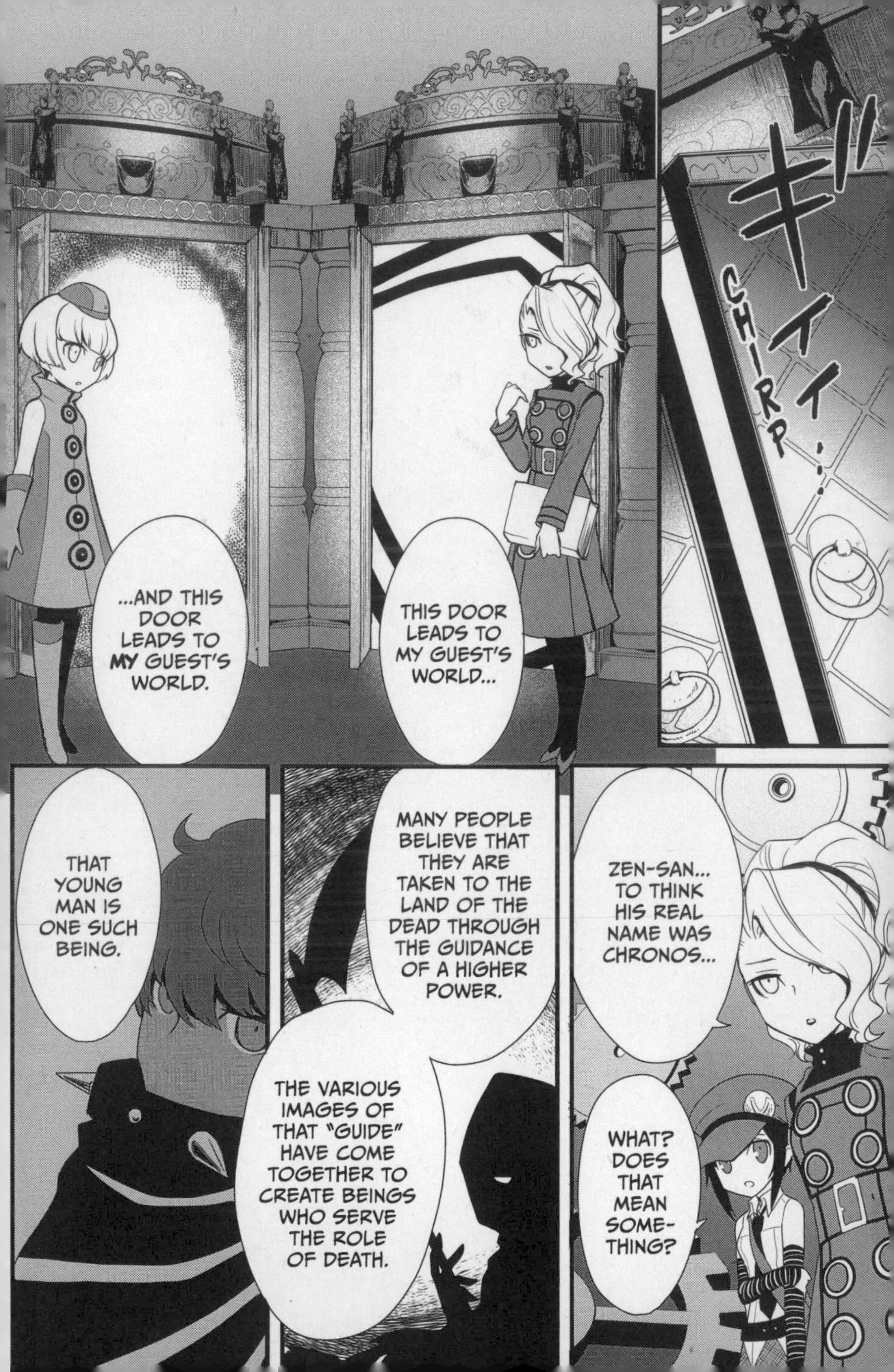
ギィィ…
CHIRP
THIS DOOR LEADS TO MY GUEST'S WORLD...
...AND THIS DOOR LEADS TO **MY** GUEST'S WORLD.
ZEN-SAN... TO THINK HIS REAL NAME WAS CHRONOS...
WHAT? DOES THAT MEAN SOME-THING?
MANY PEOPLE BELIEVE THAT THEY ARE TAKEN TO THE LAND OF THE DEAD THROUGH THE GUIDANCE OF A HIGHER POWER.
THE VARIOUS IMAGES OF THAT "GUIDE" HAVE COME TOGETHER TO CREATE BEINGS WHO SERVE THE ROLE OF DEATH.
THAT YOUNG MAN IS ONE SUCH BEING.

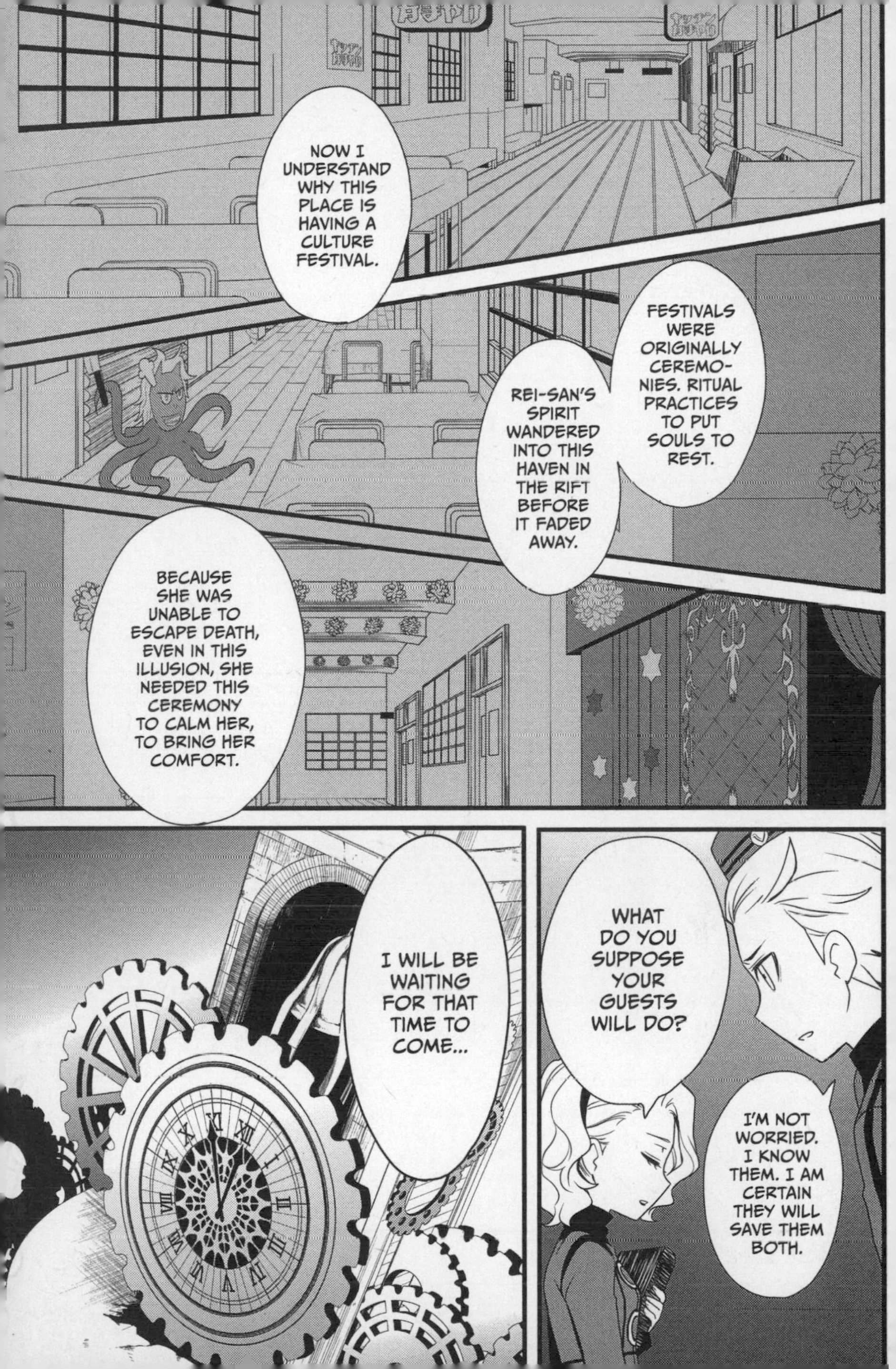
NOW I UNDERSTAND WHY THIS PLACE IS HAVING A CULTURE FESTIVAL.
FESTIVALS WERE ORIGINALLY CEREMONIES. RITUAL PRACTICES TO PUT SOULS TO REST.
REI-SAN'S SPIRIT WANDERED INTO THIS HAVEN IN THE RIFT BEFORE IT FADED AWAY.
BECAUSE SHE WAS UNABLE TO ESCAPE DEATH, EVEN IN THIS ILLUSION, SHE NEEDED THIS CEREMONY TO CALM HER, TO BRING HER COMFORT.
WHAT DO YOU SUPPOSE YOUR GUESTS WILL DO?
I'M NOT WORRIED. I KNOW THEM. I AM CERTAIN THEY WILL SAVE THEM BOTH.
I WILL BE WAITING FOR THAT TIME TO COME...

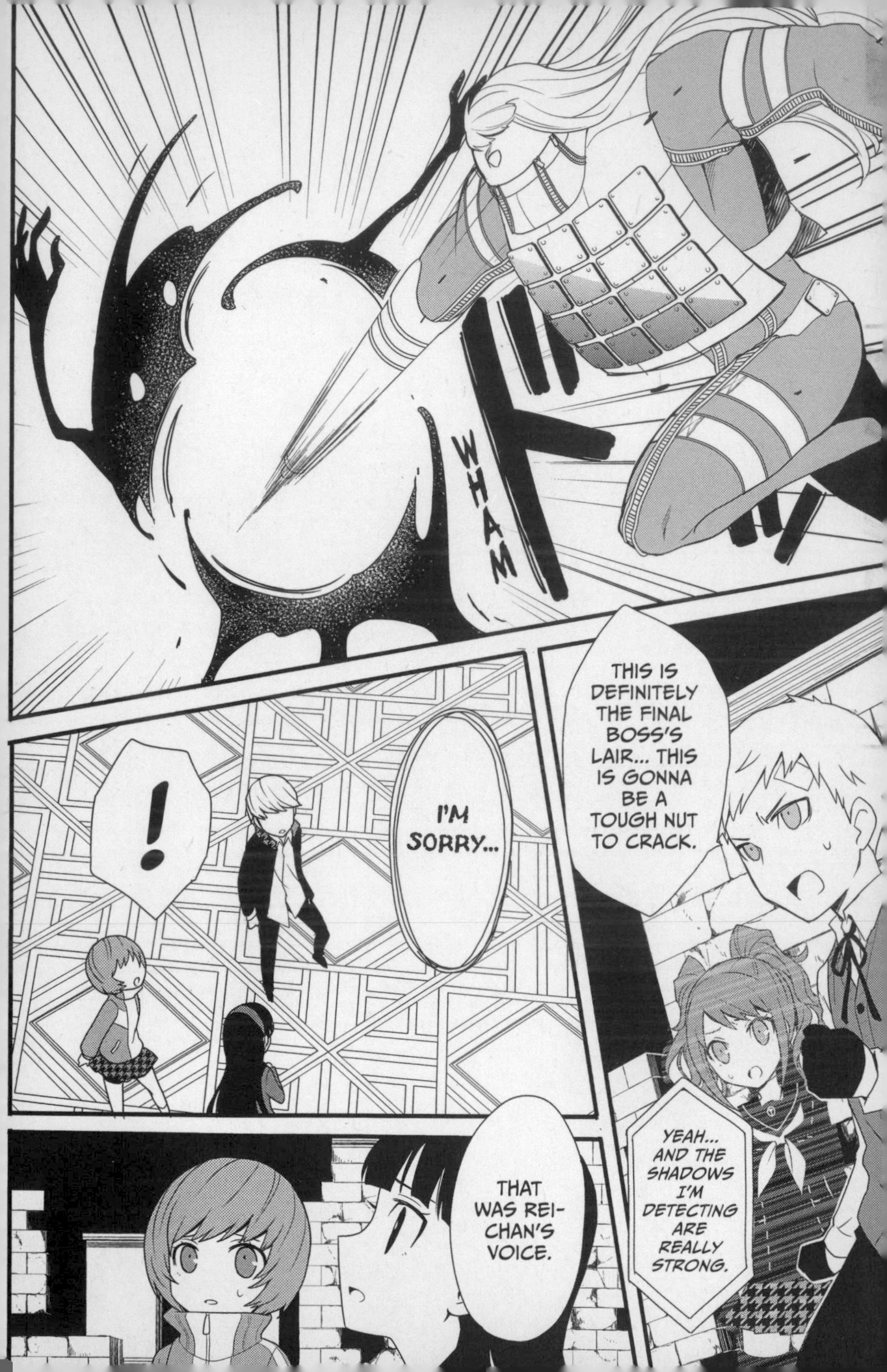
WHAM
THIS IS DEFINITELY THE FINAL BOSS'S LAIR... THIS IS GONNA BE A TOUGH NUT TO CRACK.
YEAH... AND THE SHADOWS I'M DETECTING ARE REALLY STRONG.
!
I'M SORRY...
THAT WAS REI-CHAN'S VOICE.

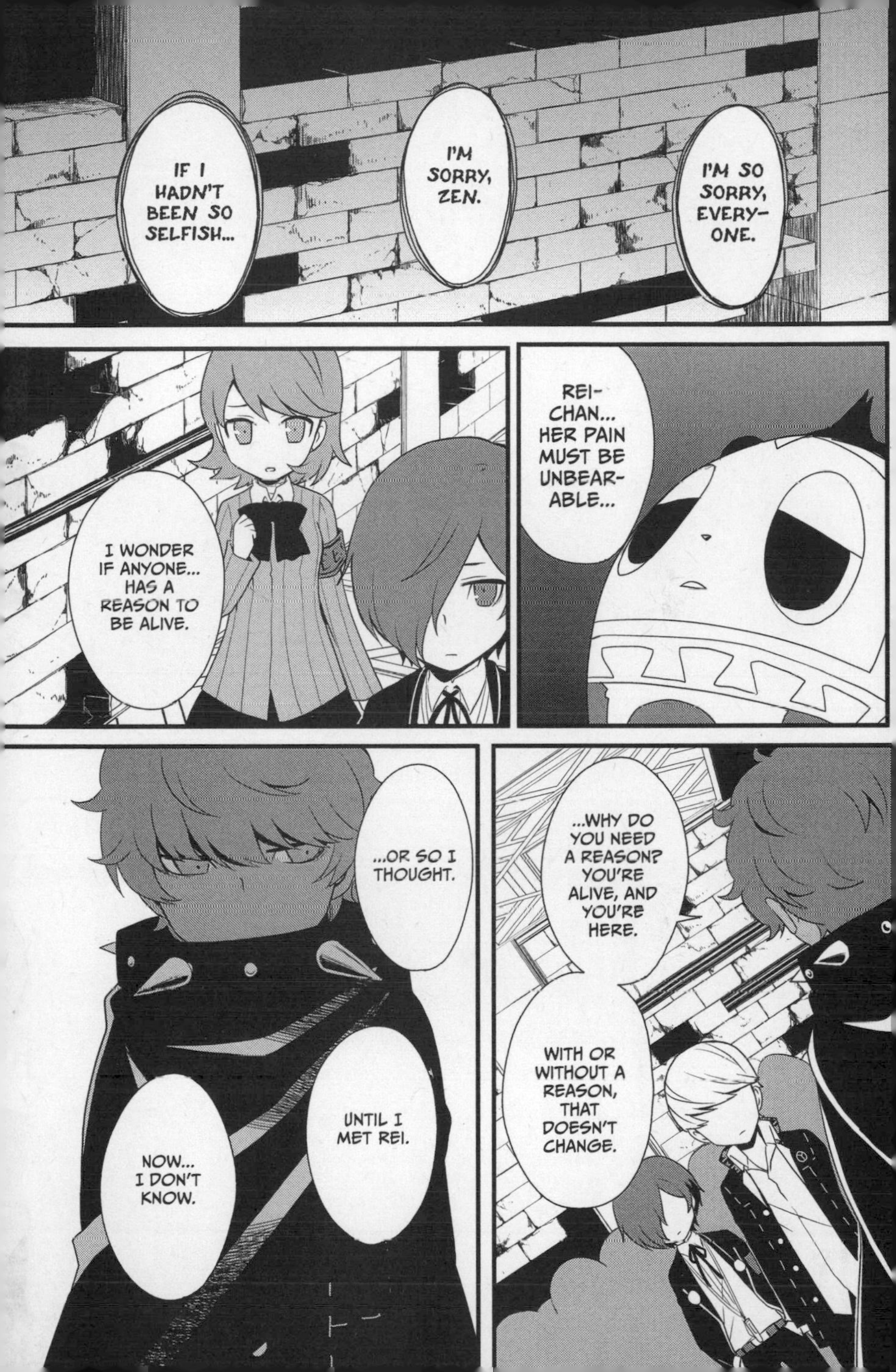
I'M SO SORRY, EVERYONE.
I'M SORRY, ZEN.
IF I HADN'T BEEN SO SELFISH...
REI-CHAN... HER PAIN MUST BE UNBEARABLE...
I WONDER IF ANYONE... HAS A REASON TO BE ALIVE.
...WHY DO YOU NEED A REASON? YOU'RE ALIVE, AND YOU'RE HERE.
WITH OR WITHOUT A REASON, THAT DOESN'T CHANGE.
...OR SO I THOUGHT.
UNTIL I MET REI.
NOW... I DON'T KNOW.

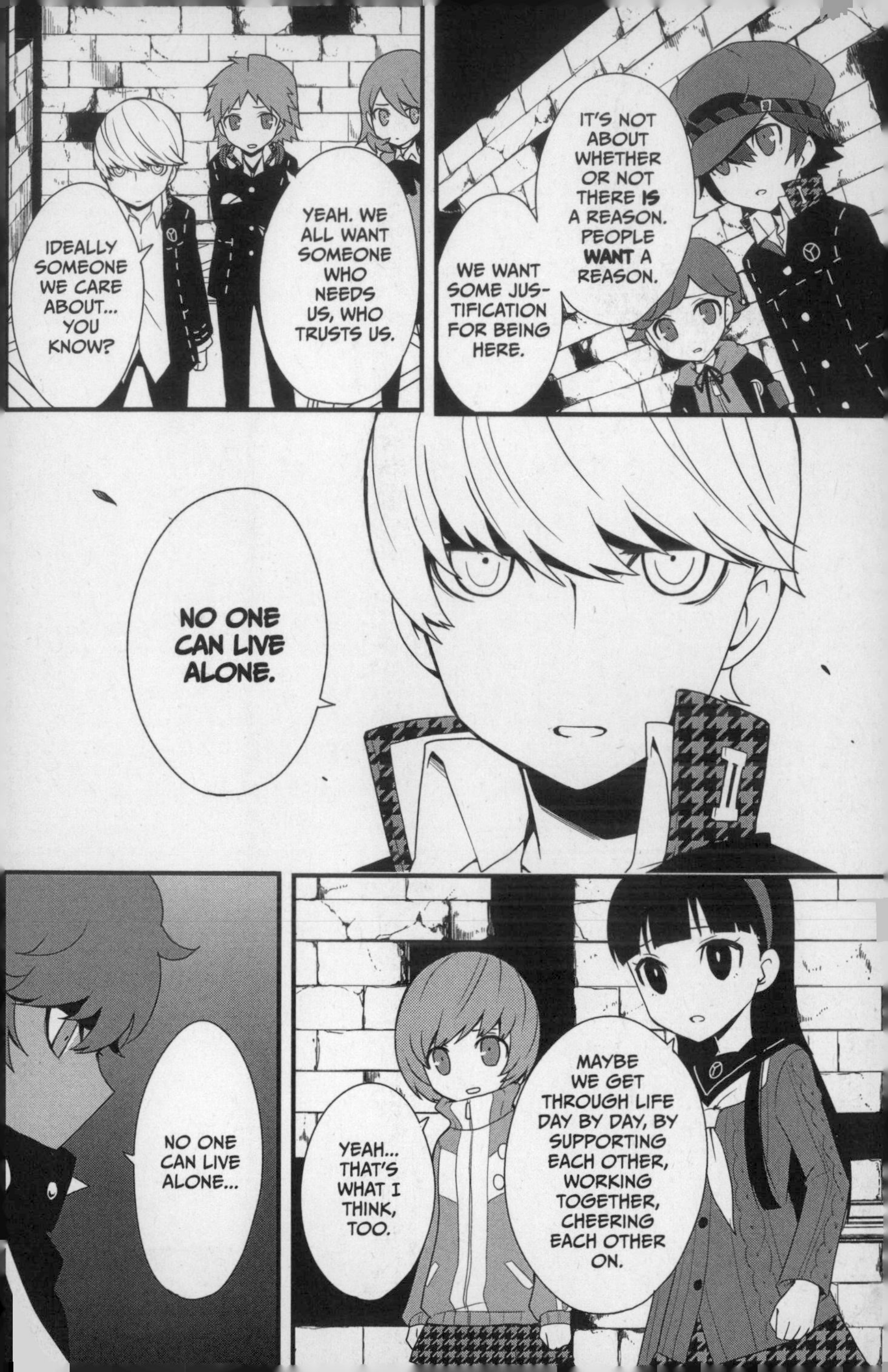
IT'S NOT ABOUT WHETHER OR NOT THERE **IS** A REASON. PEOPLE **WANT** A REASON.
WE WANT SOME JUS-TIFICATION FOR BEING HERE.
YEAH. WE ALL WANT SOMEONE WHO NEEDS US, WHO TRUSTS US.
IDEALLY SOMEONE WE CARE ABOUT... YOU KNOW?
NO ONE CAN LIVE ALONE.
MAYBE WE GET THROUGH LIFE DAY BY DAY, BY SUPPORTING EACH OTHER, WORKING TOGETHER, CHEERING EACH OTHER ON.
YEAH... THAT'S WHAT I THINK, TOO.
NO ONE CAN LIVE ALONE...

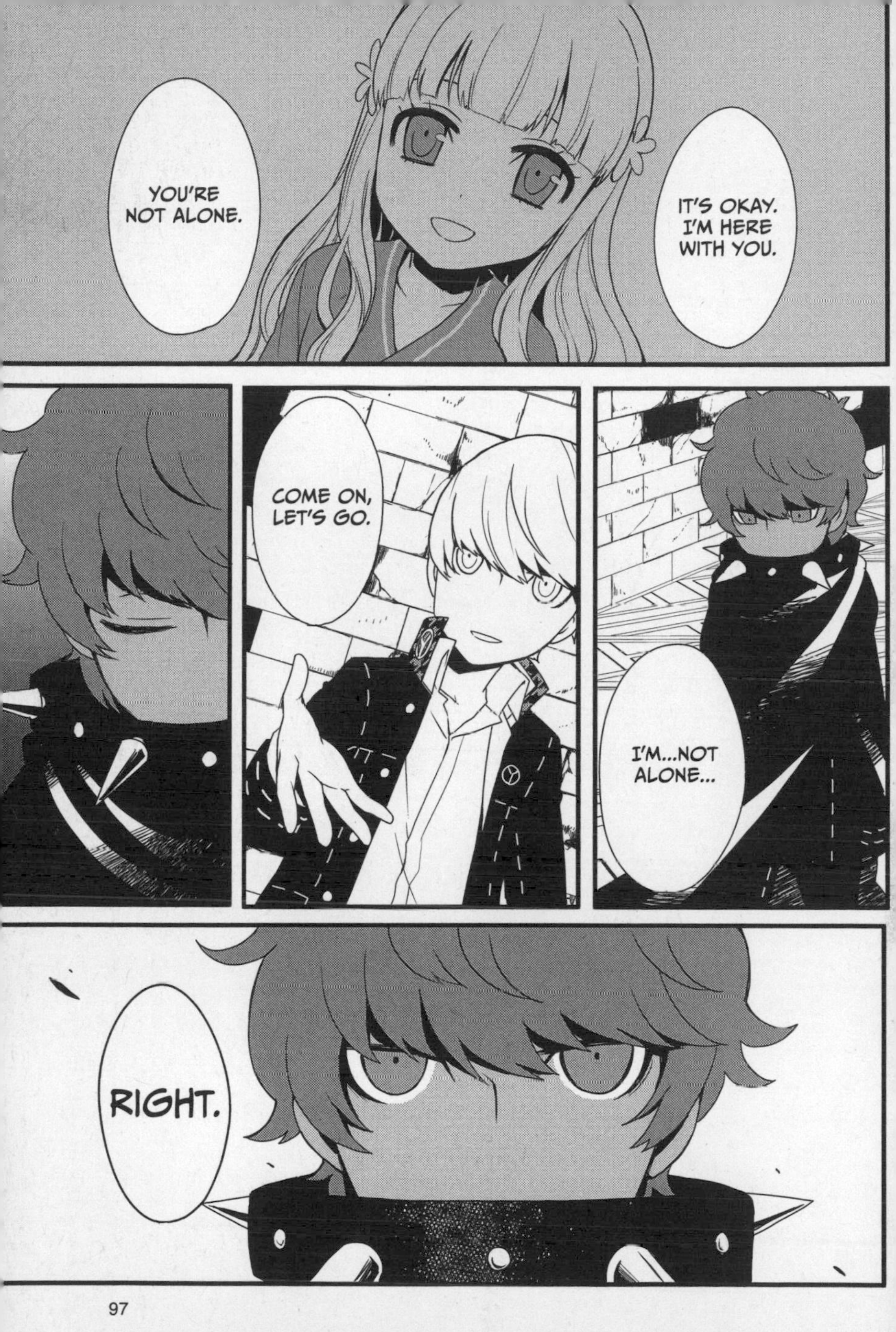
IT'S OKAY. I'M HERE WITH YOU.
YOU'RE NOT ALONE.
I'M...NOT ALONE...
COME ON, LET'S GO.
RIGHT.

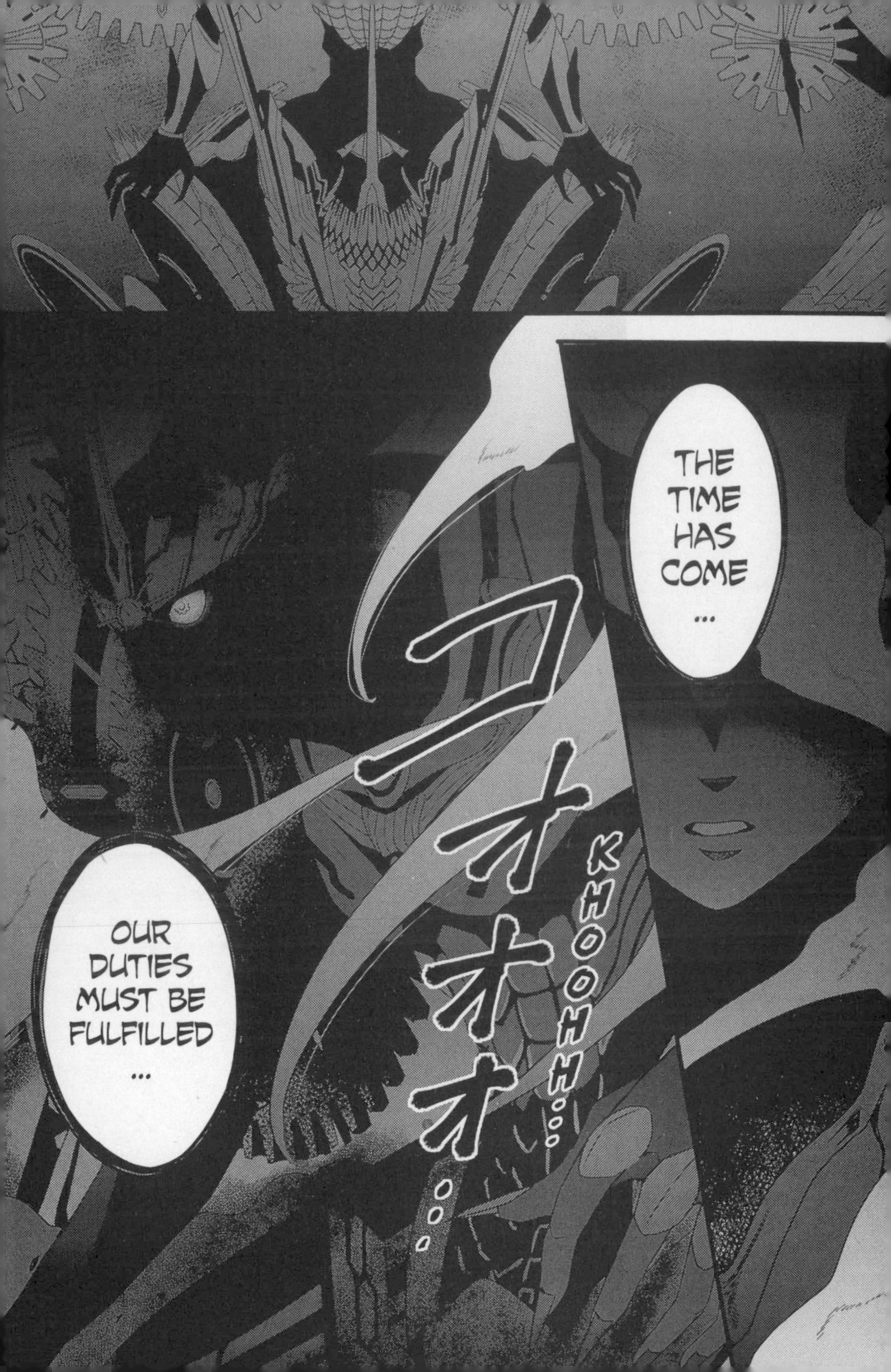
THE TIME HAS COME ...
コオオオ
KHOOHHH...
OUR DUTIES MUST BE FULFILLED ...

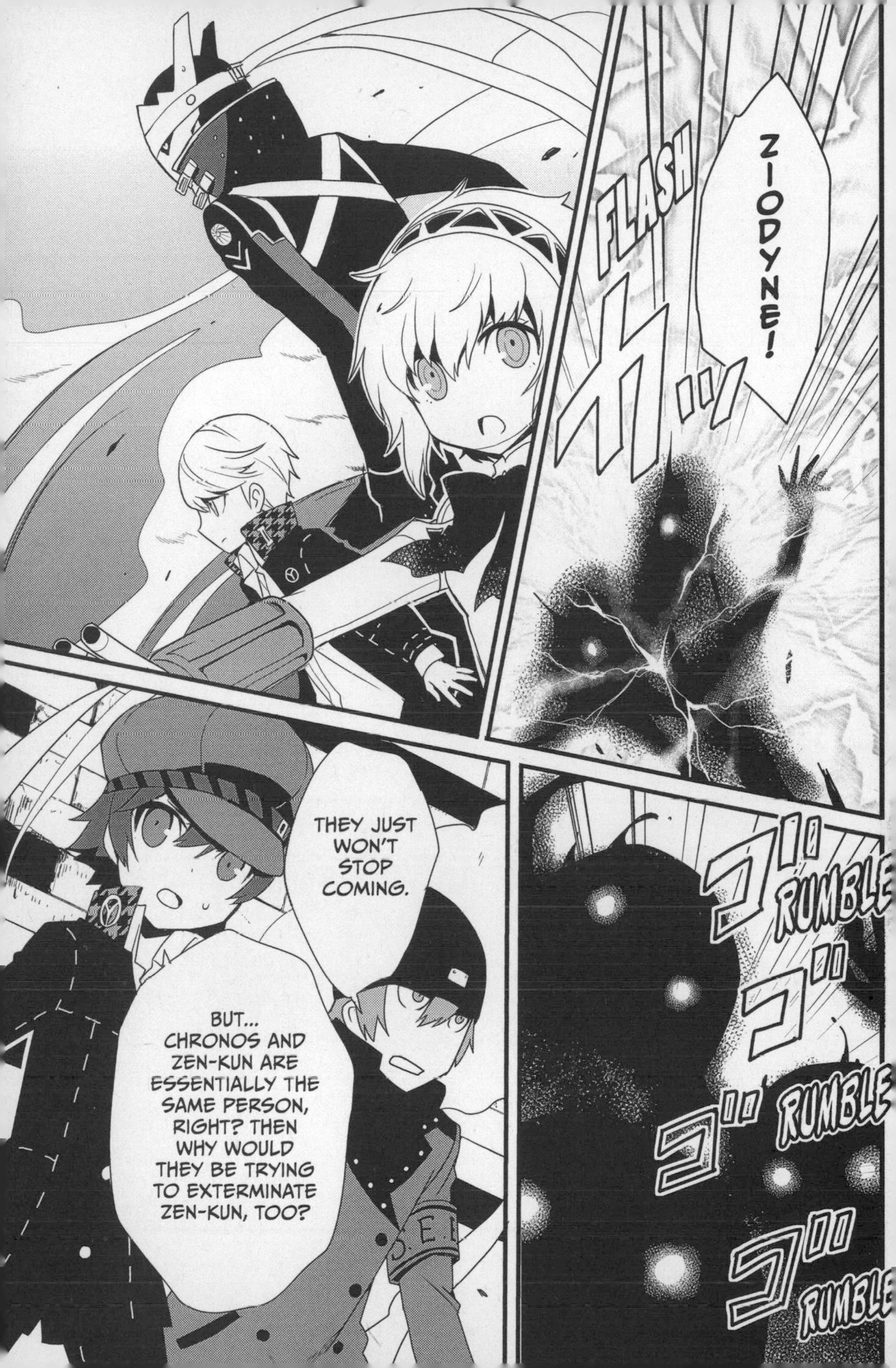
ZIODYNE!
FLASH
RUMBLE
RUMBLE
RUMBLE
THEY JUST WON'T STOP COMING.
BUT... CHRONOS AND ZEN-KUN ARE ESSENTIALLY THE SAME PERSON, RIGHT? THEN WHY WOULD THEY BE TRYING TO EXTERMINATE ZEN-KUN, TOO?

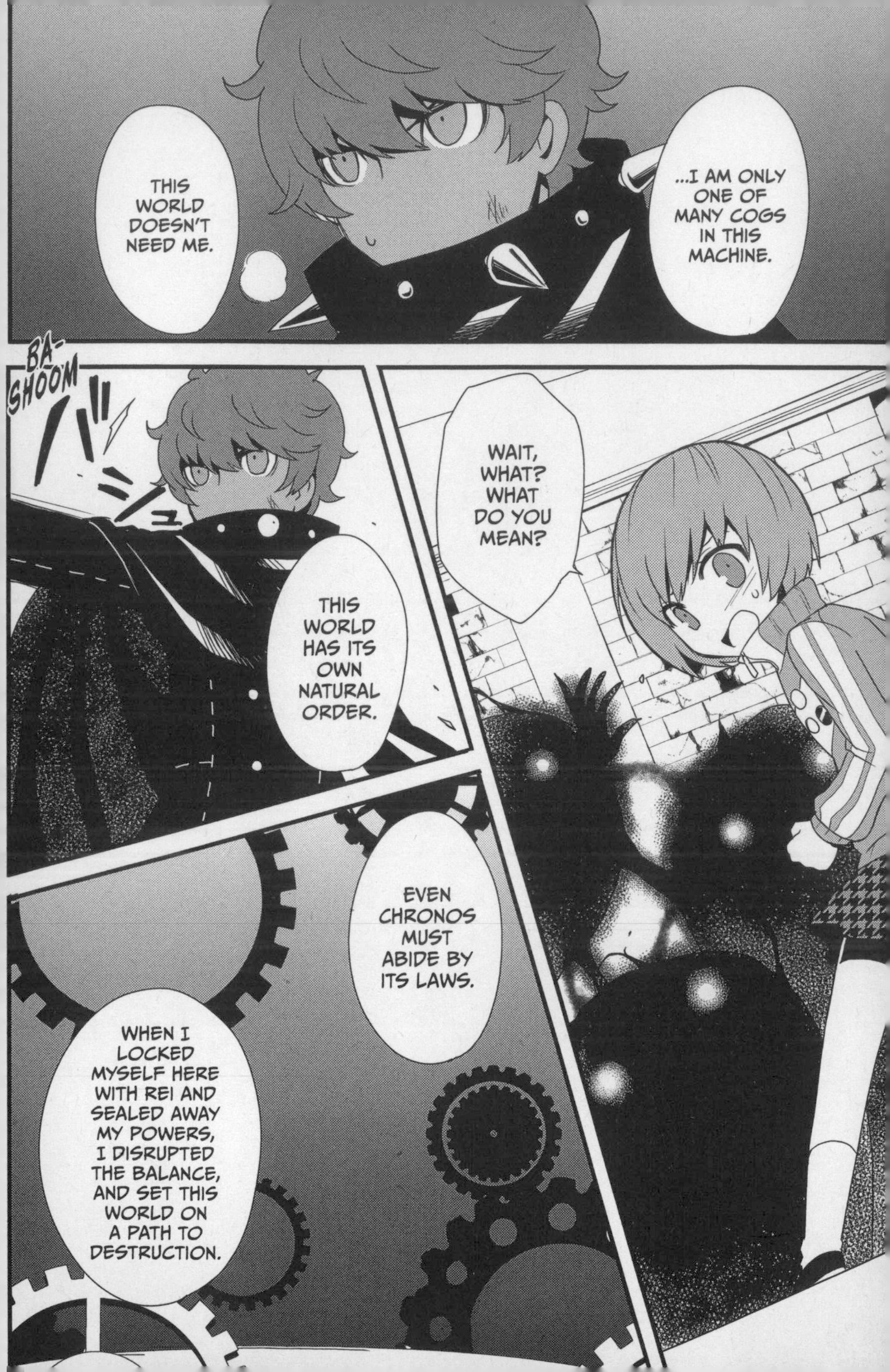
...I AM ONLY ONE OF MANY COGS IN THIS MACHINE.
THIS WORLD DOESN'T NEED ME.
WAIT, WHAT? WHAT DO YOU MEAN?
BA-SHOOM
THIS WORLD HAS ITS OWN NATURAL ORDER.
EVEN CHRONOS MUST ABIDE BY ITS LAWS.
WHEN I LOCKED MYSELF HERE WITH REI AND SEALED AWAY MY POWERS, I DISRUPTED THE BALANCE, AND SET THIS WORLD ON A PATH TO DESTRUCTION.

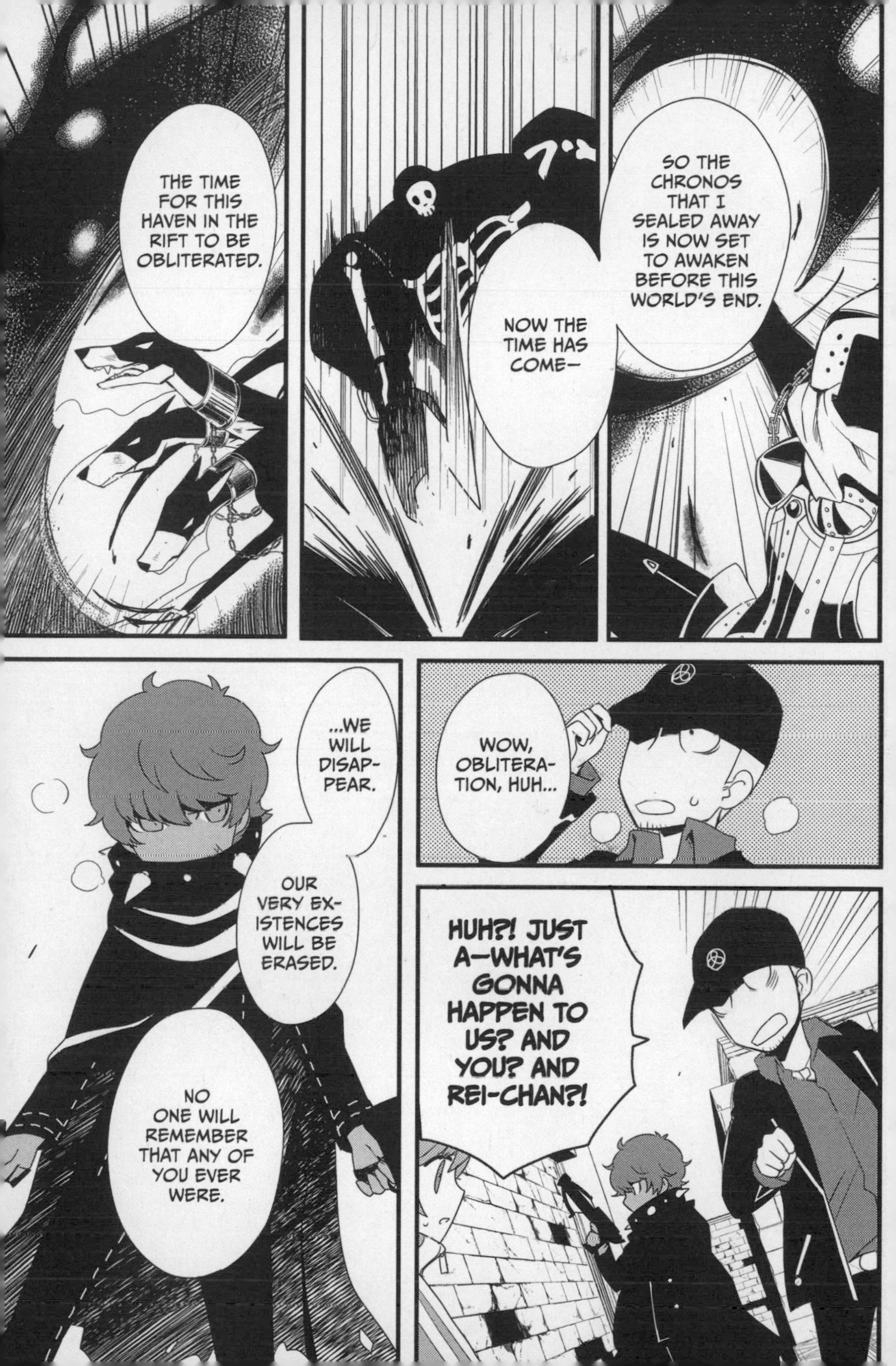

SO THE CHRONOS THAT I SEALED AWAY IS NOW SET TO AWAKEN BEFORE THIS WORLD'S END.
NOW THE TIME HAS COME—
THE TIME FOR THIS HAVEN IN THE RIFT TO BE OBLITERATED.
WOW, OBLITERATION, HUH...
HUH?! JUST A—WHAT'S GONNA HAPPEN TO US? AND YOU? AND REI-CHAN?!
...WE WILL DISAPPEAR.
OUR VERY EXISTENCES WILL BE ERASED.
NO ONE WILL REMEMBER THAT ANY OF YOU EVER WERE.

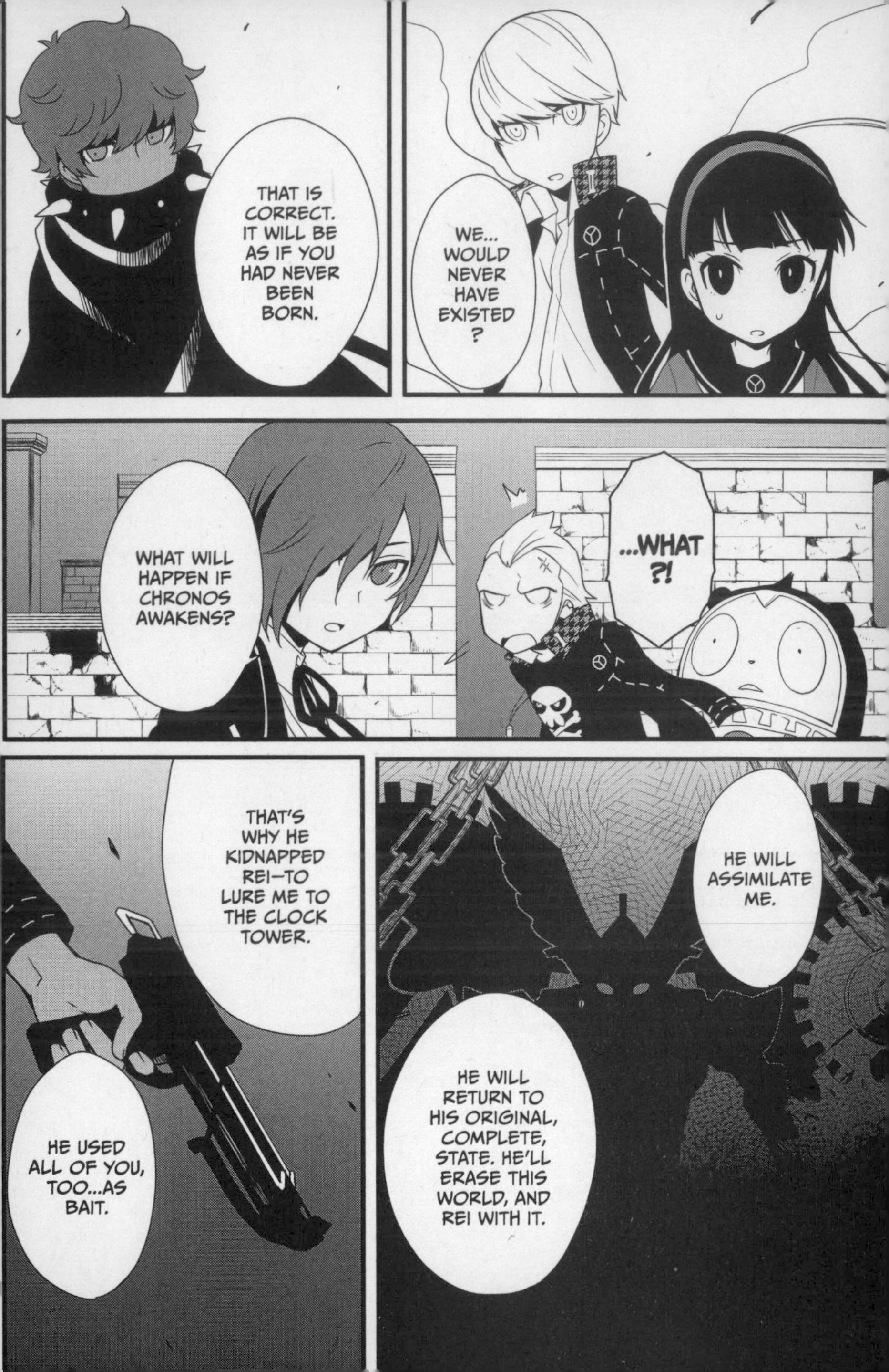
WE... WOULD NEVER HAVE EXISTED ?
THAT IS CORRECT. IT WILL BE AS IF YOU HAD NEVER BEEN BORN.
...WHAT ?!
WHAT WILL HAPPEN IF CHRONOS AWAKENS?
HE WILL ASSIMILATE ME.
HE WILL RETURN TO HIS ORIGINAL, COMPLETE, STATE. HE'LL ERASE THIS WORLD, AND REI WITH IT.
THAT'S WHY HE KIDNAPPED REI—TO LURE ME TO THE CLOCK TOWER.
HE USED ALL OF YOU, TOO...AS BAIT.

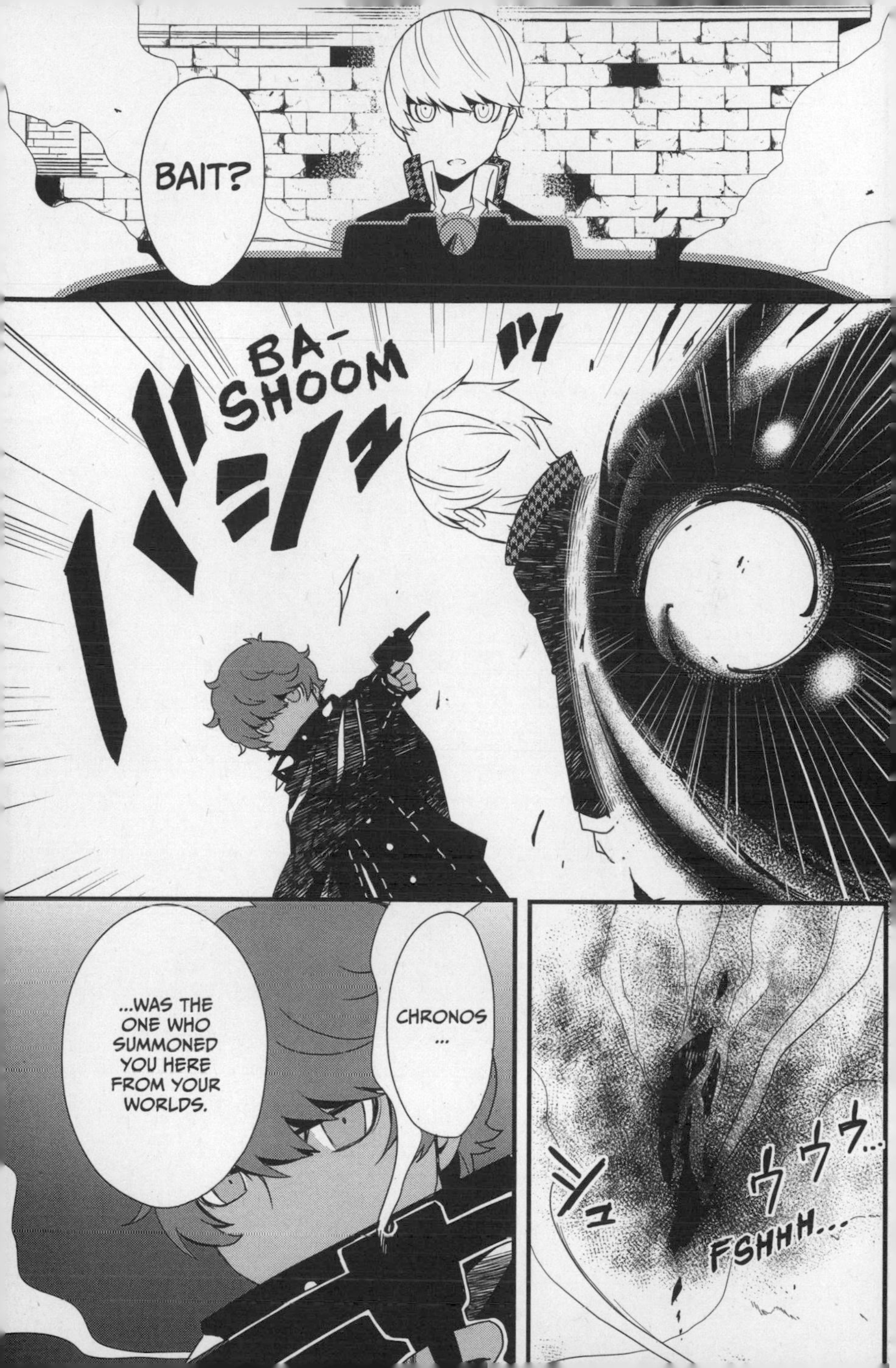
BAIT?
バシュ
BA-SHOOM
シュウウウ…
FSHHH…
CHRONOS…
…WAS THE ONE WHO SUMMONED YOU HERE FROM YOUR WORLDS.

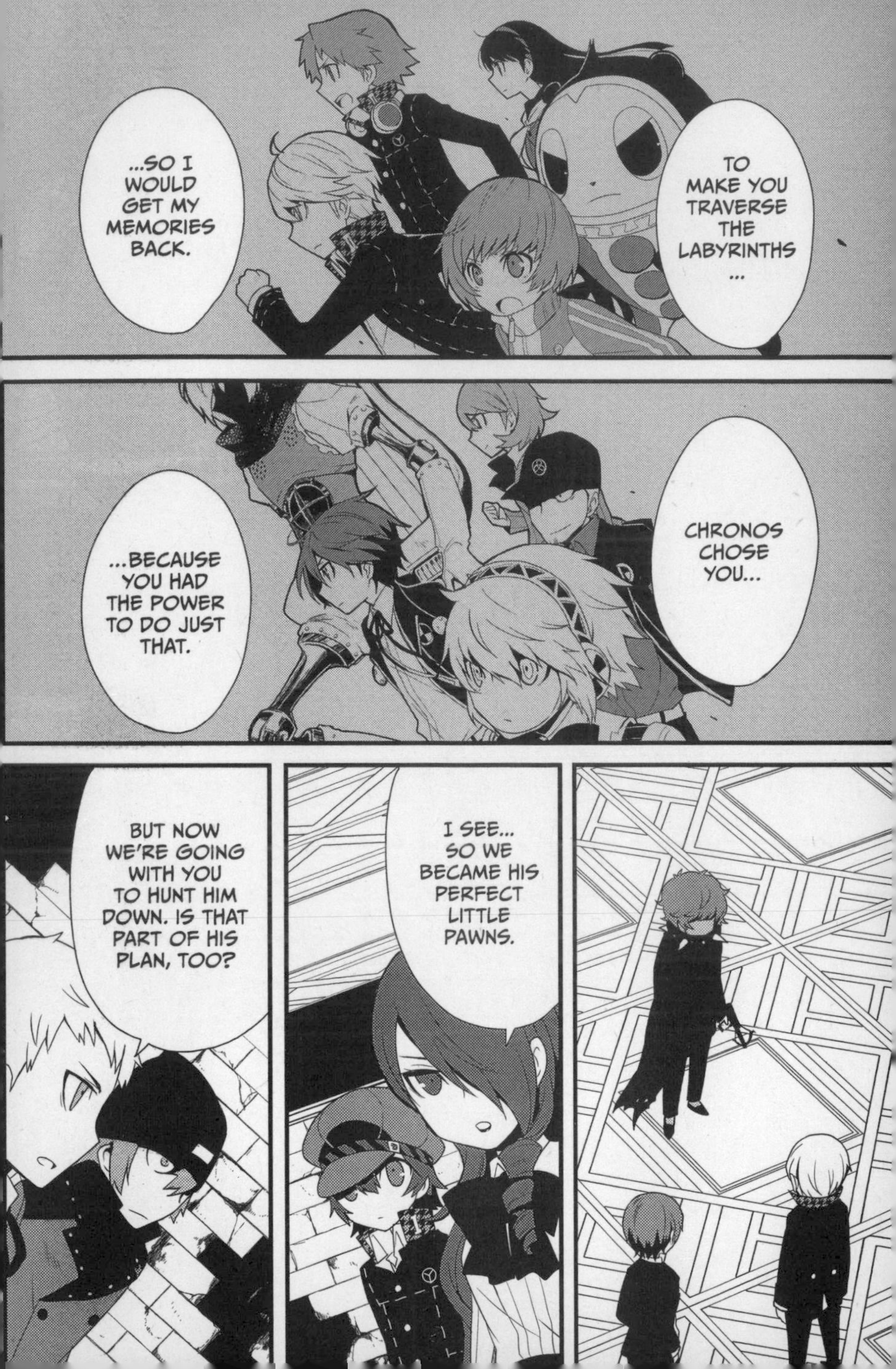
TO MAKE YOU TRAVERSE THE LABYRINTHS ...
...SO I WOULD GET MY MEMORIES BACK.
CHRONOS CHOSE YOU...
...BECAUSE YOU HAD THE POWER TO DO JUST THAT.
I SEE... SO WE BECAME HIS PERFECT LITTLE PAWNS.
BUT NOW WE'RE GOING WITH YOU TO HUNT HIM DOWN. IS THAT PART OF HIS PLAN, TOO?

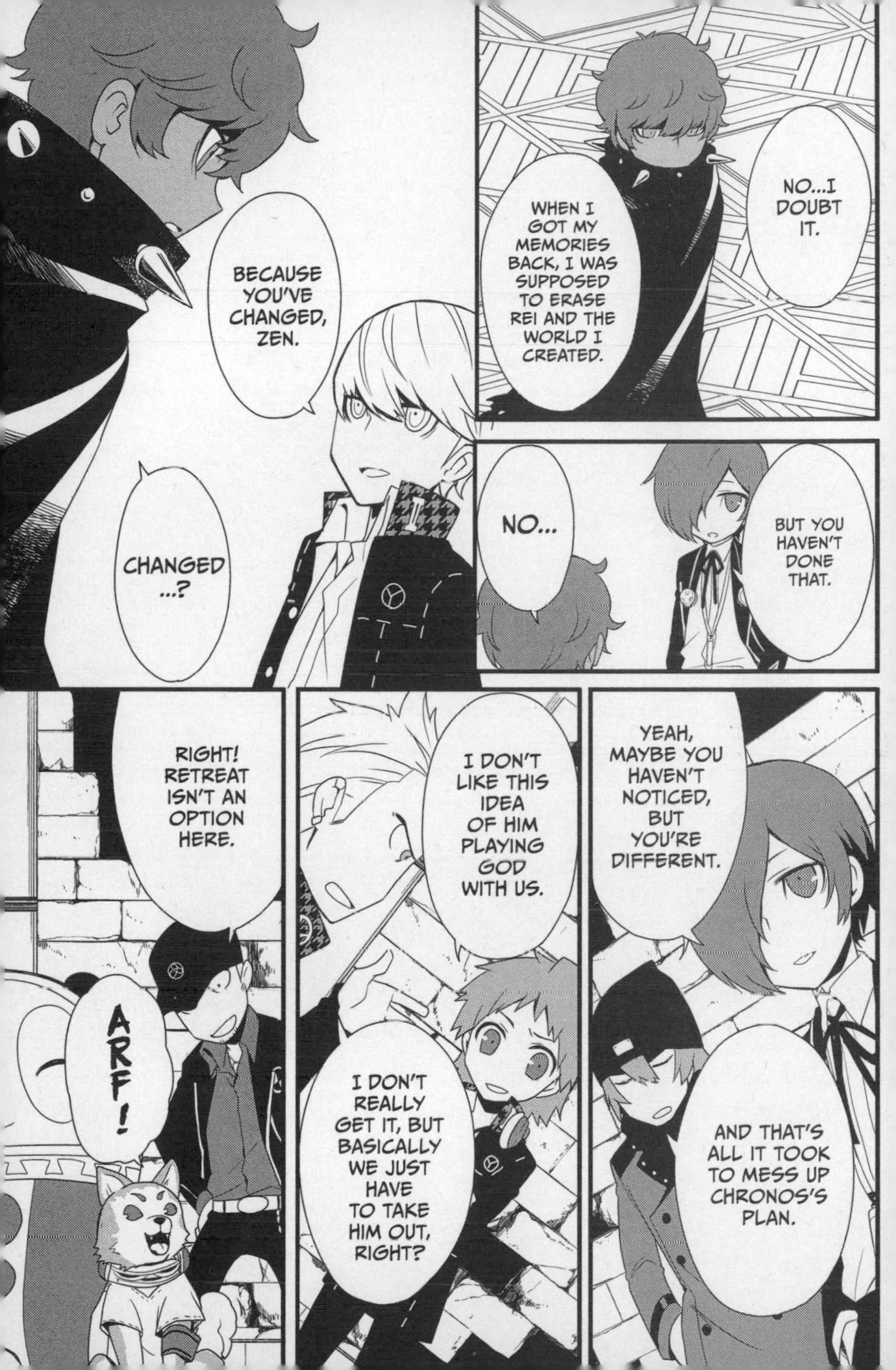
NO...I DOUBT IT.
WHEN I GOT MY MEMORIES BACK, I WAS SUPPOSED TO ERASE REI AND THE WORLD I CREATED.
BUT YOU HAVEN'T DONE THAT.
NO...
BECAUSE YOU'VE CHANGED, ZEN.
CHANGED ...?
YEAH, MAYBE YOU HAVEN'T NOTICED, BUT YOU'RE DIFFERENT.
AND THAT'S ALL IT TOOK TO MESS UP CHRONOS'S PLAN.
I DON'T LIKE THIS IDEA OF HIM PLAYING GOD WITH US.
I DON'T REALLY GET IT, BUT BASICALLY WE JUST HAVE TO TAKE HIM OUT, RIGHT?
RIGHT! RETREAT ISN'T AN OPTION HERE.
ARF!

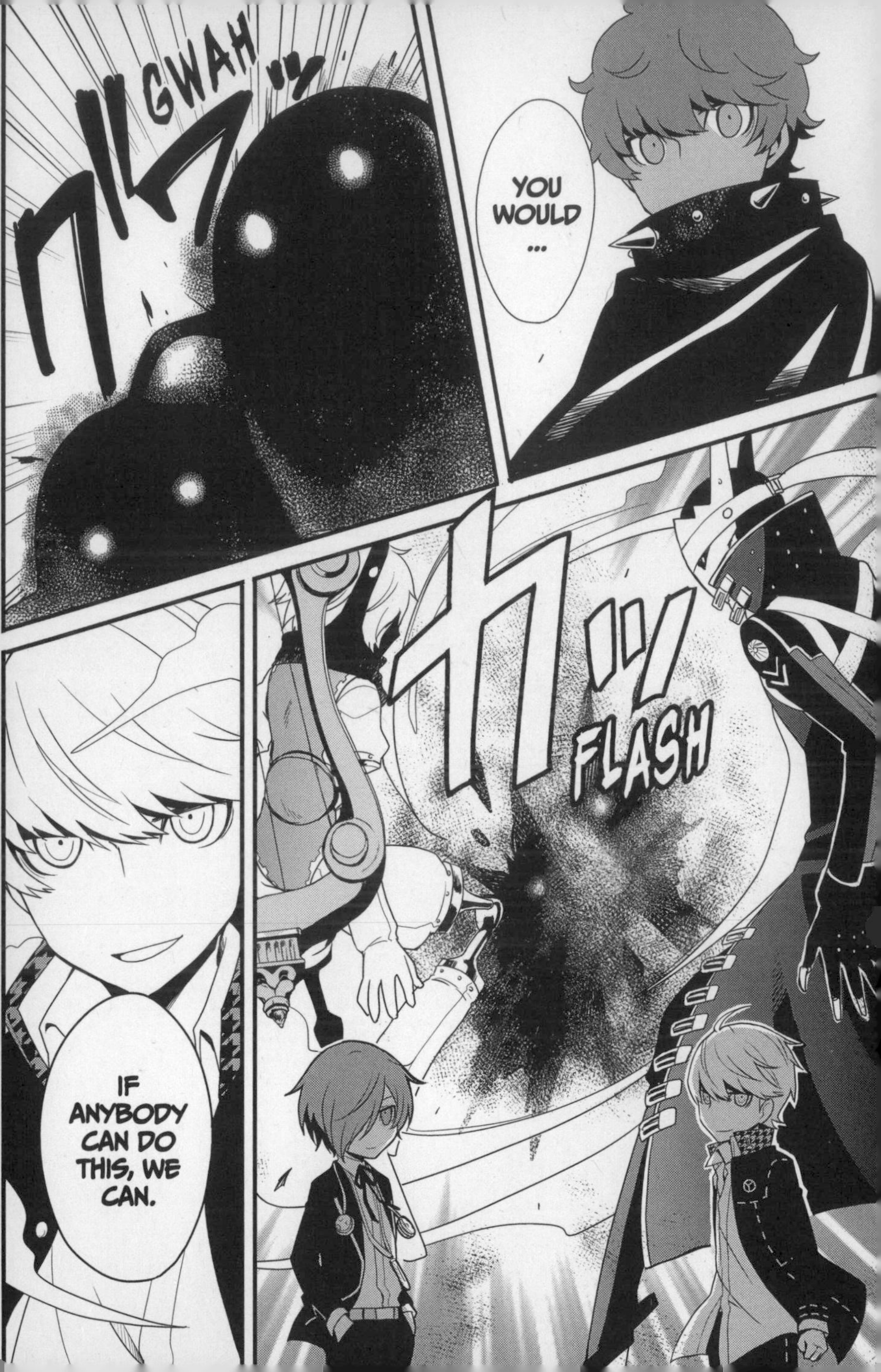
YOU WOULD ...
GWAH
FLASH
IF ANYBODY CAN DO THIS, WE CAN.

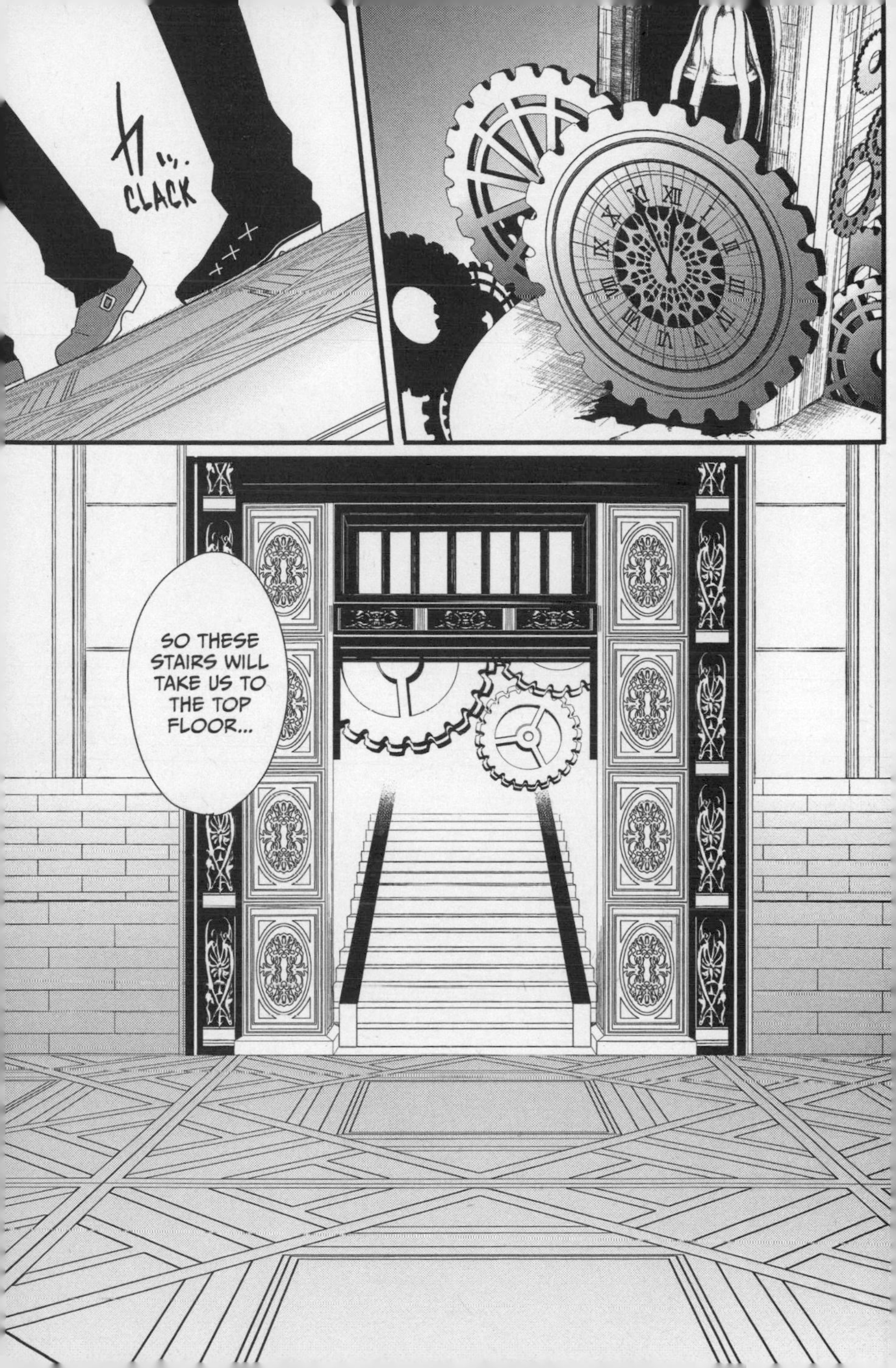
カ…
CLACK
SO THESE STAIRS WILL TAKE US TO THE TOP FLOOR...

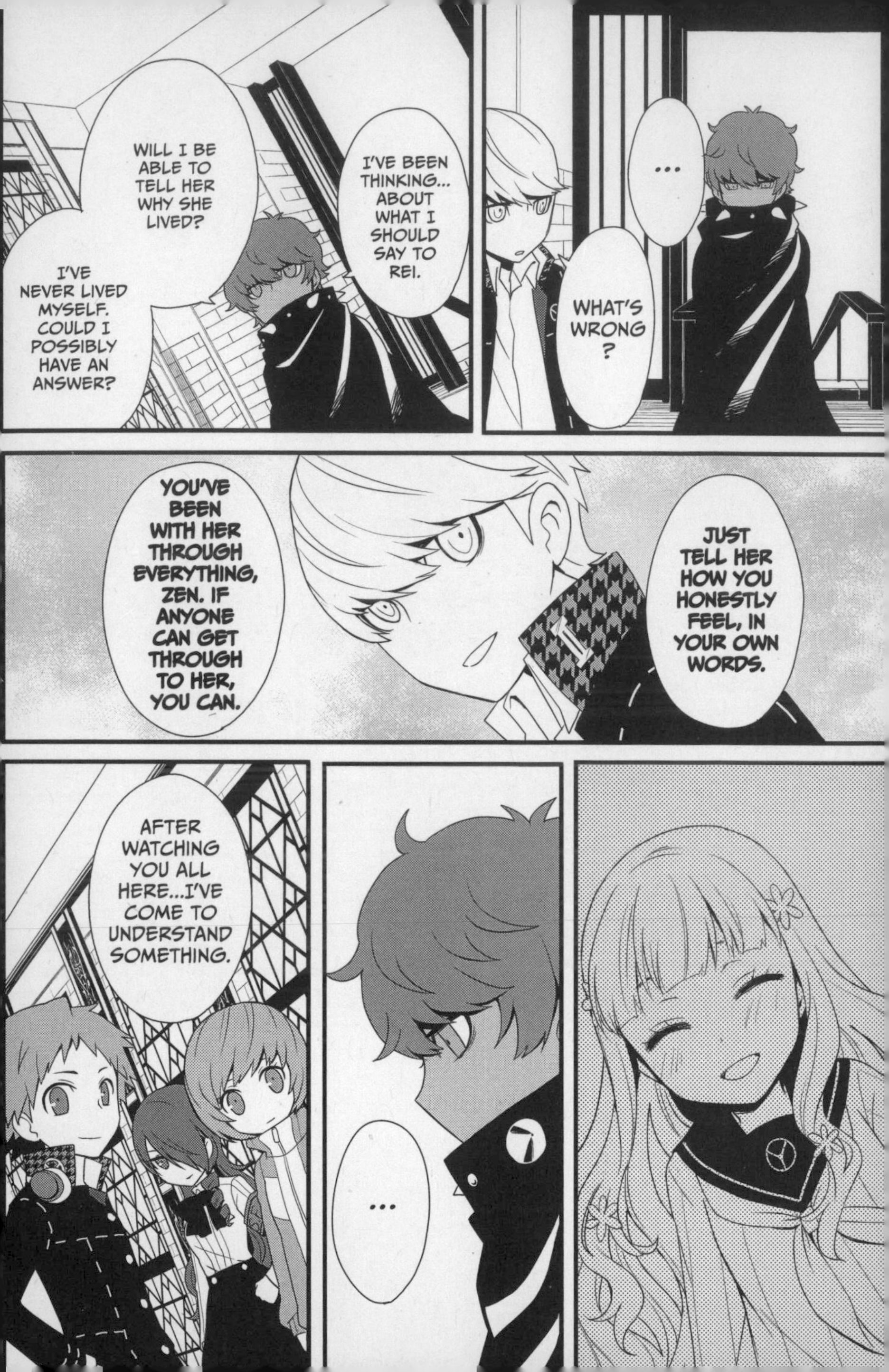
...
WHAT'S WRONG?
I'VE BEEN THINKING... ABOUT WHAT I SHOULD SAY TO REI.
WILL I BE ABLE TO TELL HER WHY SHE LIVED?
I'VE NEVER LIVED MYSELF. COULD I POSSIBLY HAVE AN ANSWER?
JUST TELL HER HOW YOU HONESTLY FEEL, IN YOUR OWN WORDS.
YOU'VE BEEN WITH HER THROUGH EVERYTHING, ZEN. IF ANYONE CAN GET THROUGH TO HER, YOU CAN.
...
AFTER WATCHING YOU ALL HERE...I'VE COME TO UNDERSTAND SOMETHING.

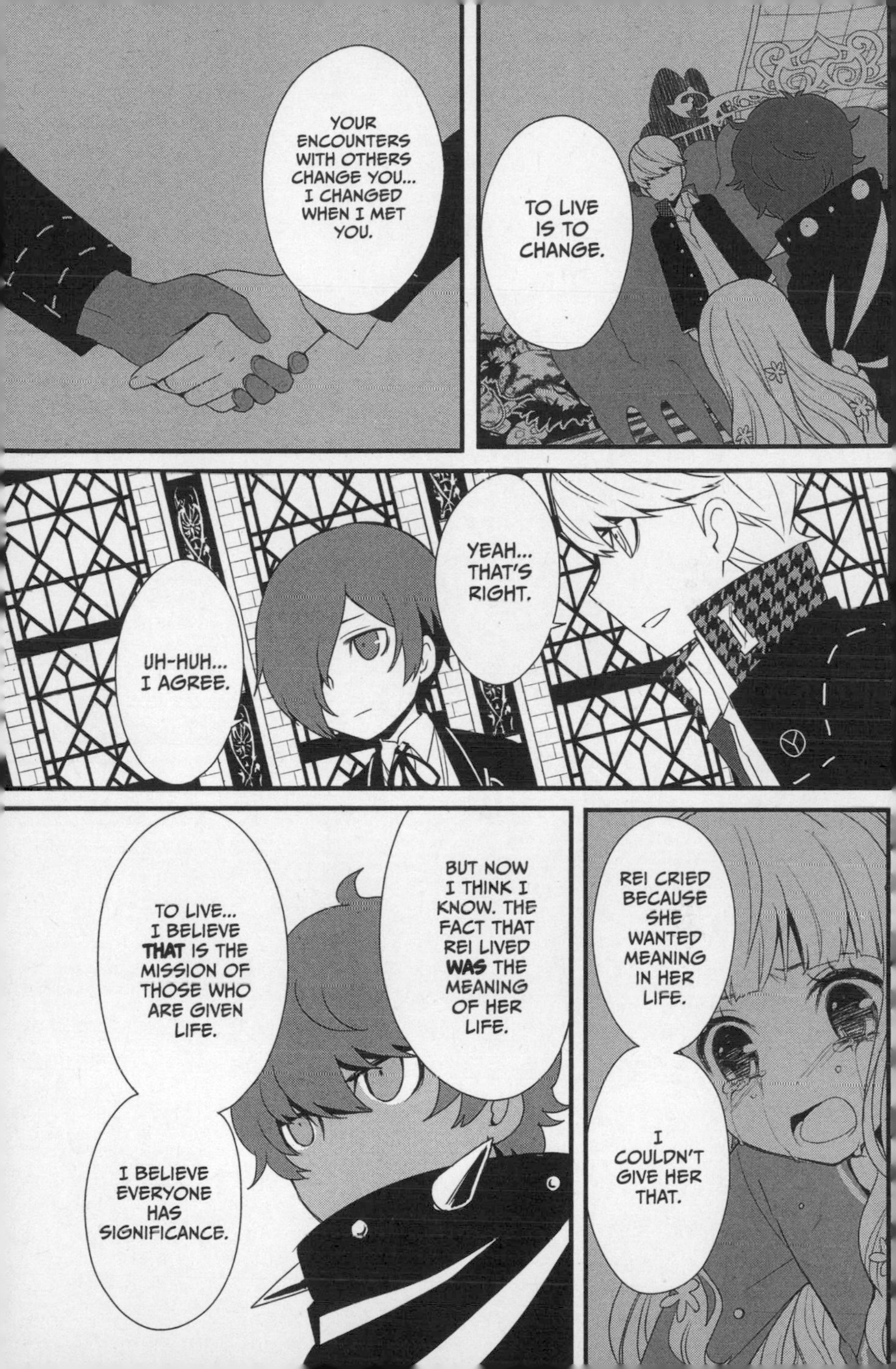
TO LIVE IS TO CHANGE.
YOUR ENCOUNTERS WITH OTHERS CHANGE YOU... I CHANGED WHEN I MET YOU.
YEAH... THAT'S RIGHT.
UH-HUH... I AGREE.
REI CRIED BECAUSE SHE WANTED MEANING IN HER LIFE.
I COULDN'T GIVE HER THAT.
BUT NOW I THINK I KNOW. THE FACT THAT REI LIVED **WAS** THE MEANING OF HER LIFE.
TO LIVE... I BELIEVE **THAT** IS THE MISSION OF THOSE WHO ARE GIVEN LIFE.
I BELIEVE EVERYONE HAS SIGNIFICANCE.

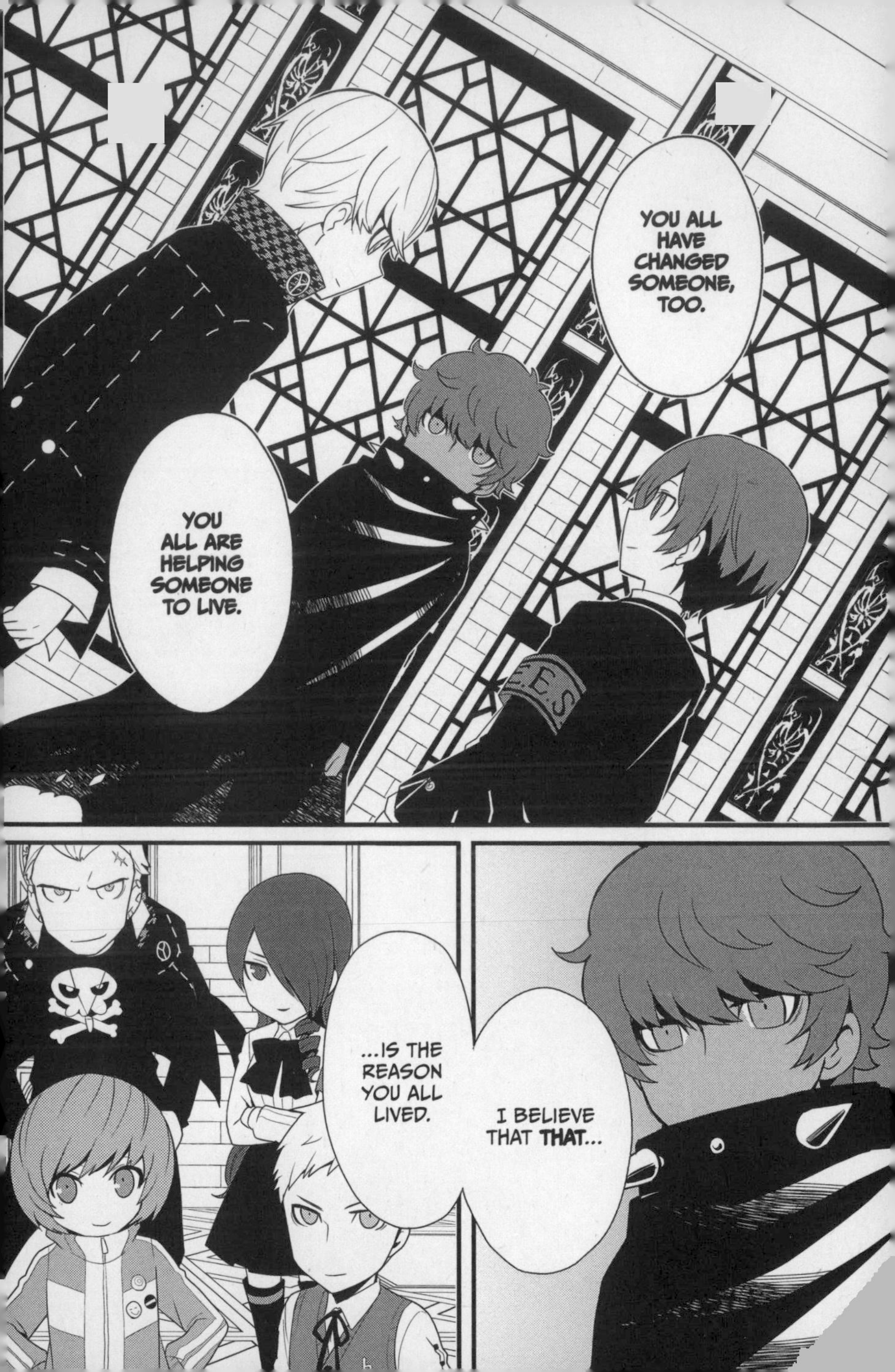
YOU ALL HAVE CHANGED SOMEONE, TOO.
YOU ALL ARE HELPING SOMEONE TO LIVE.
I BELIEVE THAT **THAT**...
...IS THE REASON YOU ALL LIVED.

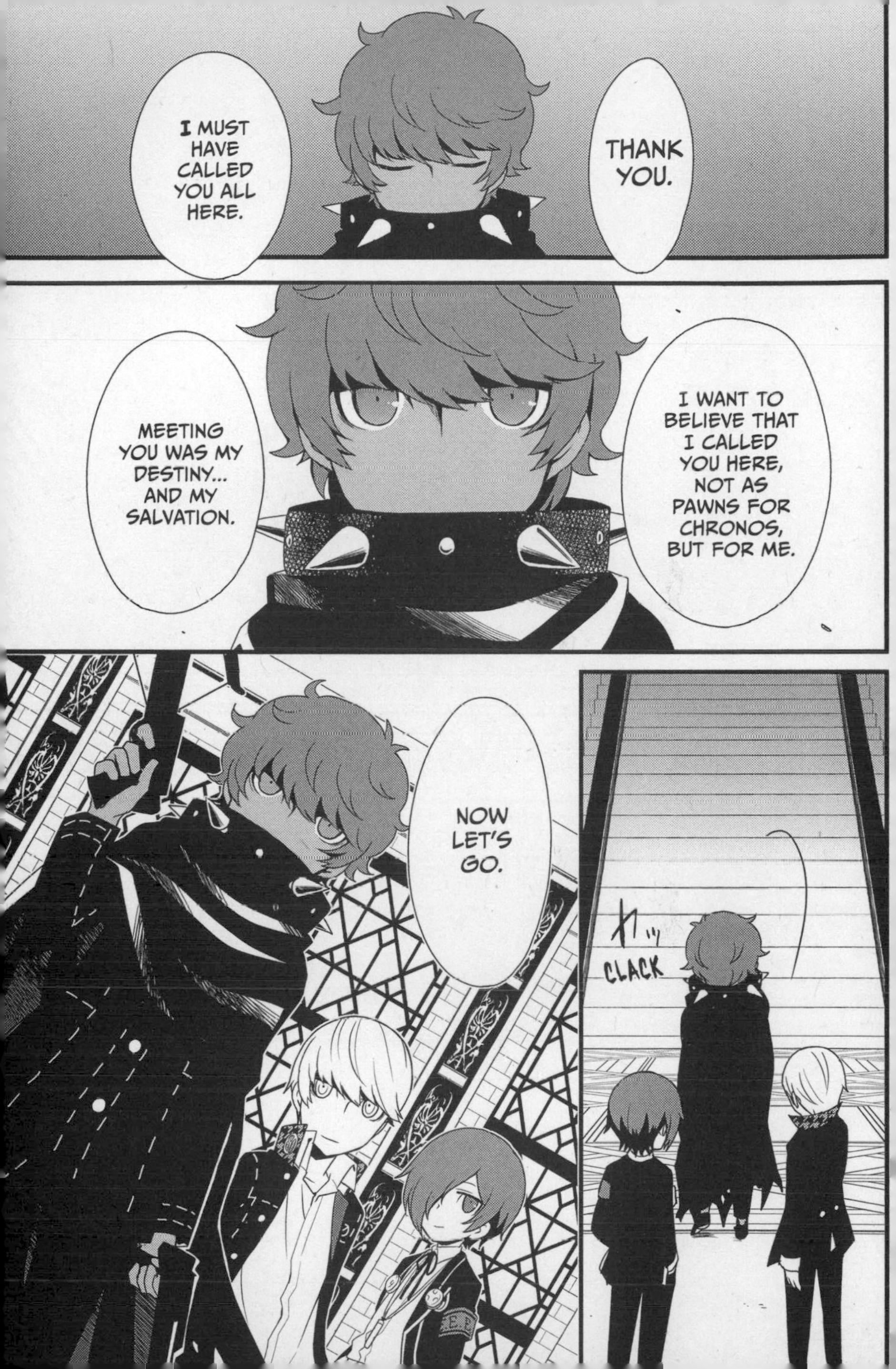
THANK YOU.
I MUST HAVE CALLED YOU ALL HERE.
I WANT TO BELIEVE THAT I CALLED YOU HERE, NOT AS PAWNS FOR CHRONOS, BUT FOR ME.
MEETING YOU WAS MY DESTINY... AND MY SALVATION.
カッ
CLACK
NOW LET'S GO.

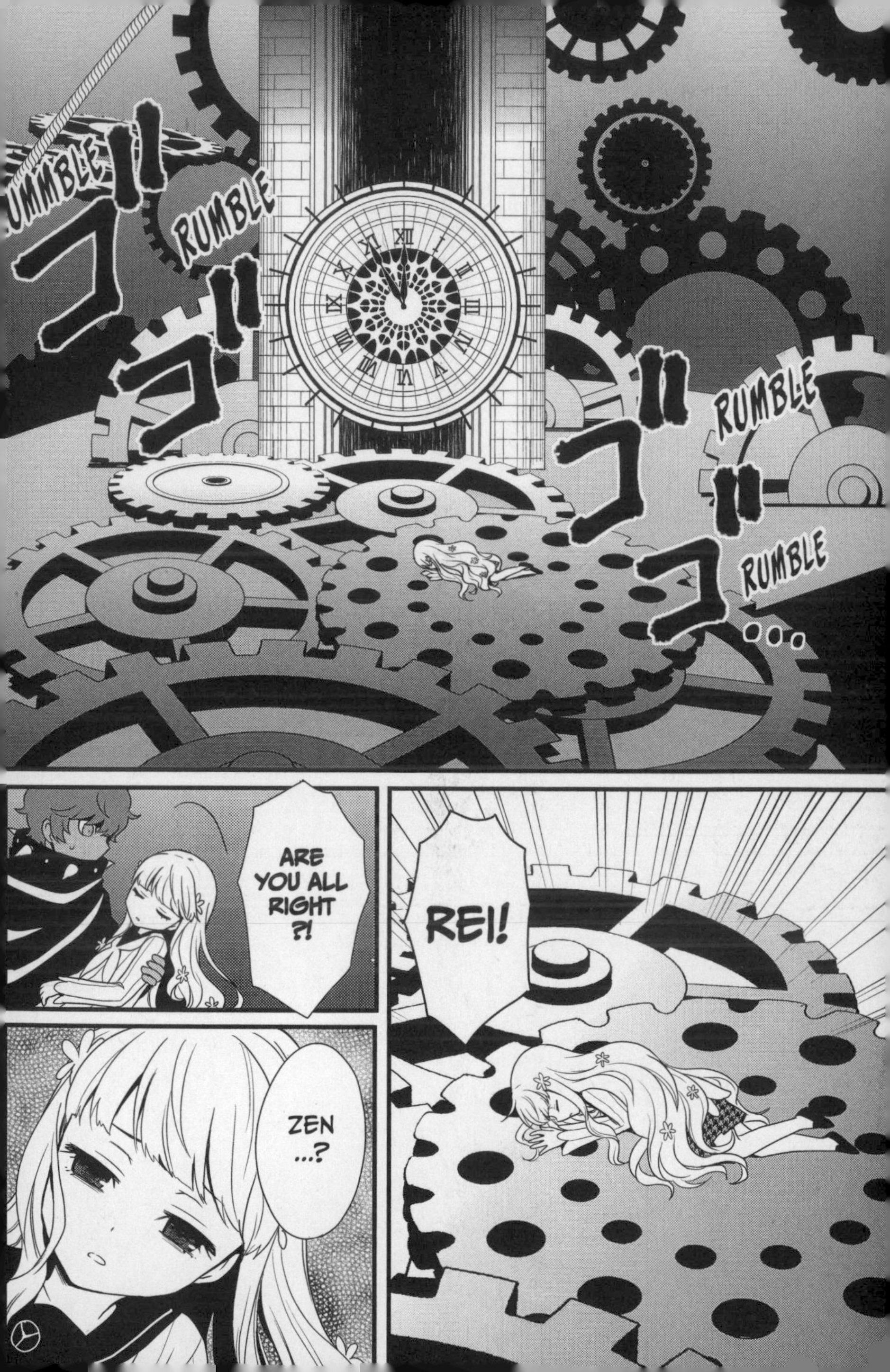
RUMBLE
ゴゴゴ…
RUMBLE
RUMBLE
ゴゴ
UMMBLE
REI!
ARE YOU ALL RIGHT ?!
ZEN ...?

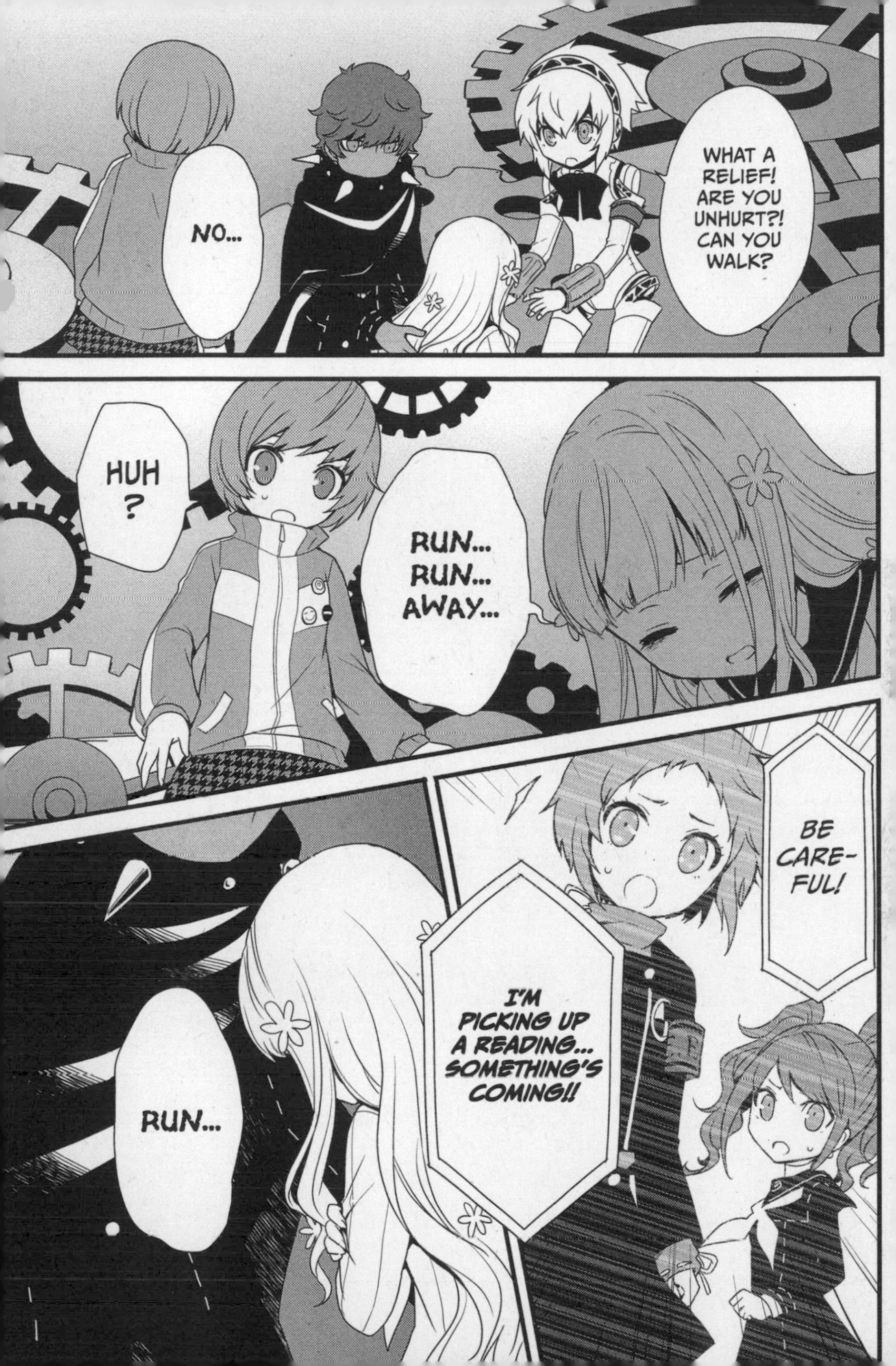
WHAT A RELIEF! ARE YOU UNHURT?! CAN YOU WALK?
NO...
RUN... RUN... AWAY...
HUH?
BE CAREFUL!
I'M PICKING UP A READING... SOMETHING'S COMING!!
RUN...

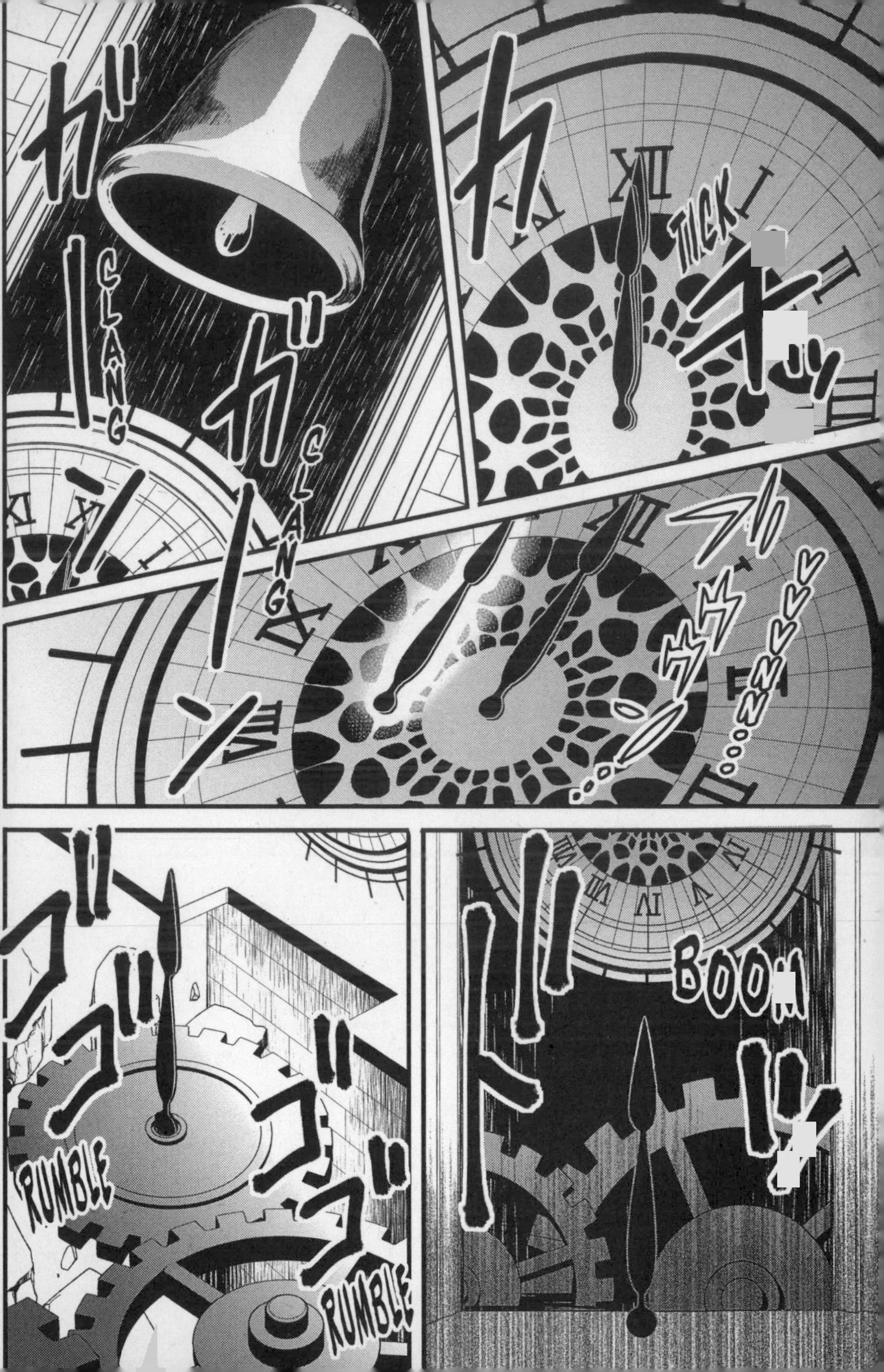
TICK
CLANG
CLANG
VVVNN...
BOOM
RUMBLE
RUMBLE

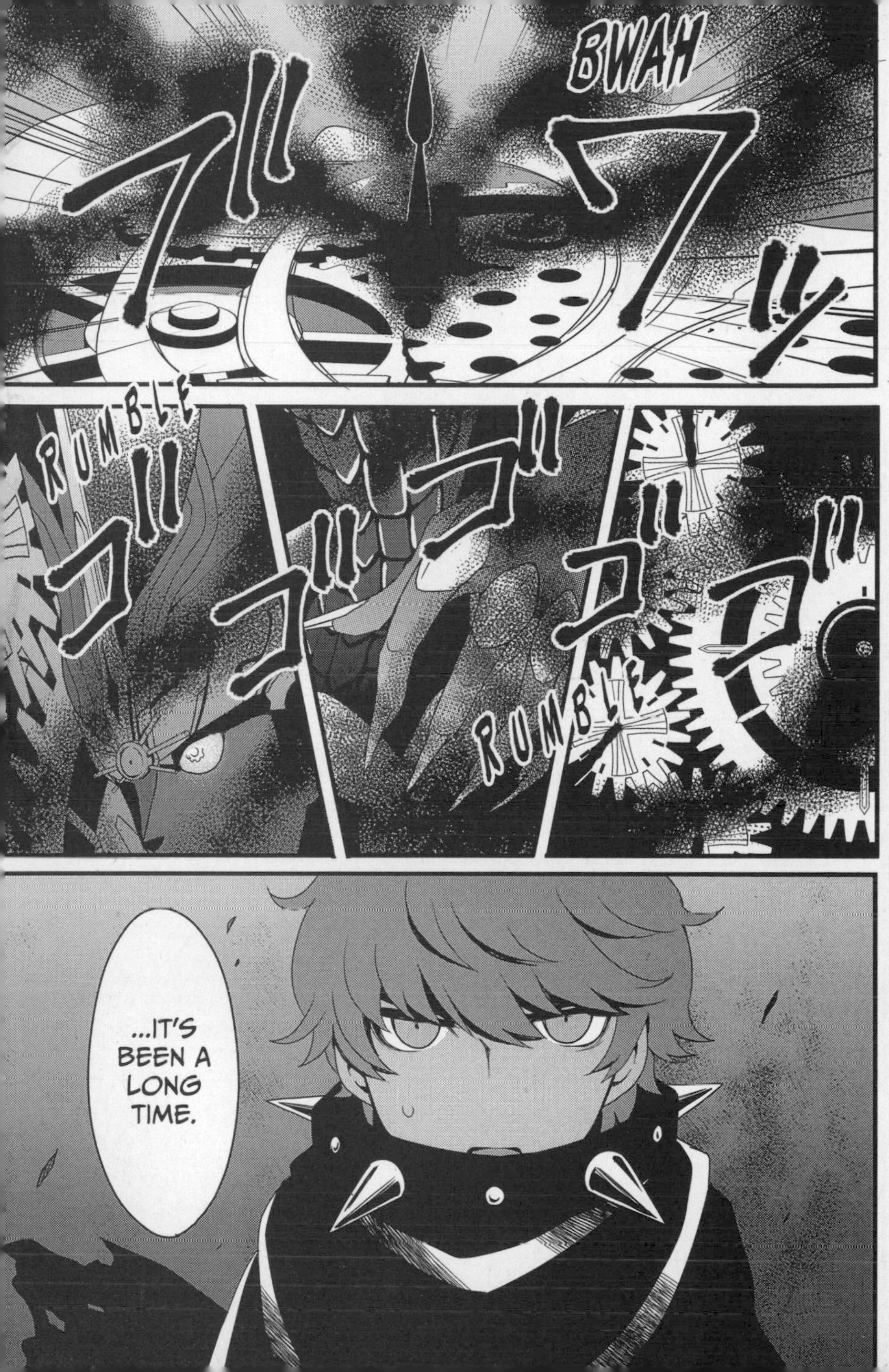
BWAH
RUMBLE
RUMBLE
...IT'S BEEN A LONG TIME.

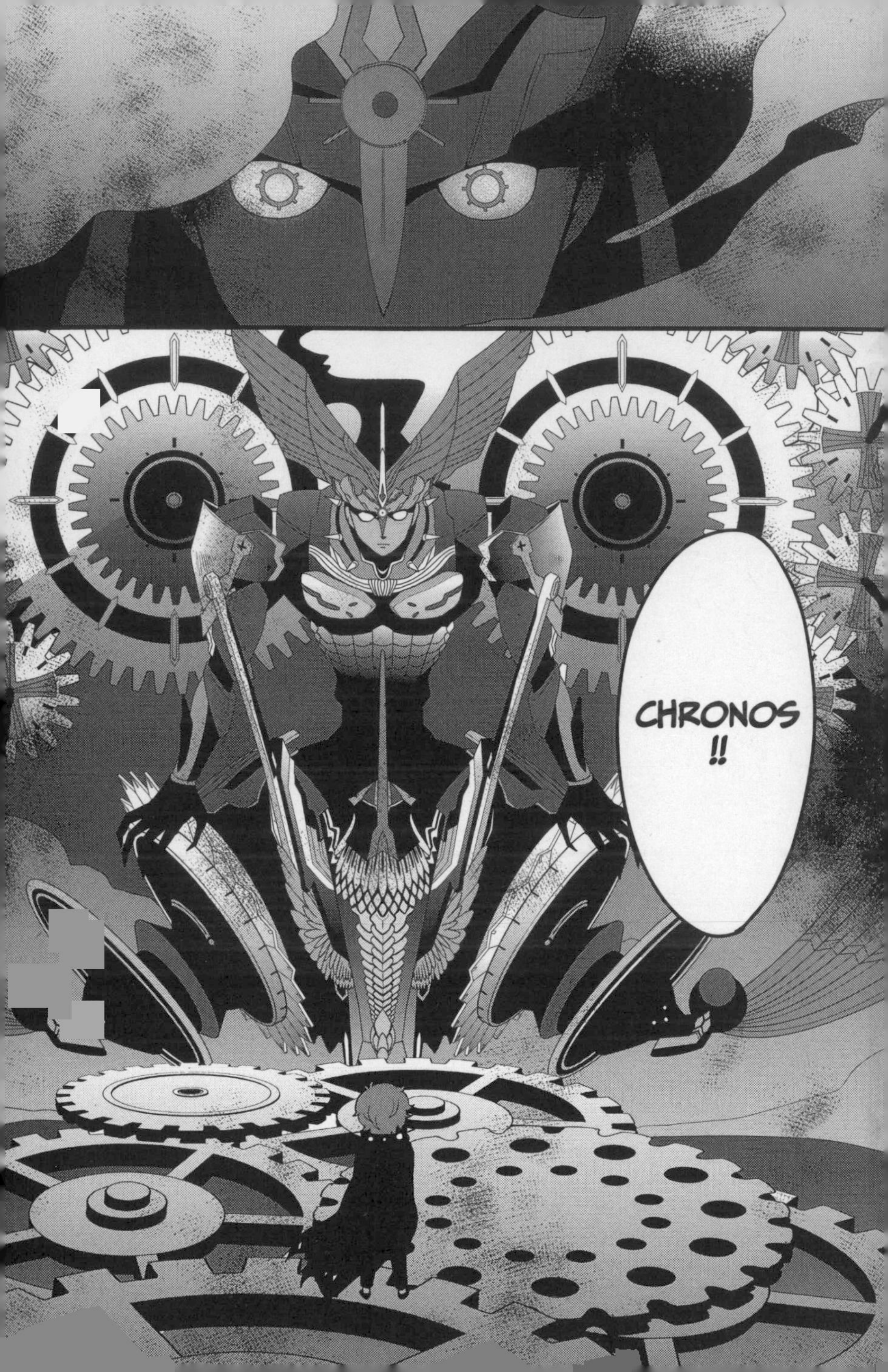
CHRONOS !!

CERBERUS (STRENGTH)

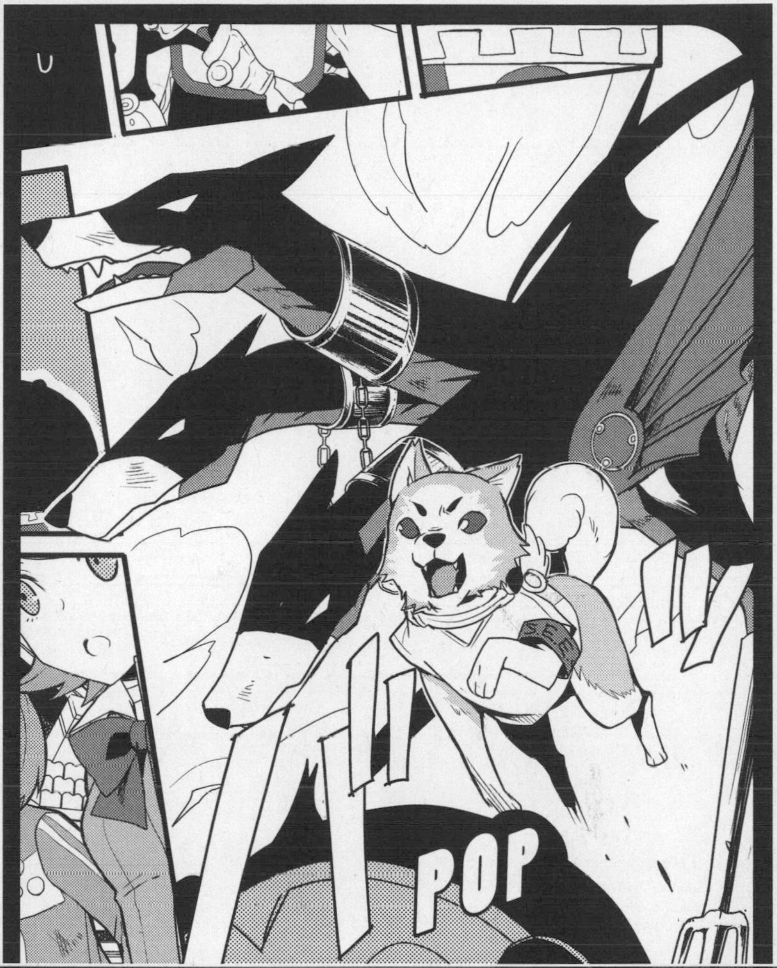
POP

A THREE-HEADED DOG OF GREEK MYTH, THE CHILD OF TYPHON AND ECHIDNA. IT IS A SIBLING TO ORTHRUS, THE HYDRA, AND THE CHIMERA. CERBERUS IS THE GUARD DOG OF THE UNDERWORLD, RULED BY HADES; IT PERMITS NEITHER THE DEAD TO LEAVE NOR THE LIVING TO ENTER. ONLY THREE PEOPLE HAVE EVADED IT: THE HERO HERCULES, ONE OF THE PROPHETESSES CALLED SIBYLS, AND THE MUSICIAN ORPHEUS.

PERSONA Q Side: P4
SHADOW OF THE LABYRINTH

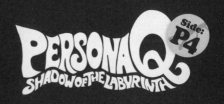

Labyrinth 23: The Gears of Time

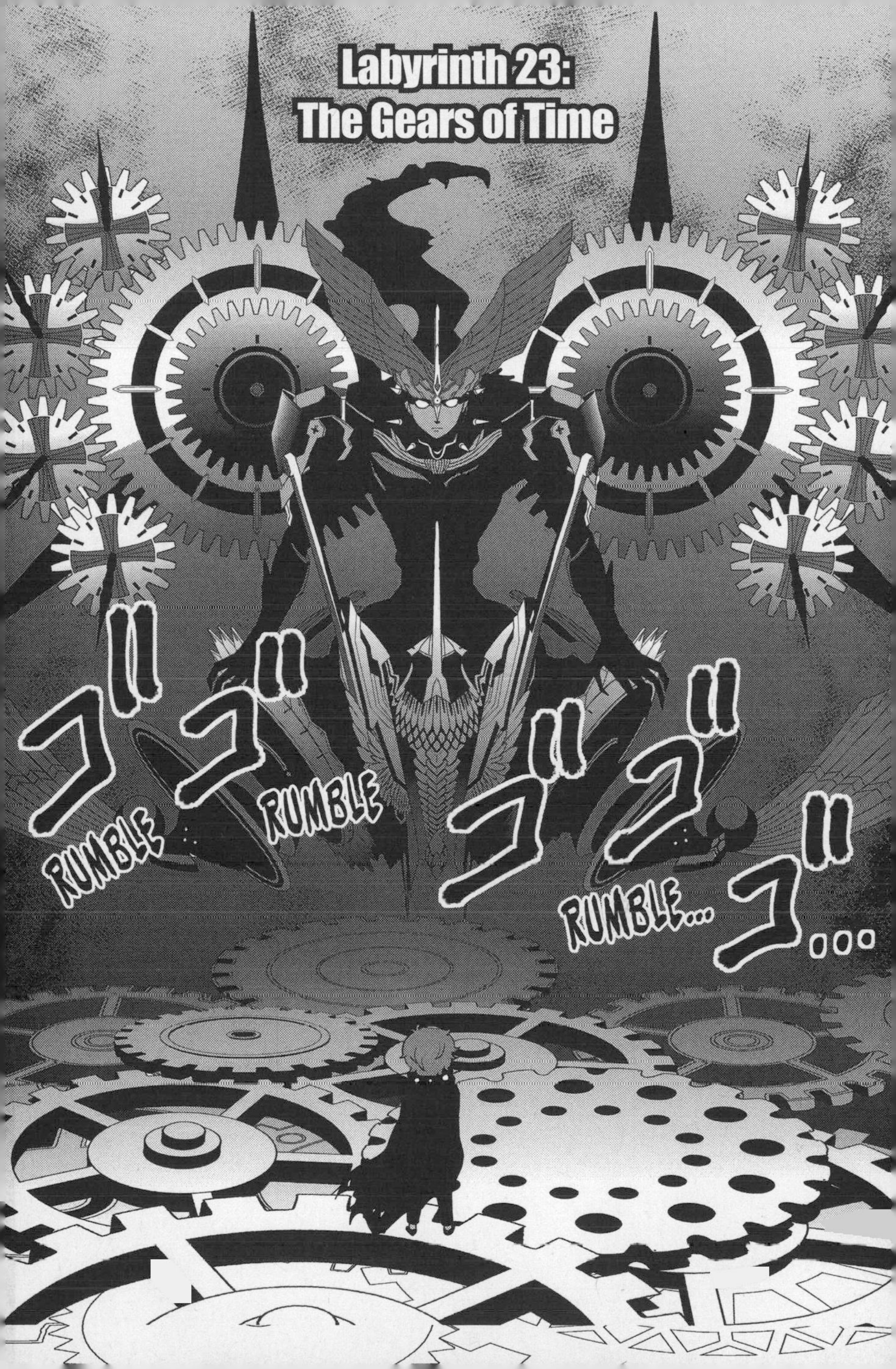

ゴ…
RUMBLE…
ゴ
ゴ
RUMBLE
ゴ
RUMBLE
ゴ

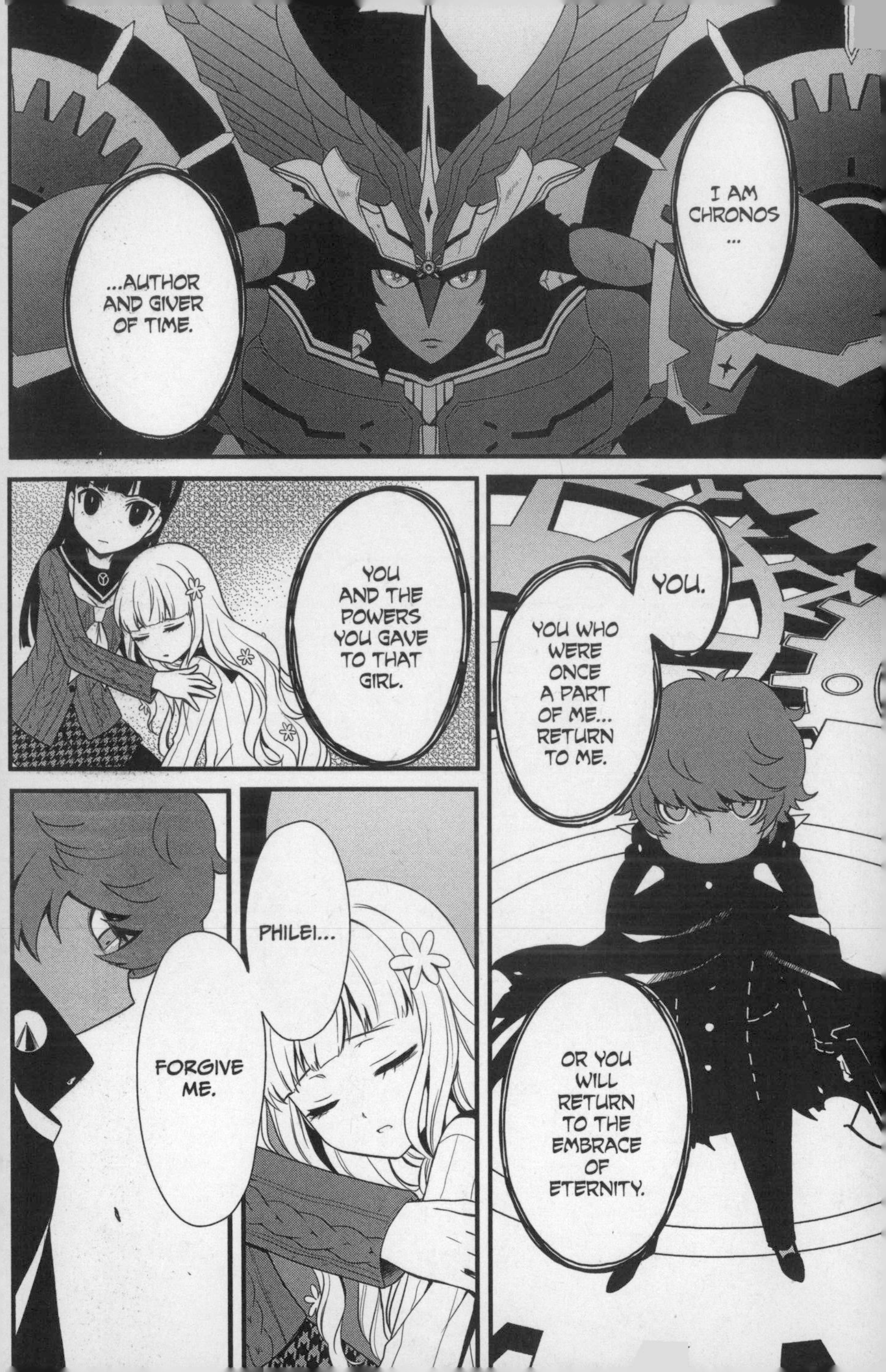
I AM CHRONOS ...
...AUTHOR AND GIVER OF TIME.
YOU.
YOU WHO WERE ONCE A PART OF ME... RETURN TO ME.
OR YOU WILL RETURN TO THE EMBRACE OF ETERNITY.
YOU AND THE POWERS YOU GAVE TO THAT GIRL.
PHILEI...
FORGIVE ME.

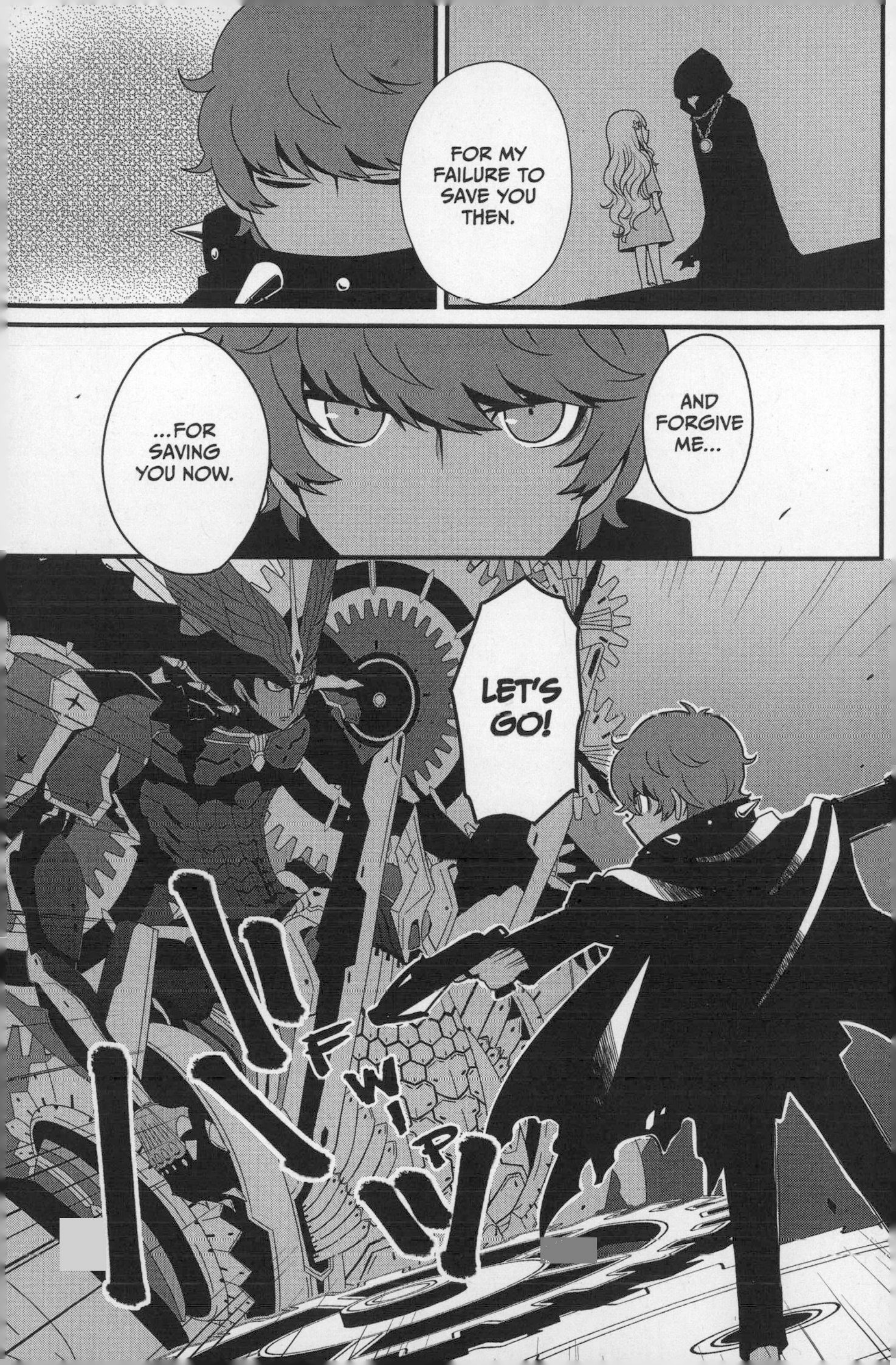
FOR MY FAILURE TO SAVE YOU THEN.
AND FORGIVE ME...
...FOR SAVING YOU NOW.
LET'S GO!
FWIP

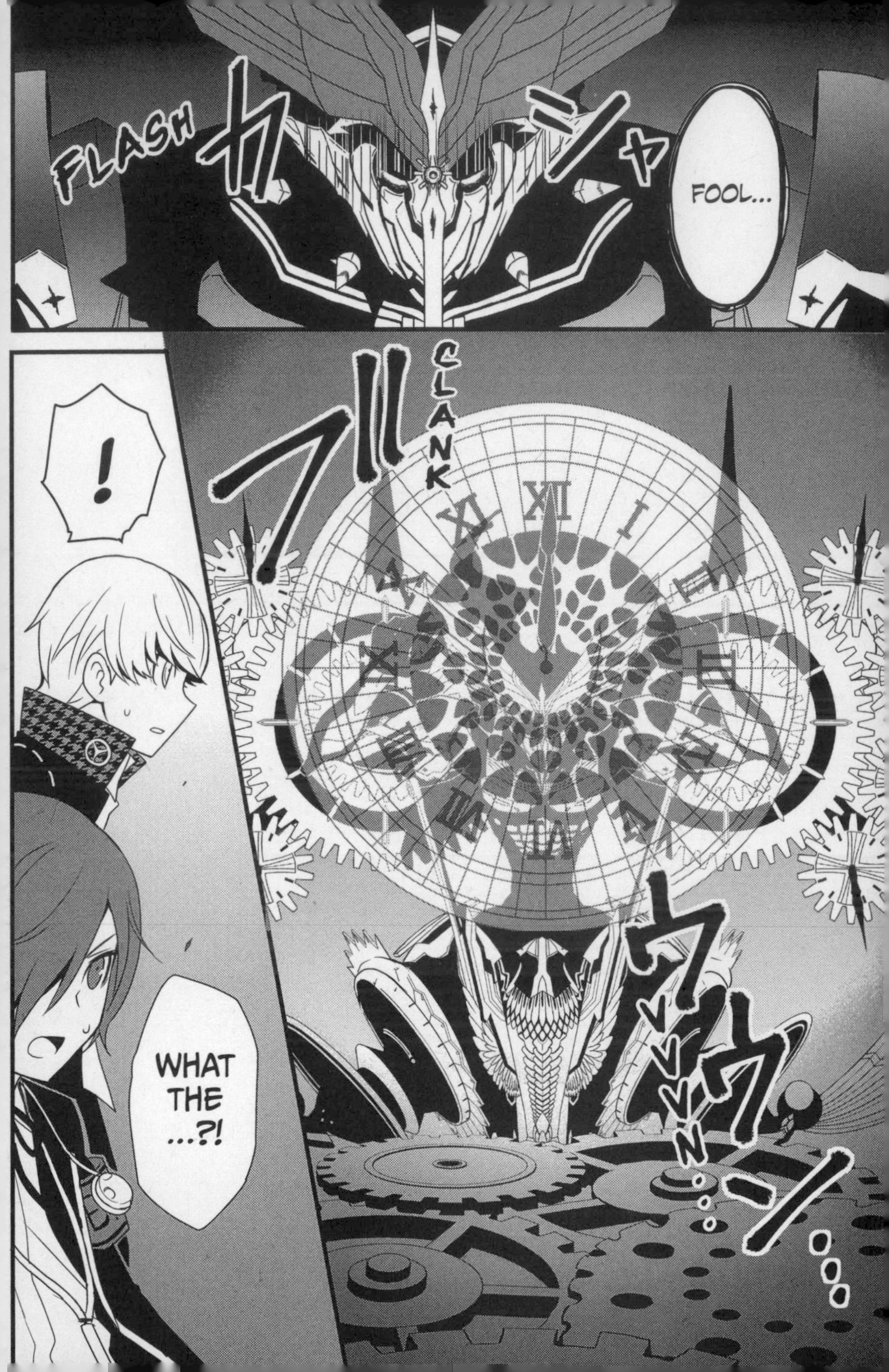
FLASH
FOOL...
CLANK
VVVVN...
!
WHAT THE ...?!

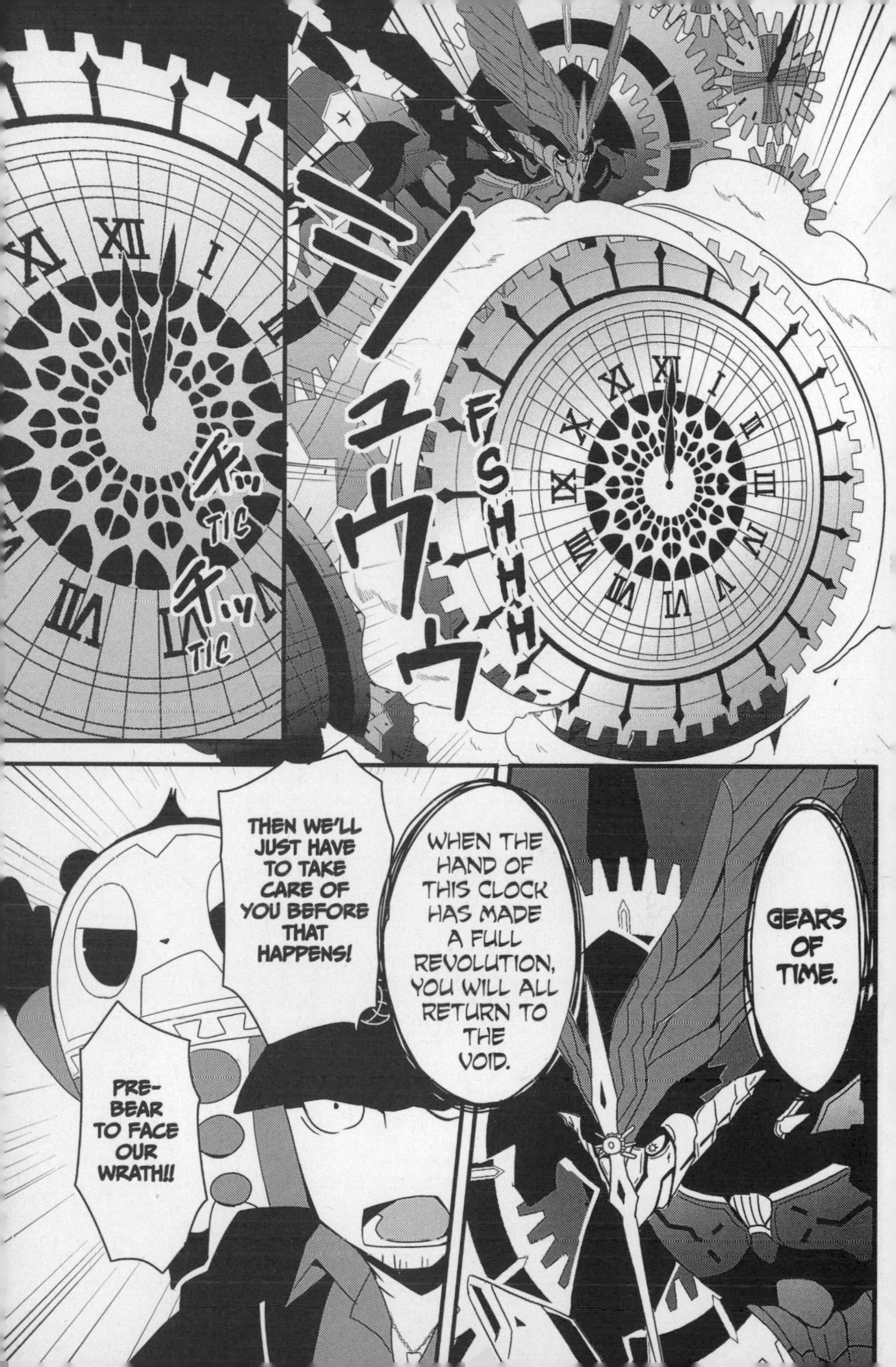
FSHHHH
TIC
TIC
GEARS OF TIME.
WHEN THE HAND OF THIS CLOCK HAS MADE A FULL REVOLUTION, YOU WILL ALL RETURN TO THE VOID.
THEN WE'LL JUST HAVE TO TAKE CARE OF YOU BEFORE THAT HAPPENS!
PRE-BEAR TO FACE OUR WRATH!!

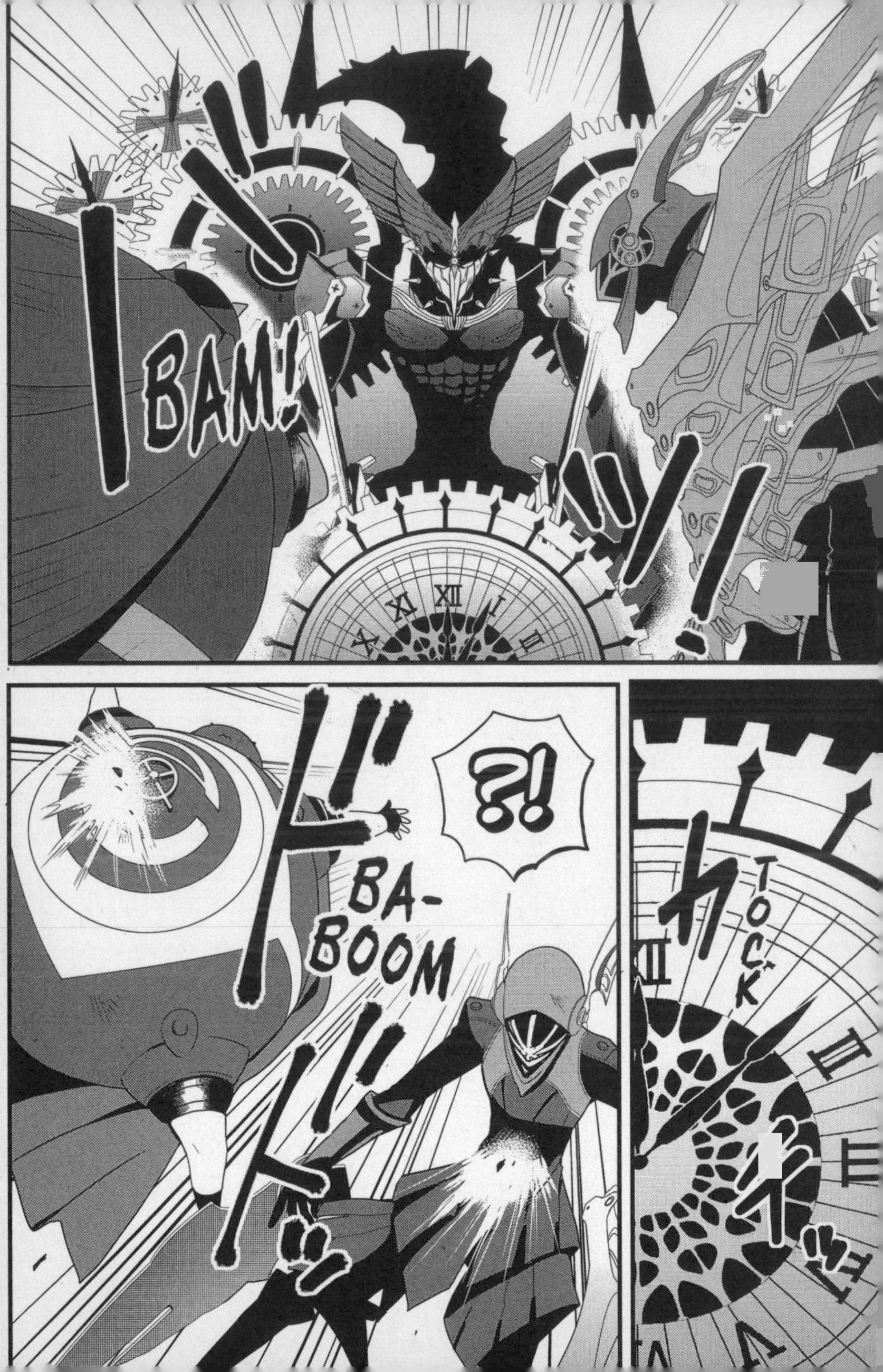
BAM!
TOCK
?!
BA-BOOM

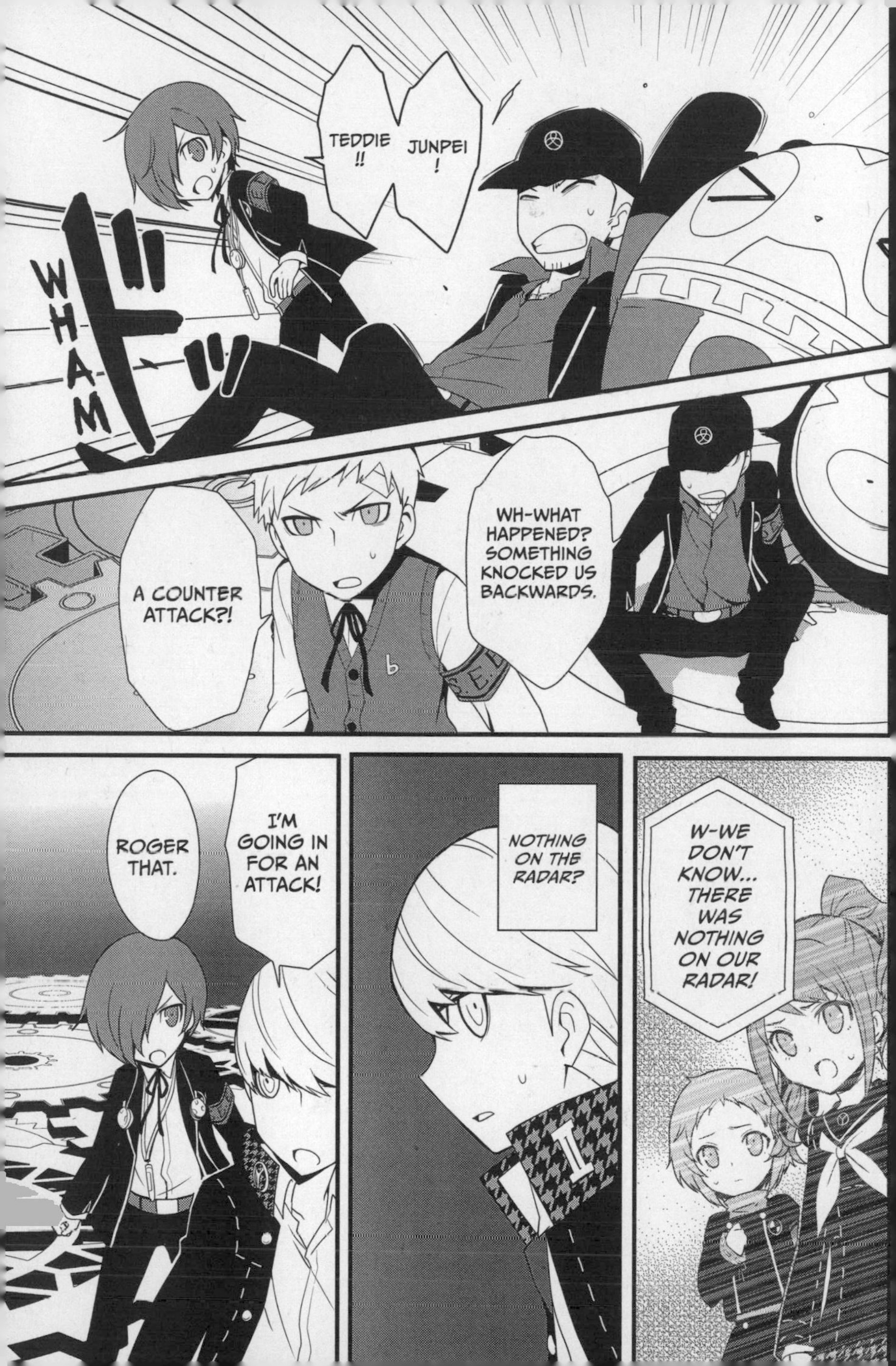
JUNPEI !
TEDDIE !!
WHAM
WH-WHAT HAPPENED? SOMETHING KNOCKED US BACKWARDS.
A COUNTER ATTACK?!
W-WE DON'T KNOW... THERE WAS NOTHING ON OUR RADAR!
NOTHING ON THE RADAR?
I'M GOING IN FOR AN ATTACK!
ROGER THAT.

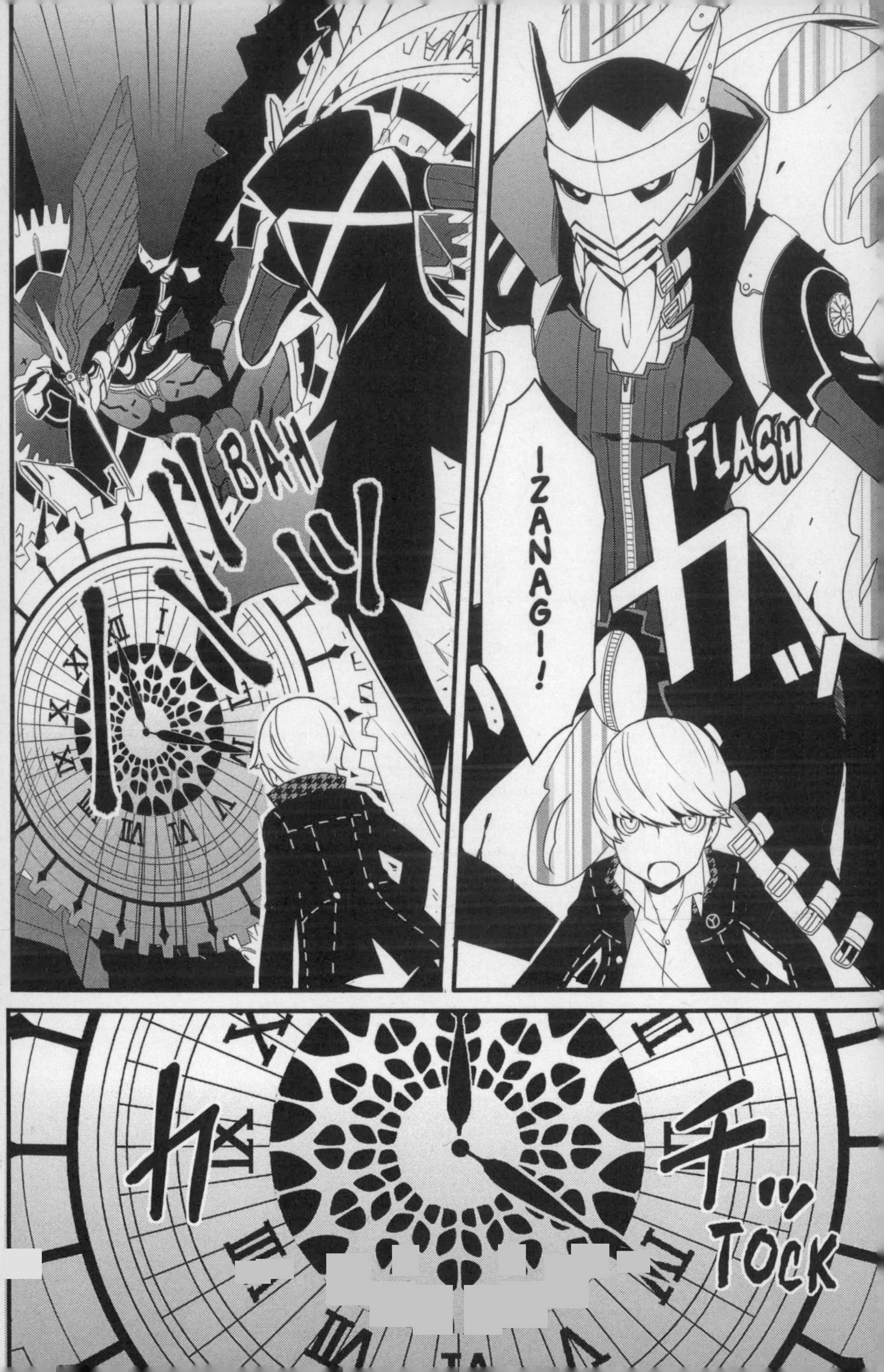
IZANAGI!
FLASH
カッ
BAH
バッ
カチッ
TOCK

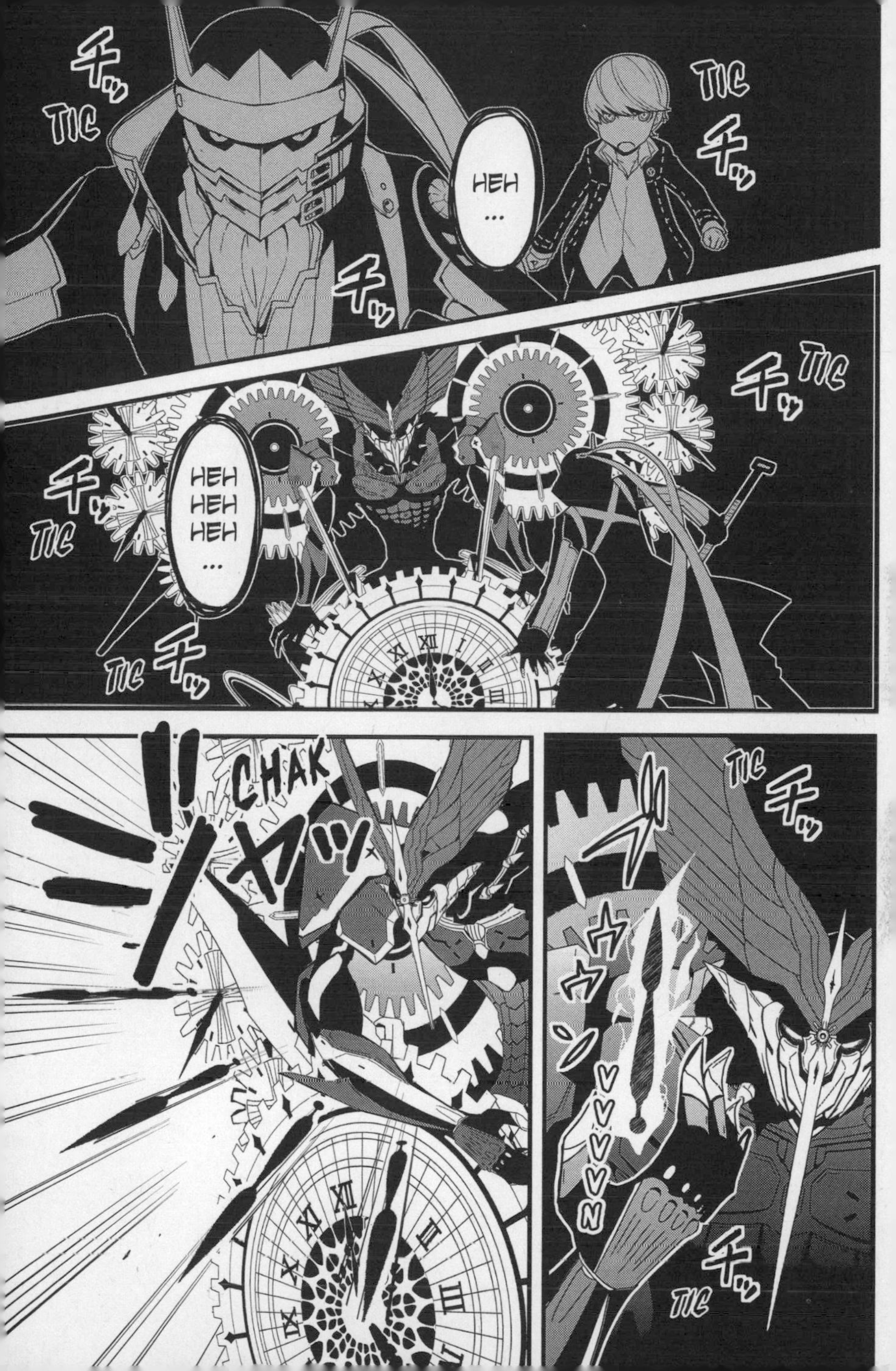
TIC
チッ
HEH
...
チッ
TIC
チッ
TIC
チッ
HEH
HEH
HEH
...
チッ
TIC
チッ
TIC
TIC
チッ
VVVVVVN
チッ
TIC
CHAK

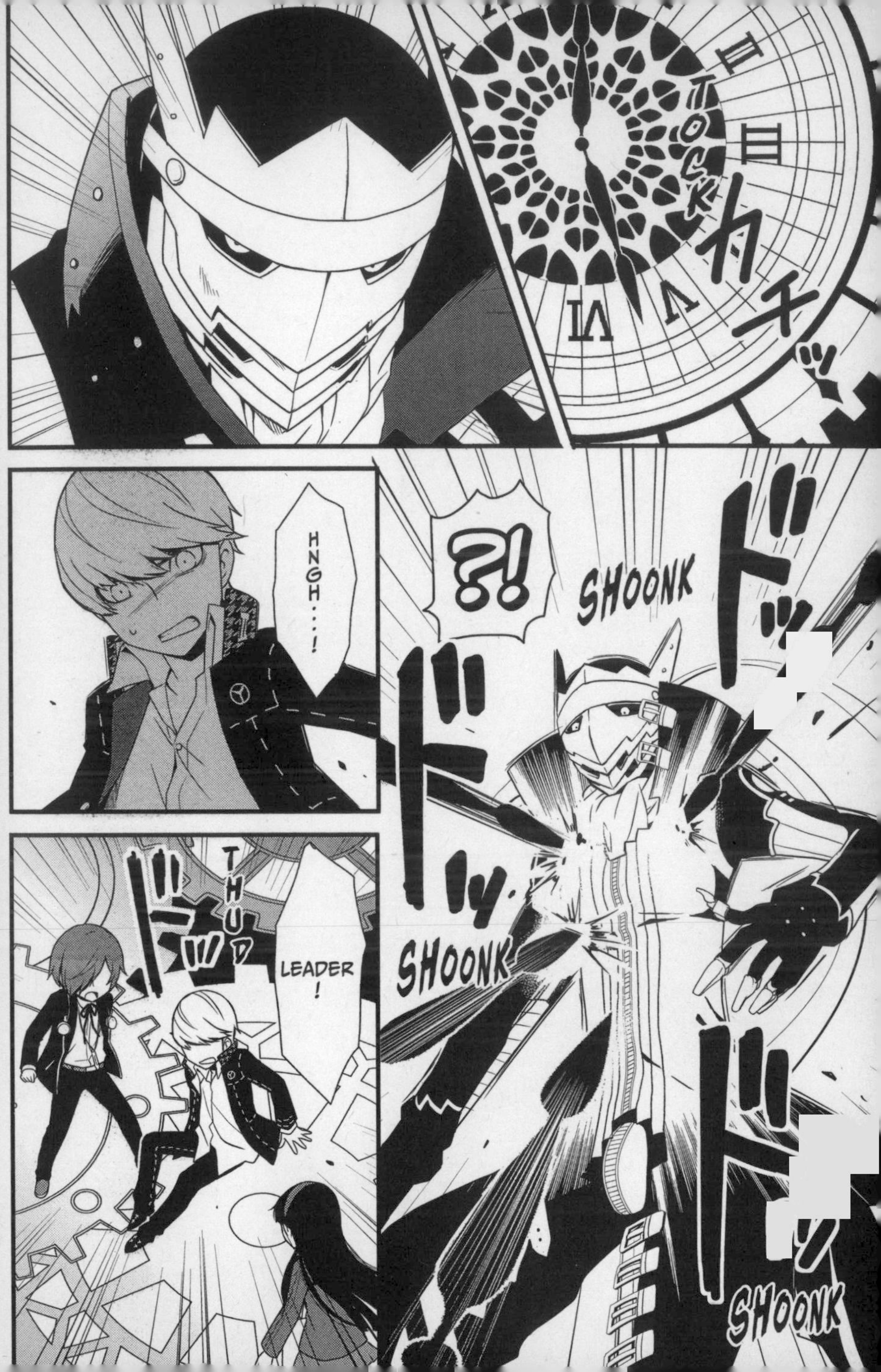
TOCK
?!
SHOONK
SHOONK
SHOONK
HNGH...!
THUD
LEADER!

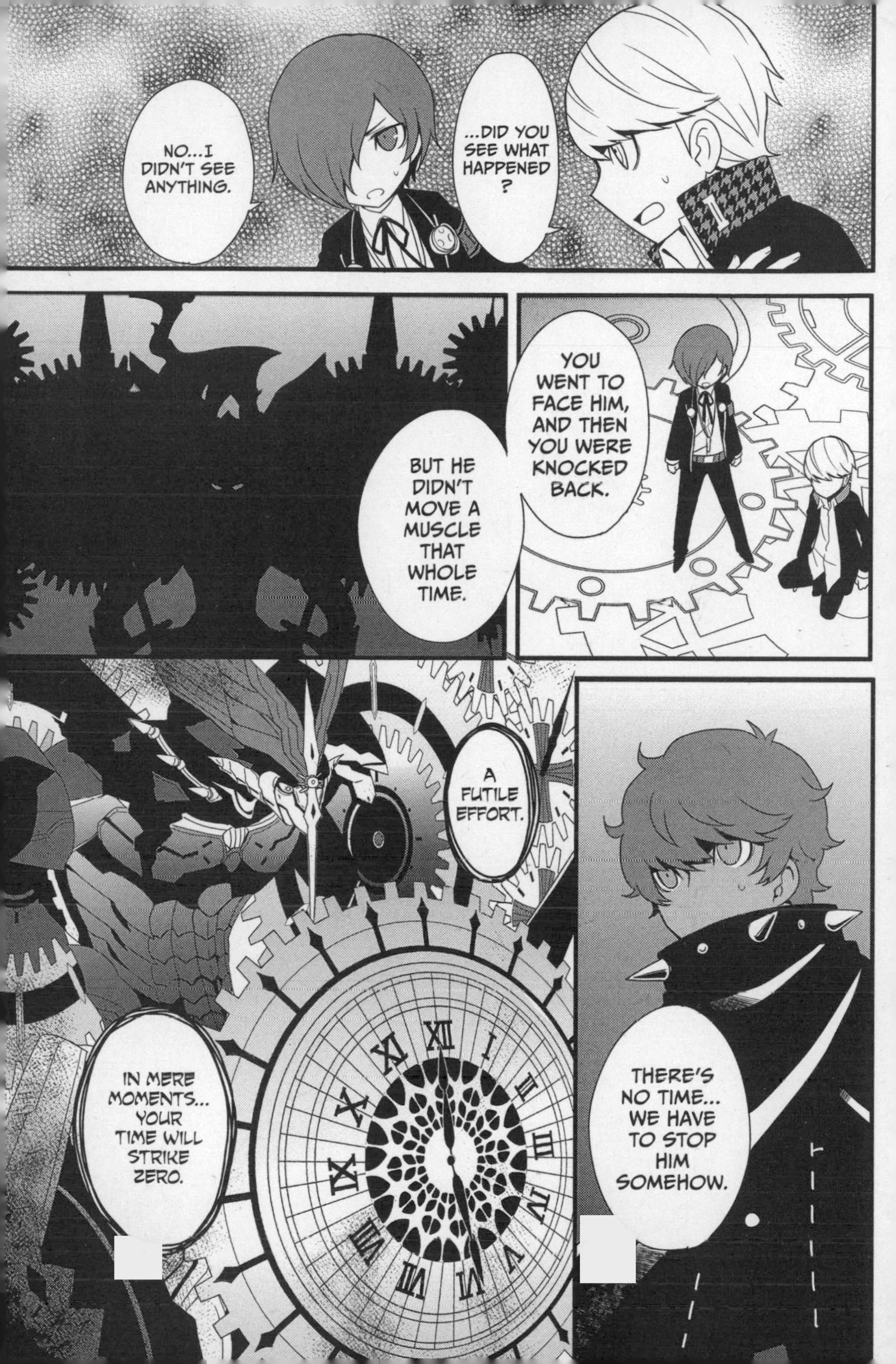
...DID YOU SEE WHAT HAPPENED?
NO...I DIDN'T SEE ANYTHING.
YOU WENT TO FACE HIM, AND THEN YOU WERE KNOCKED BACK.
BUT HE DIDN'T MOVE A MUSCLE THAT WHOLE TIME.
THERE'S NO TIME... WE HAVE TO STOP HIM SOMEHOW.
A FUTILE EFFORT.
IN MERE MOMENTS... YOUR TIME WILL STRIKE ZERO.

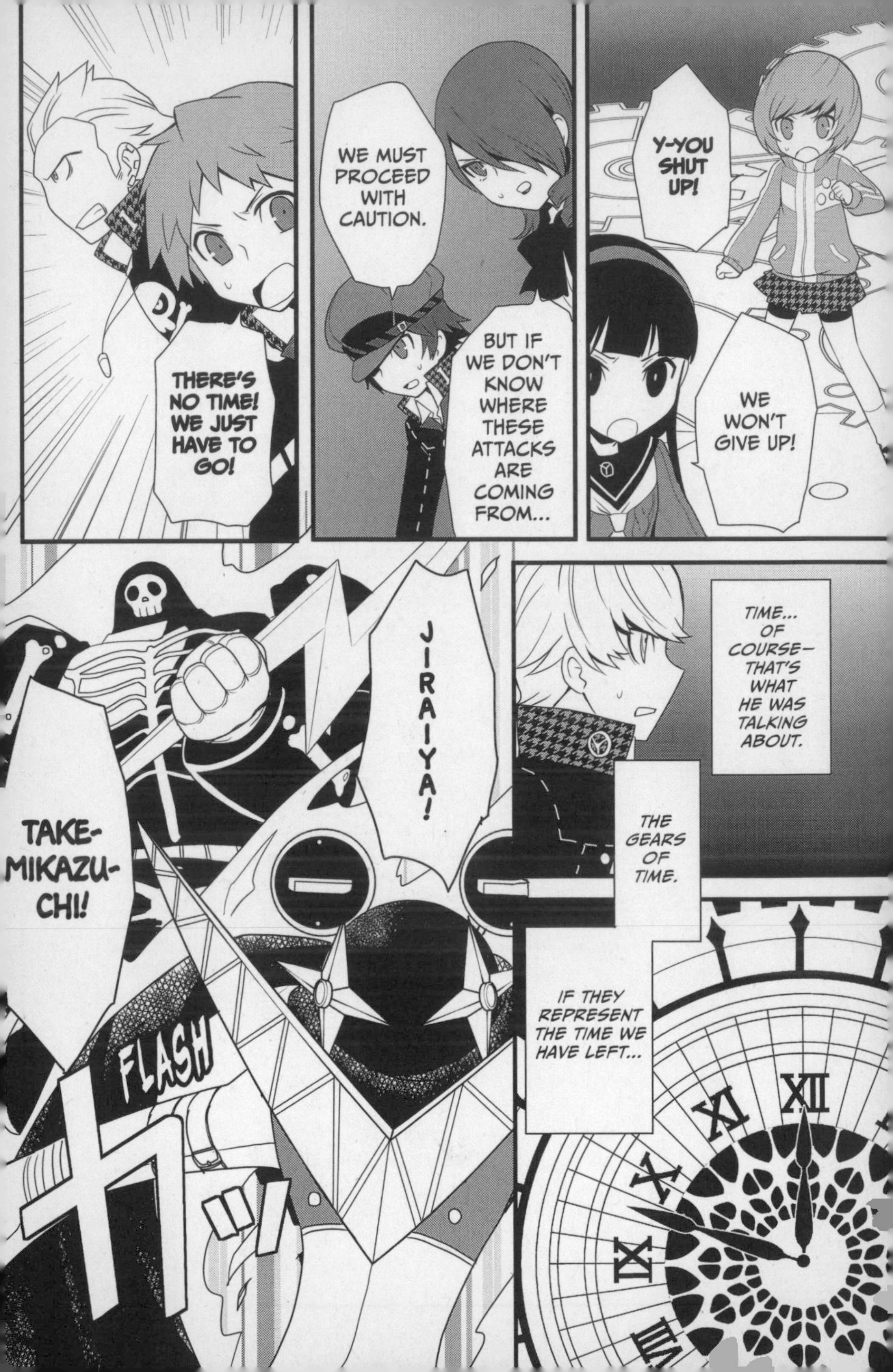
Y-YOU SHUT UP!
WE WON'T GIVE UP!
WE MUST PROCEED WITH CAUTION.
BUT IF WE DON'T KNOW WHERE THESE ATTACKS ARE COMING FROM...
THERE'S NO TIME! WE JUST HAVE TO GO!
TIME... OF COURSE—THAT'S WHAT HE WAS TALKING ABOUT.
THE GEARS OF TIME.
IF THEY REPRESENT THE TIME WE HAVE LEFT...
JIRAIYA!
TAKE-MIKAZUCHI!
FLASH

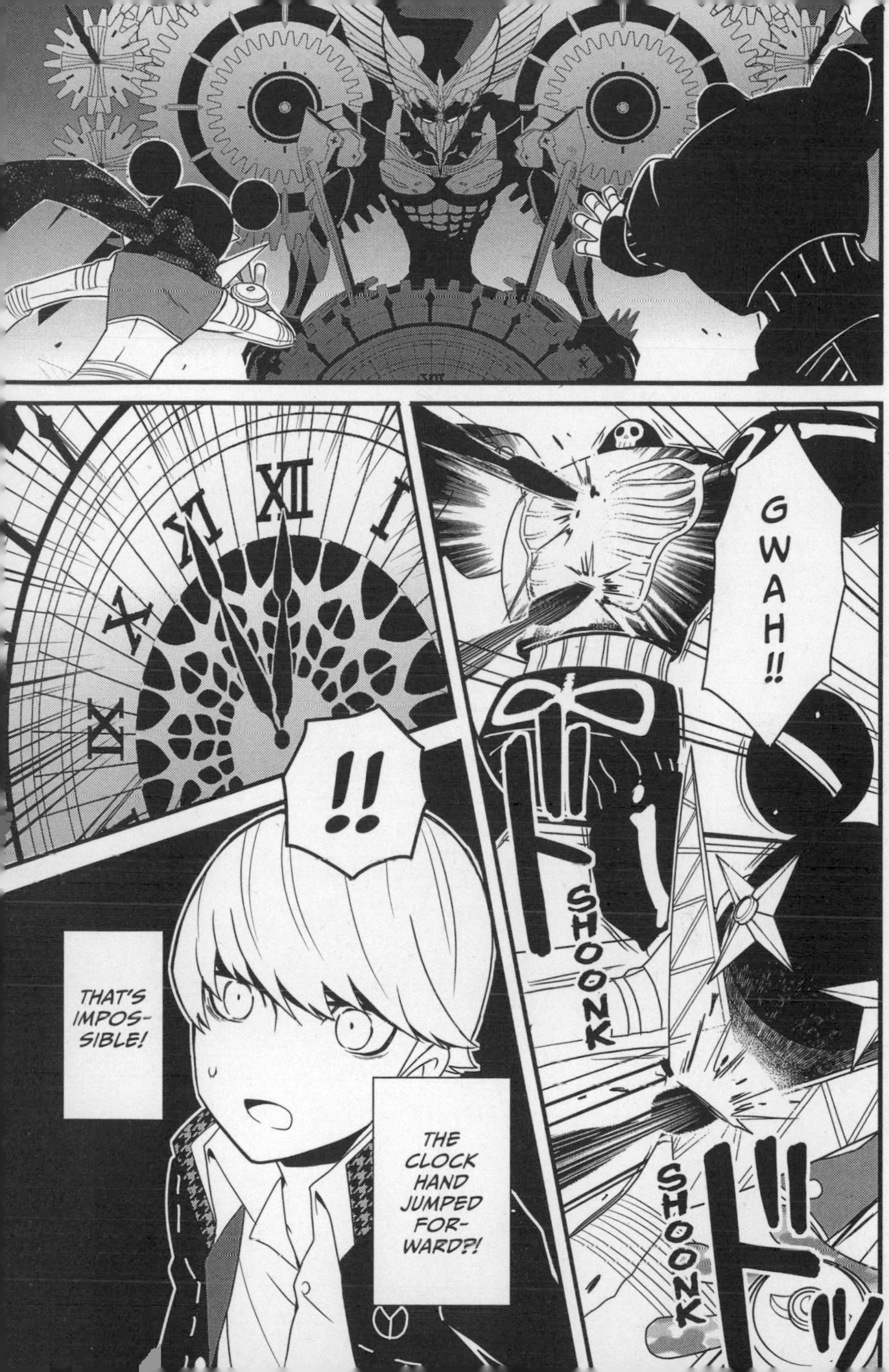
GWAH!!
SHOONK
SHOONK
!!
THAT'S IMPOS-SIBLE!
THE CLOCK HAND JUMPED FOR-WARD?!

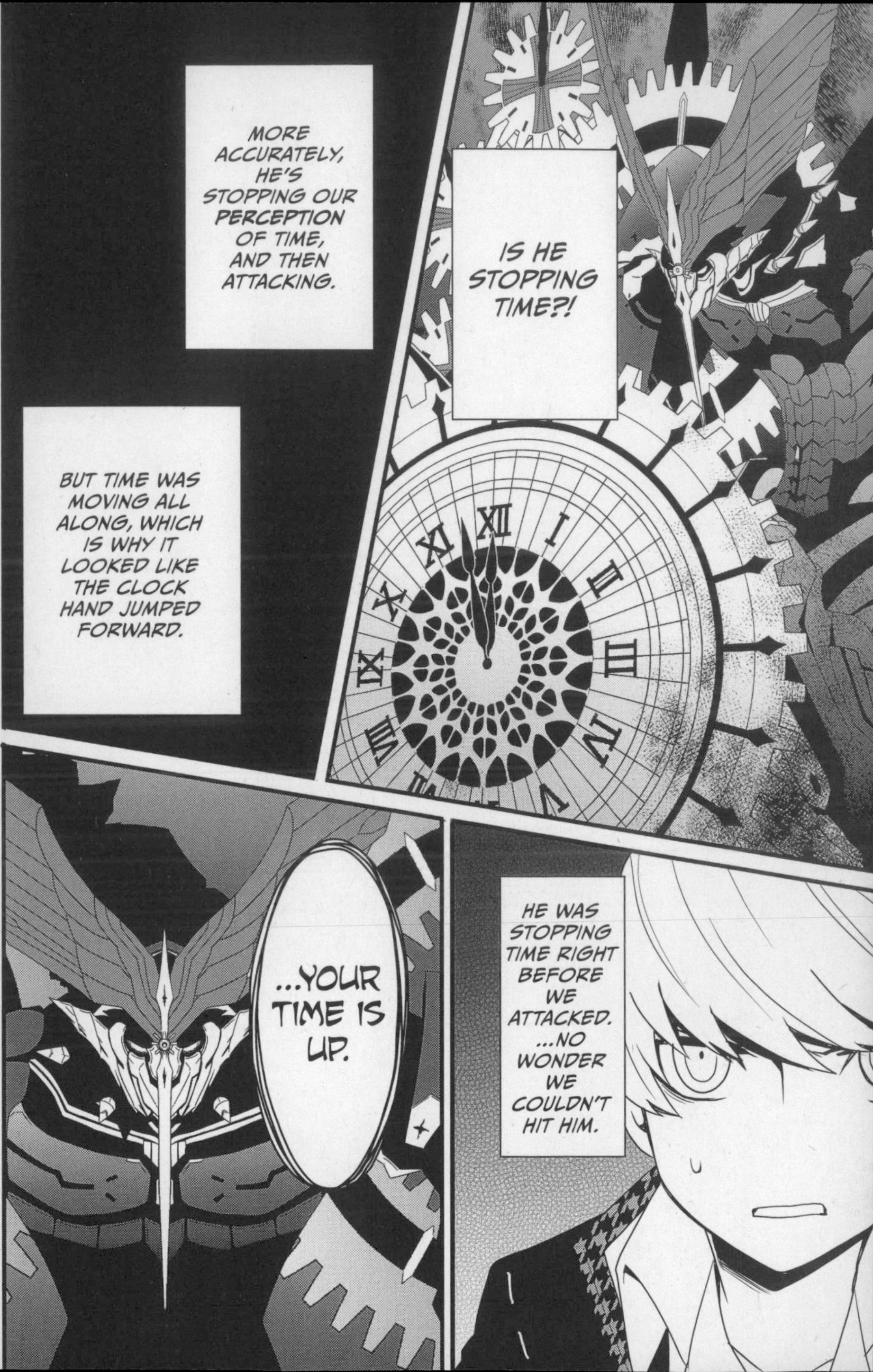
IS HE STOPPING TIME?!
MORE ACCURATELY, HE'S STOPPING OUR PERCEPTION OF TIME, AND THEN ATTACKING.
BUT TIME WAS MOVING ALL ALONG, WHICH IS WHY IT LOOKED LIKE THE CLOCK HAND JUMPED FORWARD.
HE WAS STOPPING TIME RIGHT BEFORE WE ATTACKED. ...NO WONDER WE COULDN'T HIT HIM.
...YOUR TIME IS UP.

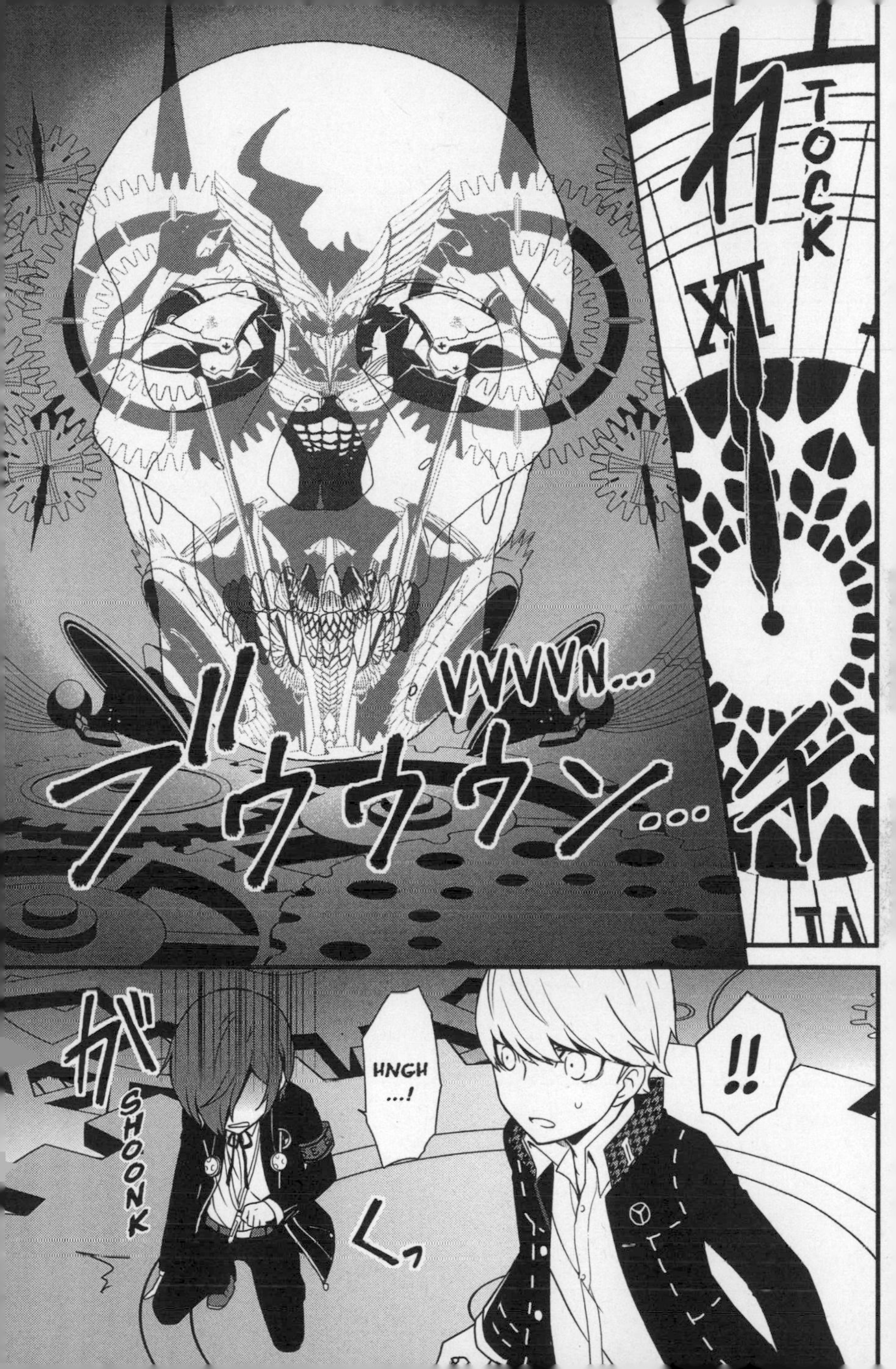
TOCK
VVVVN...
ブウウウウン…
!!
HNGH ...!
SHOONK

I'M SORRY, LEADER... I DON'T THINK I CAN GO ON.

HANG IN THERE!

SENSEI... I CAN'T MOVE A PAW...

Y-YUKIKO...

GUYS...!

YOSUKE!!

SORRY... I JUST DON'T... HAVE THE STRENGTH.

ZEN...!

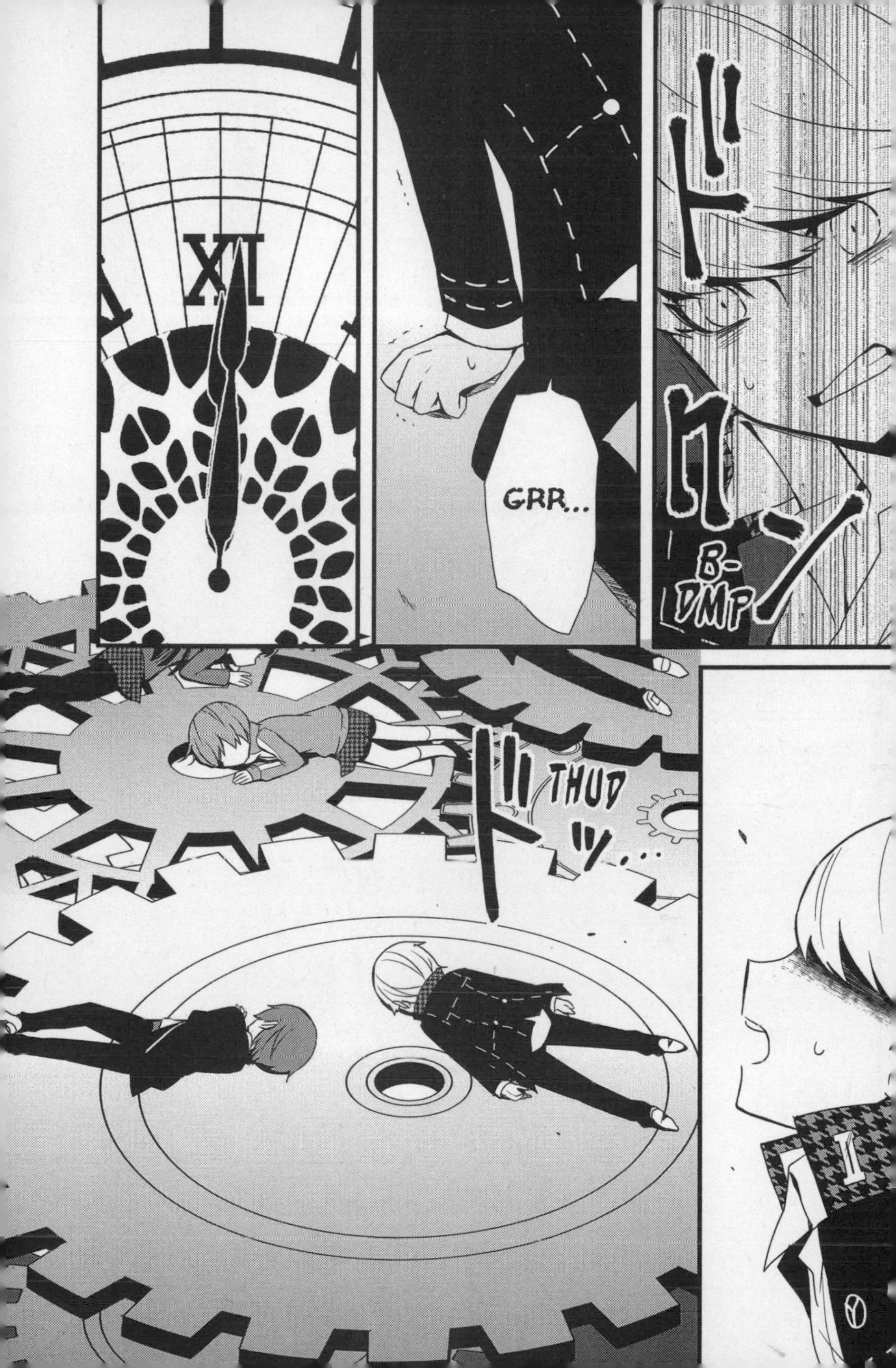
B-DMP
GRR...
THUD

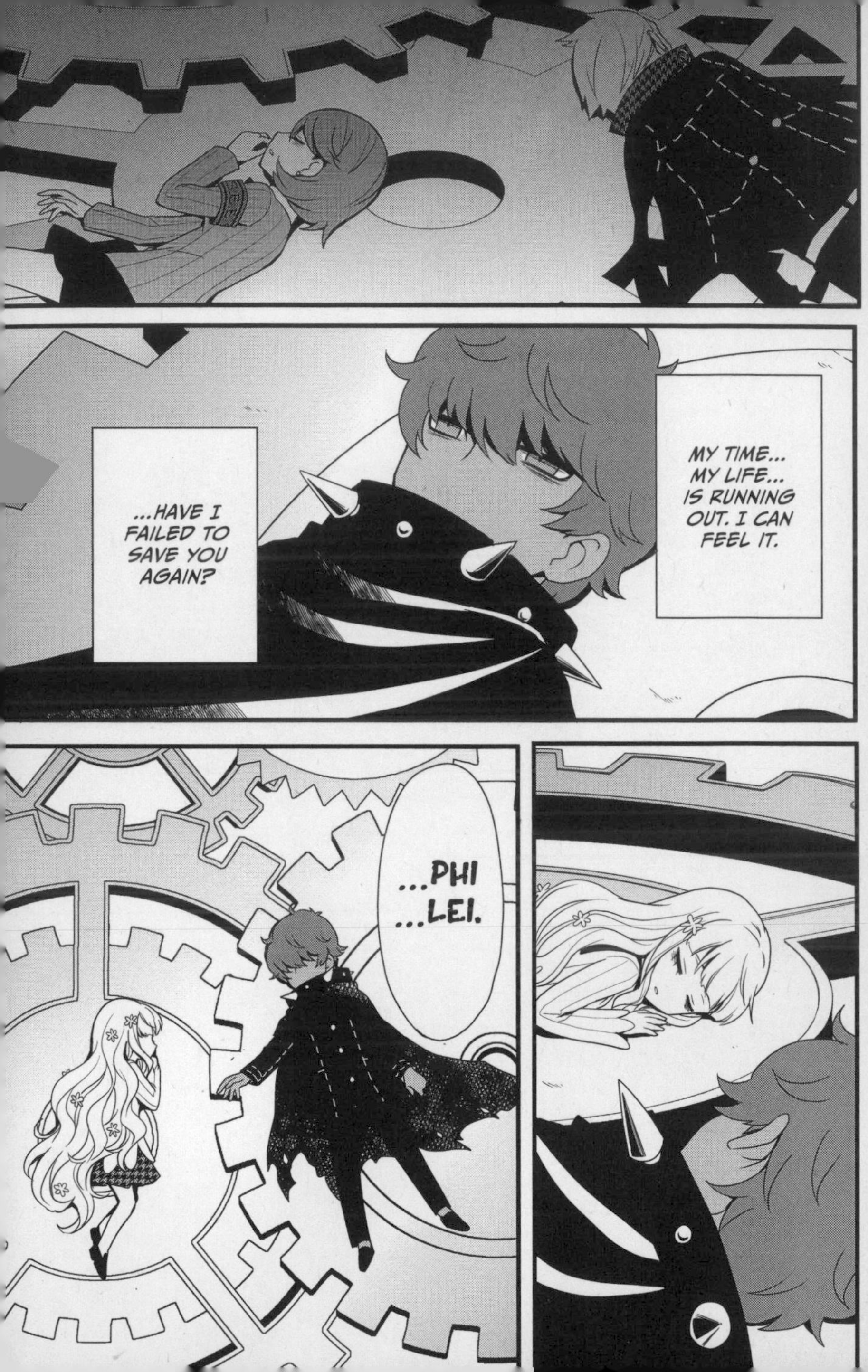
MY TIME... MY LIFE... IS RUNNING OUT. I CAN FEEL IT.
...HAVE I FAILED TO SAVE YOU AGAIN?
...PHI ...LEI.

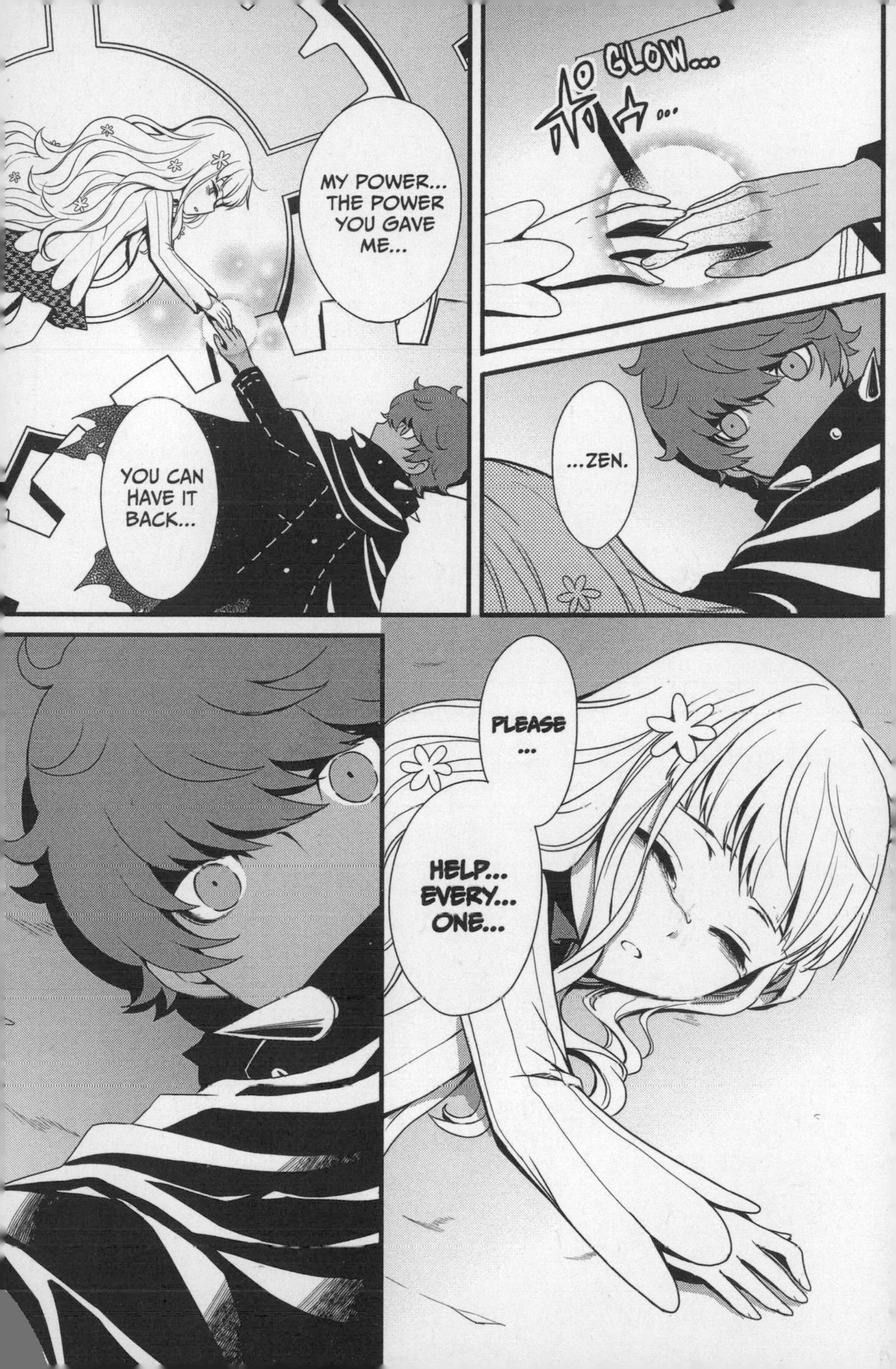
GLOW...
...ZEN.
MY POWER... THE POWER YOU GAVE ME...
YOU CAN HAVE IT BACK...
PLEASE ...
HELP... EVERY... ONE...

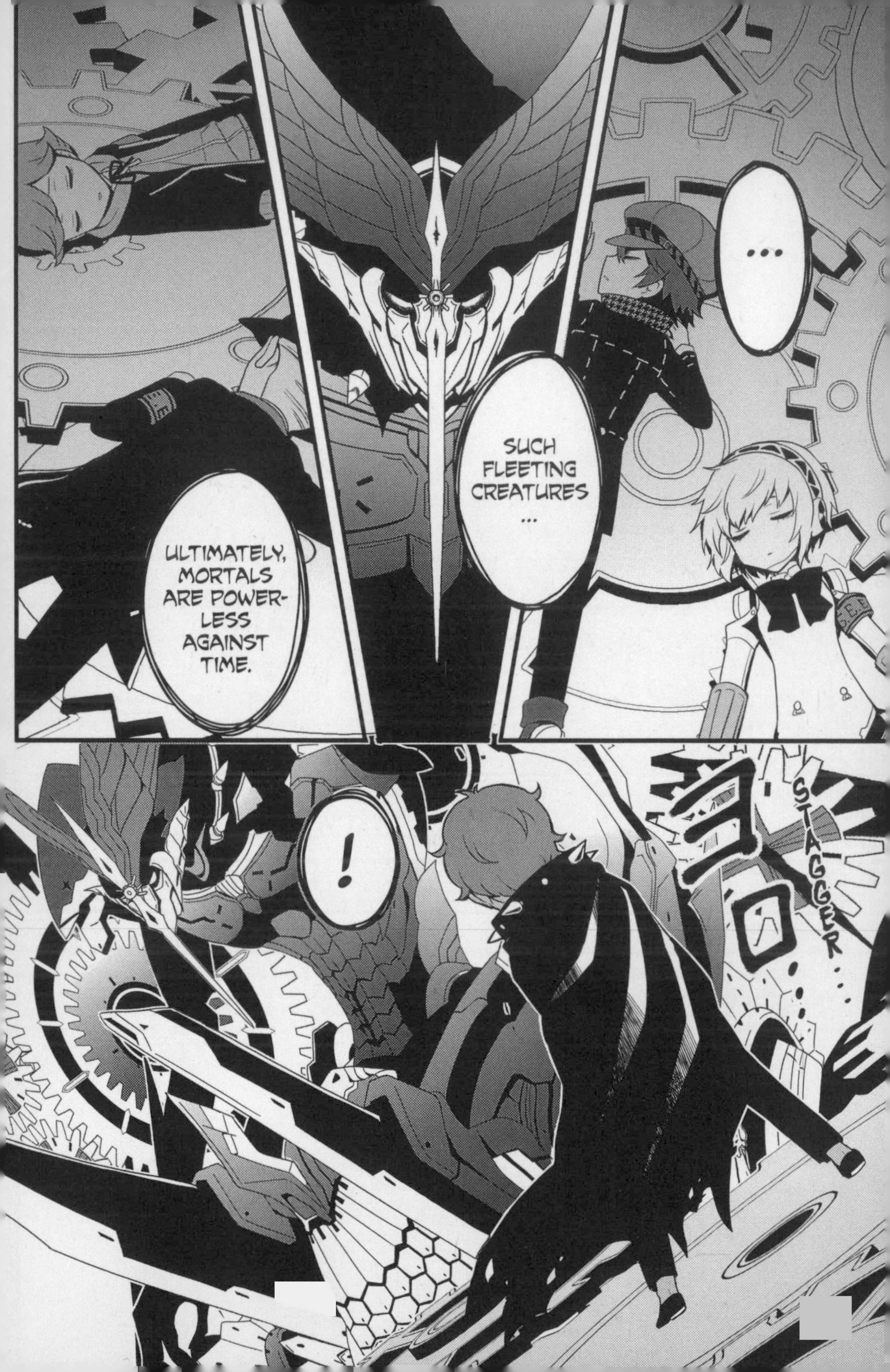
...
SUCH FLEETING CREATURES ...
ULTIMATELY, MORTALS ARE POWER-LESS AGAINST TIME.
STAGGER...
!

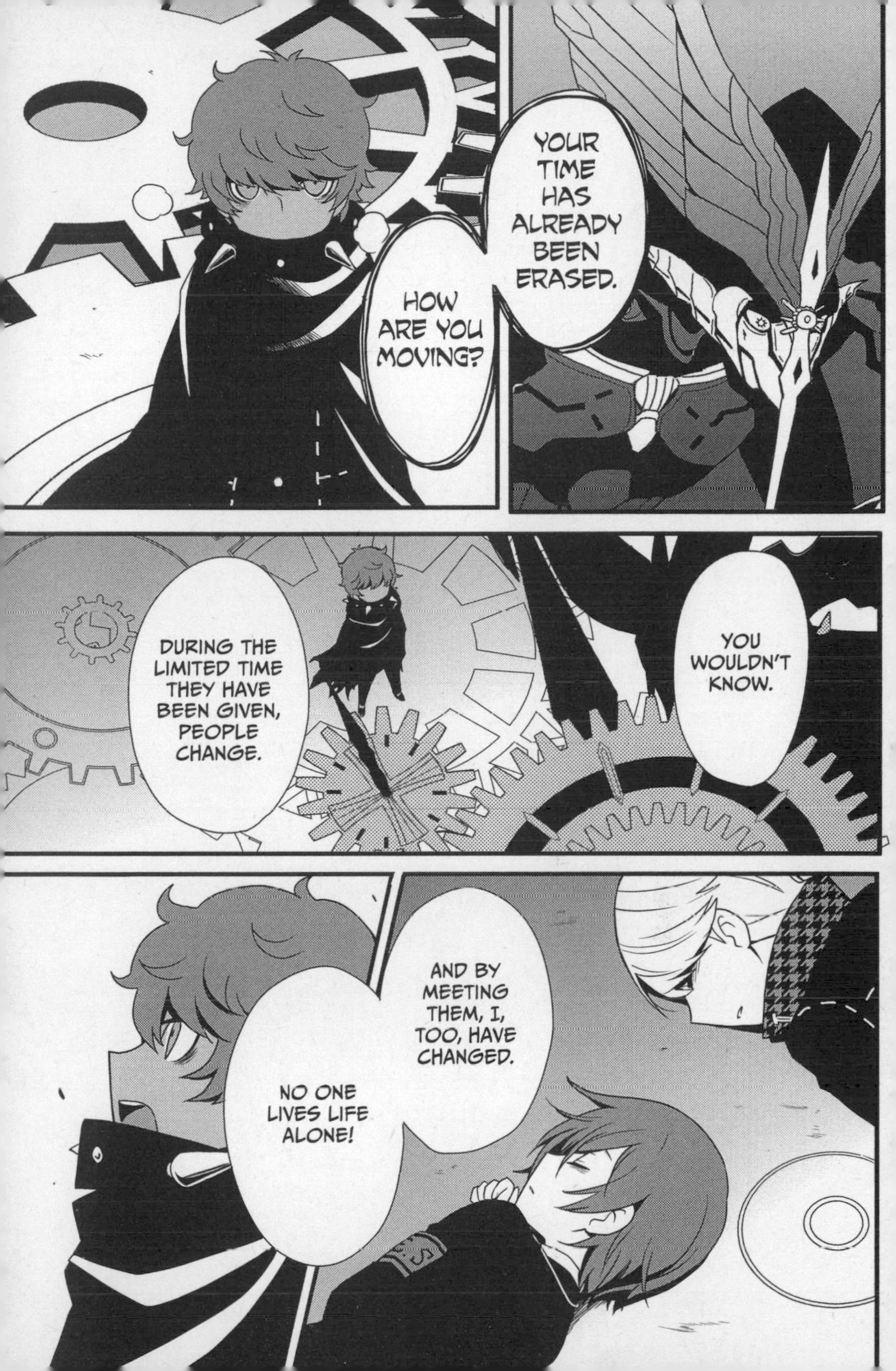
YOUR TIME HAS ALREADY BEEN ERASED.
HOW ARE YOU MOVING?
YOU WOULDN'T KNOW.
DURING THE LIMITED TIME THEY HAVE BEEN GIVEN, PEOPLE CHANGE.
AND BY MEETING THEM, I, TOO, HAVE CHANGED.
NO ONE LIVES LIFE ALONE!

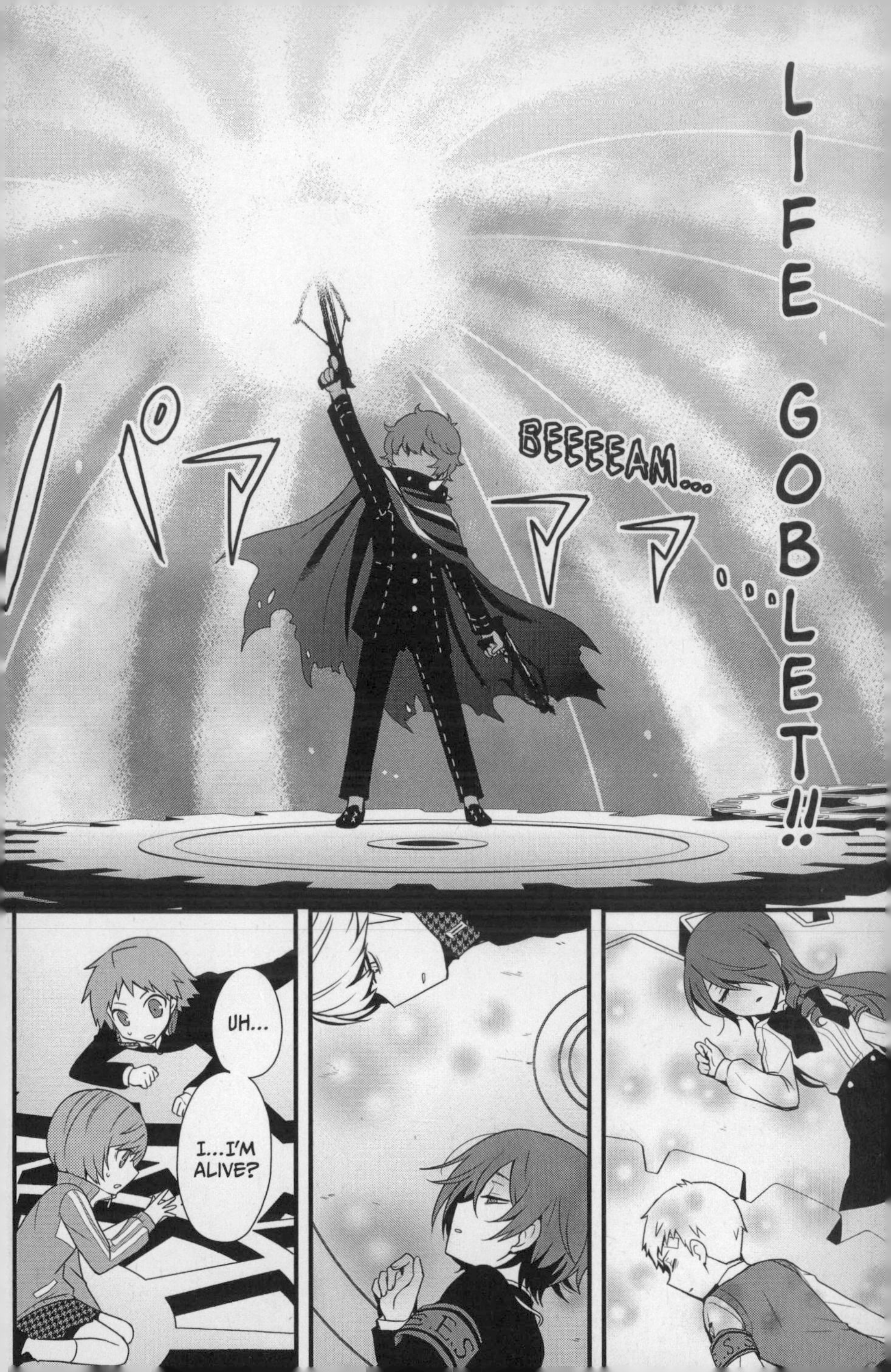
LIFE GOBLET!!
BEEEEAM...
UH...
I...I'M ALIVE?

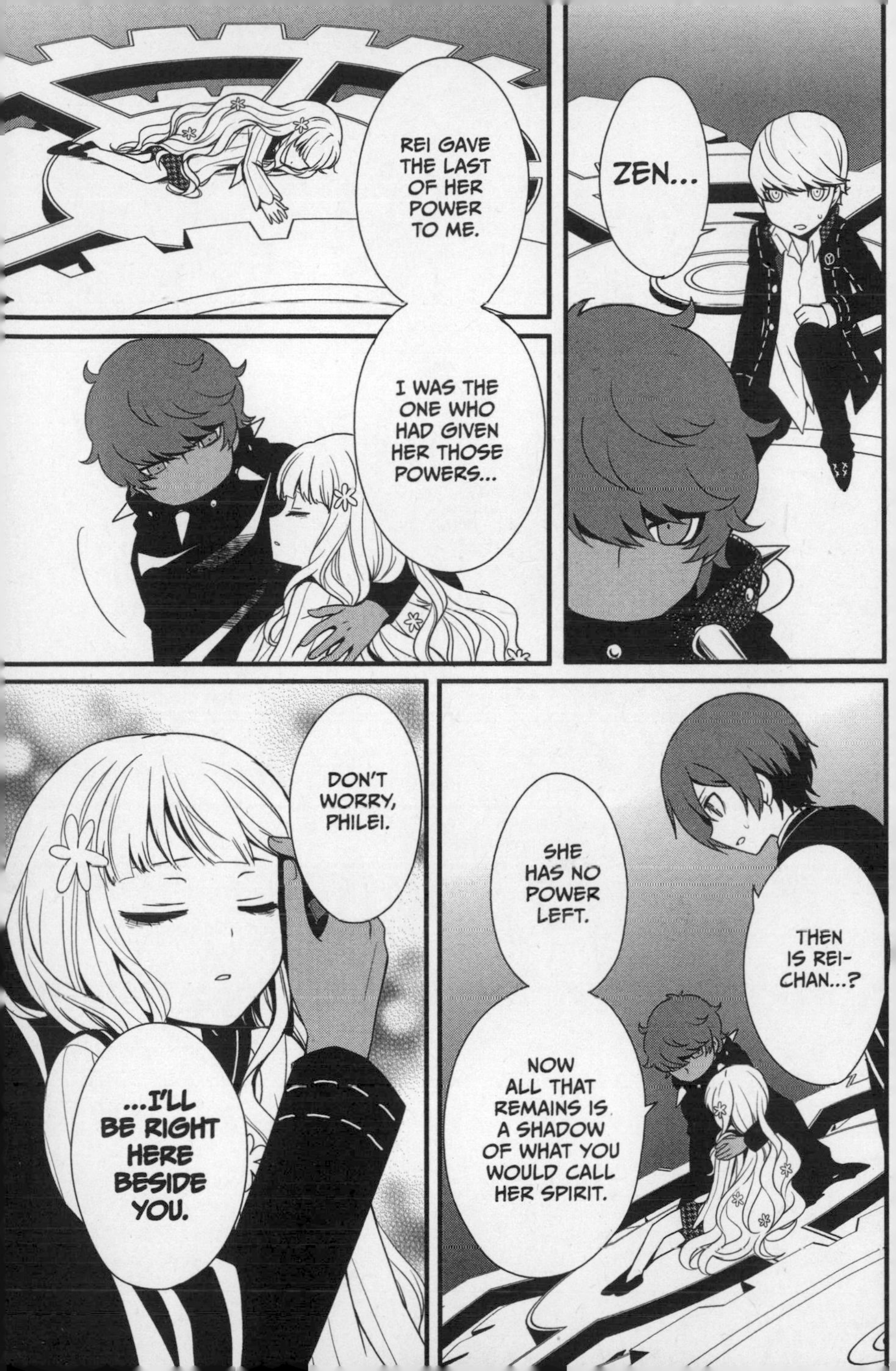

ZEN...
REI GAVE THE LAST OF HER POWER TO ME.
I WAS THE ONE WHO HAD GIVEN HER THOSE POWERS...
THEN IS REI-CHAN...?
SHE HAS NO POWER LEFT.
NOW ALL THAT REMAINS IS A SHADOW OF WHAT YOU WOULD CALL HER SPIRIT.
DON'T WORRY, PHILEI.
...I'LL BE RIGHT HERE BESIDE YOU.

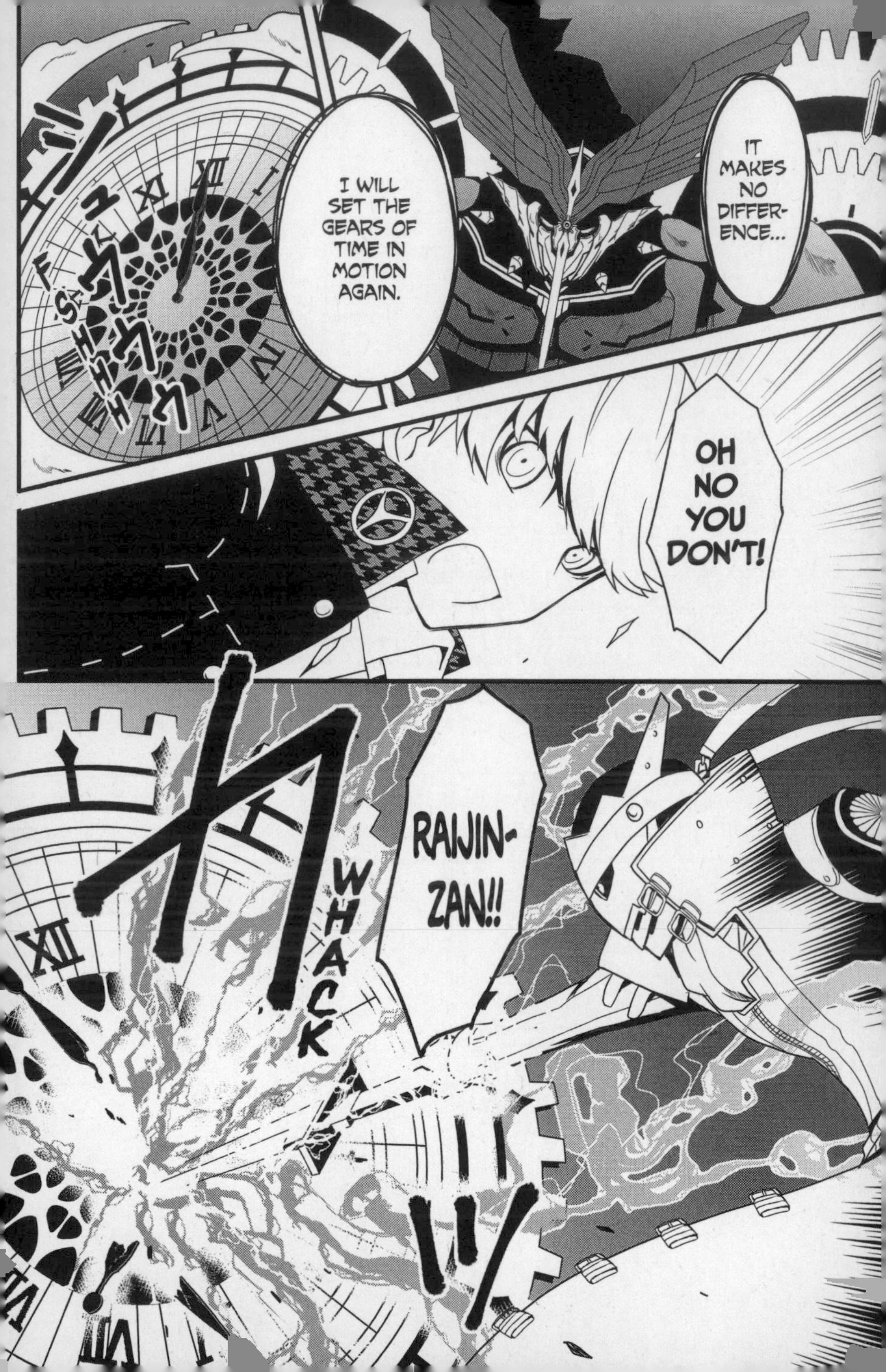
IT MAKES NO DIFFERENCE...
I WILL SET THE GEARS OF TIME IN MOTION AGAIN.
OH NO YOU DON'T!
RAIJIN-ZAN!!
WHACK

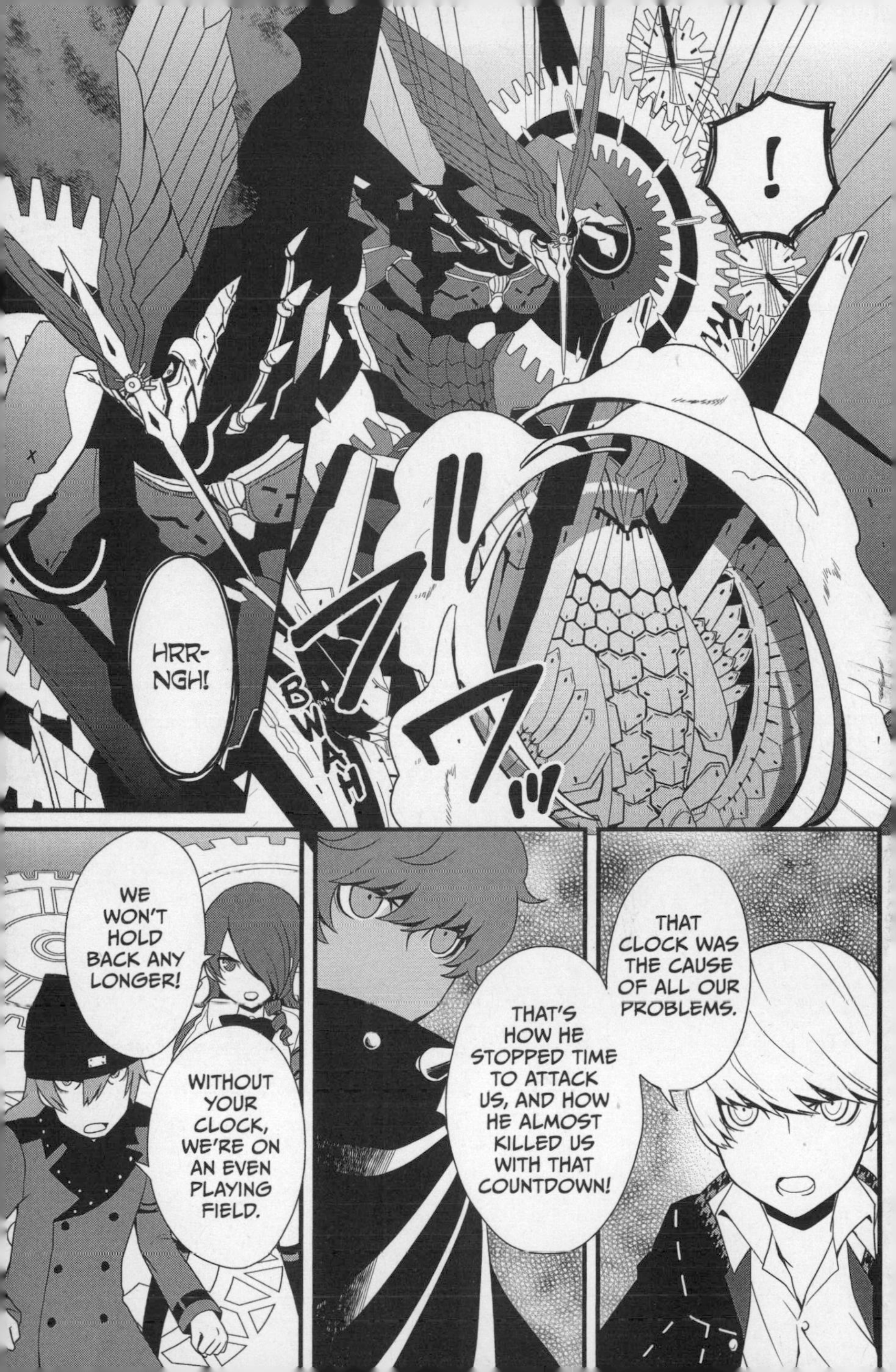
!
BWAH
HRR-NGH!
THAT CLOCK WAS THE CAUSE OF ALL OUR PROBLEMS.
THAT'S HOW HE STOPPED TIME TO ATTACK US, AND HOW HE ALMOST KILLED US WITH THAT COUNTDOWN!
WE WON'T HOLD BACK ANY LONGER!
WITHOUT YOUR CLOCK, WE'RE ON AN EVEN PLAYING FIELD.

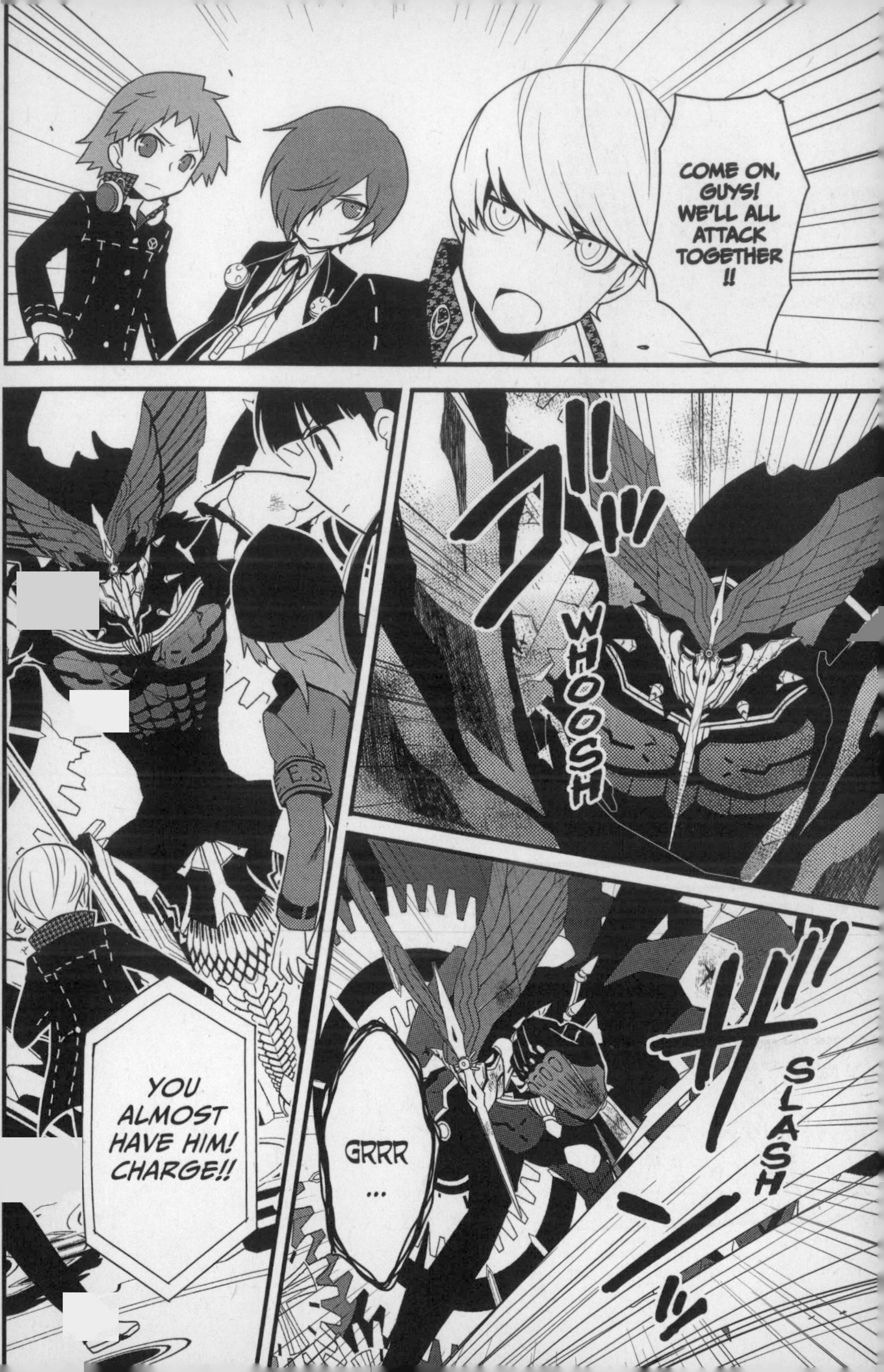
COME ON, GUYS! WE'LL ALL ATTACK TOGETHER!!
WHOOSH
SLASH
GRRR...
YOU ALMOST HAVE HIM! CHARGE!!

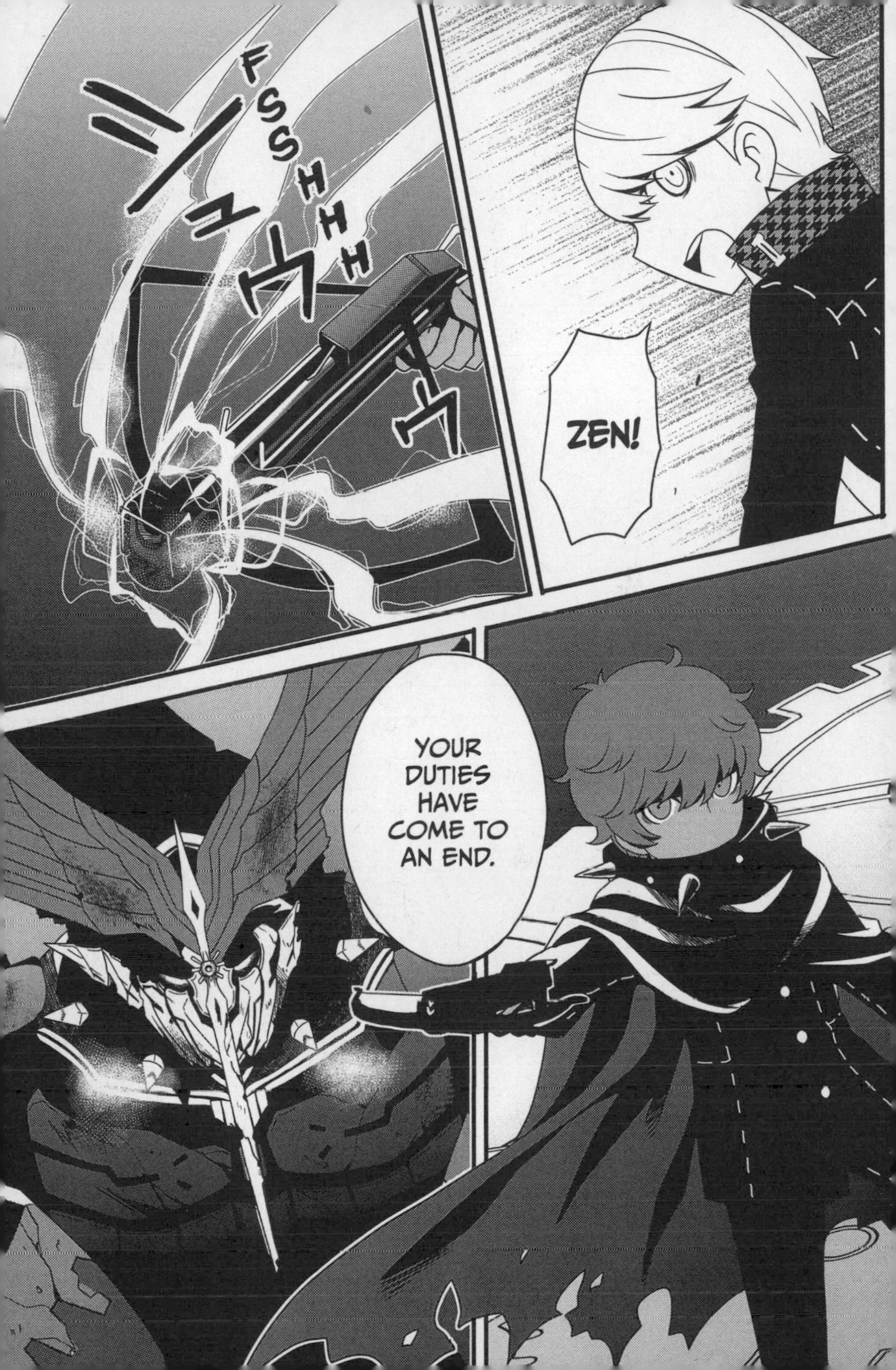
ZEN!
FSSHHH
YOUR DUTIES HAVE COME TO AN END.

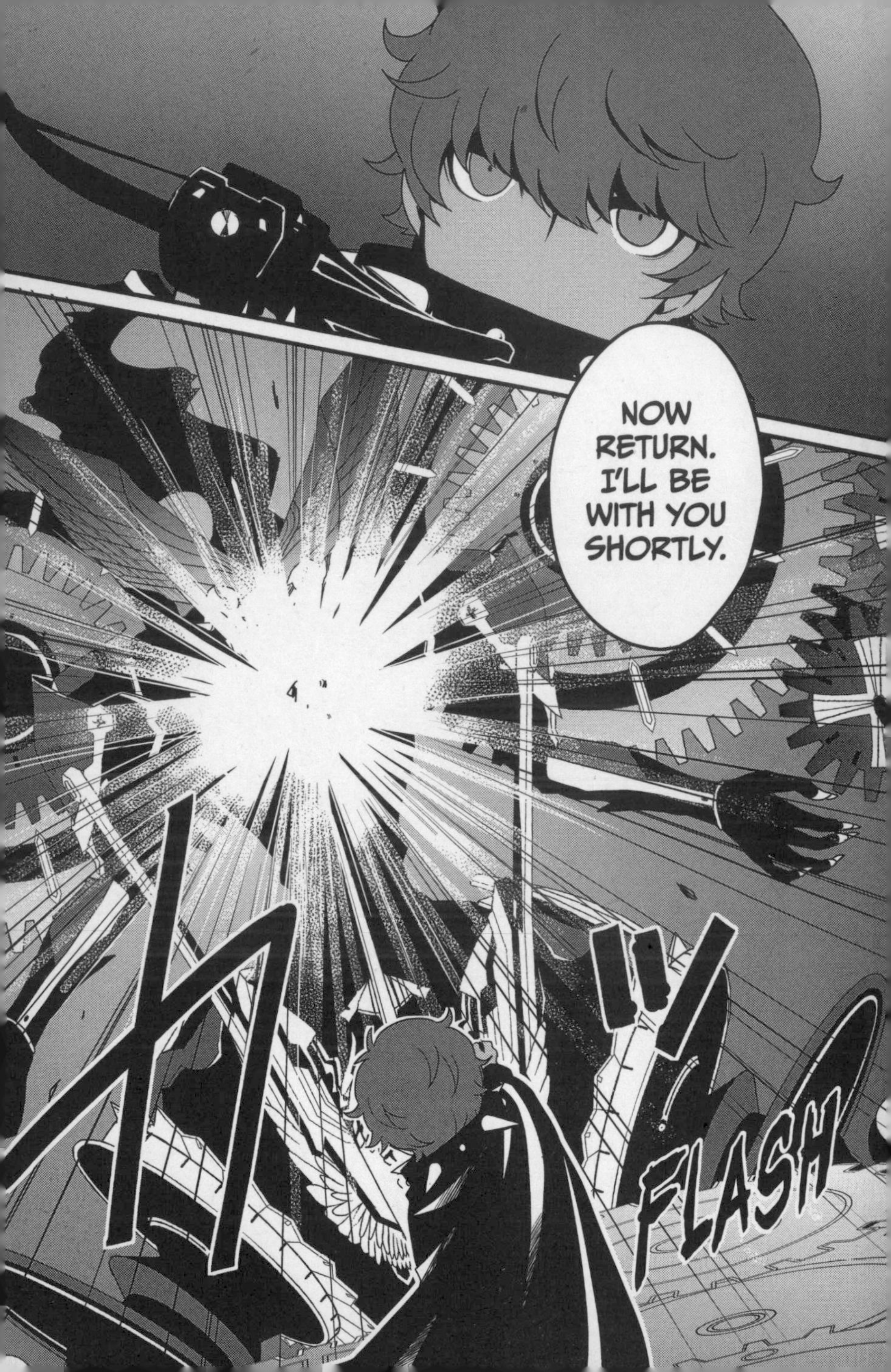
NOW RETURN. I'LL BE WITH YOU SHORTLY.
FLASH

PENTHESILEA (EMPRESS)

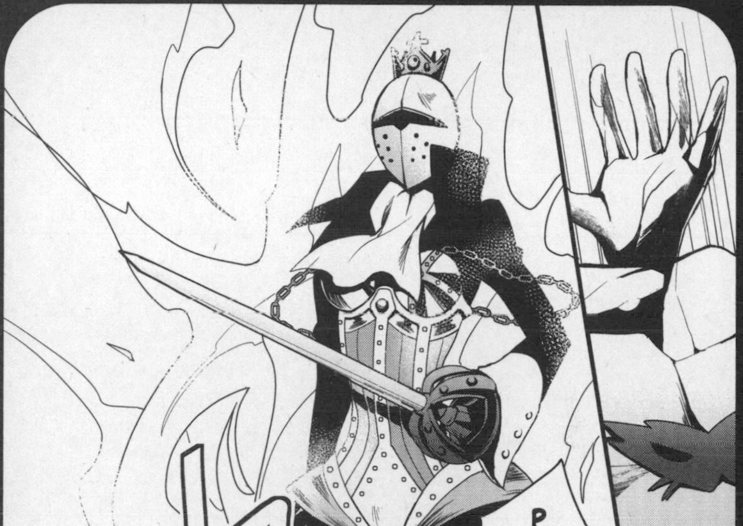
PENTHESILEA!
カッ
FLASH

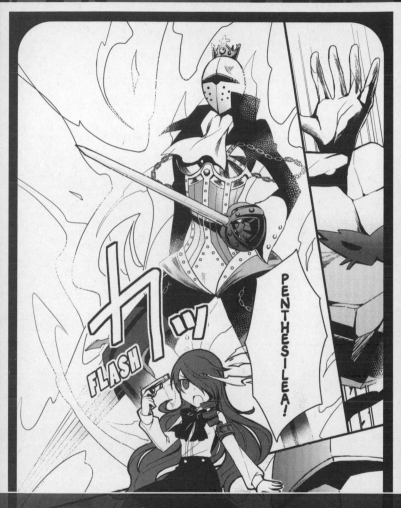

IN GREEK MYTH, PENTHESILEA IS THE DAUGHTER OF ARES AND OTRERA, AND IS THE QUEEN OF THE AMAZONS. SHE AND 12 OF HER AMAZONESSES FOUGHT TO SAVE TROY IN ITS HOUR OF NEED; THEY DID MANY GREAT DEEDS, BUT WERE KILLED BY GREECE'S HERO ACHILLES. WHEN, UPON HER DEATH, HE DISCOVERED HOW BEAUTIFUL PENTHESILEA WAS, ACHILLES RUED HAVING KILLED HER.

PERSONA Q
SHADOW OF THE LABYRINTH
Side: P4

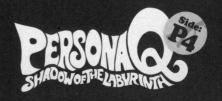

Final Labyrinth: A Reason for Life

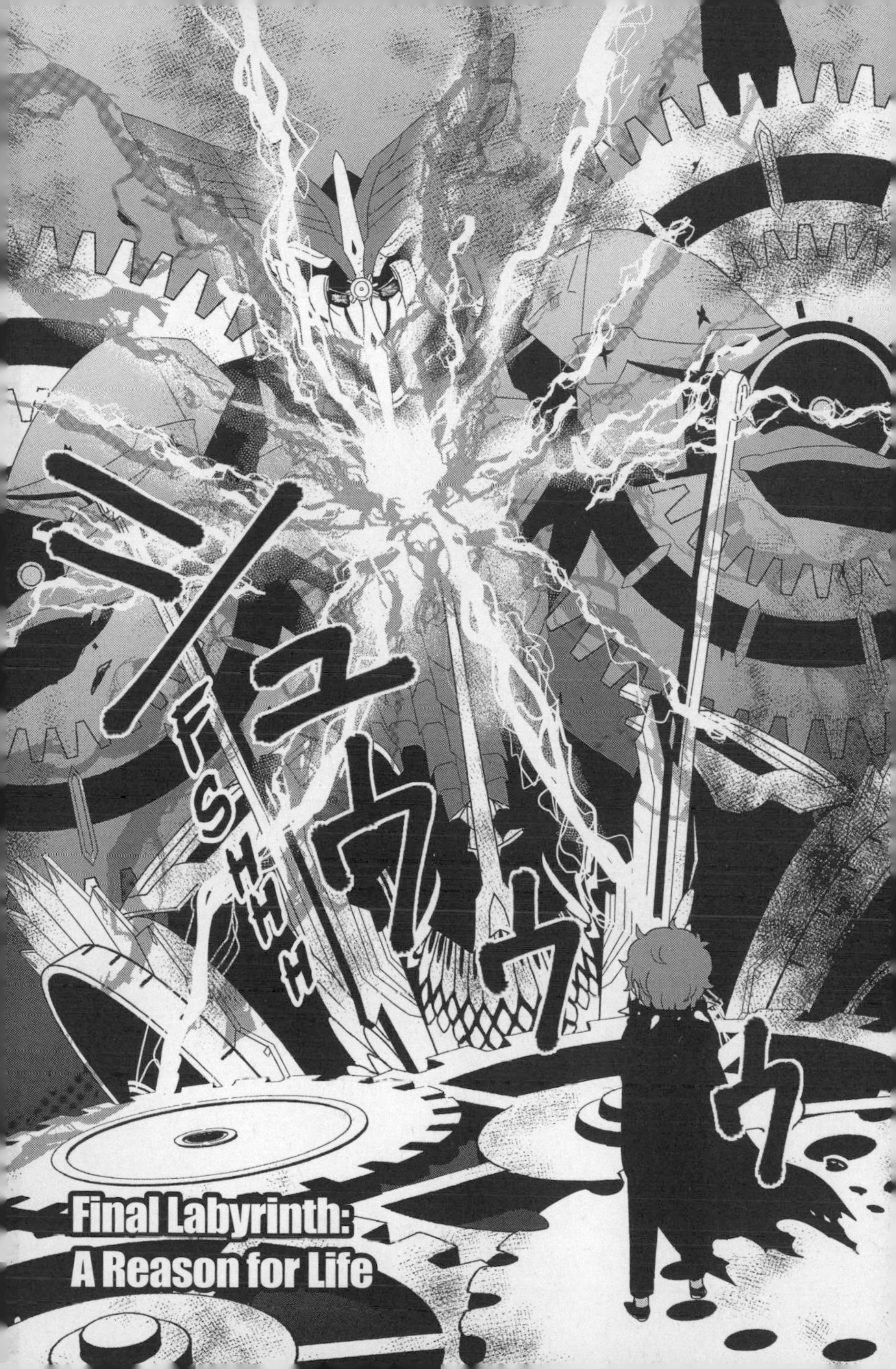
シュウウウ
FSHHH

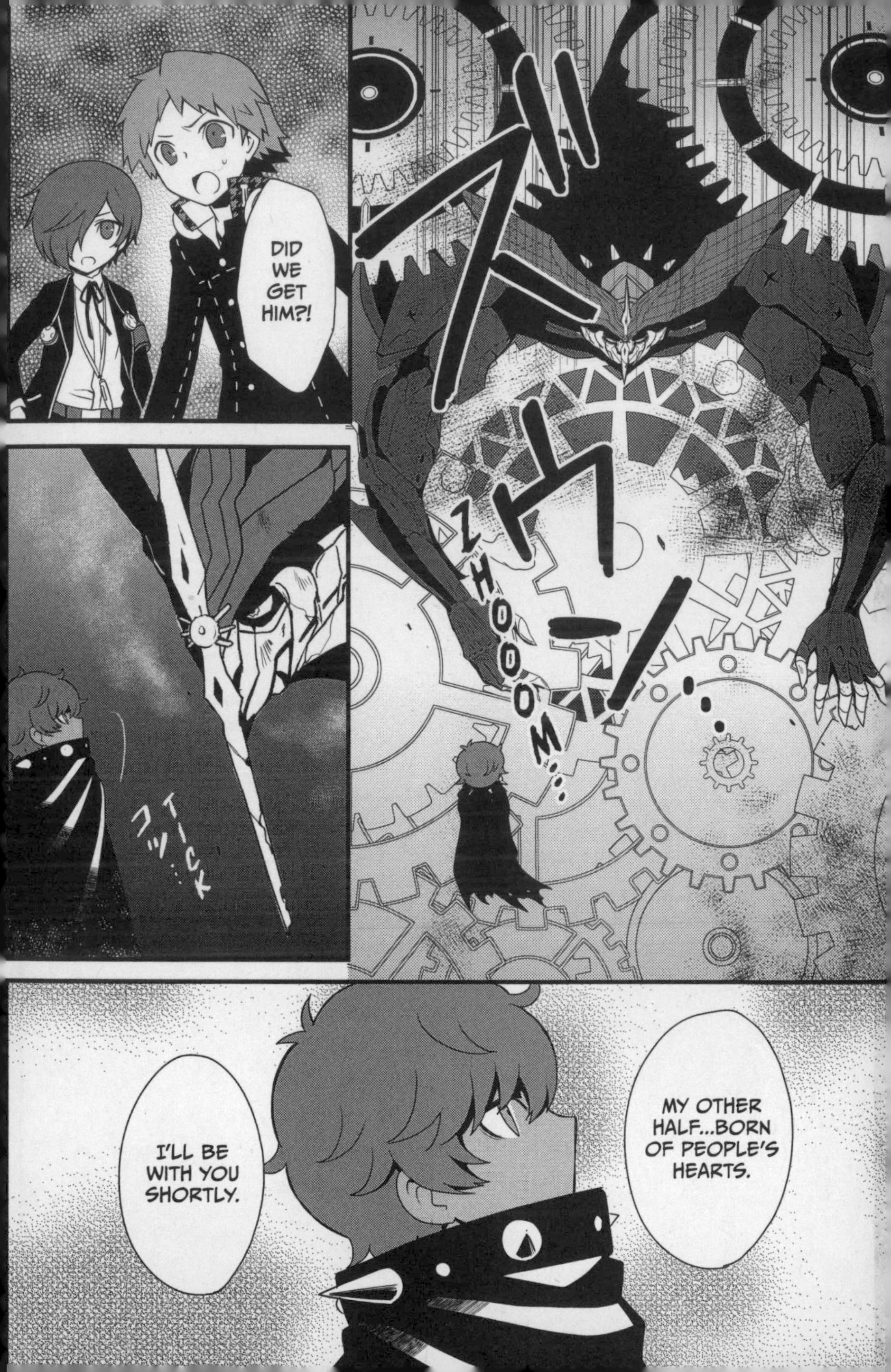
ZHOOOOM...
DID WE GET HIM?!
コッ
TICK...
MY OTHER HALF...BORN OF PEOPLE'S HEARTS.
I'LL BE WITH YOU SHORTLY.

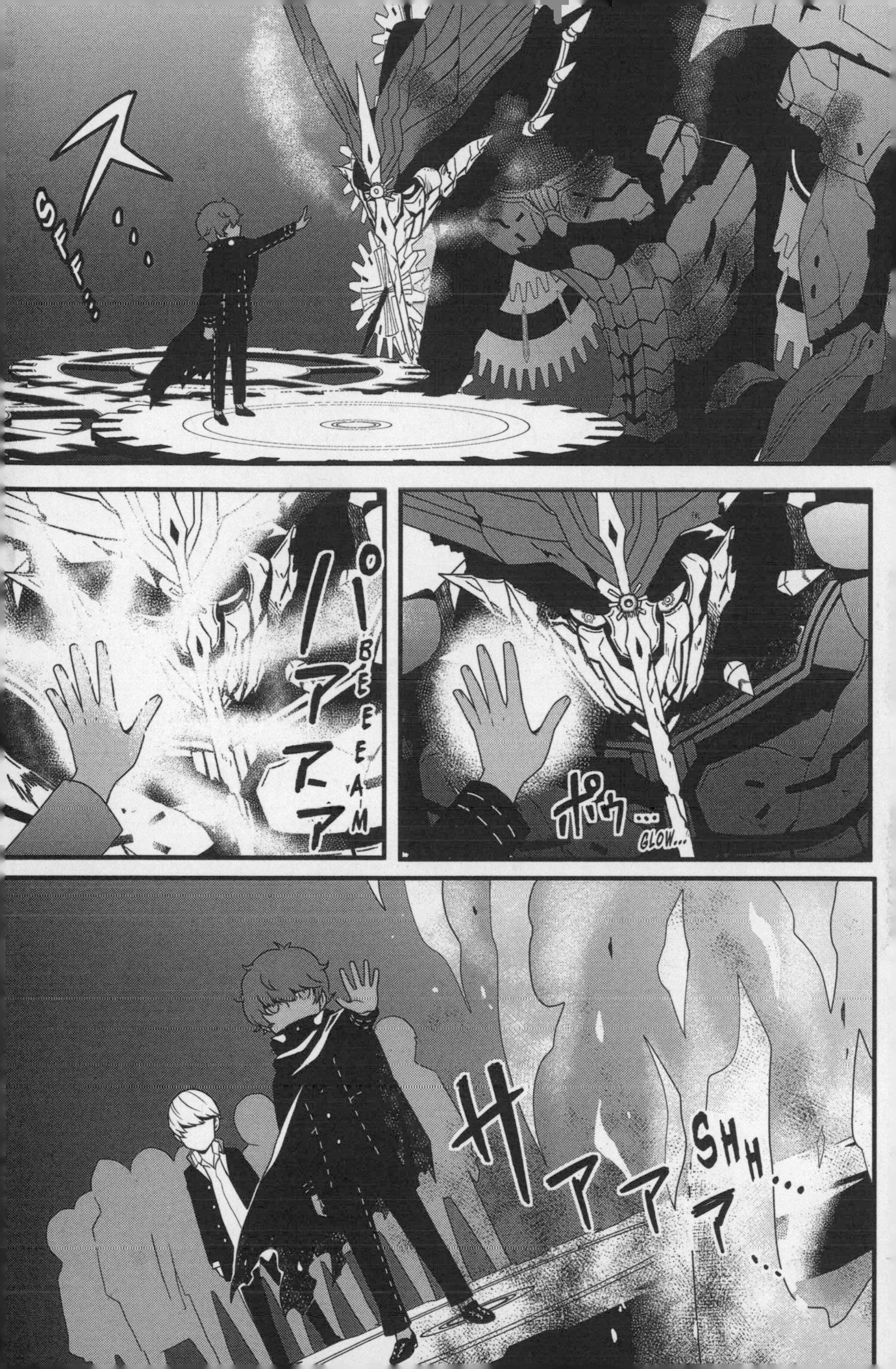
ス…
SFF...
ポウ…
GLOW...
ピーアーア
BEEEAM
サアアア…
SHH...

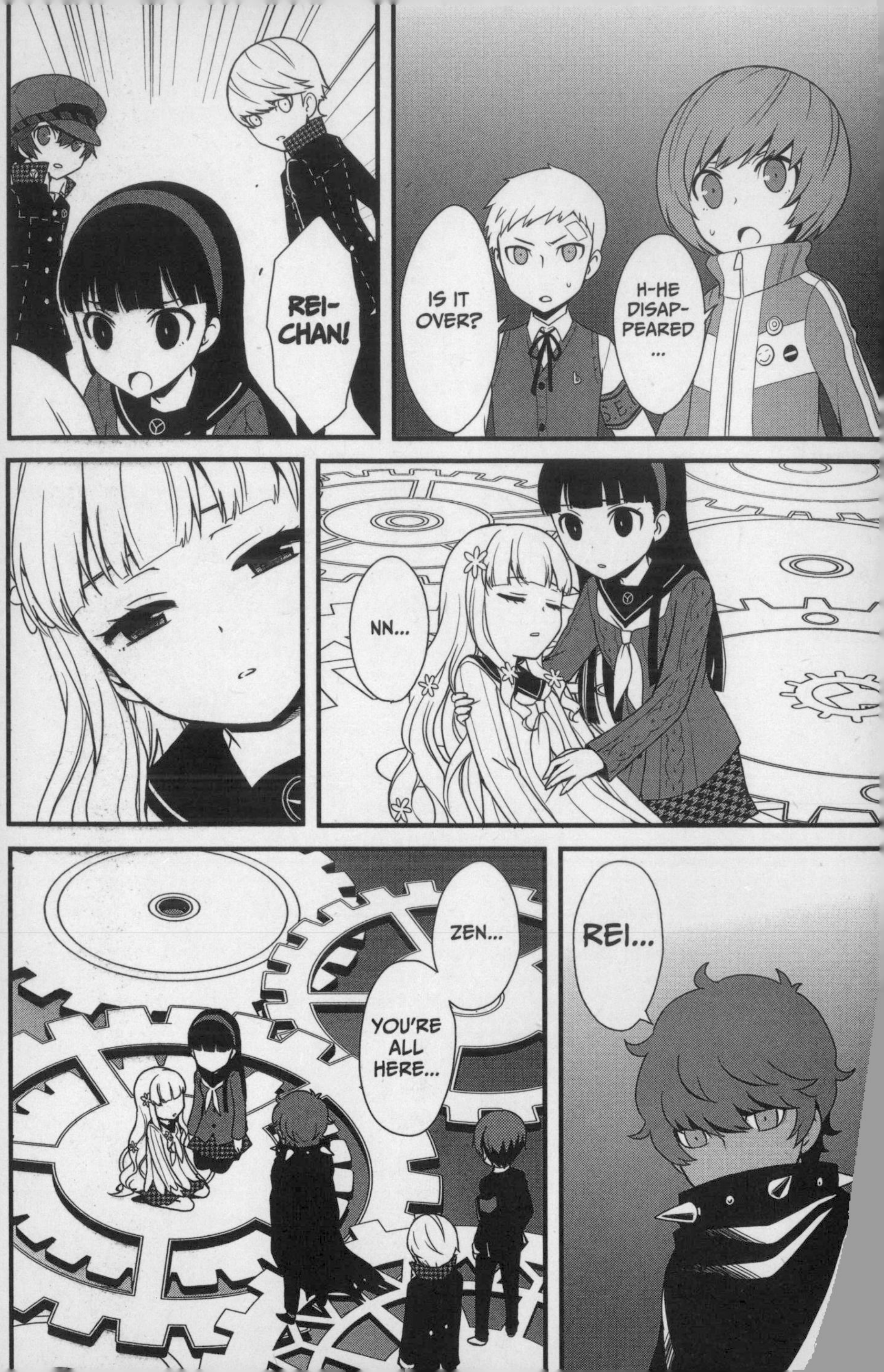
H-HE DISAP-PEARED ...
IS IT OVER?
REI-CHAN!
NN...
REI...
ZEN...
YOU'RE ALL HERE...

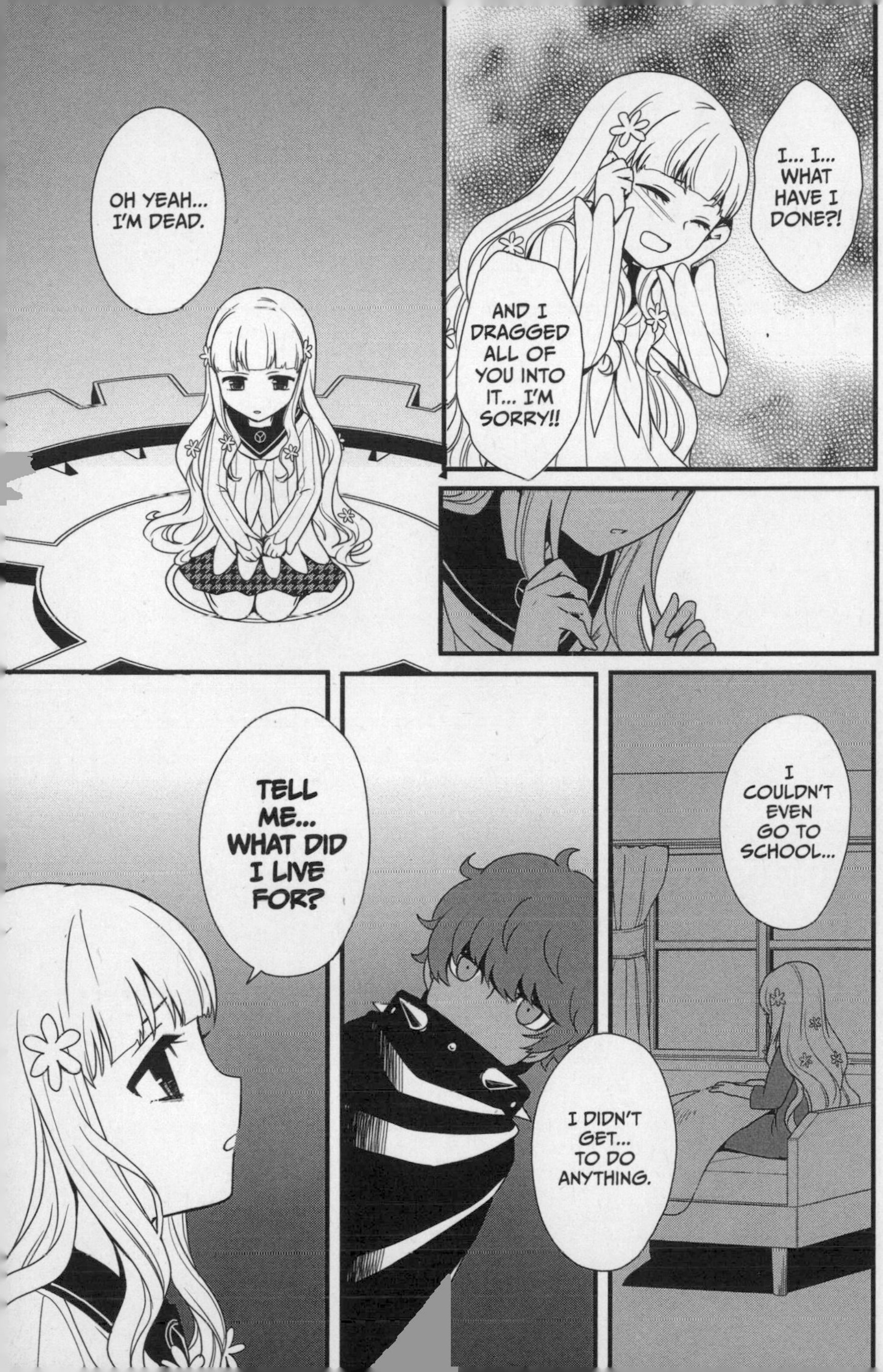
I... I... WHAT HAVE I DONE?!
AND I DRAGGED ALL OF YOU INTO IT... I'M SORRY!!
OH YEAH... I'M DEAD.
I COULDN'T EVEN GO TO SCHOOL...
I DIDN'T GET... TO DO ANYTHING.
TELL ME... WHAT DID I LIVE FOR?

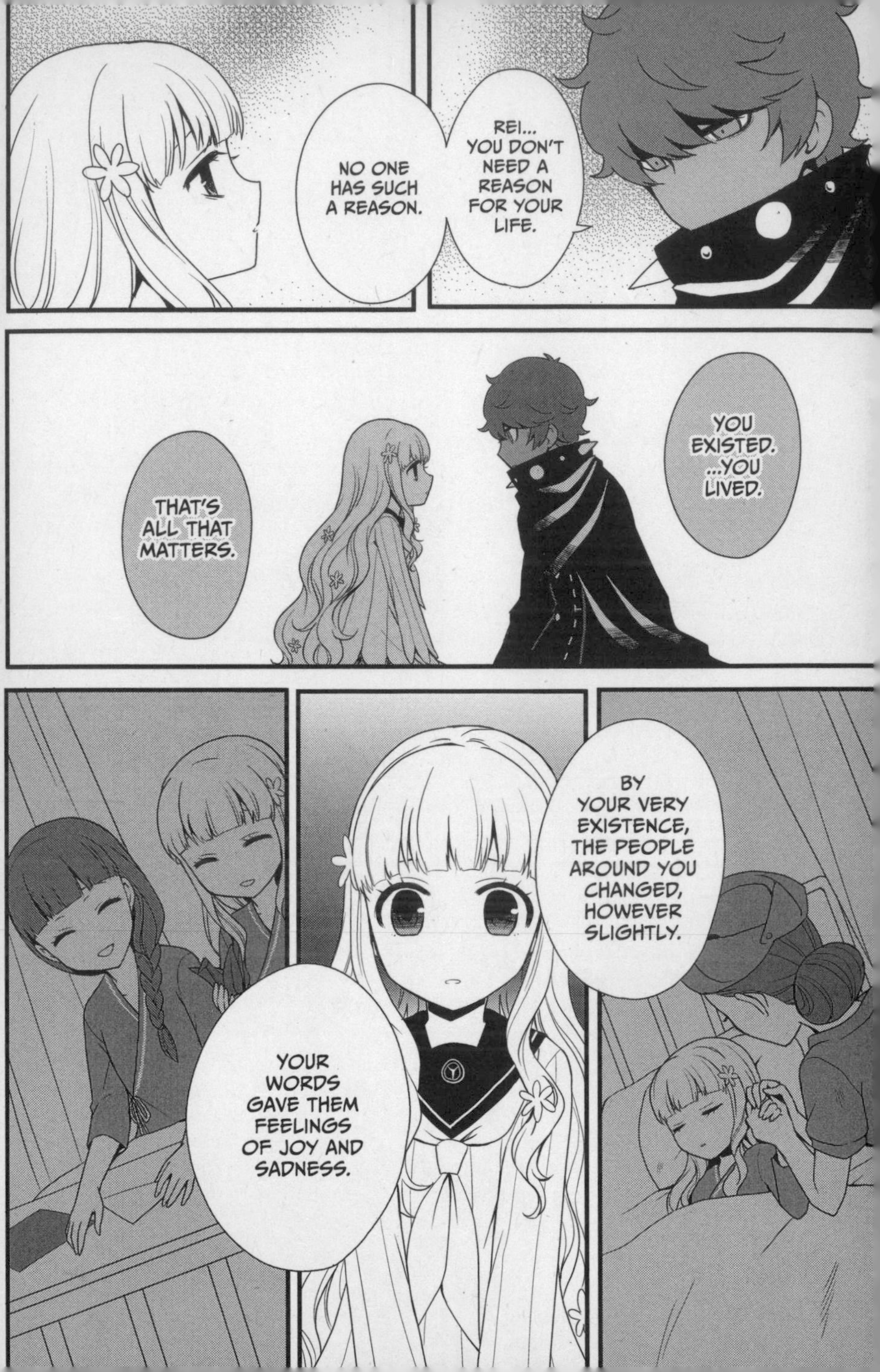
REI... YOU DON'T NEED A REASON FOR YOUR LIFE.
NO ONE HAS SUCH A REASON.
YOU EXISTED. ...YOU LIVED.
THAT'S ALL THAT MATTERS.
BY YOUR VERY EXISTENCE, THE PEOPLE AROUND YOU CHANGED, HOWEVER SLIGHTLY.
YOUR WORDS GAVE THEM FEELINGS OF JOY AND SADNESS.

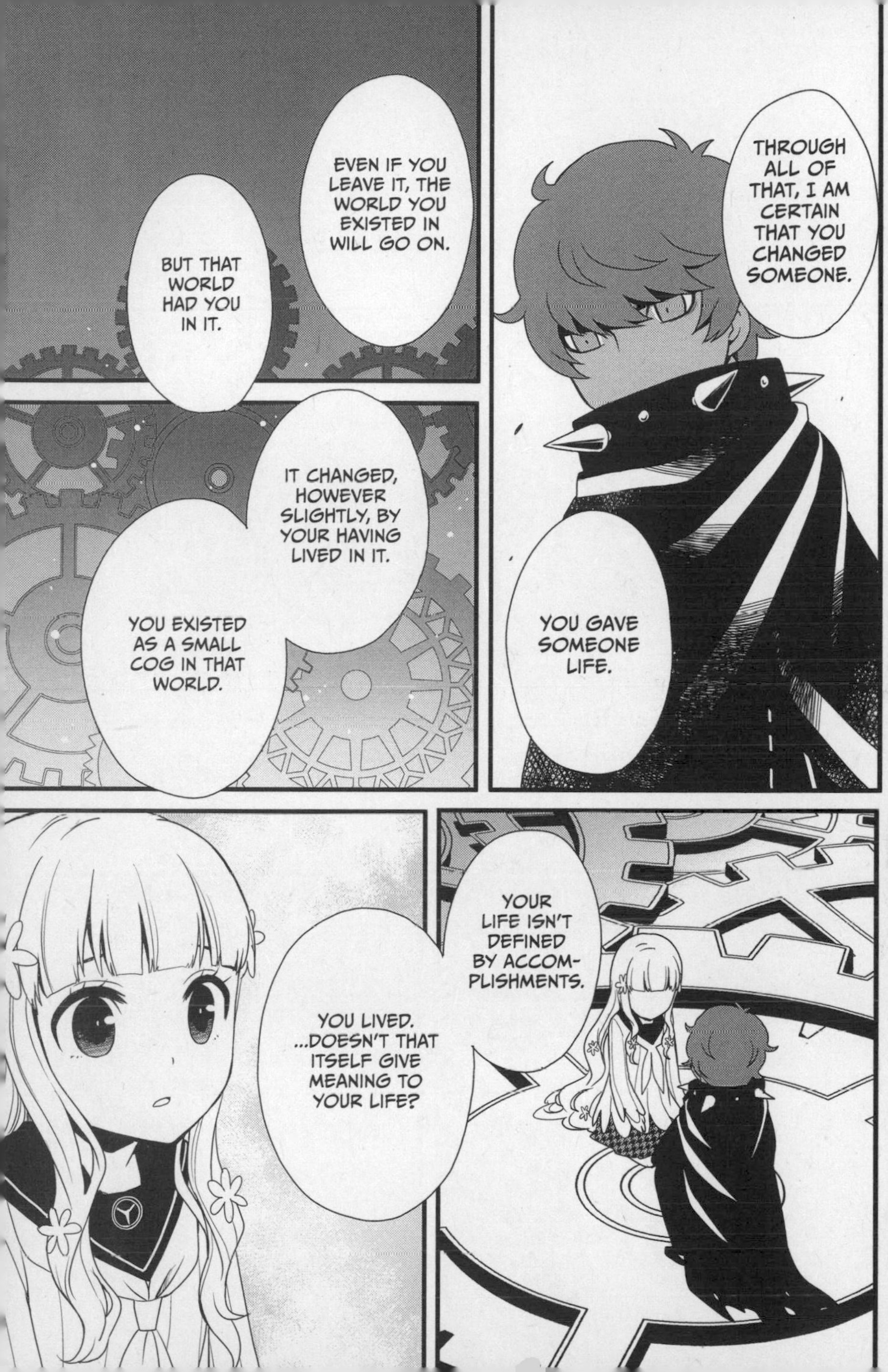
THROUGH ALL OF THAT, I AM CERTAIN THAT YOU CHANGED SOMEONE.
YOU GAVE SOMEONE LIFE.
EVEN IF YOU LEAVE IT, THE WORLD YOU EXISTED IN WILL GO ON.
BUT THAT WORLD HAD YOU IN IT.
IT CHANGED, HOWEVER SLIGHTLY, BY YOUR HAVING LIVED IN IT.
YOU EXISTED AS A SMALL COG IN THAT WORLD.
YOUR LIFE ISN'T DEFINED BY ACCOM-PLISHMENTS.
YOU LIVED. ...DOESN'T THAT ITSELF GIVE MEANING TO YOUR LIFE?

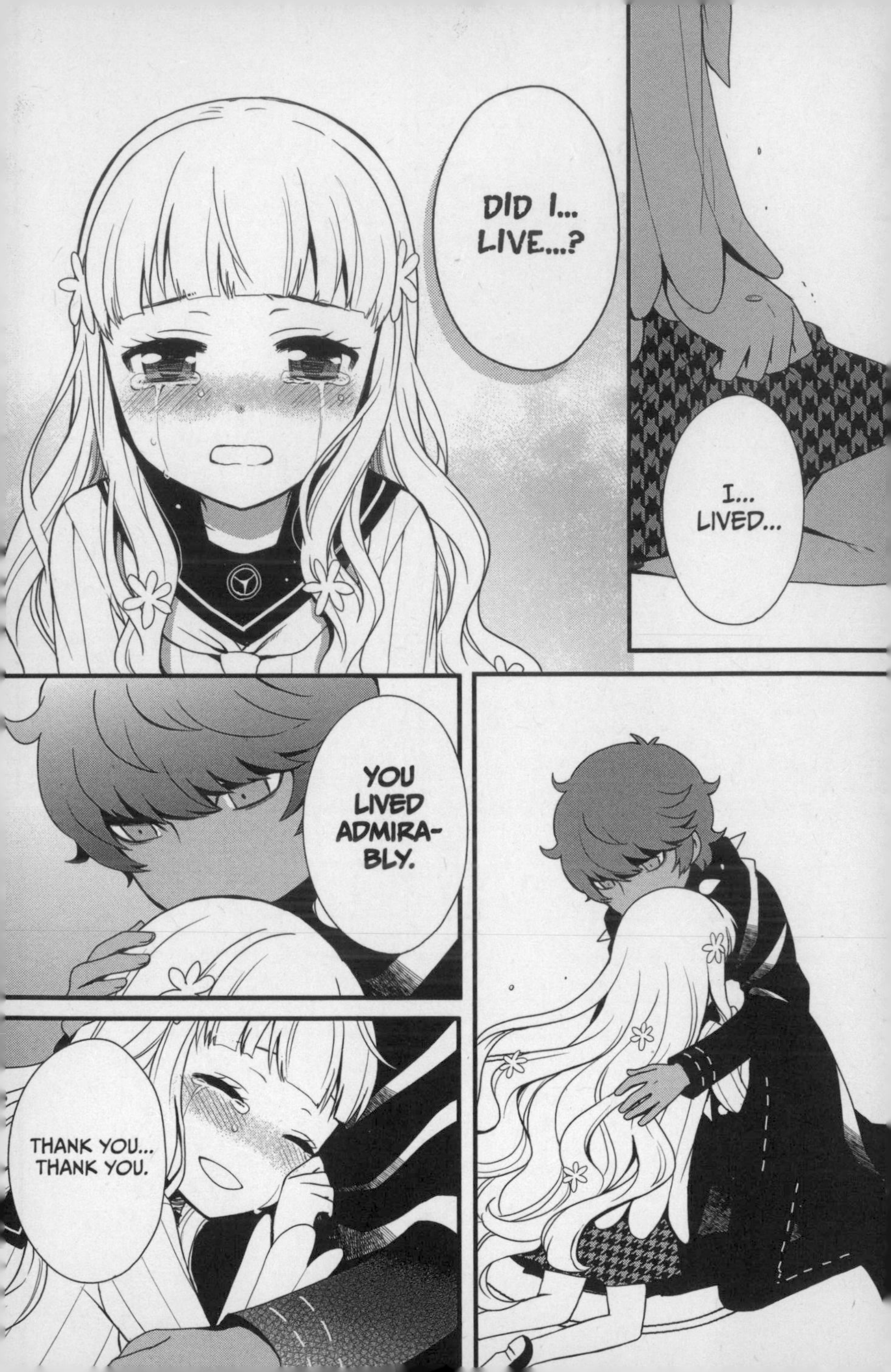
I... LIVED...
DID I... LIVE...?
YOU LIVED ADMIRA-BLY.
THANK YOU... THANK YOU.

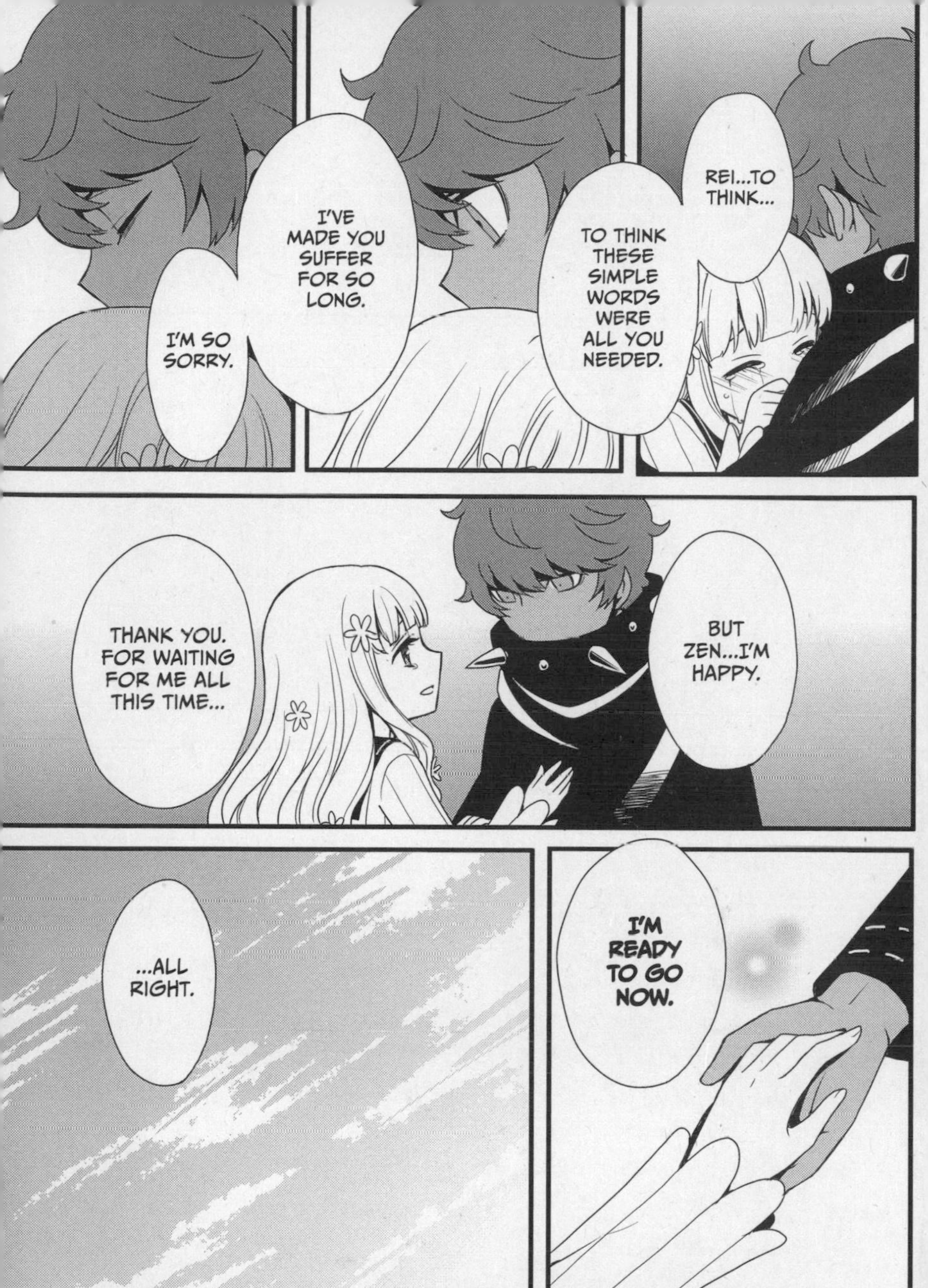
REI...TO THINK...
TO THINK THESE SIMPLE WORDS WERE ALL YOU NEEDED.
I'VE MADE YOU SUFFER FOR SO LONG.
I'M SO SORRY.
BUT ZEN...I'M HAPPY.
THANK YOU. FOR WAITING FOR ME ALL THIS TIME...
I'M READY TO GO NOW.
...ALL RIGHT.

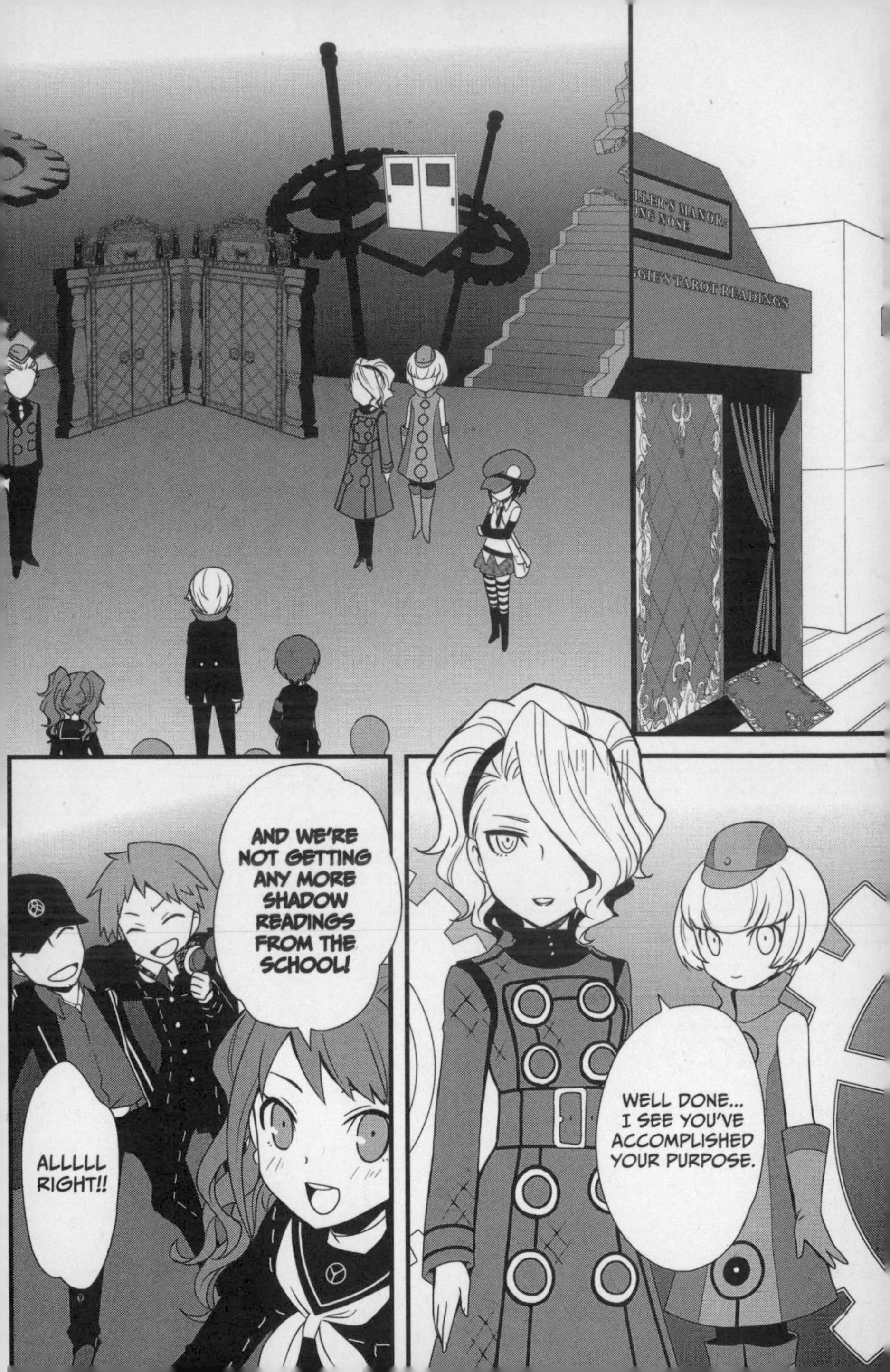
GGIE'S TAROT READINGS
WELL DONE... I SEE YOU'VE ACCOMPLISHED YOUR PURPOSE.
AND WE'RE NOT GETTING ANY MORE SHADOW READINGS FROM THE SCHOOL!
ALLLLL RIGHT!!

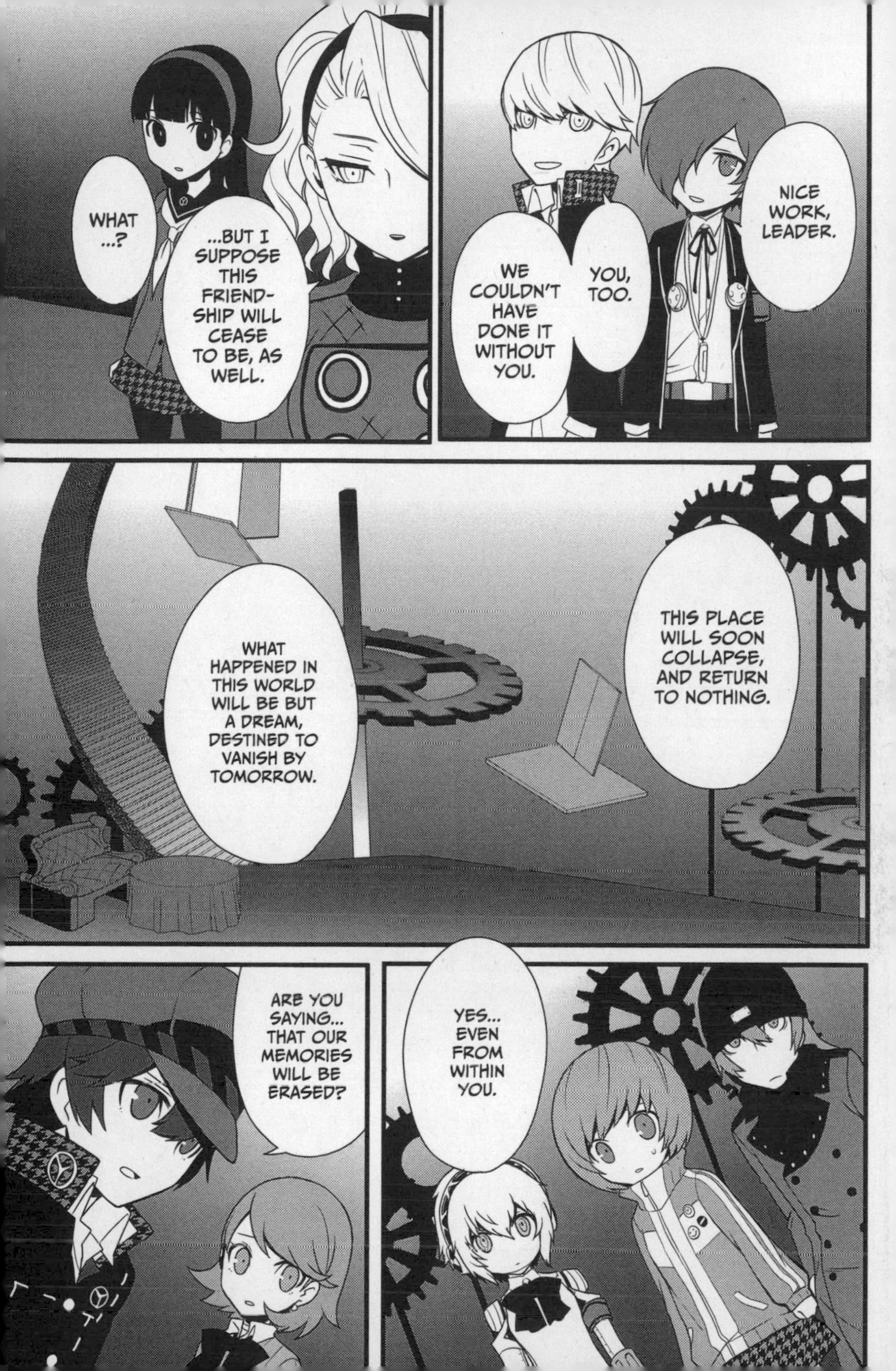
NICE WORK, LEADER.
YOU, TOO.
WE COULDN'T HAVE DONE IT WITHOUT YOU.
...BUT I SUPPOSE THIS FRIEND-SHIP WILL CEASE TO BE, AS WELL.
WHAT ...?
THIS PLACE WILL SOON COLLAPSE, AND RETURN TO NOTHING.
WHAT HAPPENED IN THIS WORLD WILL BE BUT A DREAM, DESTINED TO VANISH BY TOMORROW.
YES... EVEN FROM WITHIN YOU.
ARE YOU SAYING... THAT OUR MEMORIES WILL BE ERASED?

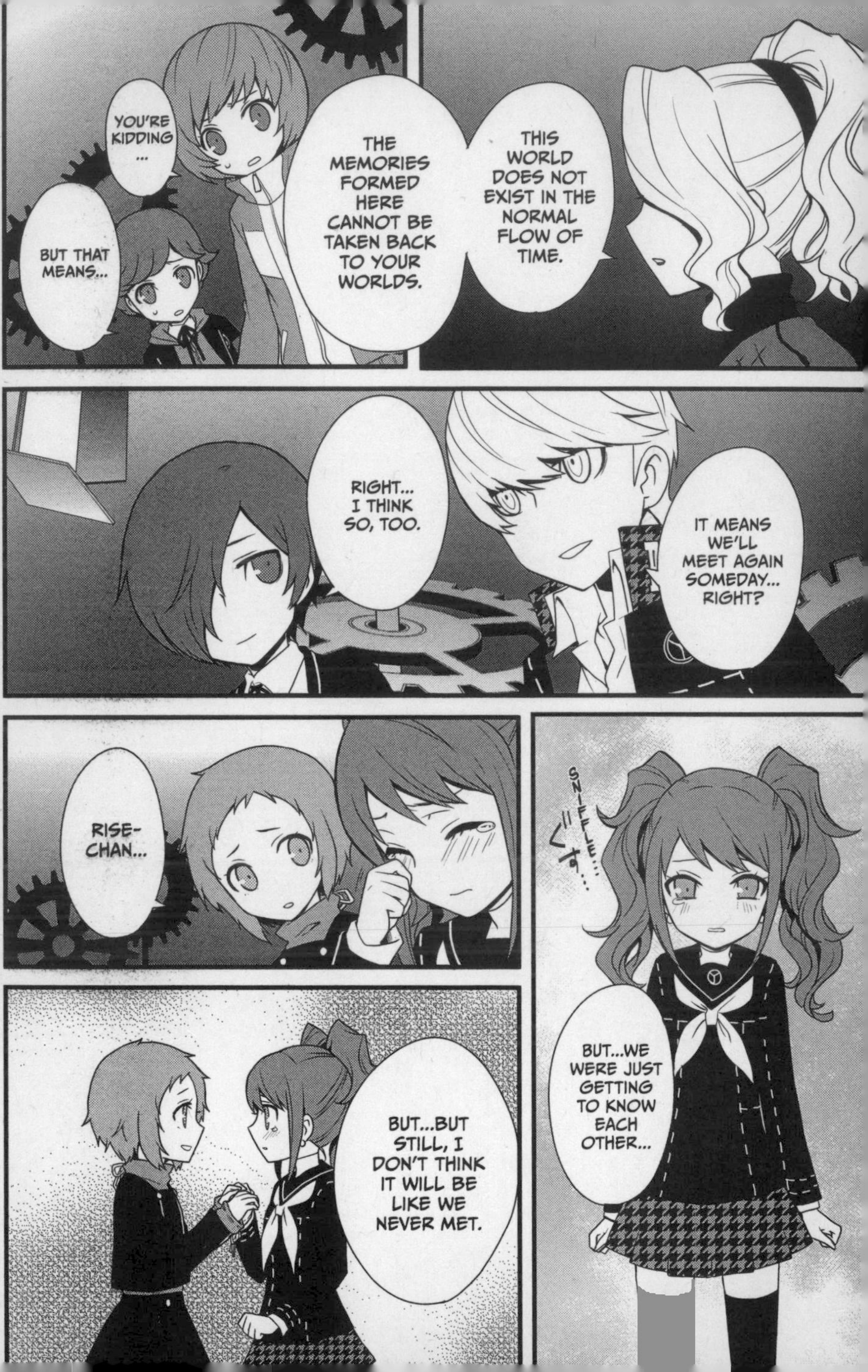
THIS WORLD DOES NOT EXIST IN THE NORMAL FLOW OF TIME.
THE MEMORIES FORMED HERE CANNOT BE TAKEN BACK TO YOUR WORLDS.
YOU'RE KIDDING ...
BUT THAT MEANS...
IT MEANS WE'LL MEET AGAIN SOMEDAY... RIGHT?
RIGHT... I THINK SO, TOO.
SNIFFLE...
BUT...WE WERE JUST GETTING TO KNOW EACH OTHER...
RISE-CHAN...
BUT...BUT STILL, I DON'T THINK IT WILL BE LIKE WE NEVER MET.

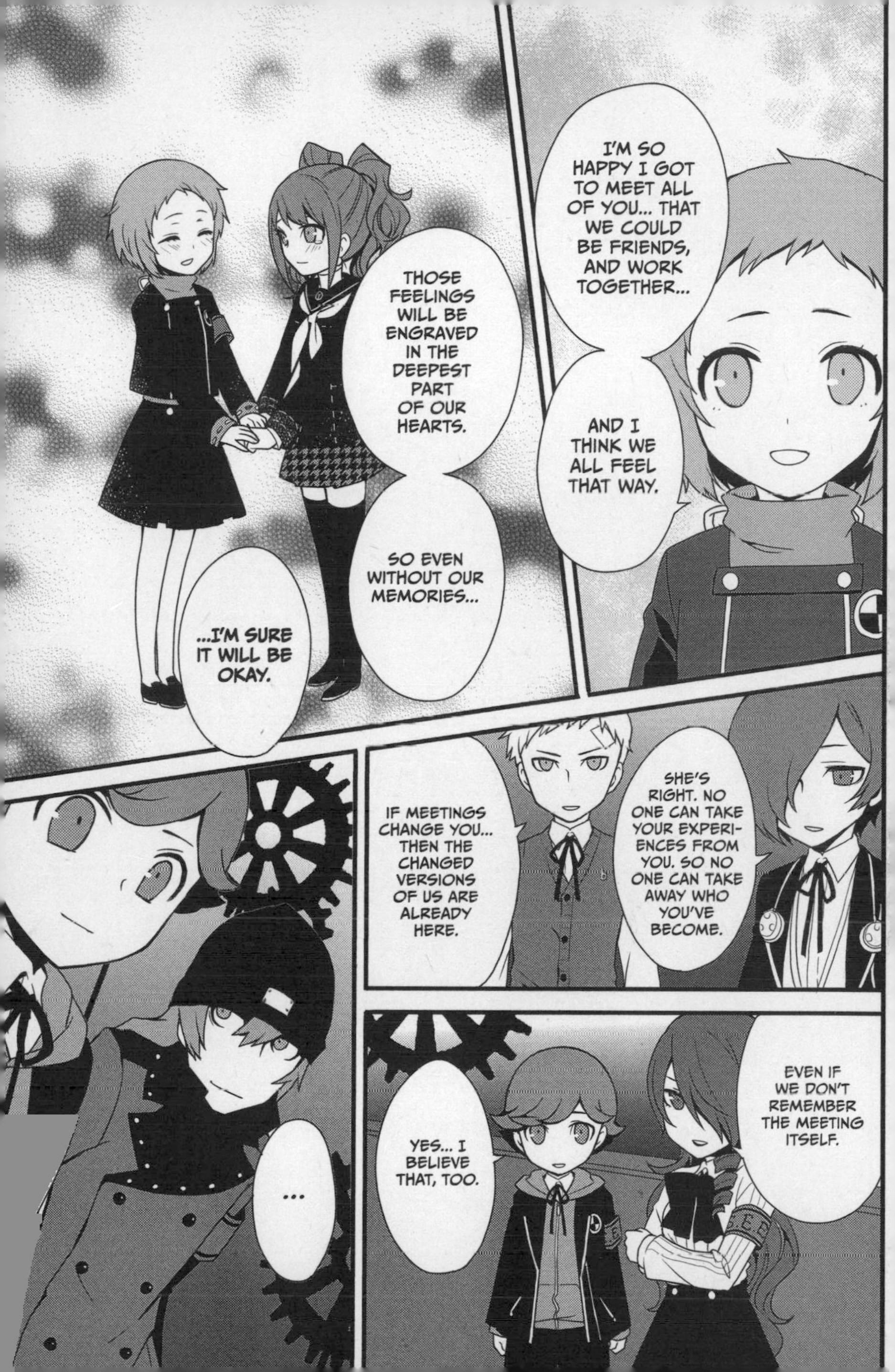
I'M SO HAPPY I GOT TO MEET ALL OF YOU... THAT WE COULD BE FRIENDS, AND WORK TOGETHER...
AND I THINK WE ALL FEEL THAT WAY.
THOSE FEELINGS WILL BE ENGRAVED IN THE DEEPEST PART OF OUR HEARTS.
SO EVEN WITHOUT OUR MEMORIES...
...I'M SURE IT WILL BE OKAY.
SHE'S RIGHT. NO ONE CAN TAKE YOUR EXPERI-ENCES FROM YOU. SO NO ONE CAN TAKE AWAY WHO YOU'VE BECOME.
IF MEETINGS CHANGE YOU... THEN THE CHANGED VERSIONS OF US ARE ALREADY HERE.
EVEN IF WE DON'T REMEMBER THE MEETING ITSELF.
YES... I BELIEVE THAT, TOO.
...

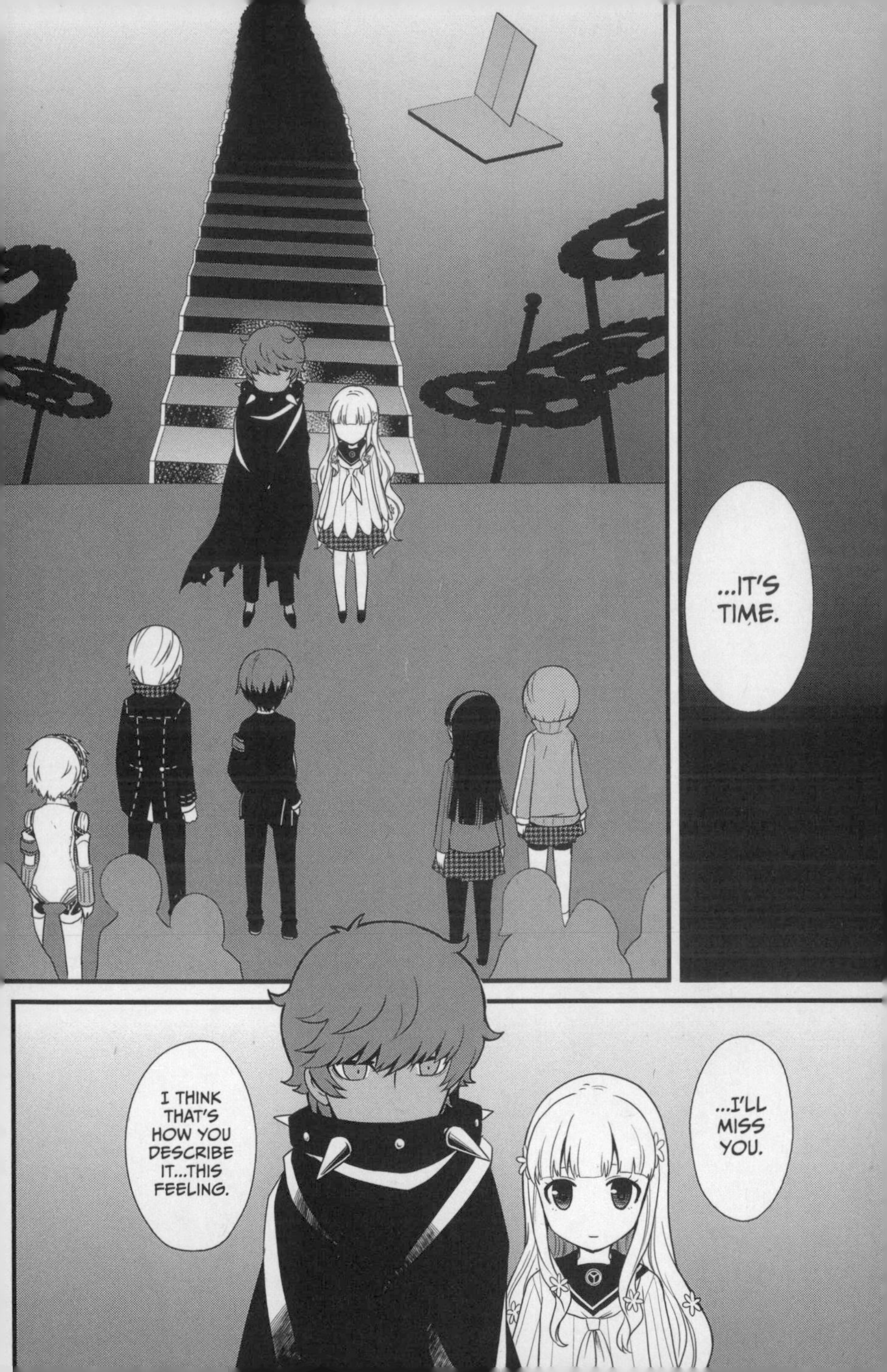
...IT'S TIME.
...I'LL MISS YOU.
I THINK THAT'S HOW YOU DESCRIBE IT...THIS FEELING.

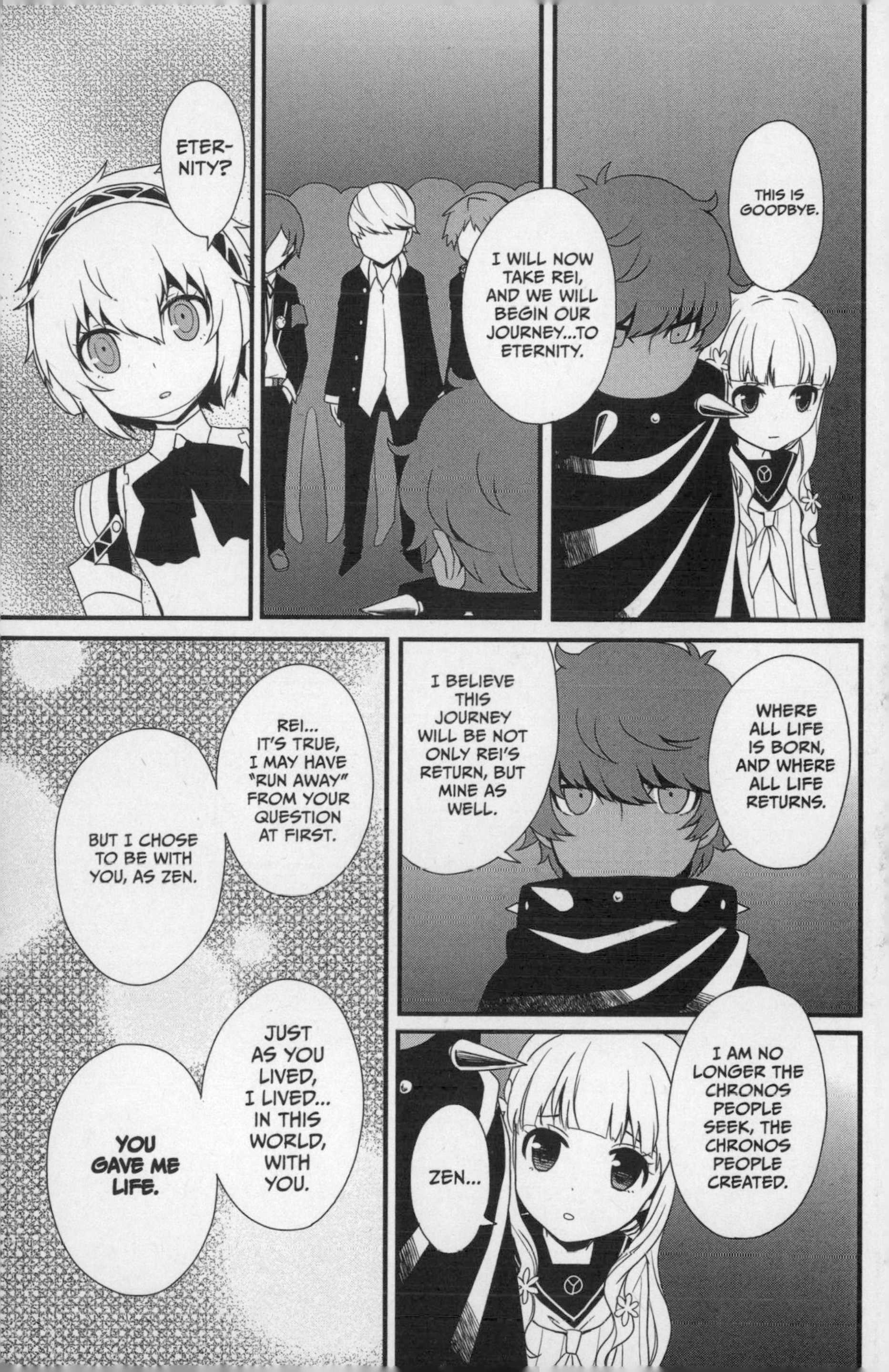
THIS IS GOODBYE.
I WILL NOW TAKE REI, AND WE WILL BEGIN OUR JOURNEY...TO ETERNITY.
ETER-NITY?
WHERE ALL LIFE IS BORN, AND WHERE ALL LIFE RETURNS.
I BELIEVE THIS JOURNEY WILL BE NOT ONLY REI'S RETURN, BUT MINE AS WELL.
I AM NO LONGER THE CHRONOS PEOPLE SEEK, THE CHRONOS PEOPLE CREATED.
ZEN...
REI... IT'S TRUE, I MAY HAVE "RUN AWAY" FROM YOUR QUESTION AT FIRST.
BUT I CHOSE TO BE WITH YOU, AS ZEN.
JUST AS YOU LIVED, I LIVED... IN THIS WORLD, WITH YOU.
YOU GAVE ME LIFE.

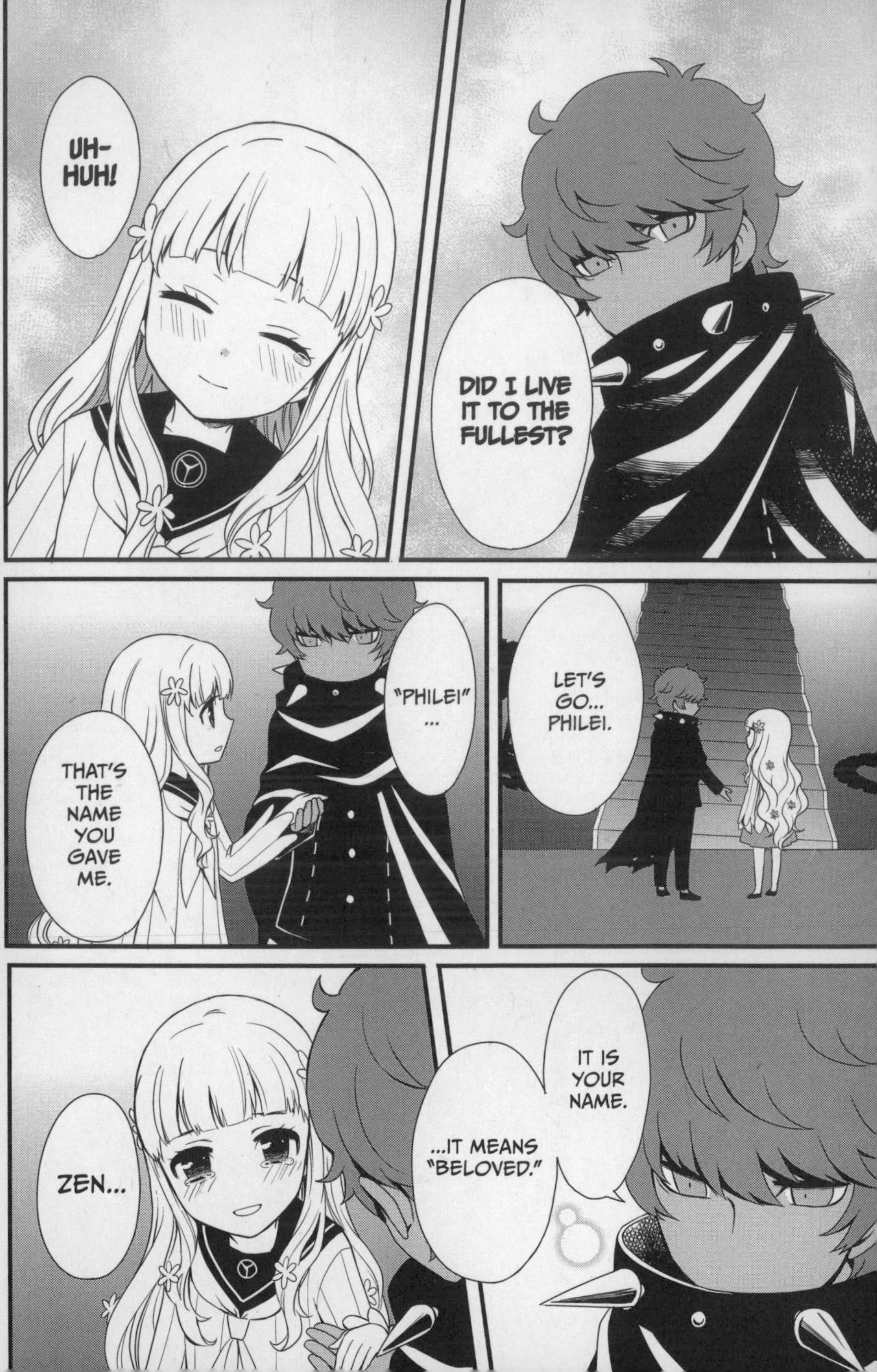
DID I LIVE IT TO THE FULLEST?
UH-HUH!
LET'S GO... PHILEI.
"PHILEI" ...
THAT'S THE NAME YOU GAVE ME.
IT IS YOUR NAME.
...IT MEANS "BELOVED."
ZEN...

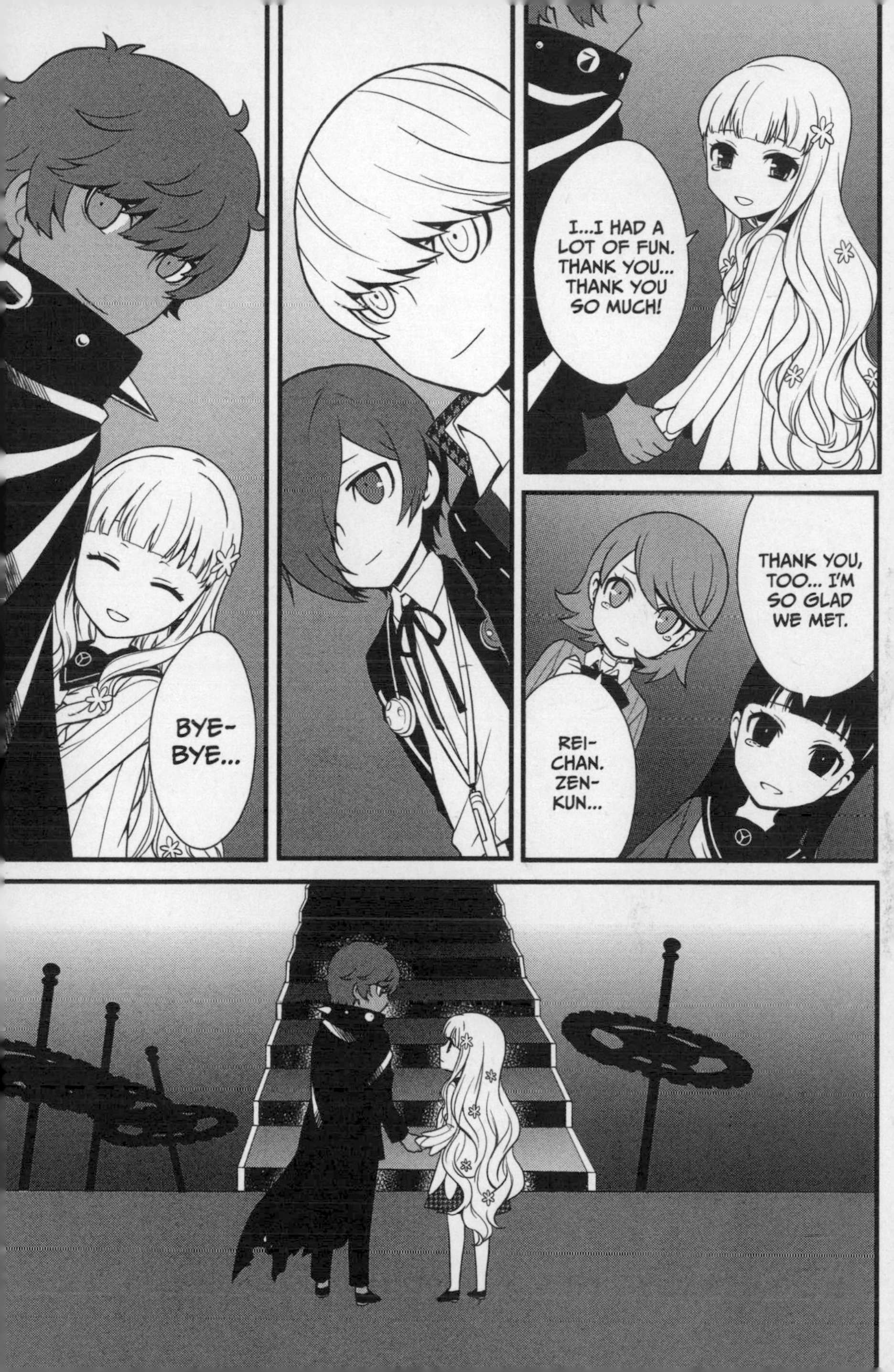
I...I HAD A LOT OF FUN. THANK YOU... THANK YOU SO MUCH!
THANK YOU, TOO... I'M SO GLAD WE MET.
REI-CHAN. ZEN-KUN...
BYE-BYE...

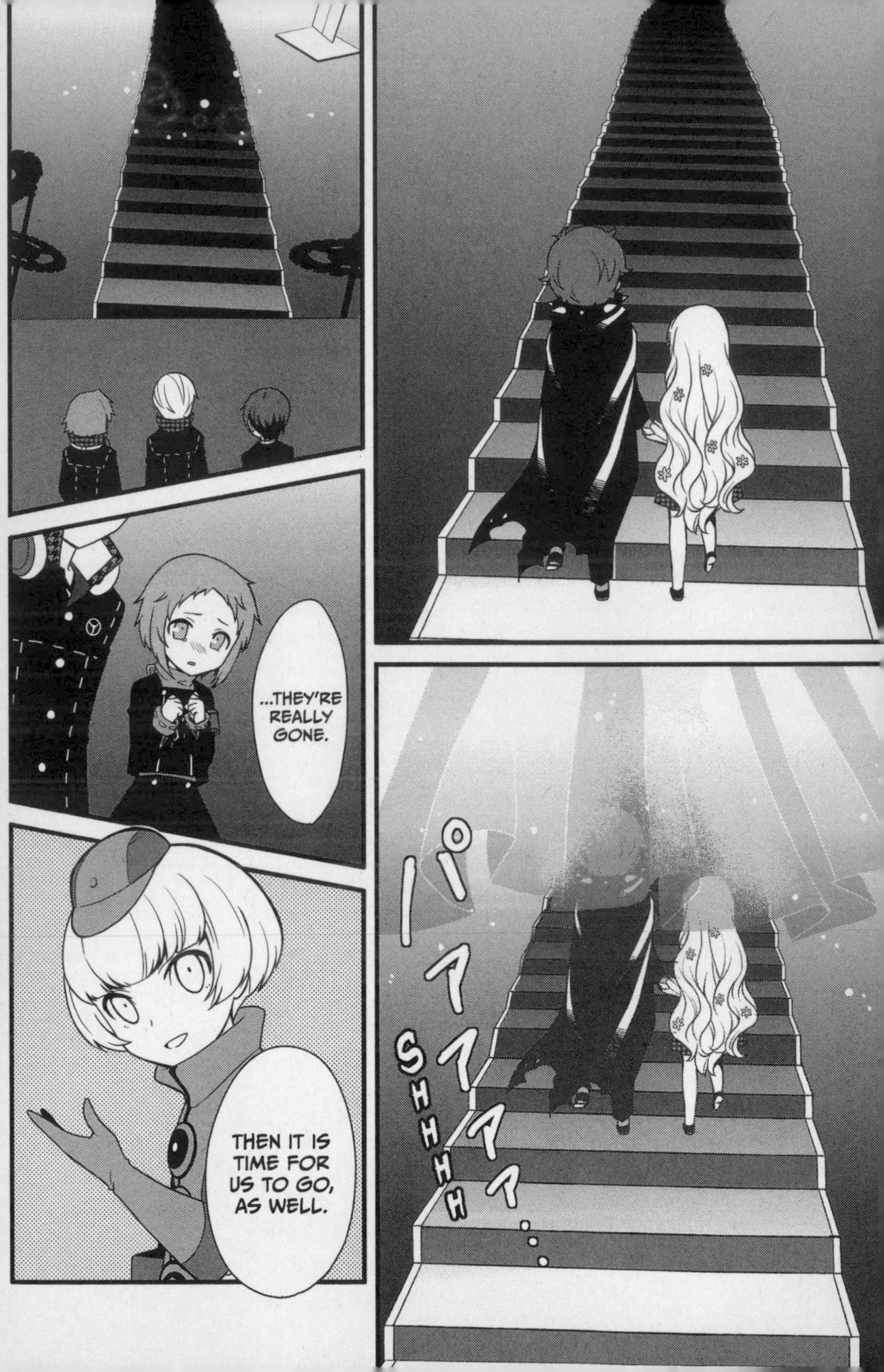
パーアアアア
SHHHHH
...THEY'RE REALLY GONE.
THEN IT IS TIME FOR US TO GO, AS WELL.

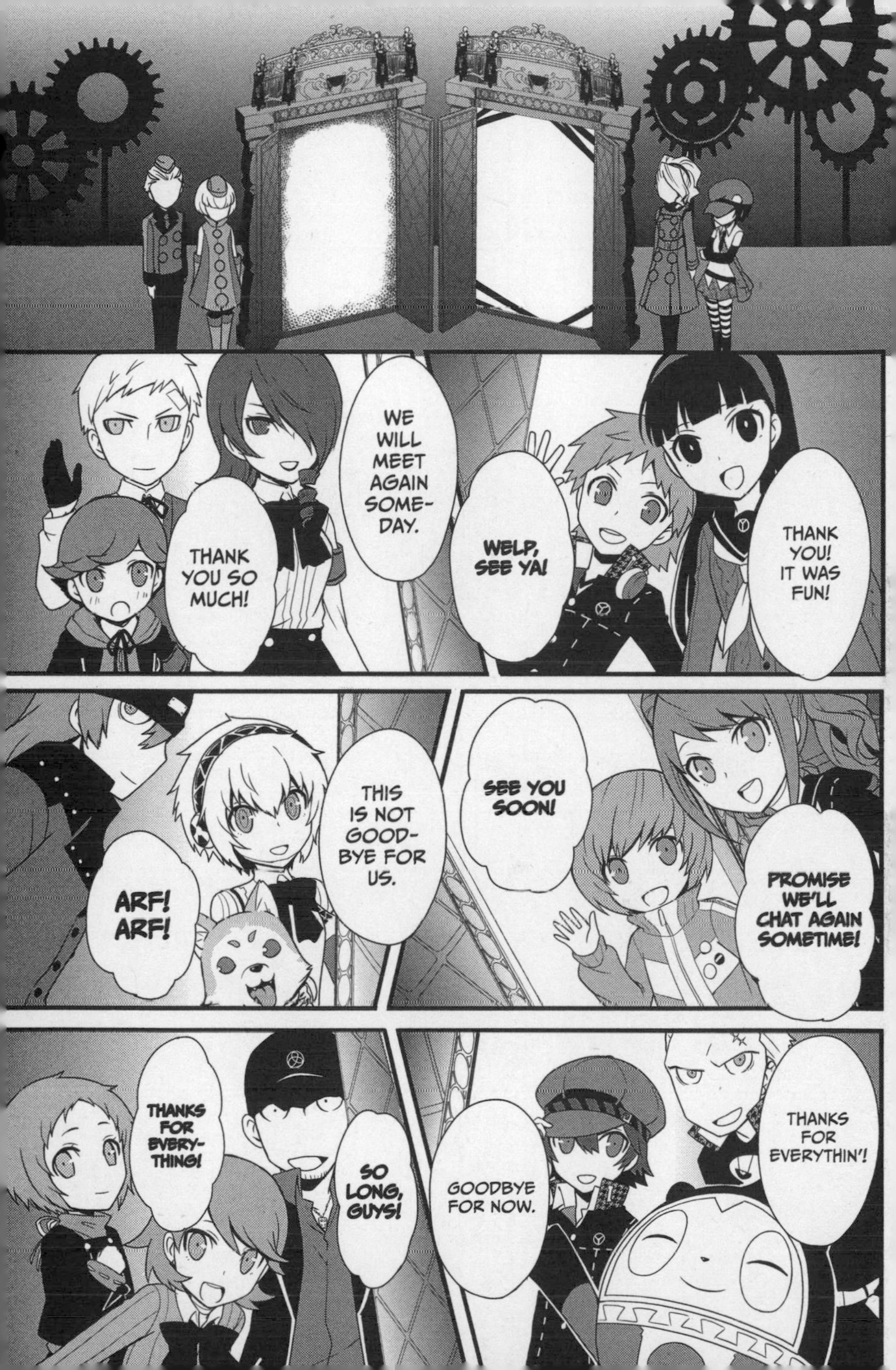
THANK YOU! IT WAS FUN!
WELP, SEE YA!
WE WILL MEET AGAIN SOME-DAY.
THANK YOU SO MUCH!
PROMISE WE'LL CHAT AGAIN SOMETIME!
SEE YOU SOON!
THIS IS NOT GOOD-BYE FOR US.
ARF! ARF!
THANKS FOR EVERYTHIN'!
GOODBYE FOR NOW.
SO LONG, GUYS!
THANKS FOR EVERY-THING!

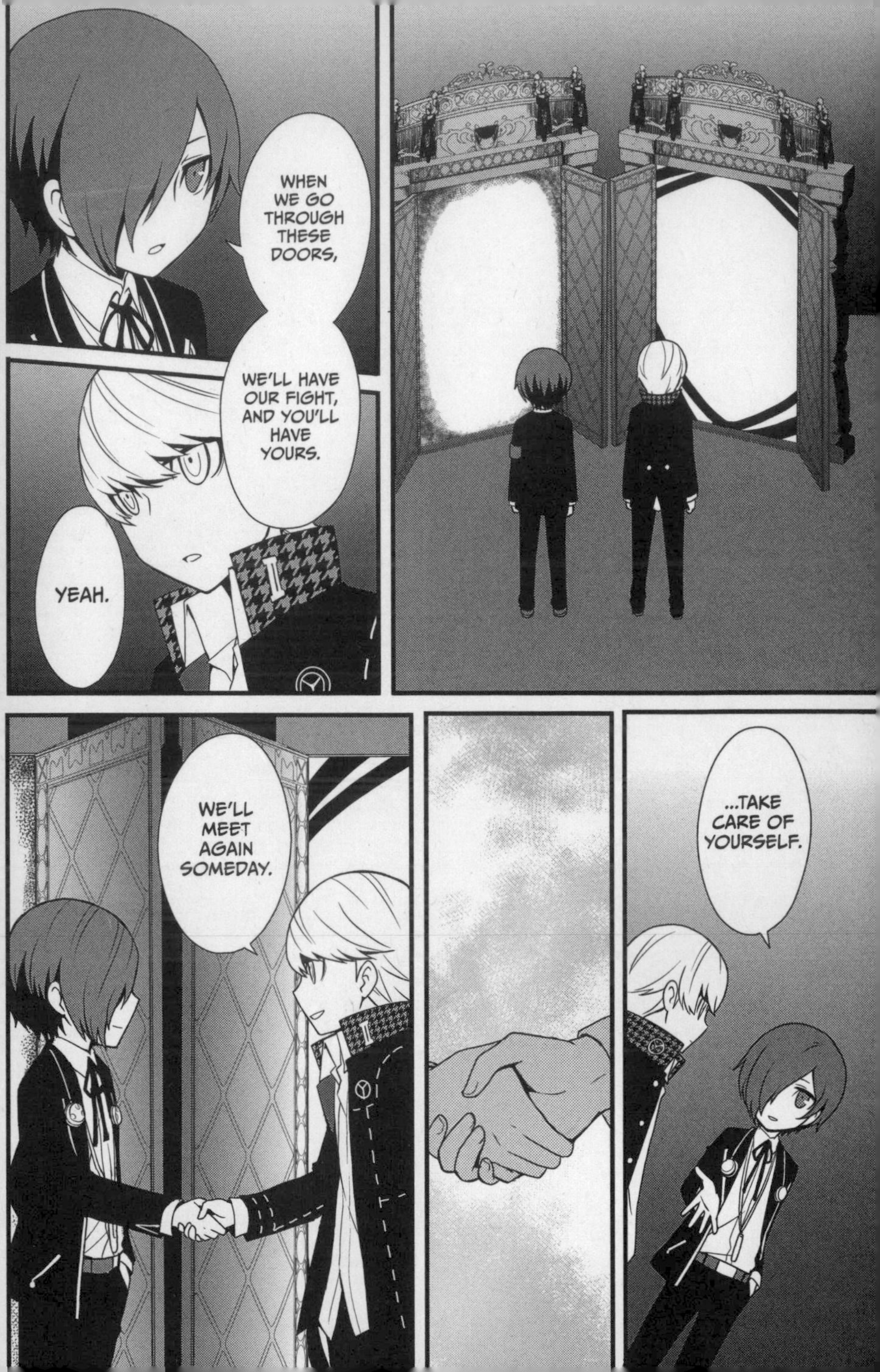
WHEN WE GO THROUGH THESE DOORS,
WE'LL HAVE OUR FIGHT, AND YOU'LL HAVE YOURS.
YEAH.
...TAKE CARE OF YOURSELF.
WE'LL MEET AGAIN SOMEDAY.

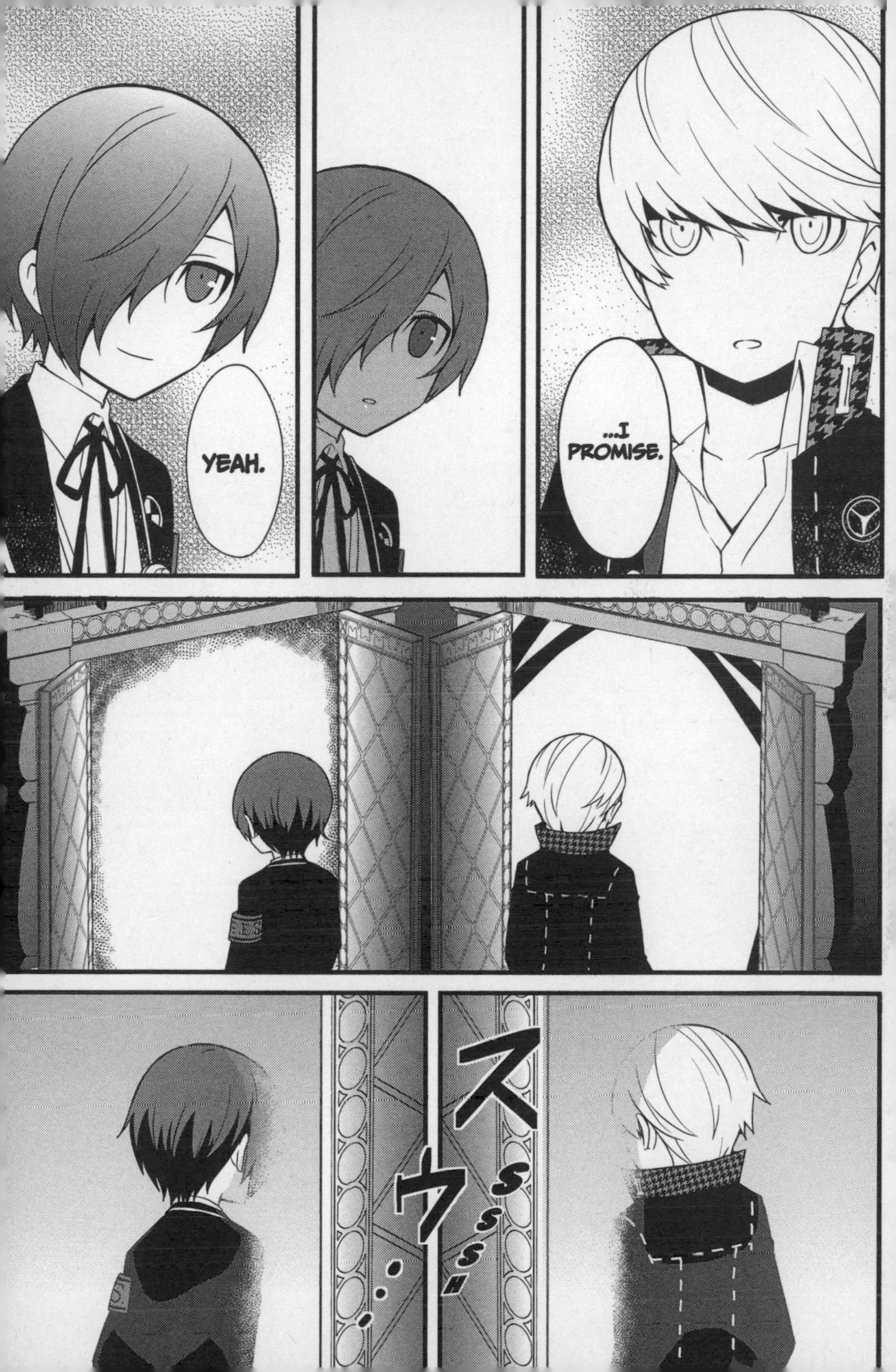
...I PROMISE.
YEAH.
スウ…
SSSH

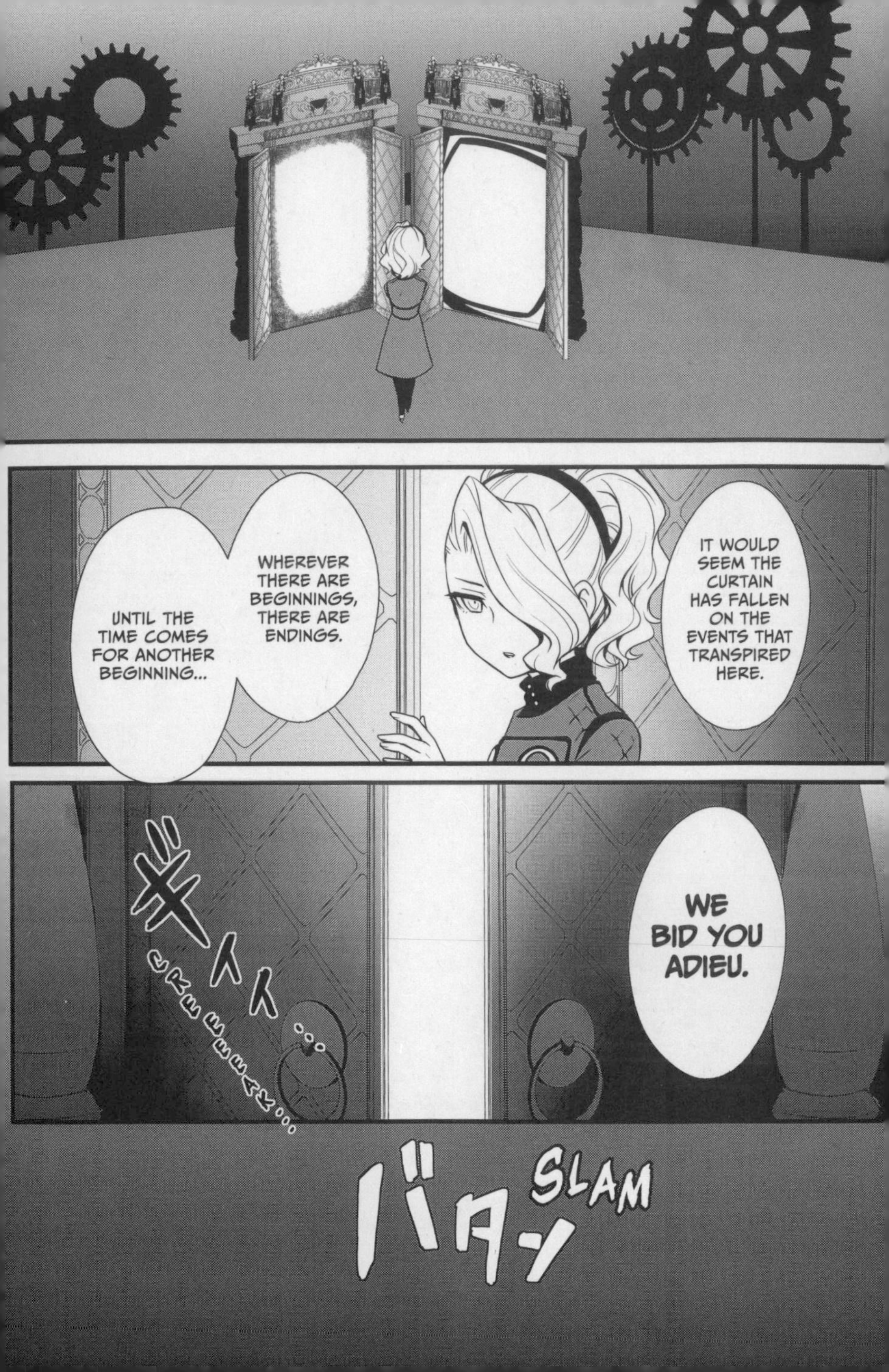
IT WOULD SEEM THE CURTAIN HAS FALLEN ON THE EVENTS THAT TRANSPIRED HERE.
WHEREVER THERE ARE BEGINNINGS, THERE ARE ENDINGS.
UNTIL THE TIME COMES FOR ANOTHER BEGINNING...
WE BID YOU ADIEU.
ギィィ…
CREEEEAK...
バタン
SLAM

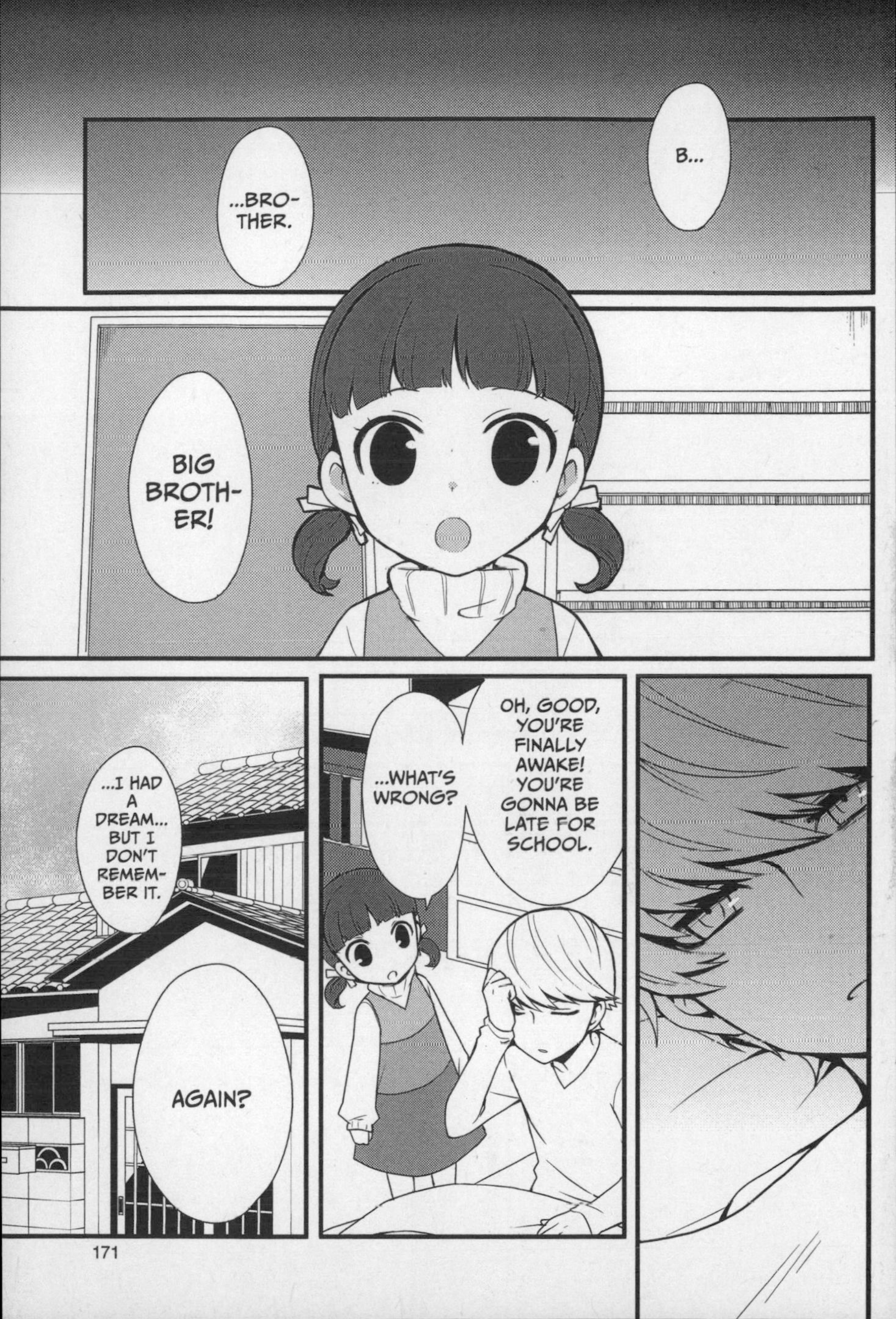
B...
...BROTHER.
BIG BROTHER!
OH, GOOD, YOU'RE FINALLY AWAKE! YOU'RE GONNA BE LATE FOR SCHOOL.
...WHAT'S WRONG?
...I HAD A DREAM... BUT I DON'T REMEMBER IT.
AGAIN?

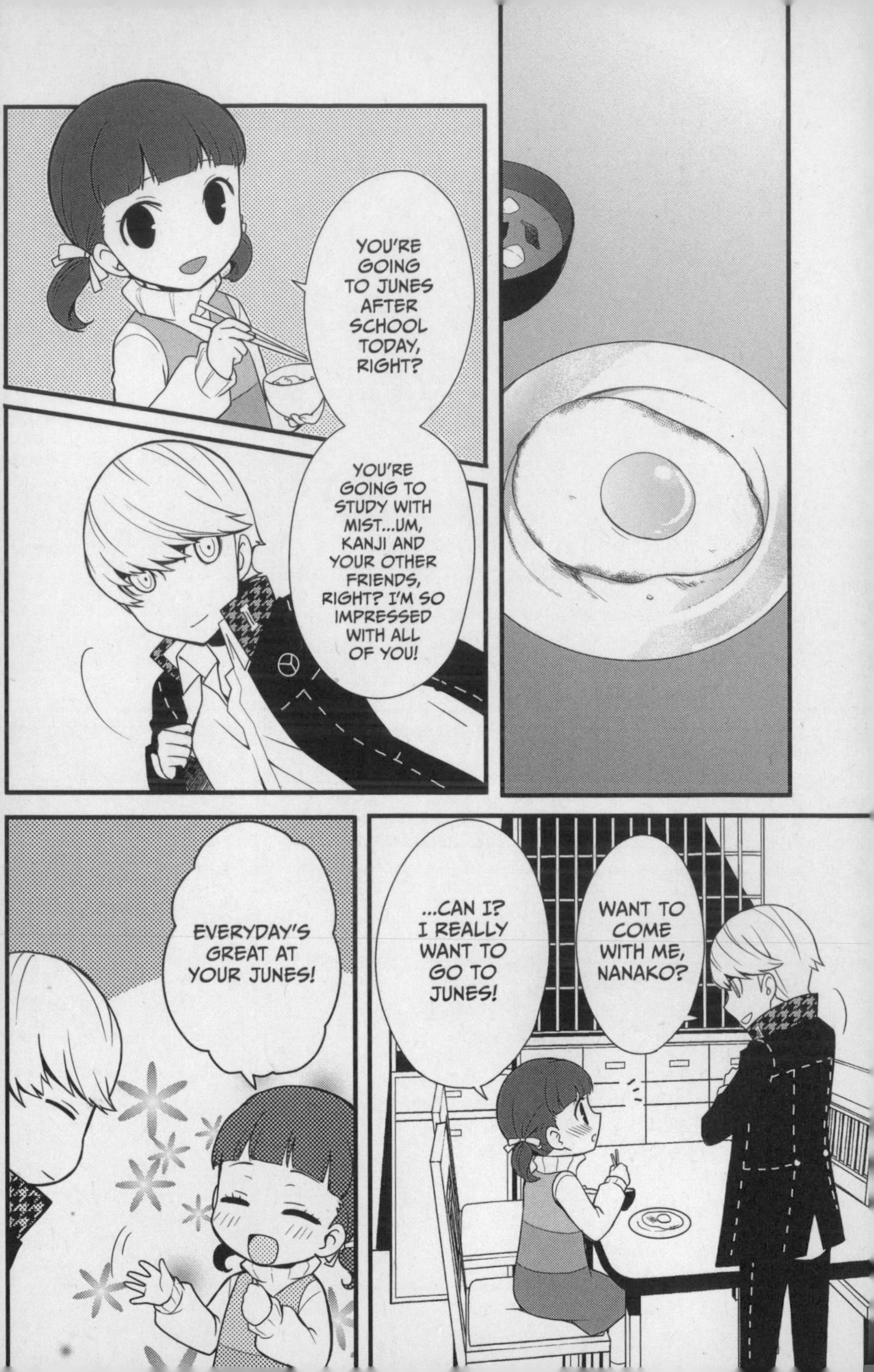
YOU'RE GOING TO JUNES AFTER SCHOOL TODAY, RIGHT?
YOU'RE GOING TO STUDY WITH MIST...UM, KANJI AND YOUR OTHER FRIENDS, RIGHT? I'M SO IMPRESSED WITH ALL OF YOU!
WANT TO COME WITH ME, NANAKO?
...CAN I? I REALLY WANT TO GO TO JUNES!
EVERYDAY'S GREAT AT YOUR JUNES!

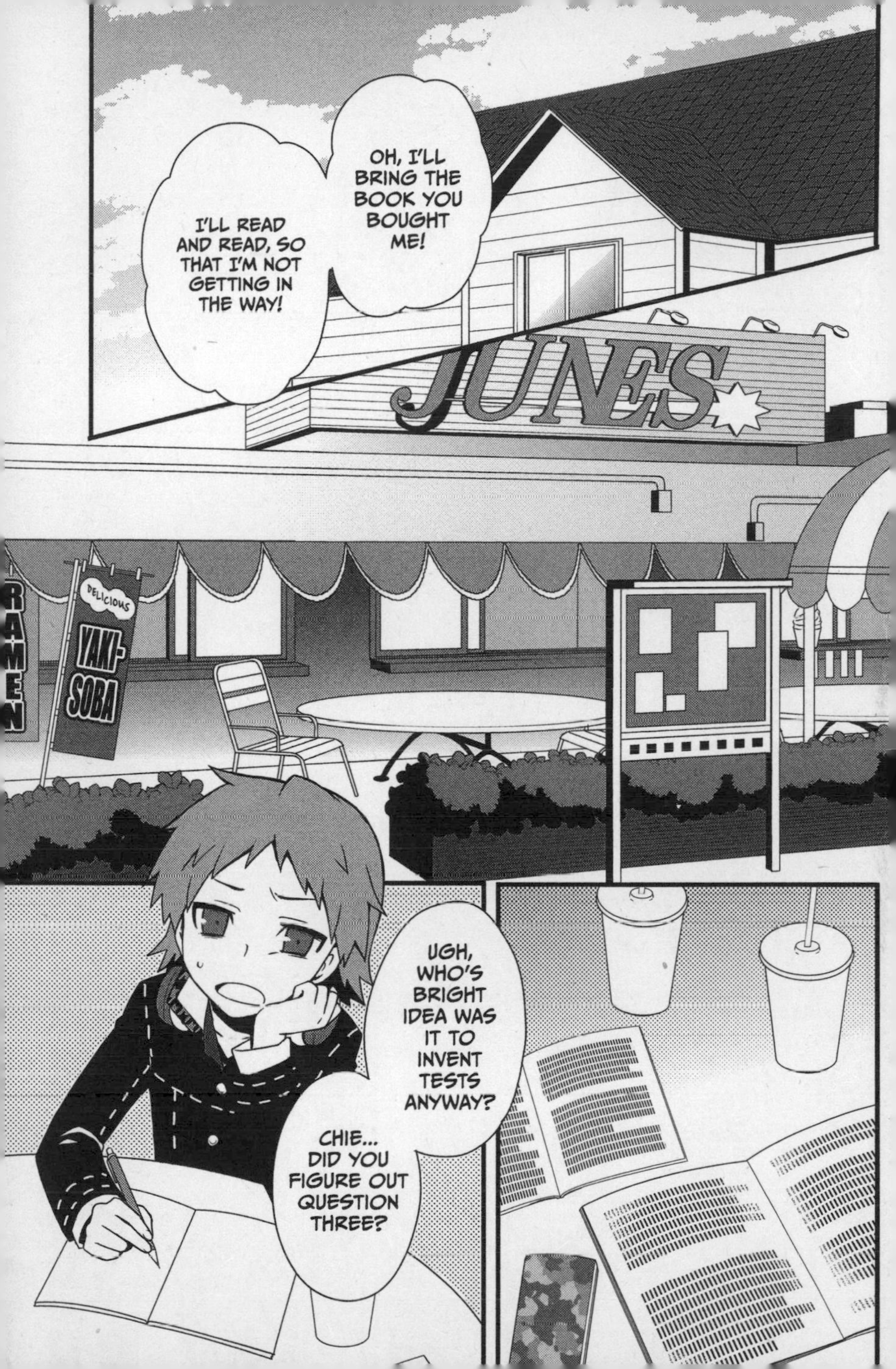
OH, I'LL BRING THE BOOK YOU BOUGHT ME!
I'LL READ AND READ, SO THAT I'M NOT GETTING IN THE WAY!
JUNES
RAMEN
DELICIOUS
YAKI-SOBA
UGH, WHO'S BRIGHT IDEA WAS IT TO INVENT TESTS ANYWAY?
CHIE... DID YOU FIGURE OUT QUESTION THREE?

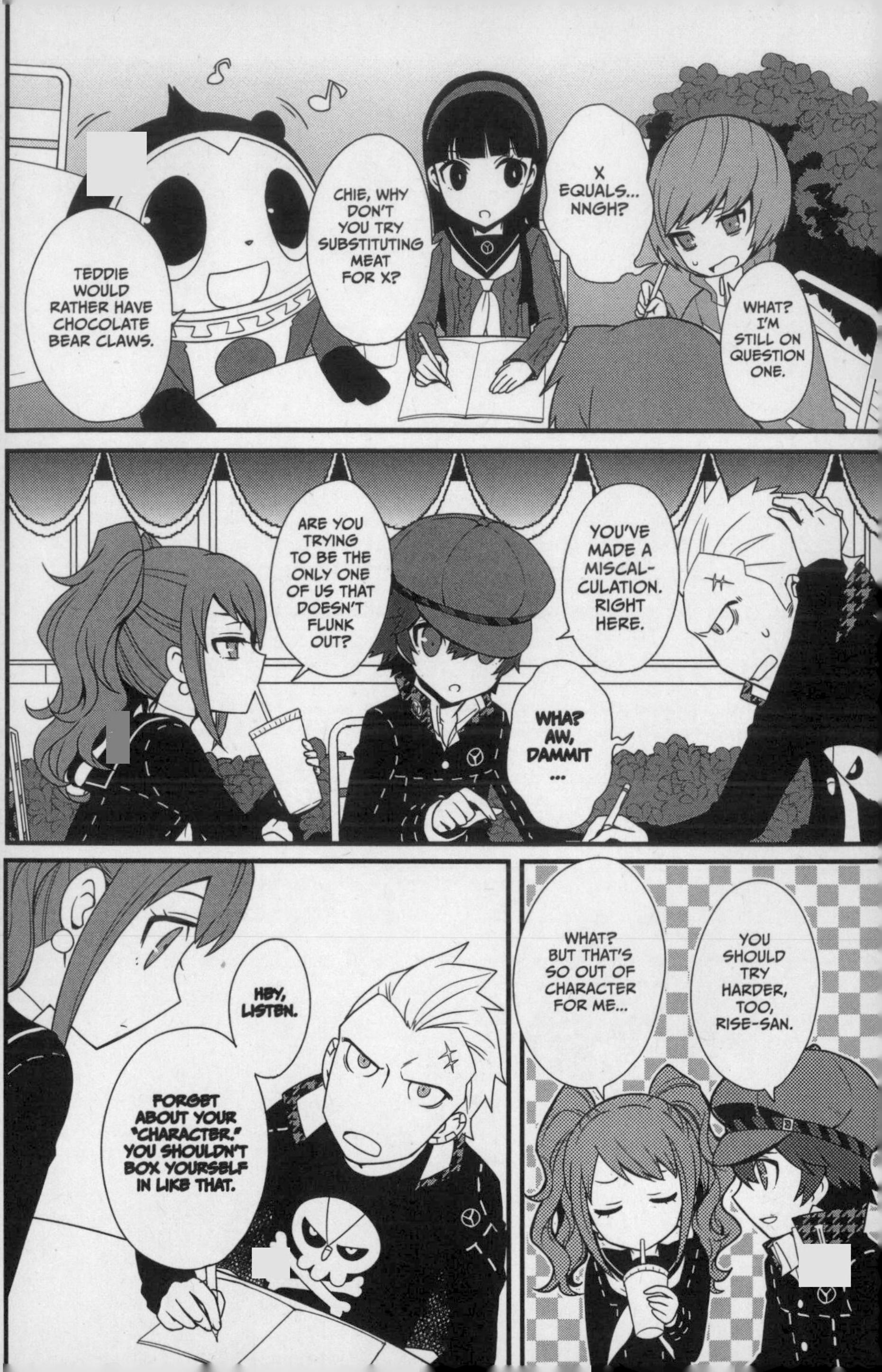
X EQUALS... NNGH?
WHAT? I'M STILL ON QUESTION ONE.
CHIE, WHY DON'T YOU TRY SUBSTITUTING MEAT FOR X?
TEDDIE WOULD RATHER HAVE CHOCOLATE BEAR CLAWS.
YOU'VE MADE A MISCAL-CULATION. RIGHT HERE.
WHA? AW, DAMMIT ...
ARE YOU TRYING TO BE THE ONLY ONE OF US THAT DOESN'T FLUNK OUT?
YOU SHOULD TRY HARDER, TOO, RISE-SAN.
WHAT? BUT THAT'S SO OUT OF CHARACTER FOR ME...
HEY, LISTEN.
FORGET ABOUT YOUR "CHARACTER." YOU SHOULDN'T BOX YOURSELF IN LIKE THAT.

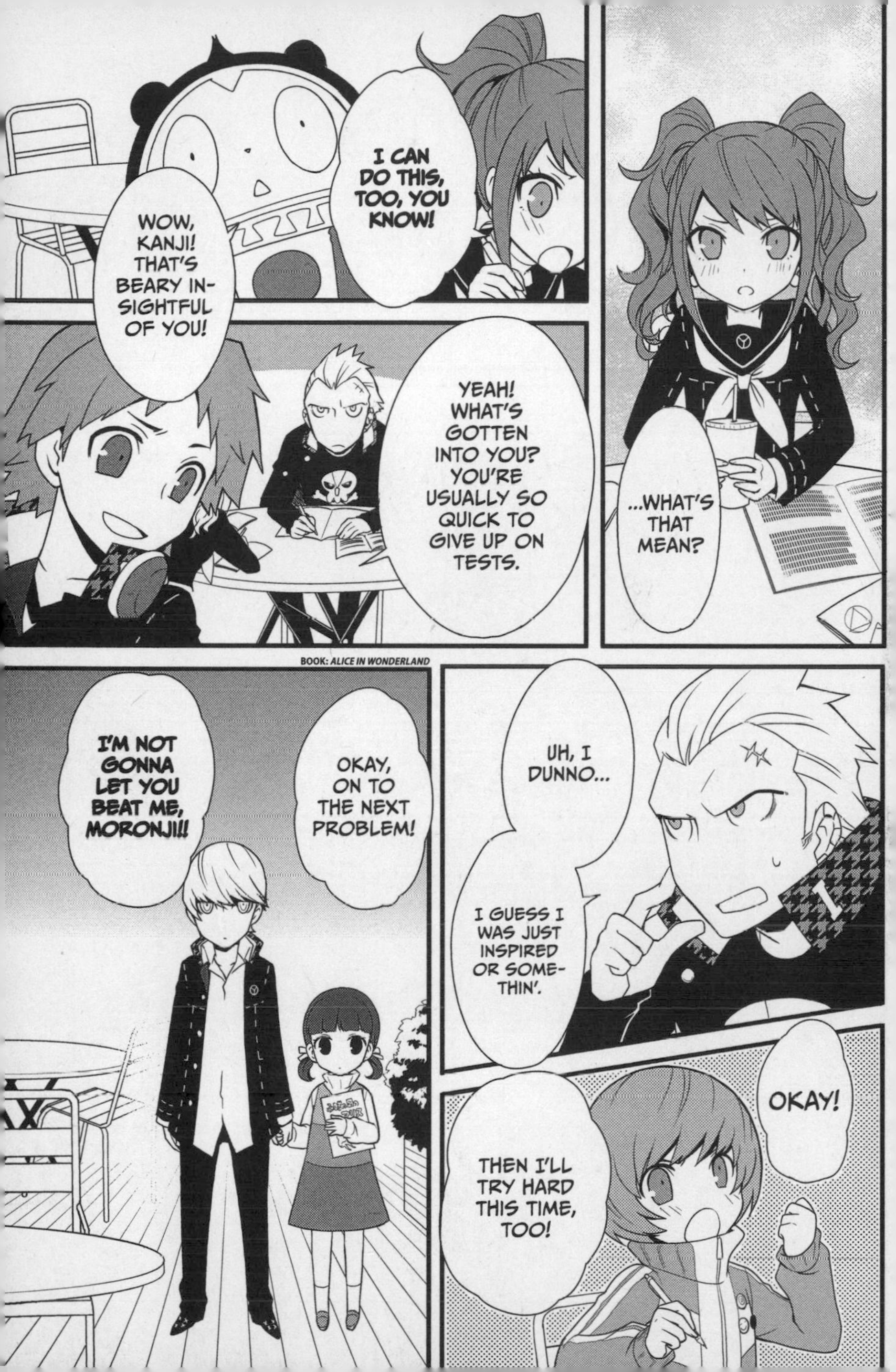
...WHAT'S THAT MEAN?
I CAN DO THIS, TOO, YOU KNOW!
WOW, KANJI! THAT'S BEARY IN-SIGHTFUL OF YOU!
YEAH! WHAT'S GOTTEN INTO YOU? YOU'RE USUALLY SO QUICK TO GIVE UP ON TESTS.
UH, I DUNNO...
I GUESS I WAS JUST INSPIRED OR SOME-THIN'.
OKAY!
THEN I'LL TRY HARD THIS TIME, TOO!
BOOK: *ALICE IN WONDERLAND*
OKAY, ON TO THE NEXT PROBLEM!
I'M NOT GONNA LET YOU BEAT ME, MORONJI!!

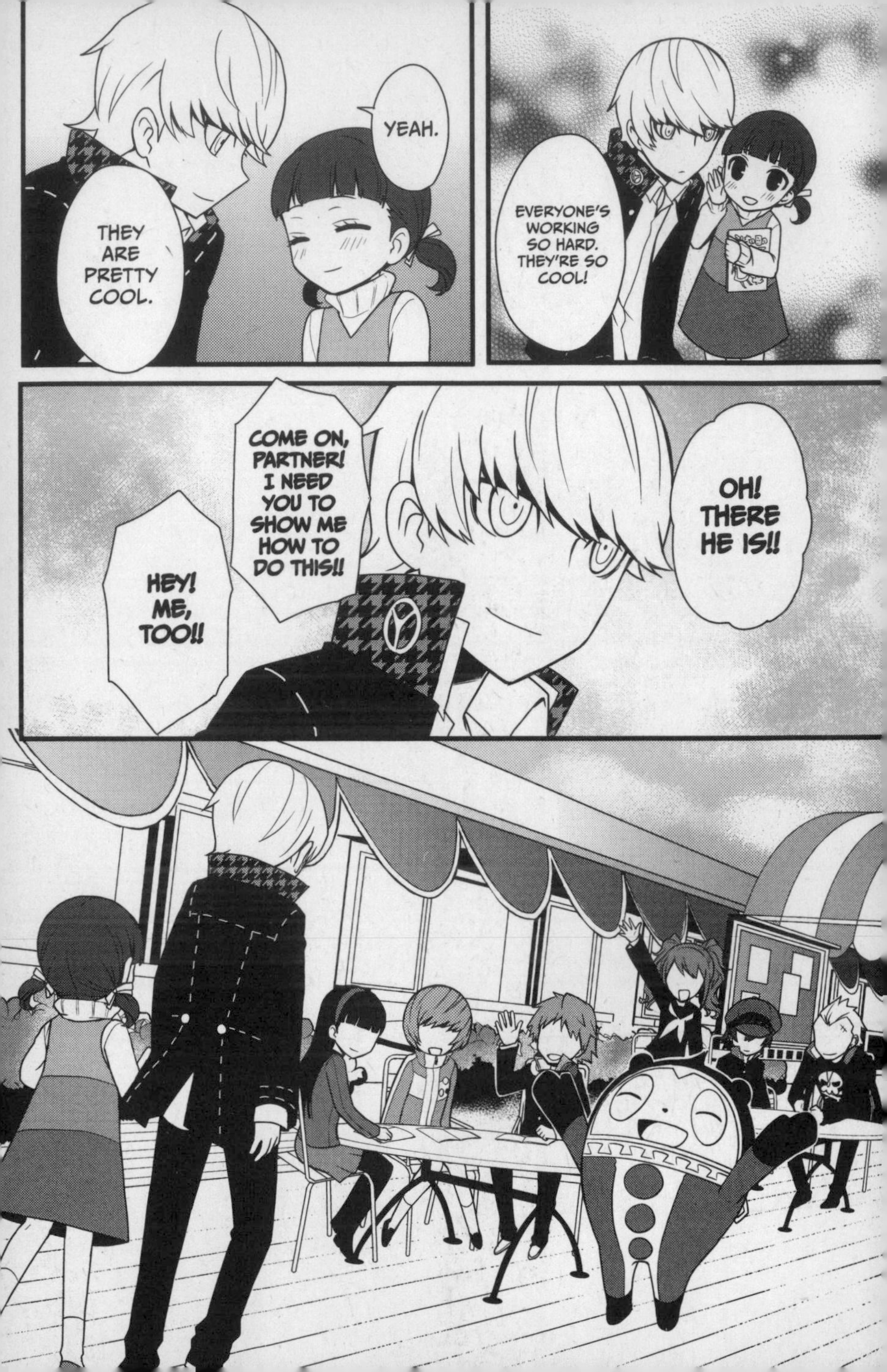
EVERYONE'S WORKING SO HARD. THEY'RE SO COOL!
YEAH.
THEY ARE PRETTY COOL.
OH! THERE HE IS!!
COME ON, PARTNER! I NEED YOU TO SHOW ME HOW TO DO THIS!!
HEY! ME, TOO!!

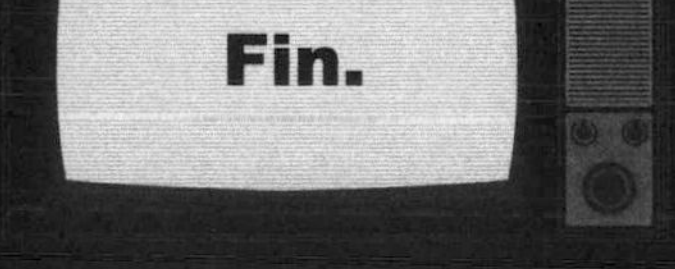
Fin.

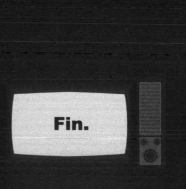

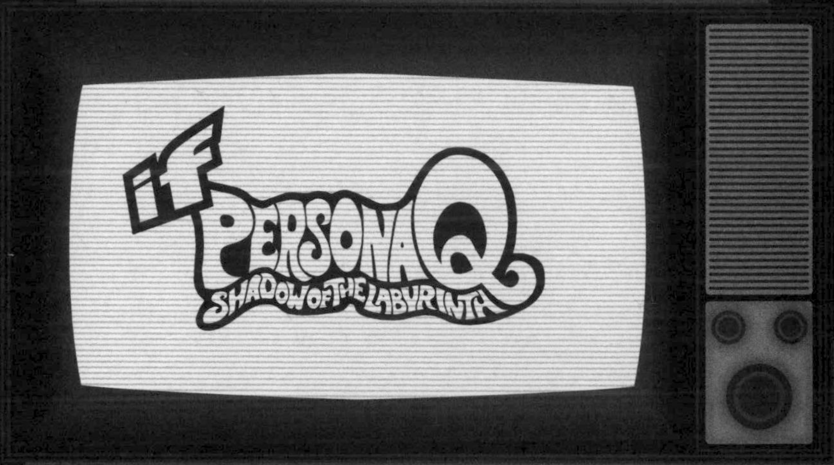
if
PERSONA Q
SHADOW OF THE LABYRINTH

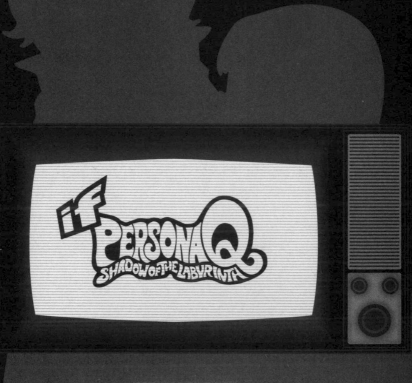

IF REI HAD BEEN HEALTHY,
I'M SURE THAT THE CULTURE FESTIVAL
WOULD NEVER HAVE TURNED INTO THE TWISTED MAZE IT DID.

PERHAPS IT WOULD HAVE BEEN NOT ZEN,
BUT REI WHO STAYED HER HAND.

IT WAS WITH THAT THOUGHT, AND THE HOPE OF WHAT IT
MIGHT BRING,
THAT I PENNED THIS "IF" STORY.

DAISUKE KANEDA

DIRECTOR

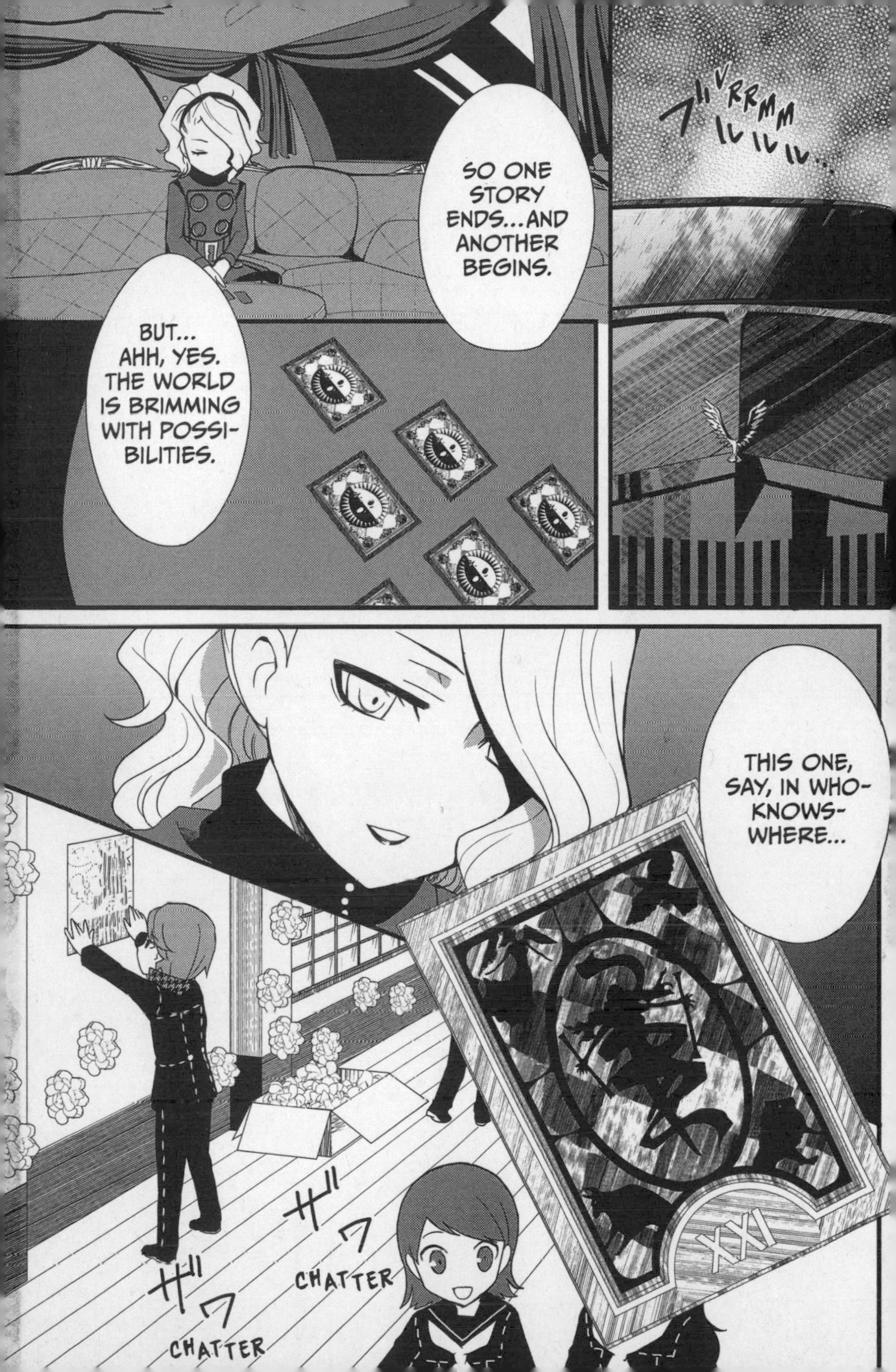
VRRMM
SO ONE STORY ENDS...AND ANOTHER BEGINS.
BUT... AHH, YES. THE WORLD IS BRIMMING WITH POSSIBILITIES.
THIS ONE, SAY, IN WHO-KNOWS-WHERE...
CHATTER
CHATTER

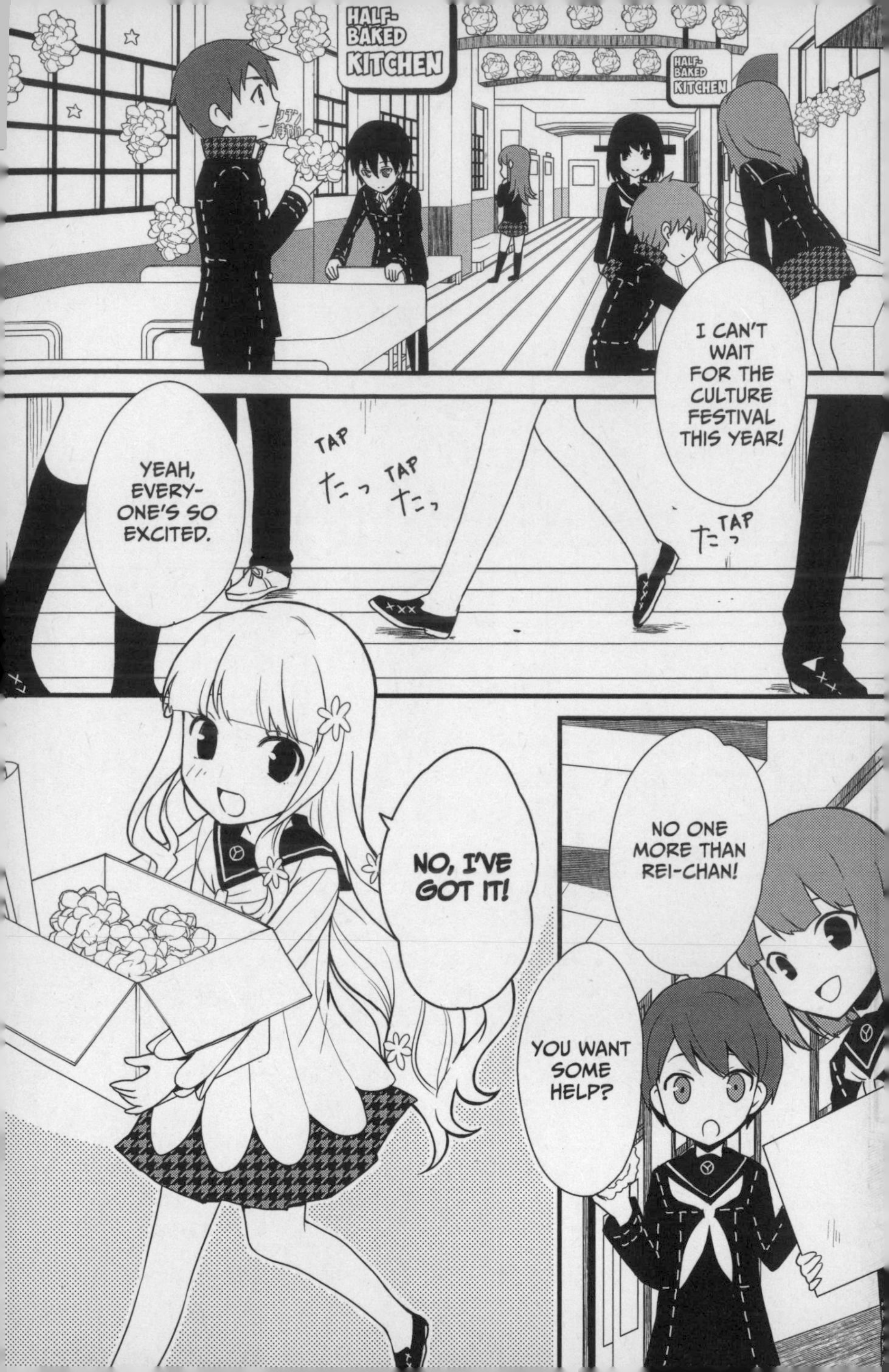
HALF-BAKED KITCHEN
HALF-BAKED KITCHEN
I CAN'T WAIT FOR THE CULTURE FESTIVAL THIS YEAR!
TAP たっ
TAP たっ
TAP たっ
YEAH, EVERY-ONE'S SO EXCITED.
NO ONE MORE THAN REI-CHAN!
YOU WANT SOME HELP?
NO, I'VE GOT IT!

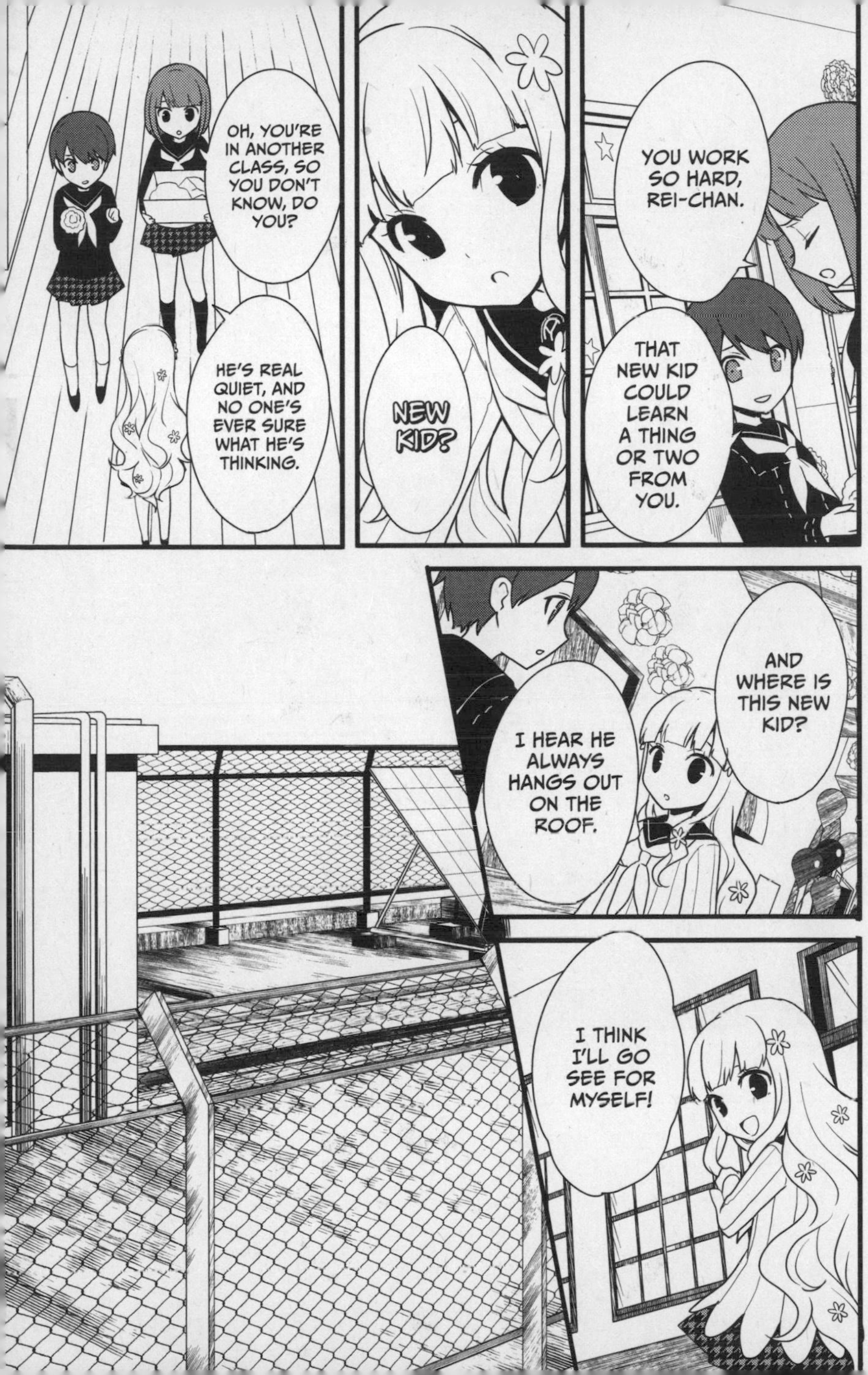

YOU WORK SO HARD, REI-CHAN.
THAT NEW KID COULD LEARN A THING OR TWO FROM YOU.
NEW KID?
OH, YOU'RE IN ANOTHER CLASS, SO YOU DON'T KNOW, DO YOU?
HE'S REAL QUIET, AND NO ONE'S EVER SURE WHAT HE'S THINKING.
AND WHERE IS THIS NEW KID?
I HEAR HE ALWAYS HANGS OUT ON THE ROOF.
I THINK I'LL GO SEE FOR MYSELF!

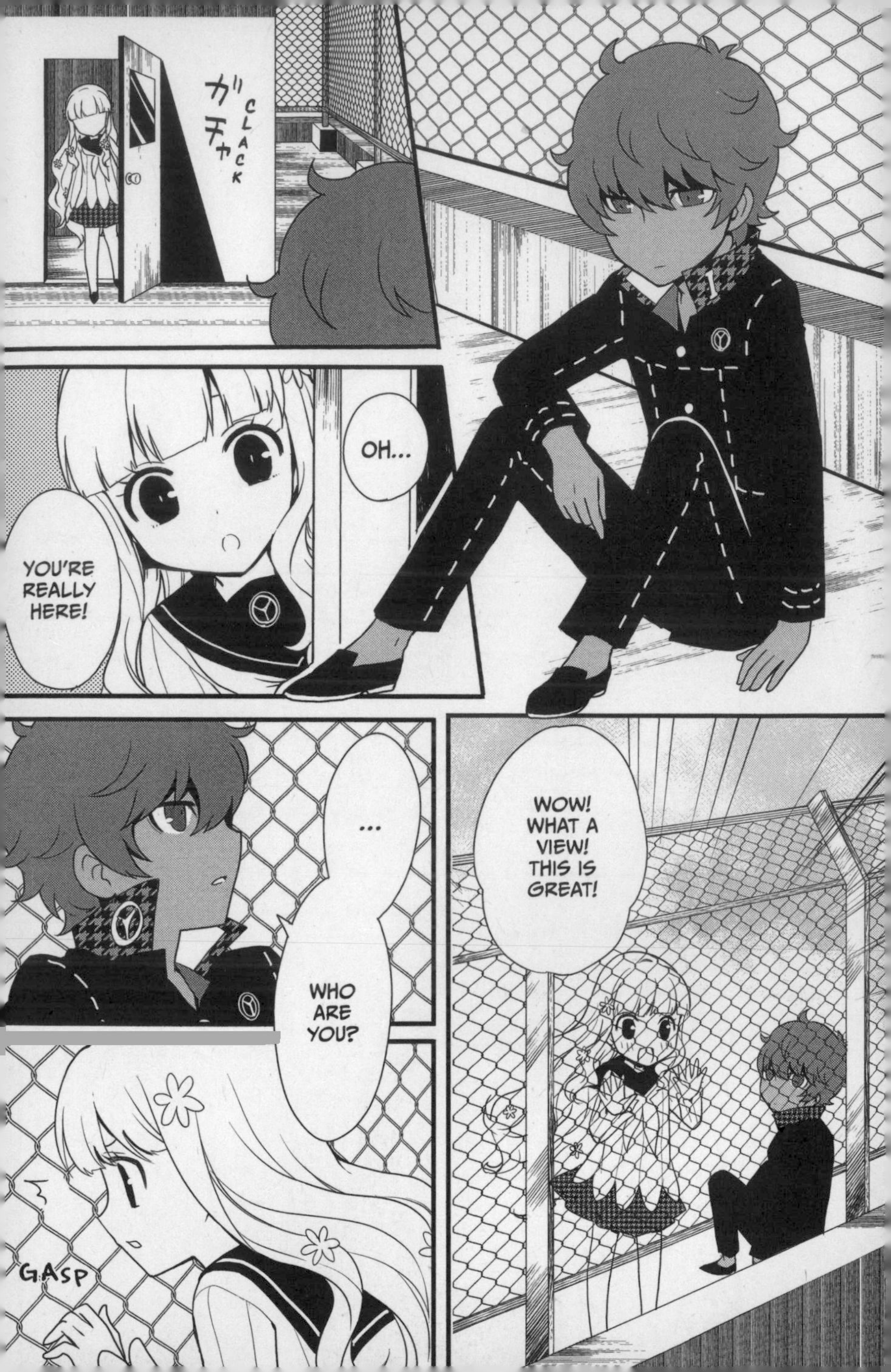
ガチャ
CLACK
OH...
YOU'RE REALLY HERE!
WOW! WHAT A VIEW! THIS IS GREAT!
...
WHO ARE YOU?
GASP

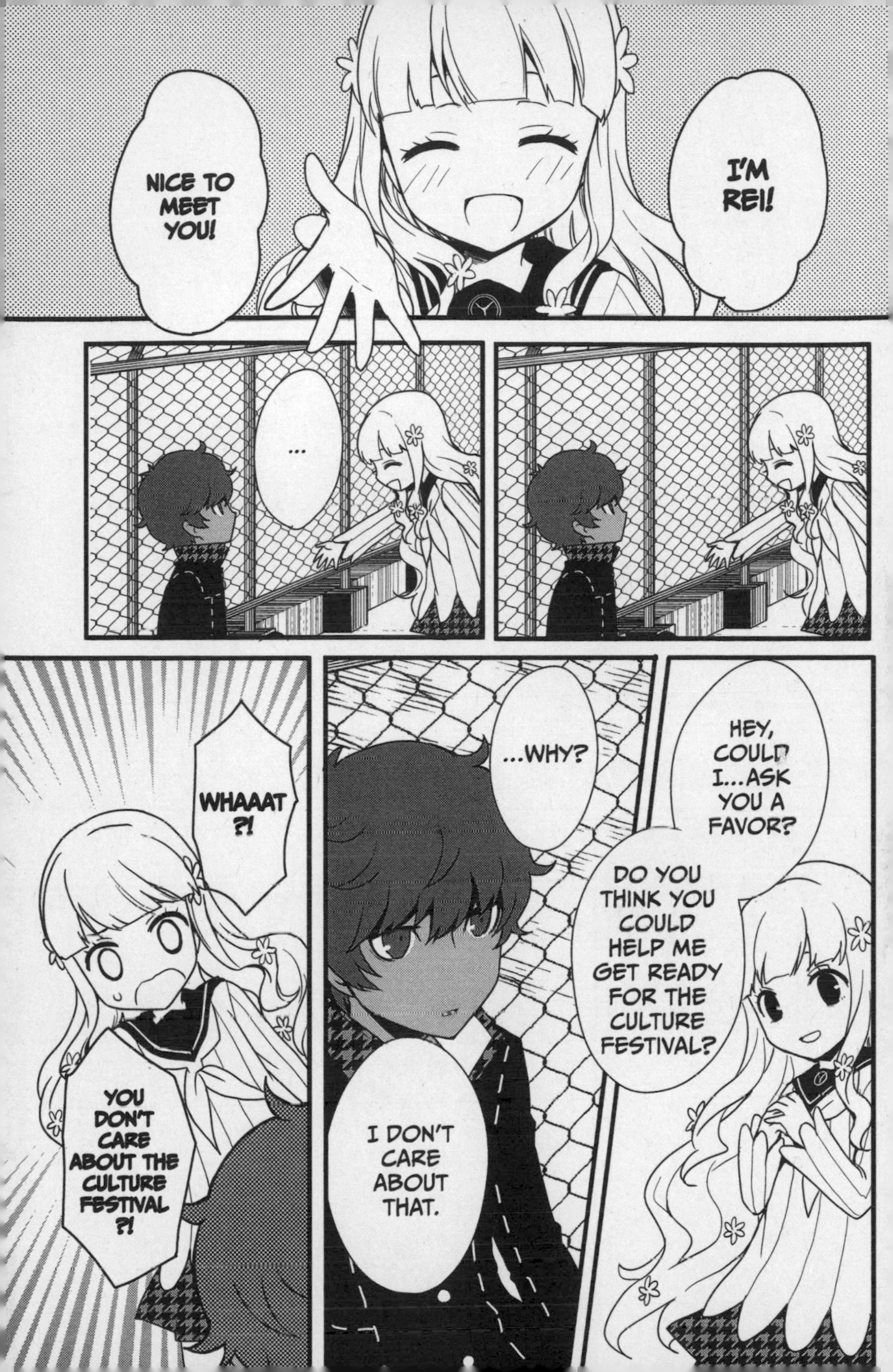
I'M REI!
NICE TO MEET YOU!
...
HEY, COULD I...ASK YOU A FAVOR?
DO YOU THINK YOU COULD HELP ME GET READY FOR THE CULTURE FESTIVAL?
...WHY?
I DON'T CARE ABOUT THAT.
WHAAAT?!
YOU DON'T CARE ABOUT THE CULTURE FESTIVAL?!

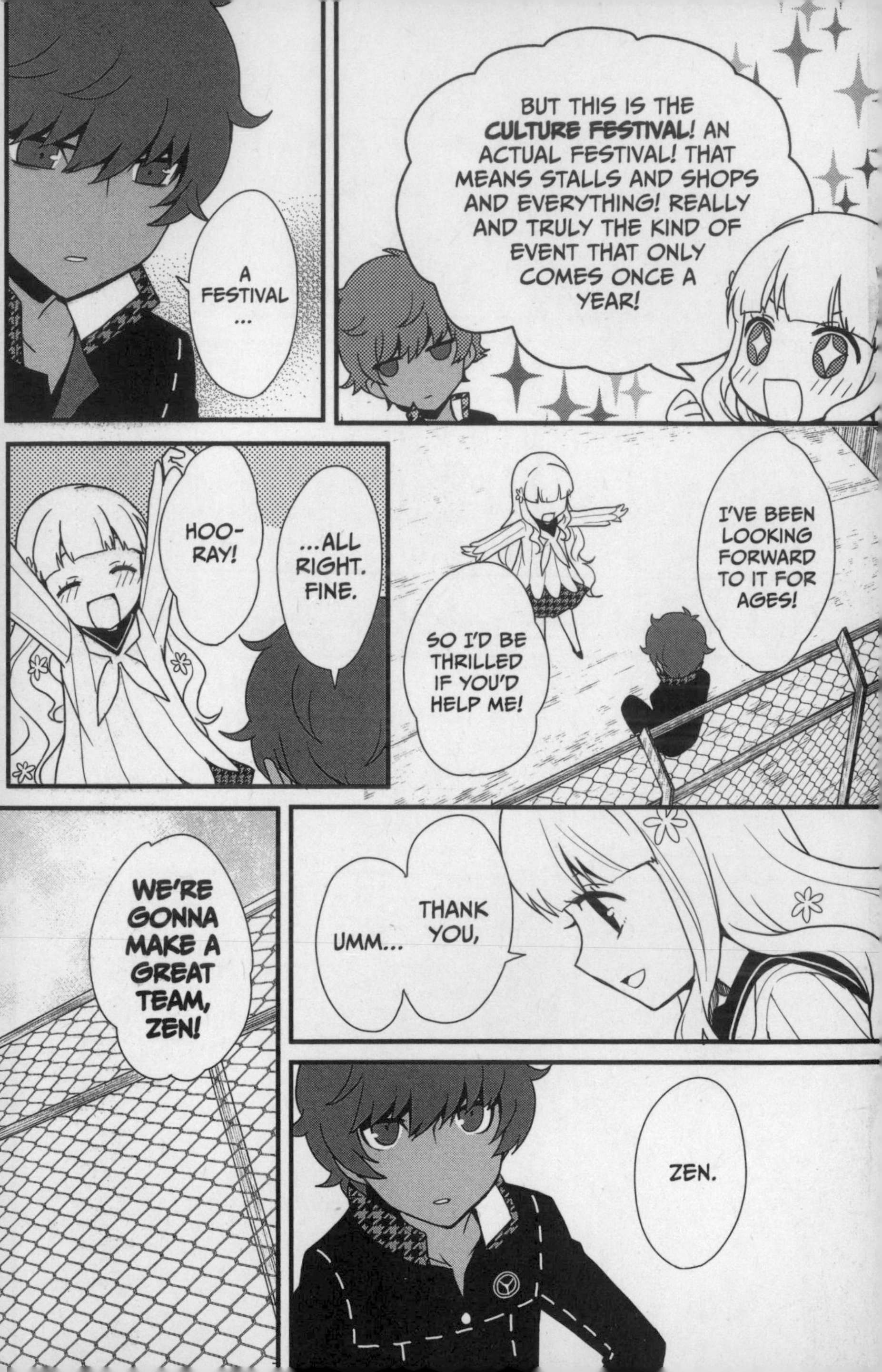
BUT THIS IS THE CULTURE FESTIVAL! AN ACTUAL FESTIVAL! THAT MEANS STALLS AND SHOPS AND EVERYTHING! REALLY AND TRULY THE KIND OF EVENT THAT ONLY COMES ONCE A YEAR!
A FESTIVAL ...
I'VE BEEN LOOKING FORWARD TO IT FOR AGES!
SO I'D BE THRILLED IF YOU'D HELP ME!
...ALL RIGHT. FINE.
HOO-RAY!
THANK YOU,
UMM...
ZEN.
WE'RE GONNA MAKE A GREAT TEAM, ZEN!

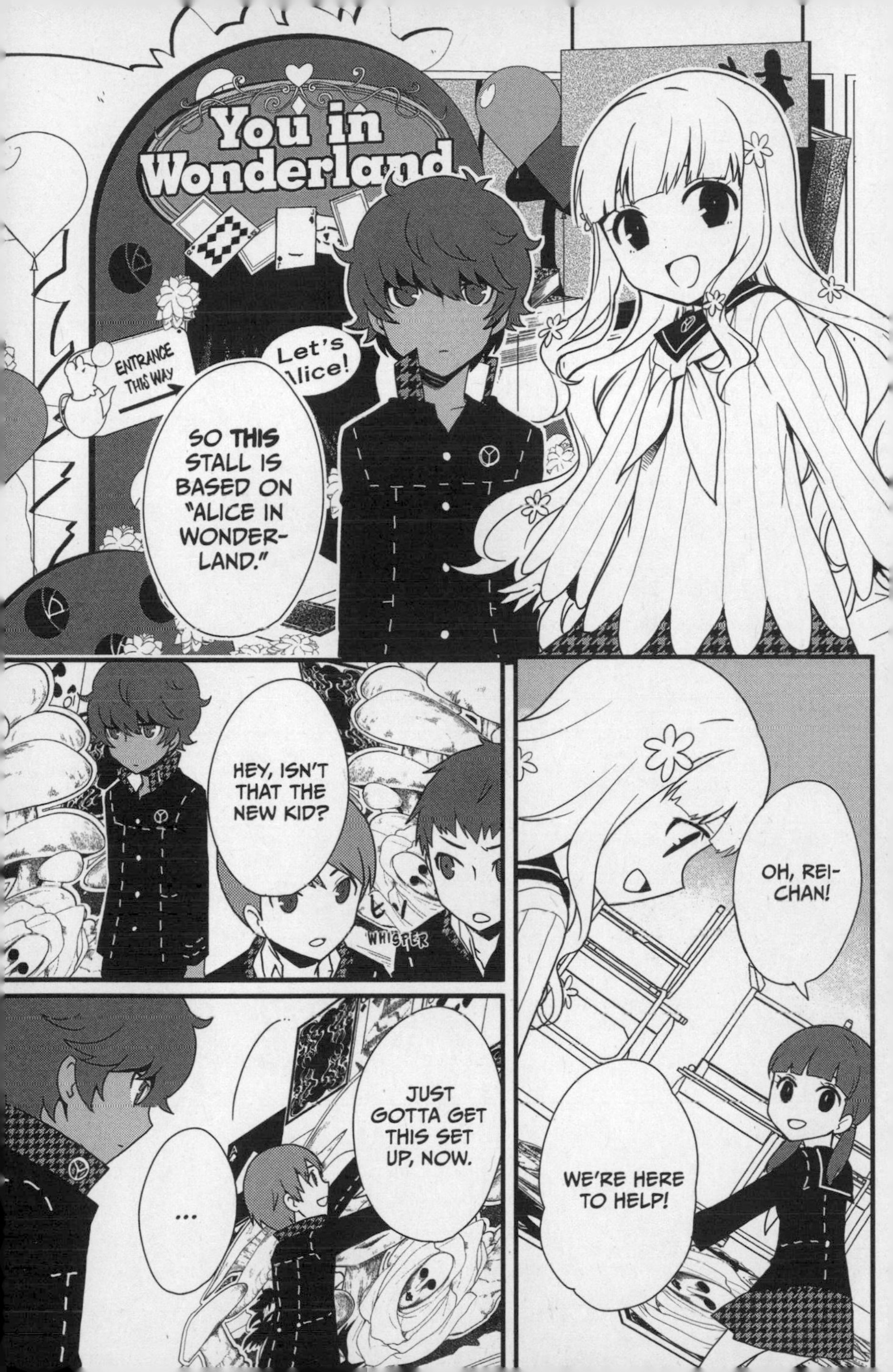
You in Wonderland
ENTRANCE THIS WAY
Let's Alice!
SO THIS STALL IS BASED ON "ALICE IN WONDERLAND."
OH, REI-CHAN!
WE'RE HERE TO HELP!
HEY, ISN'T THAT THE NEW KID?
WHISPER
JUST GOTTA GET THIS SET UP, NOW.
...
...

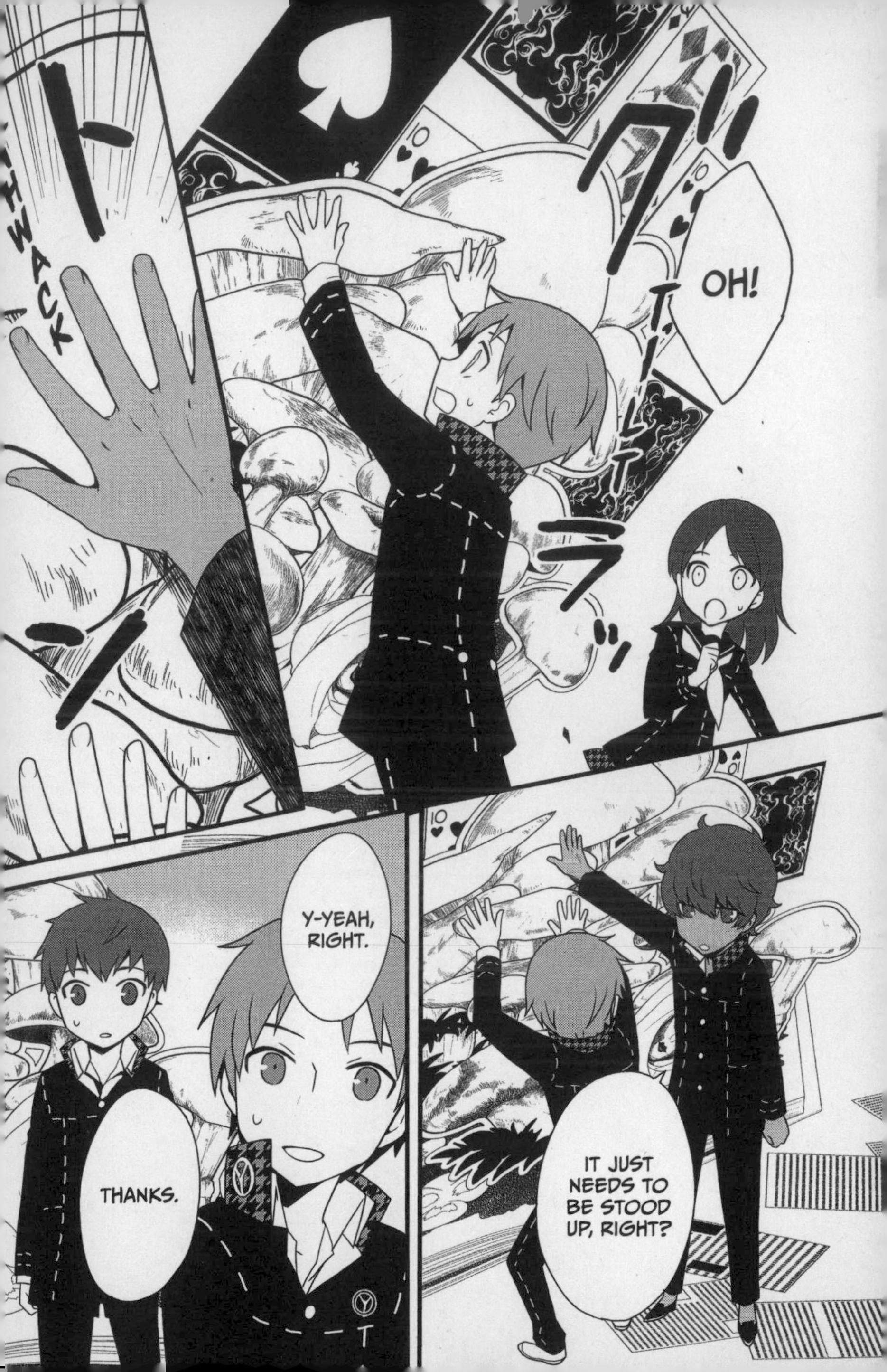
OH!
THWACK
IT JUST NEEDS TO BE STOOD UP, RIGHT?
Y-YEAH, RIGHT.
THANKS.

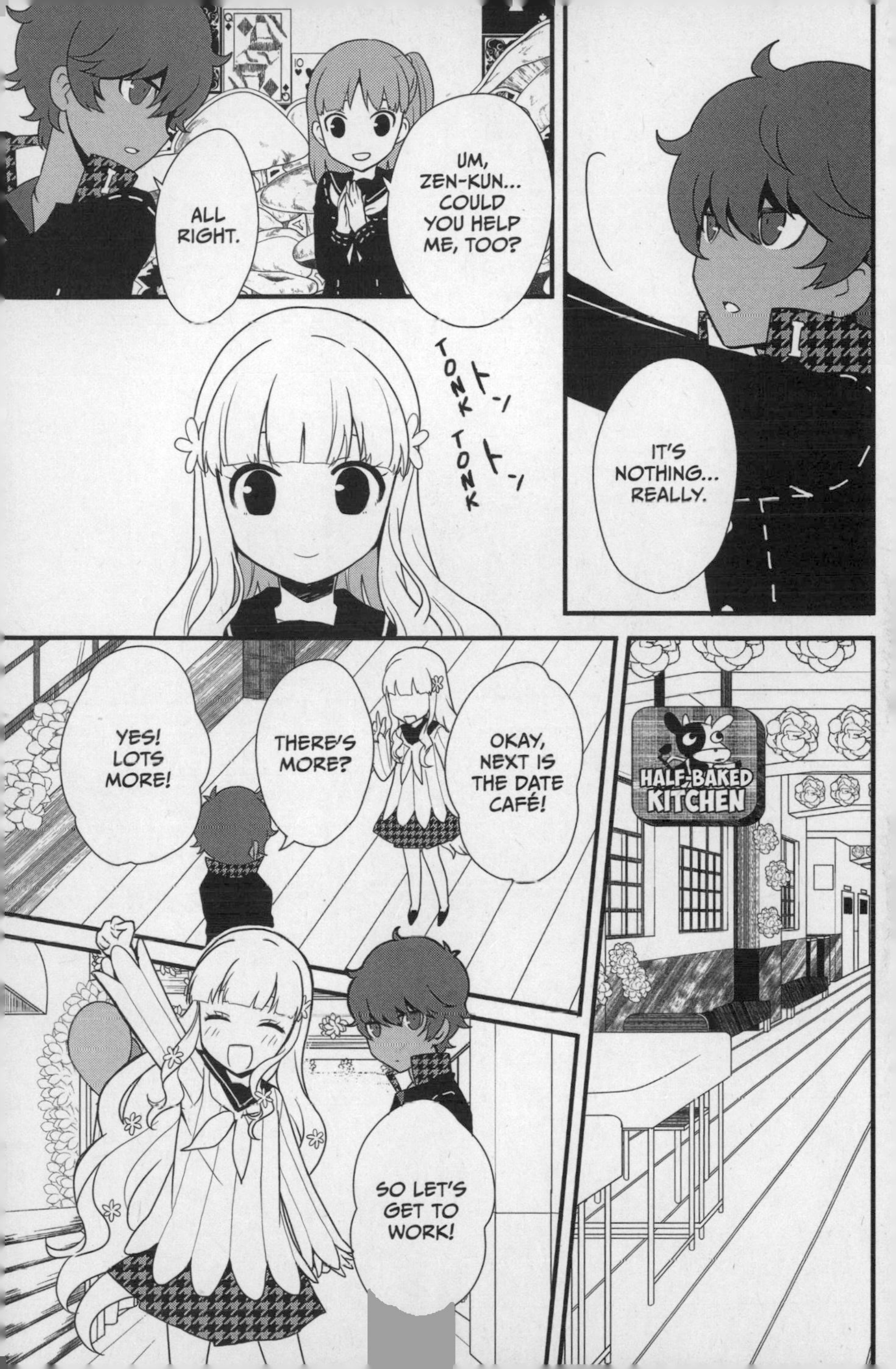
IT'S NOTHING... REALLY.
UM, ZEN-KUN... COULD YOU HELP ME, TOO?
ALL RIGHT.
TONK TONK
HALF-BAKED KITCHEN
OKAY, NEXT IS THE DATE CAFÉ!
THERE'S MORE?
YES! LOTS MORE!
SO LET'S GET TO WORK!

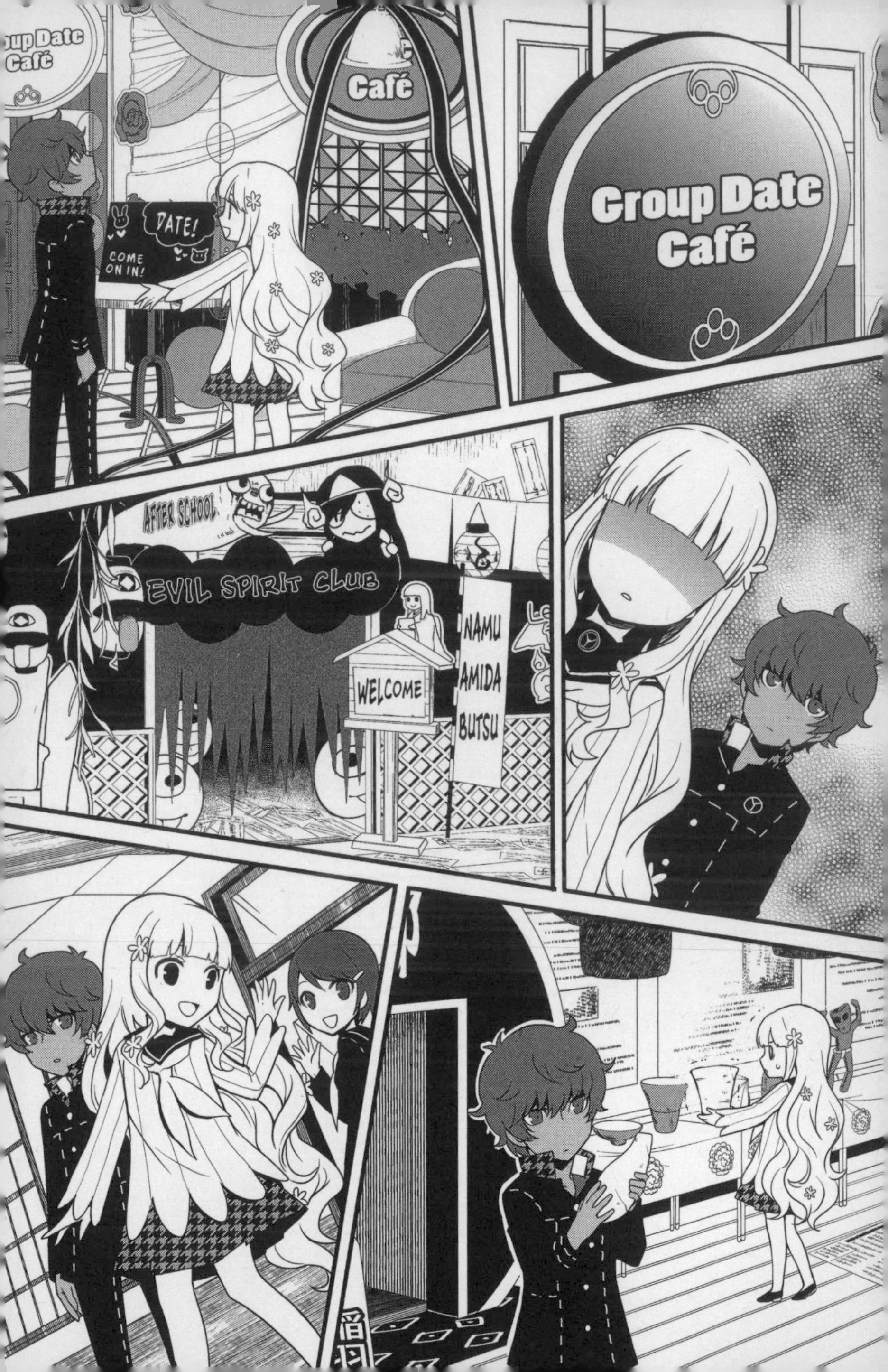
Group Date Café
Café
DATE!
COME ON IN!
AFTER SCHOOL
EVIL SPIRIT CLUB
NAMU AMIDA BUTSU
WELCOME

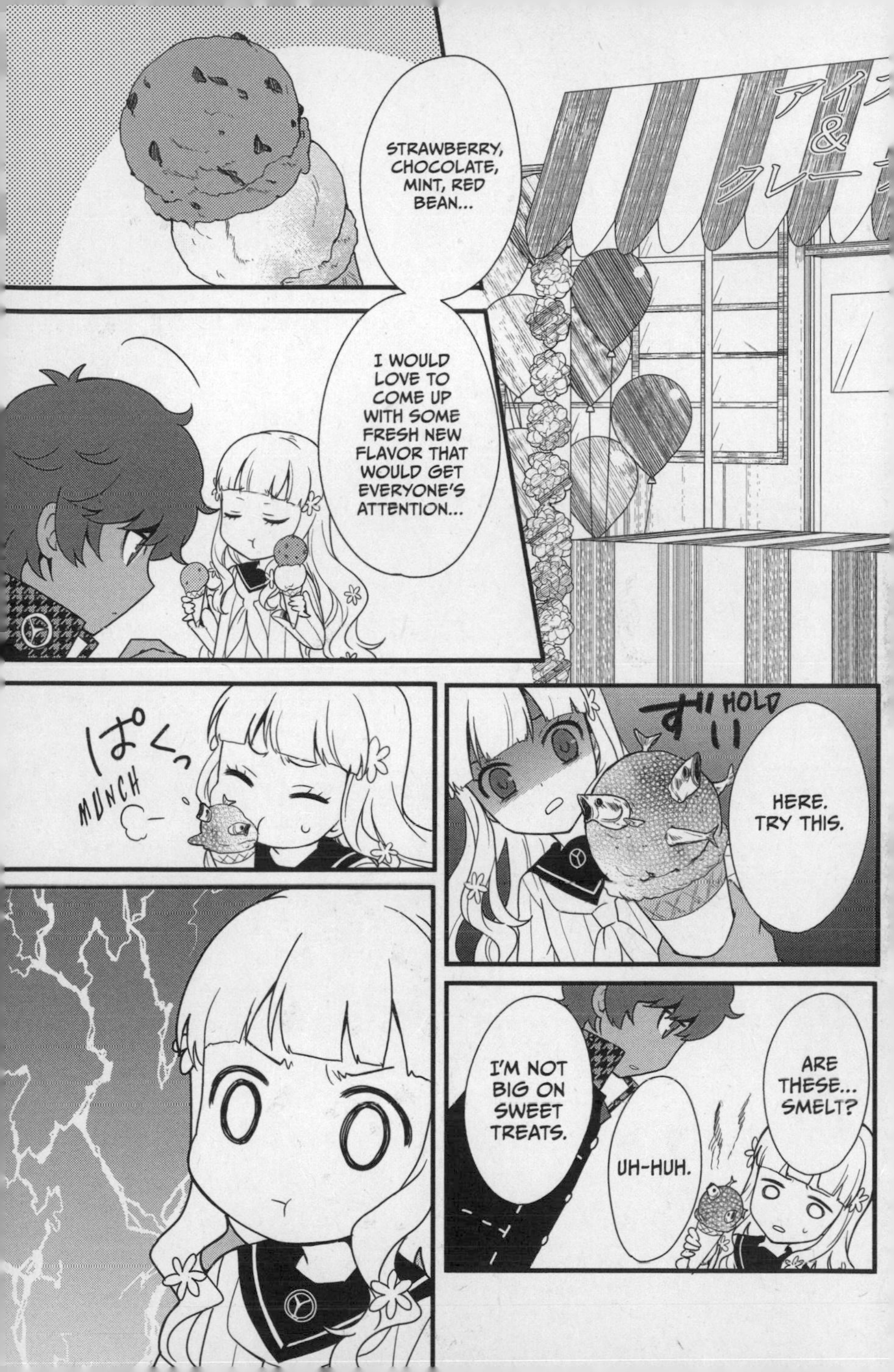
STRAWBERRY, CHOCOLATE, MINT, RED BEAN...
I WOULD LOVE TO COME UP WITH SOME FRESH NEW FLAVOR THAT WOULD GET EVERYONE'S ATTENTION...
すい HOLD
HERE. TRY THIS.
ARE THESE... SMELT?
UH-HUH.
I'M NOT BIG ON SWEET TREATS.
ぱくっ MUNCH

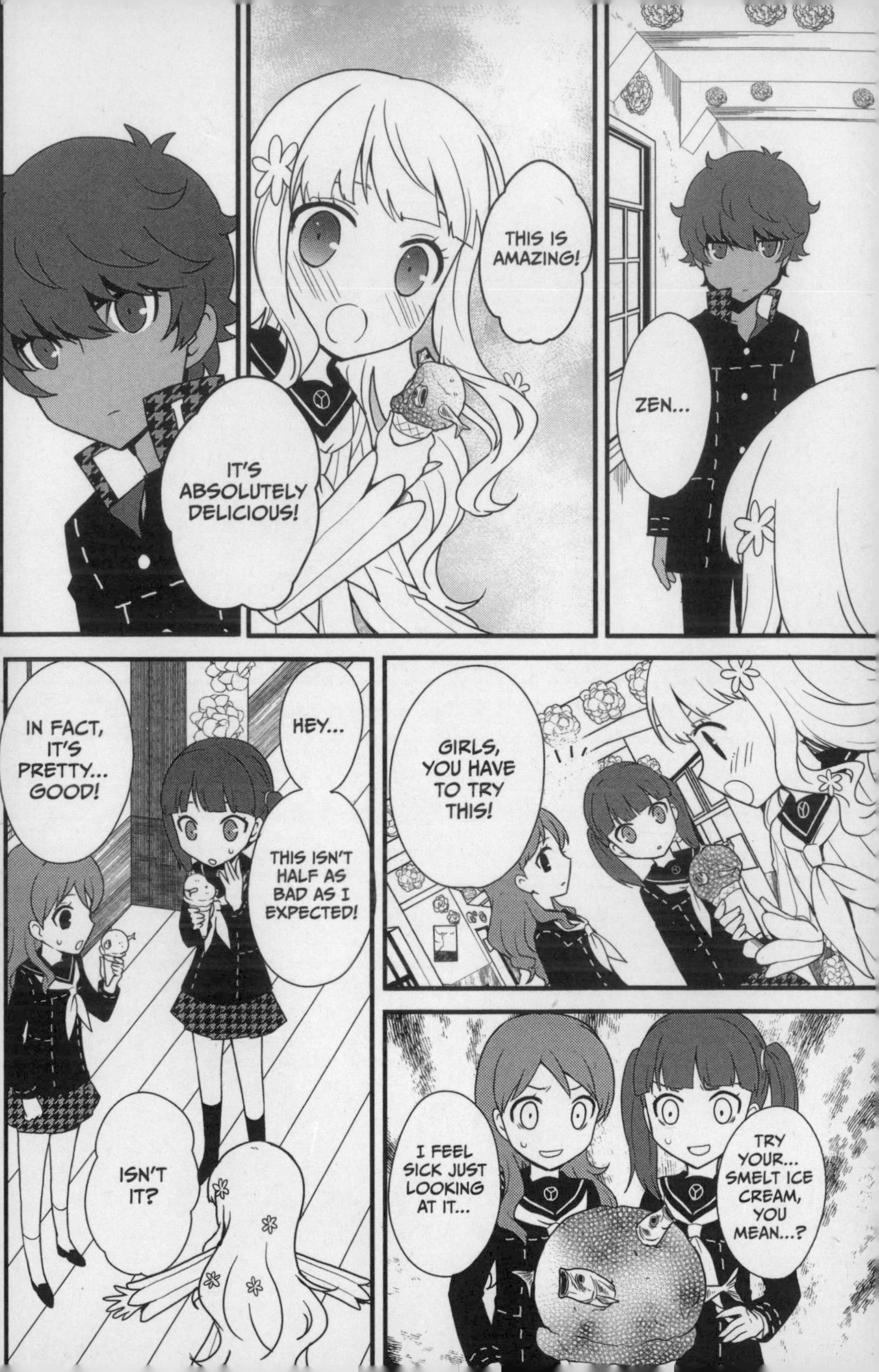
ZEN...
THIS IS AMAZING!
IT'S ABSOLUTELY DELICIOUS!
GIRLS, YOU HAVE TO TRY THIS!
TRY YOUR... SMELT ICE CREAM, YOU MEAN...?
I FEEL SICK JUST LOOKING AT IT...
HEY...
THIS ISN'T HALF AS BAD AS I EXPECTED!
IN FACT, IT'S PRETTY... GOOD!
ISN'T IT?

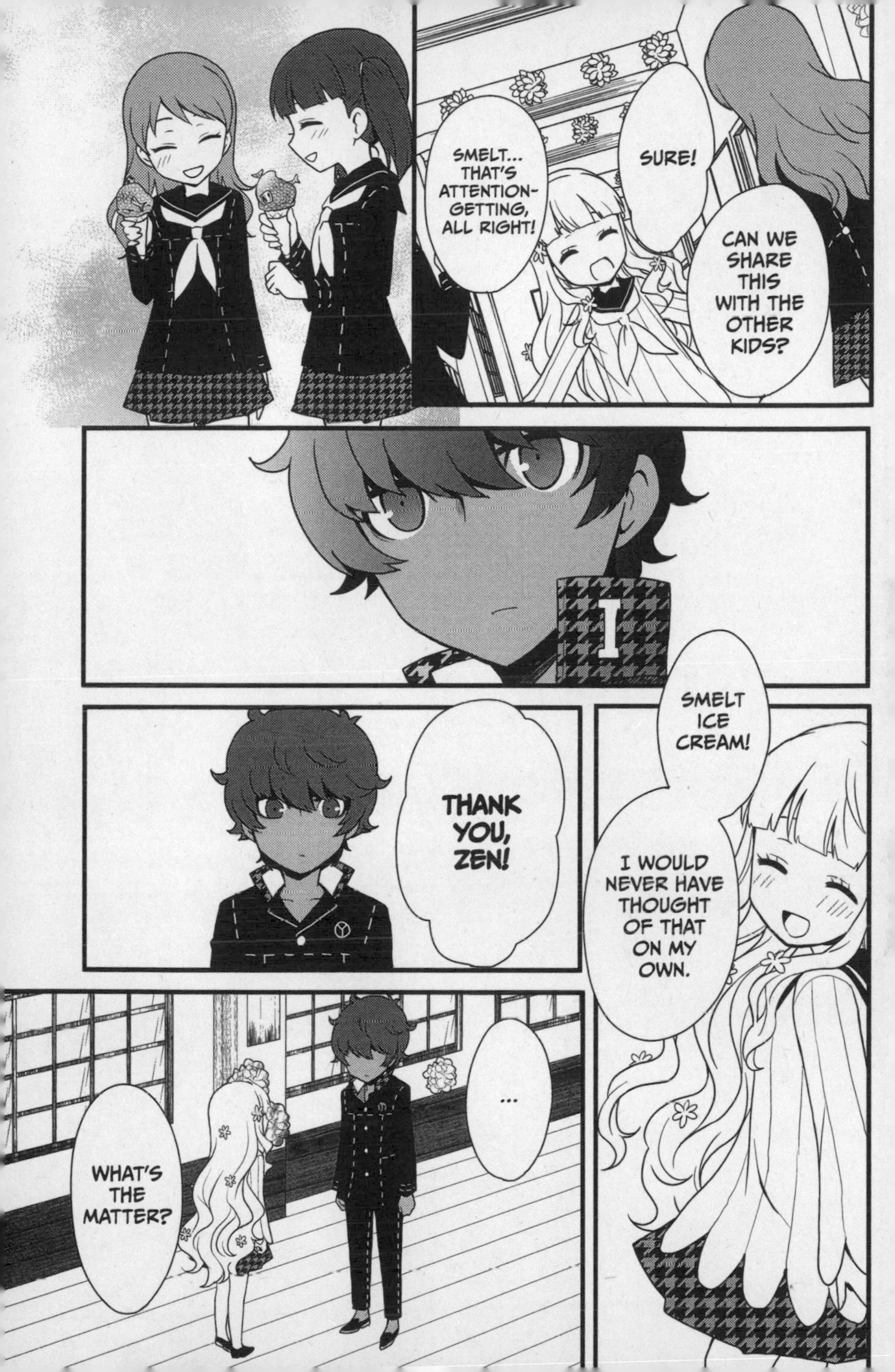
SURE!
SMELT... THAT'S ATTENTION-GETTING, ALL RIGHT!
CAN WE SHARE THIS WITH THE OTHER KIDS?
SMELT ICE CREAM!
I WOULD NEVER HAVE THOUGHT OF THAT ON MY OWN.
THANK YOU, ZEN!
...
WHAT'S THE MATTER?

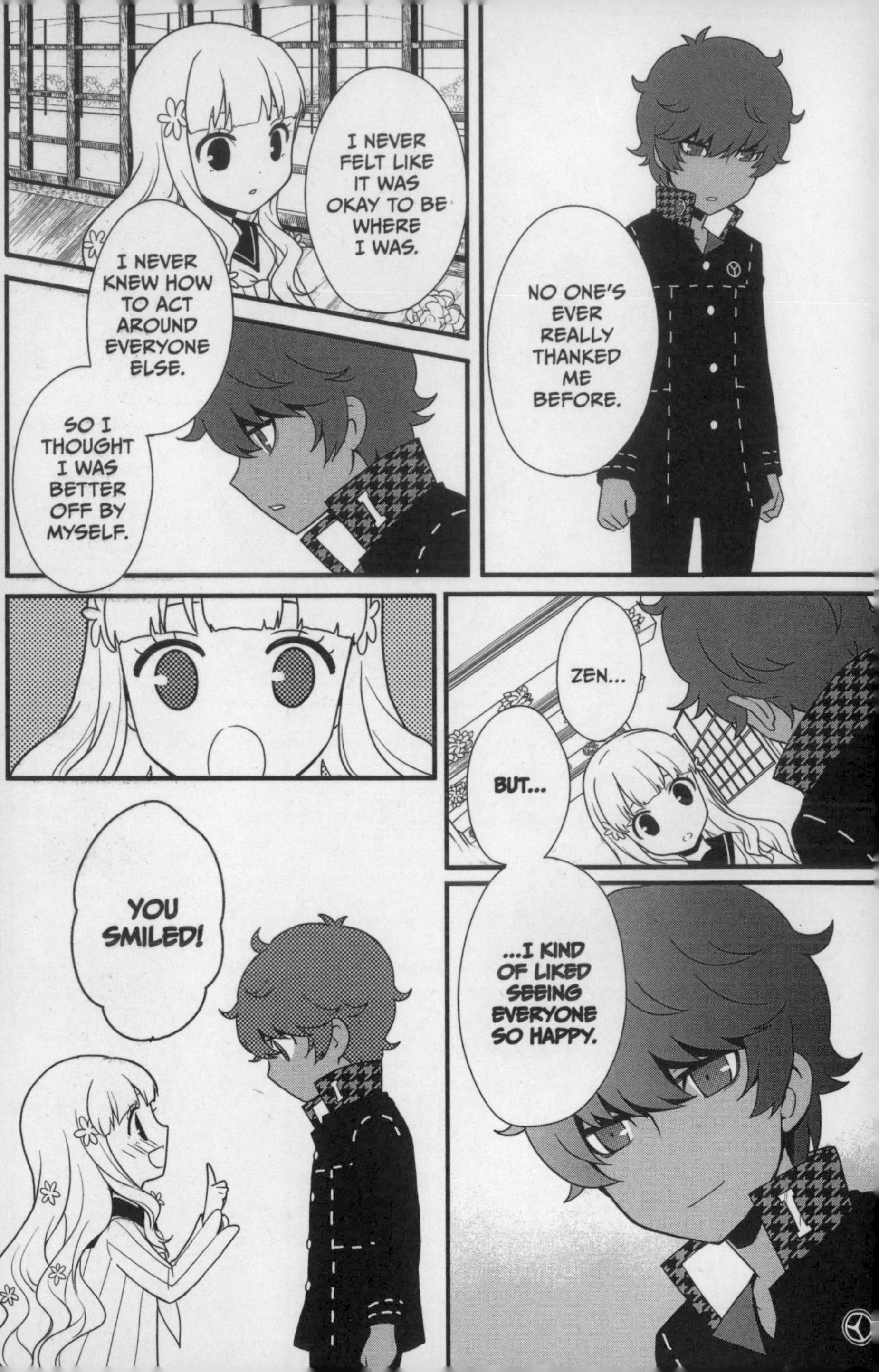

NO ONE'S EVER REALLY THANKED ME BEFORE.
I NEVER FELT LIKE IT WAS OKAY TO BE WHERE I WAS.
I NEVER KNEW HOW TO ACT AROUND EVERYONE ELSE.
SO I THOUGHT I WAS BETTER OFF BY MYSELF.
ZEN...
BUT...
...I KIND OF LIKED SEEING EVERYONE SO HAPPY.
YOU SMILED!

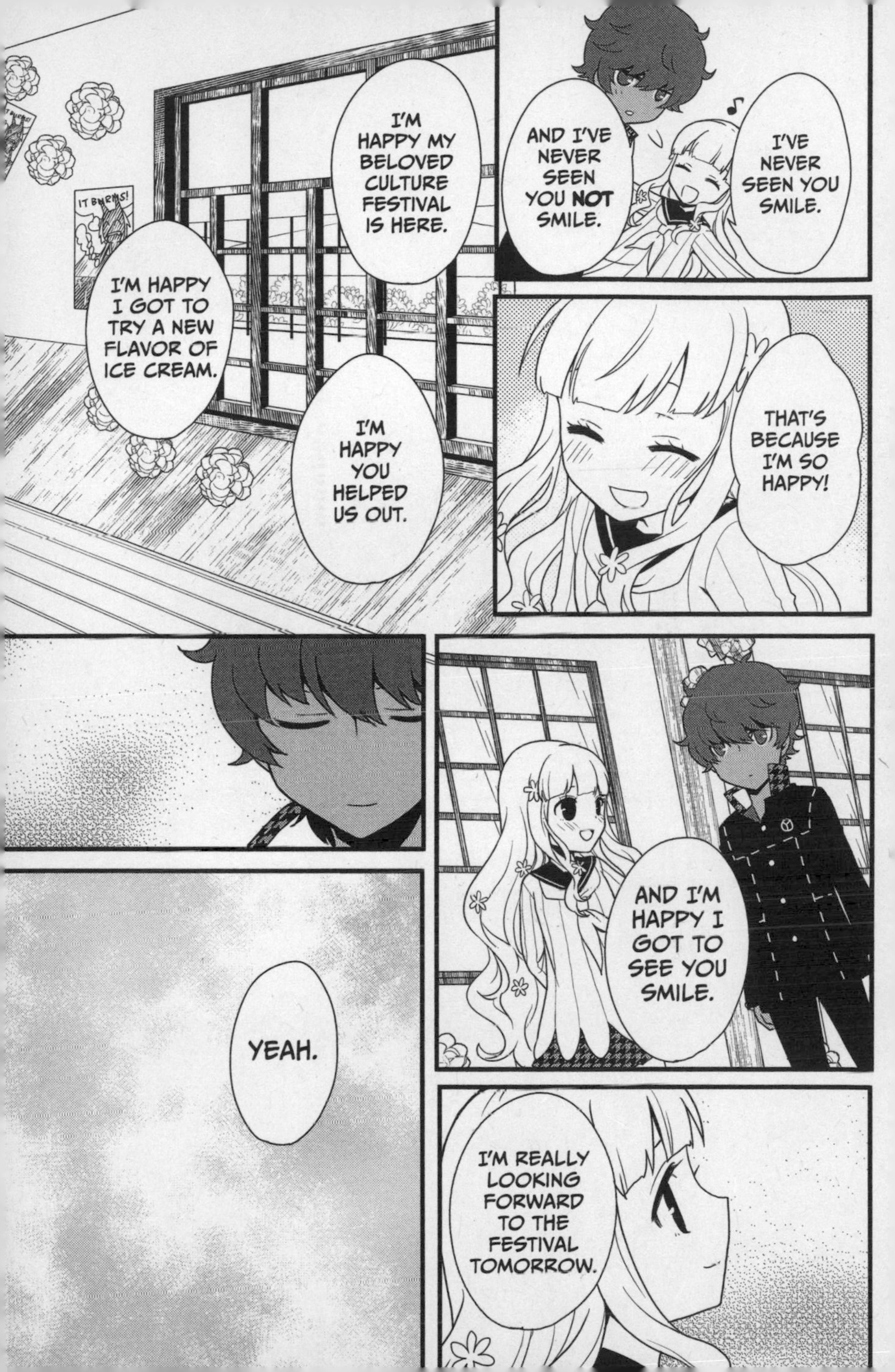
I'VE NEVER SEEN YOU SMILE.
AND I'VE NEVER SEEN YOU **NOT** SMILE.
THAT'S BECAUSE I'M SO HAPPY!
I'M HAPPY MY BELOVED CULTURE FESTIVAL IS HERE.
IT BURNS!
I'M HAPPY I GOT TO TRY A NEW FLAVOR OF ICE CREAM.
I'M HAPPY YOU HELPED US OUT.
AND I'M HAPPY I GOT TO SEE YOU SMILE.
I'M REALLY LOOKING FORWARD TO THE FESTIVAL TOMORROW.
YEAH.

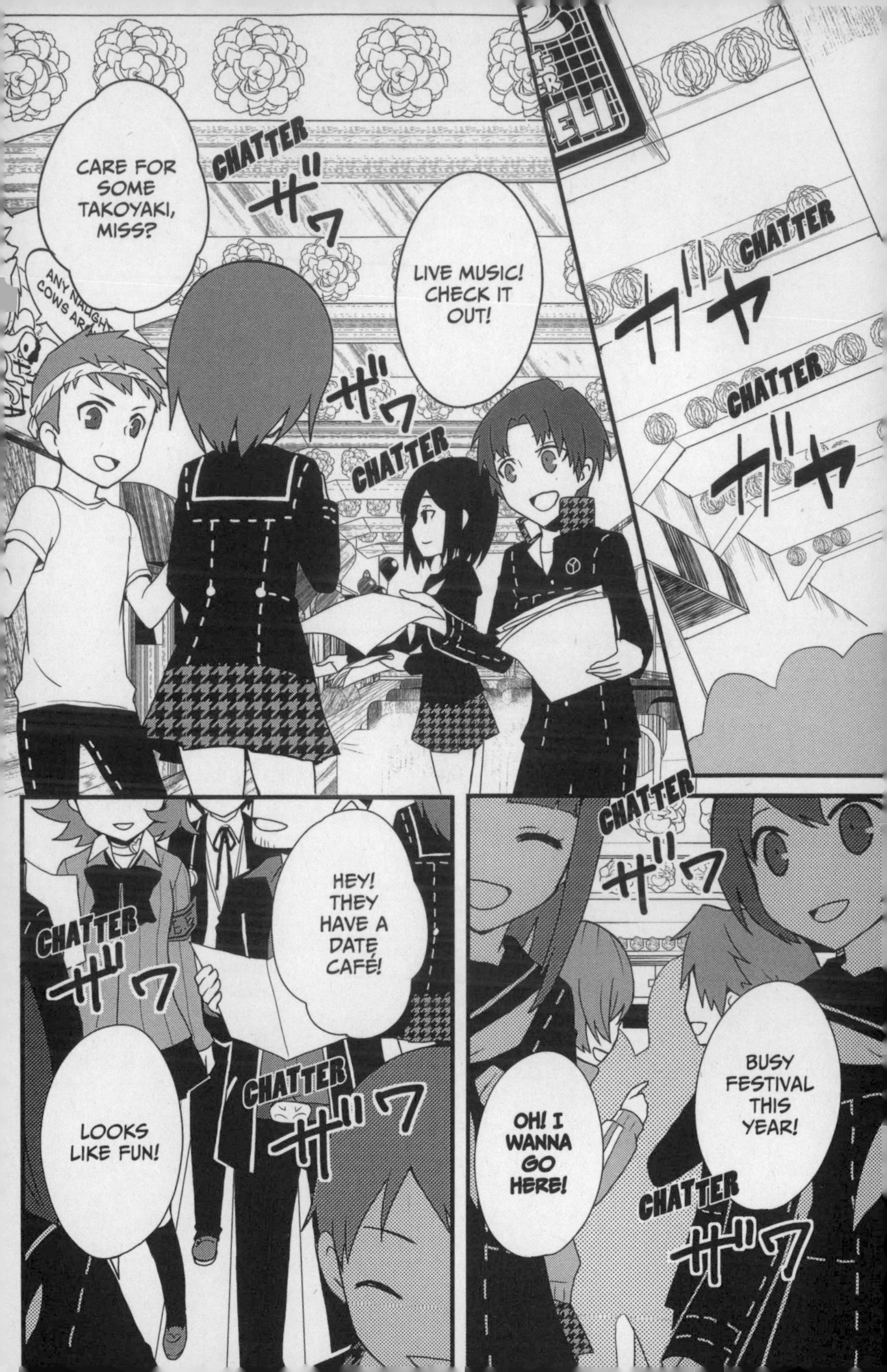
CHATTER
ガヤ
CHATTER
ガヤ
LIVE MUSIC! CHECK IT OUT!
CHATTER
ザワ
CARE FOR SOME TAKOYAKI, MISS?
ザワ
CHATTER
CHATTER
ザワ
BUSY FESTIVAL THIS YEAR!
OH! I WANNA GO HERE!
CHATTER
ザワ
HEY! THEY HAVE A DATE CAFÉ!
CHATTER
ザワ
CHATTER
ザワ
LOOKS LIKE FUN!

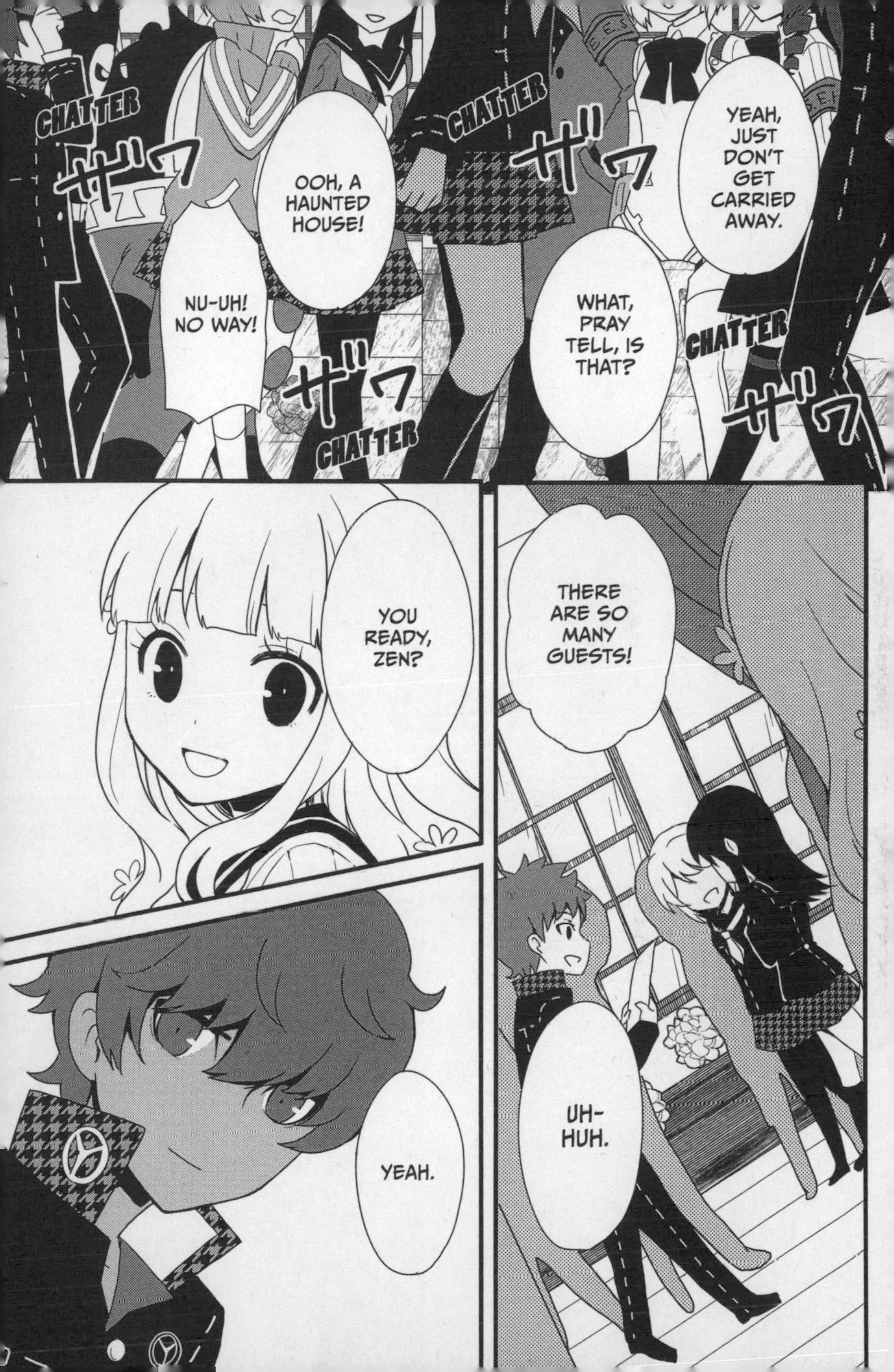
CHATTER
ザワ
YEAH, JUST DON'T GET CARRIED AWAY.
CHATTER
ザワ
WHAT, PRAY TELL, IS THAT?
CHATTER
ザワ
OOH, A HAUNTED HOUSE!
CHATTER
ザワ
NU-UH! NO WAY!
CHATTER
ザワ
THERE ARE SO MANY GUESTS!
UH-HUH.
YOU READY, ZEN?
YEAH.

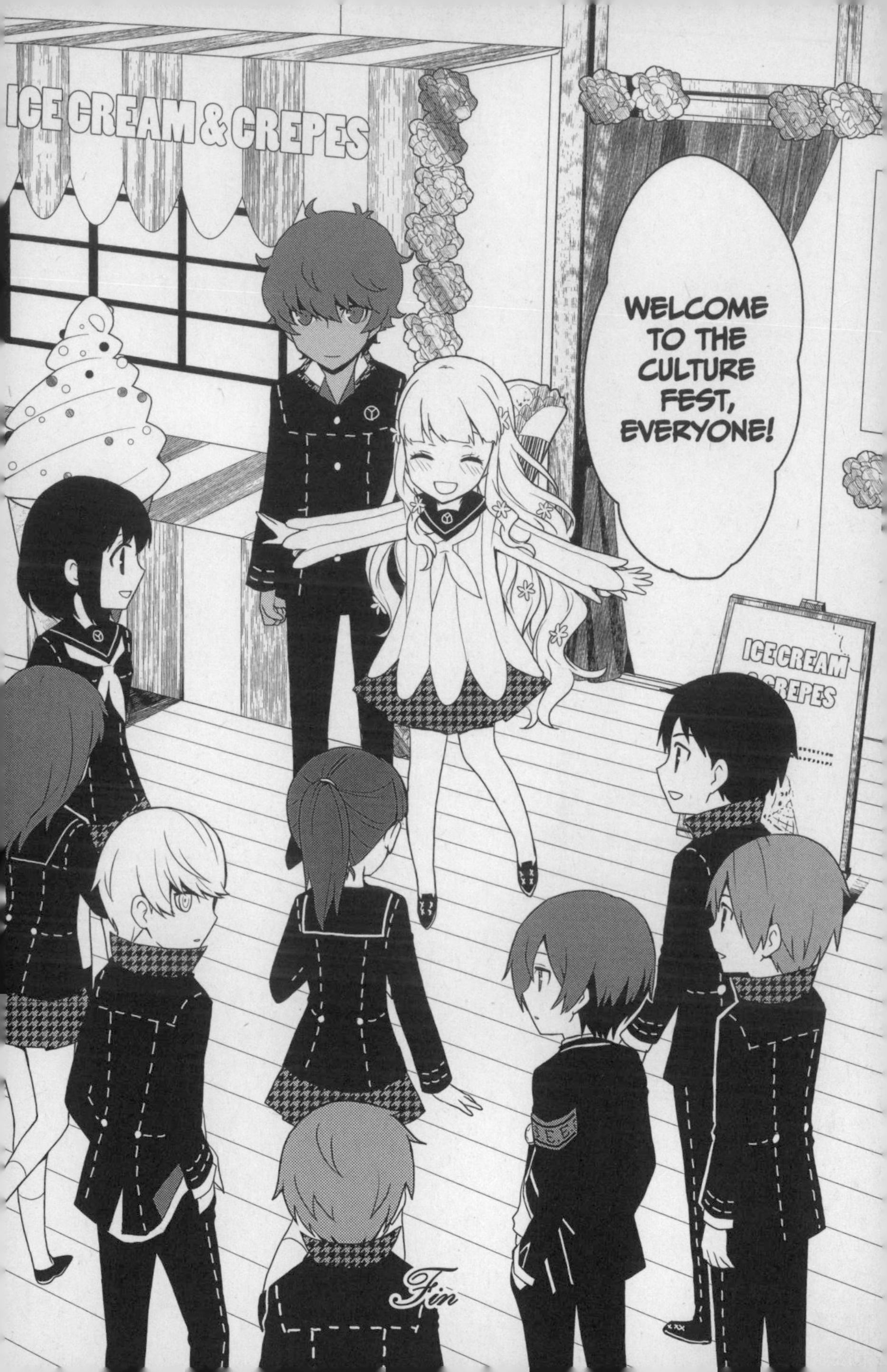
ICE CREAM & CREPES
WELCOME TO THE CULTURE FEST, EVERYONE!
ICE CREAM & CREPES
Fin

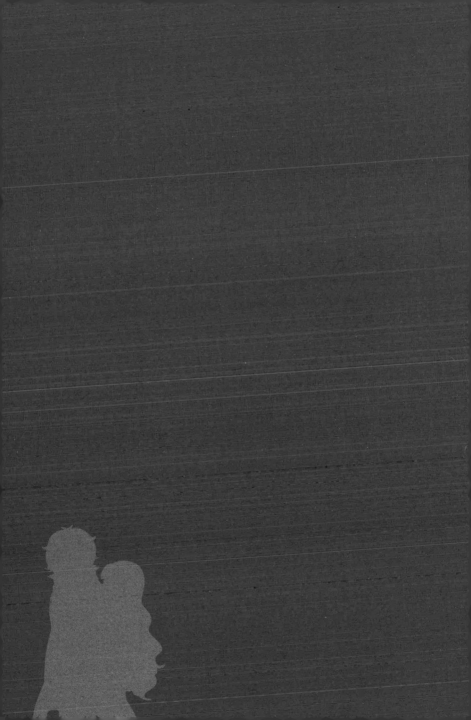

TRANSLATION NOTES

Niko, page 70

In Japanese, *niko niko* is a phrase that represents the "sound" of someone smiling, which is where the nurses' confusion may have come from. However, Niko's name is written 二子, which is the character for "two" or "second," followed by the character for "child." Names that indicate birth rank of the child have not been uncommon throughout Japanese history.

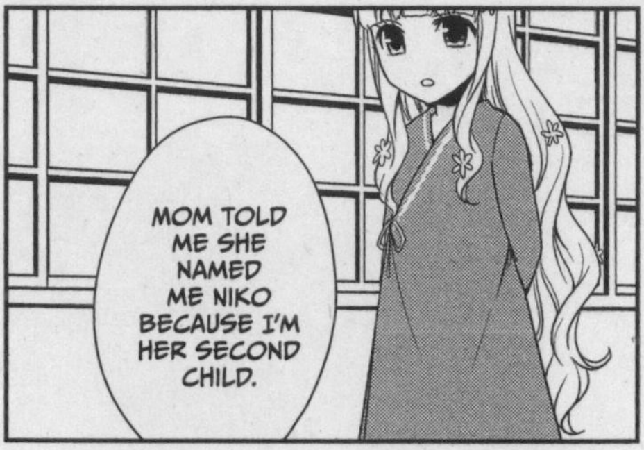
MOM TOLD ME SHE NAMED ME NIKO BECAUSE I'M HER SECOND CHILD.

Zen, page 78

Though Zen originally takes Greek names for himself (Zhn) and Rei (Philei), Rei mishears him and imagines Zen to be written with the Japanese character 善, meaning "good" or "right."

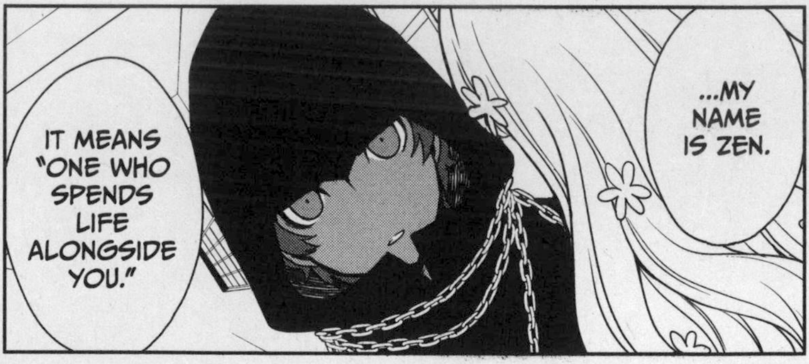
...MY NAME IS ZEN.
IT MEANS "ONE WHO SPENDS LIFE ALONGSIDE YOU."

ANIME COMING SUMMER 2018

The award-winning manga about what happens inside you!

"Far more entertaining than it ought to be... What kid doesn't want to think that every time they sneeze, a torpedo shoots out their nose?"

—Anime News Network

Strep throat! Hay fever! Influenza! The world is a dangerous place for a red blood cell just trying to get her deliveries finished. Fortunately, she's not alone. She's got a whole human body's worth of cells ready to help out! The mysterious white blood cell, the buff and brash killer T cell, the nerdy neuron, even the cute little platelets— everyone's got to come together if they want to keep you healthy!

Cells at Work!

By Akane Shimizu

ABOUT MITSUROU KUBO

Mitsurou Kubo is a manga artist born in Nagasaki prefecture. Her series *3.3.7 Byoshi!!* (2001-2003), *Tokkyu!!* (2004-2008), and *Again!!* (2011-2014) were published in *Weekly Shonen Magazine*, and *Moteki* (2008-2010) was published in the seinen comics magazine *Evening*. After the publication of *Again!!* concluded, she met Sayo Yamamoto, director of the global smash-hit anime ***Yuri!!! on ICE***. Working with Yamamoto, Kubo contributed the original concept, original character designs, and initial script for ***Yuri!!! on ICE***. *Again!!* is her first manga to be published in English.

A new series from the creator of *Soul Eater*, the megahit manga and anime seen on Toonami!

"Fun and lively... a great start!"
-Adventures in Poor Taste

FIRE FORCE

By **Atsushi Ohkubo**

The city of Tokyo is plagued by a deadly phenomenon: spontaneous human combustion! Luckily, a special team is there to quench the inferno: The Fire Force! The fire soldiers at Special Fire Cathedral 8 are about to get a unique addition. Enter Shinra, a boy who possesses the power to run at the speed of a rocket, leaving behind the famous "devil's footprints" (and destroying his shoes in the process). Can Shinra and his colleagues discover the source of this strange epidemic before the city burns to ashes?

From the creator of *The Ancient Magus' Bride*
comes a supernatural action manga in the
vein of *Fullmetal Alchemist*!

More than a century after an eccentric scholar made an infamous deal with a
devil, the story of Faust has passed into legend. However, the true Faust is not
the stuffy, professorial man known in fairy tales, but a charismatic, bespectacled
woman named Johanna Faust, who happens to still be alive. Searching for
pieces of her long-lost demon, Johanna passes through a provincial town, where
she saves a young boy named Marion from a criminal's fate. In exchange, she
asks a simple favor of Marion, but Marion soon finds himself intrigued by
the peculiar Doctor Faust and joins her on her journey. Thus begins the strange
and wonderful adventures of *Frau Faust*!

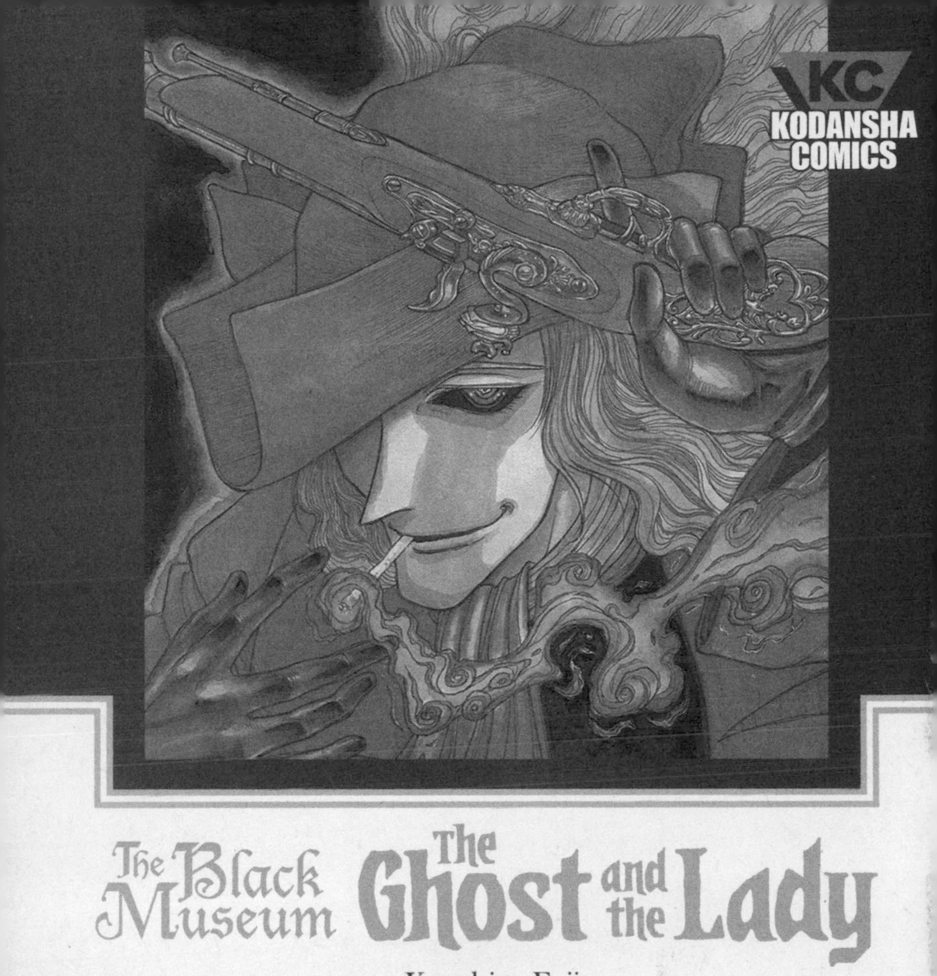

KODANSHA COMICS

The Black Museum: The Ghost and the Lady

By Kazuhiro Fujita

Deep in Scotland Yard in London sits an evidence room dedicated to the greatest mysteries of British history. In this "Black Museum" sits a misshapen hunk of lead—two bullets fused together—the key to a wartime encounter between Florence Nightingale, the mother of modern nursing, and a supernatural Man in Grey. This story is unknown to most scholars of history, but a special guest of the museum will tell the tale of *The Ghost and the Lady*...

Praise for Kazuhiro Fujita's *Ushio and Tora*

"A charming revival that combines a classic look with modern depth and pacing... **Essential viewing both for curmudgeons and new fans alike.**" — Anime News Network

"**GREAT!** The first episode of *Ushio and Tora* captures the essence of '90s anime." — IGN

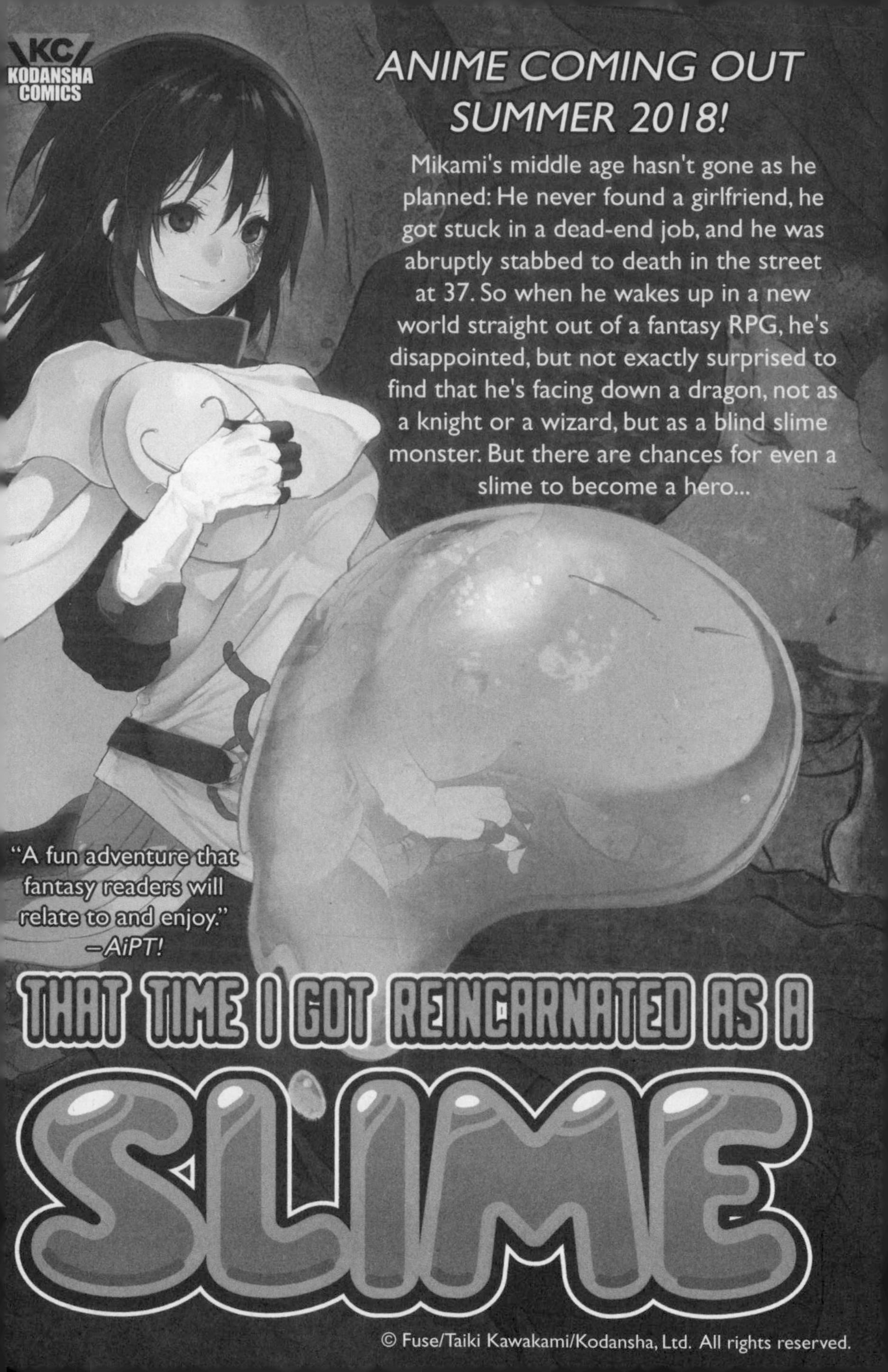
KC KODANSHA COMICS
ANIME COMING OUT SUMMER 2018!
Mikami's middle age hasn't gone as he planned: He never found a girlfriend, he got stuck in a dead-end job, and he was abruptly stabbed to death in the street at 37. So when he wakes up in a new world straight out of a fantasy RPG, he's disappointed, but not exactly surprised to find that he's facing down a dragon, not as a knight or a wizard, but as a blind slime monster. But there are chances for even a slime to become a hero...
"A fun adventure that fantasy readers will relate to and enjoy." —AiPT!
THAT TIME I GOT REINCARNATED AS A
SLIME
© Fuse/Taiki Kawakami/Kodansha, Ltd. All rights reserved.

"An emotional and artistic tour de force! We see incredible triumph, and crushing defeat... each panel [is] a thrill!"
—Anitay

"A journey that's instantly compelling."
—Anime News Network

WELCOME TO THE BALLROOM

By Tomo Takeuchi

Feckless high school student Tatara Fujita wants to be good at something—anything. Unfortunately, he's about as average as a slouchy teen can be. The local bullies know this, and make it a habit to hit him up for cash, but all that changes when the debonair Kaname Sengoku sends them packing. Sengoku's not the neighborhood watch, though. He's a professional ballroom dancer. And once Tatara Fujita gets pulled into the world of ballroom, his life will never be the same.

KC KODANSHA COMICS

KC KODANSHA COMICS

In love, there are no save points.

NOW AN ANIME!

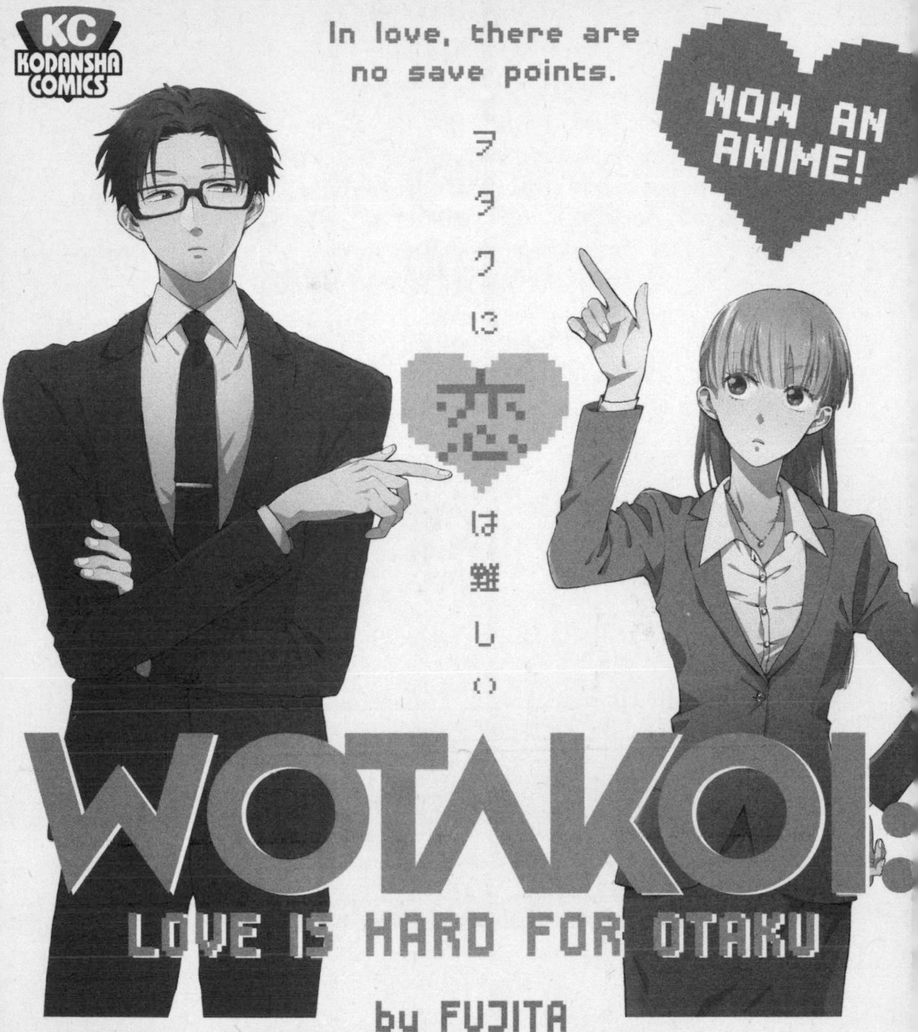
ヲタクに恋は難しい

WOTAKOI: LOVE IS HARD FOR OTAKU

by FUJITA

Narumi has had it rough: Every boyfriend she's had dumped her once they found out she was an otaku, so she's gone to great lengths to hide it. At her new job, she bumps into Hirotaka, her childhood friend and fellow otaku. When Hirotaka almost gets her secret outed at work, she comes up with a plan to keep him quiet. But he comes up with a counter-proposal: Why doesn't she just date him instead?

A Kodansha Comics Trade Paperback Original.

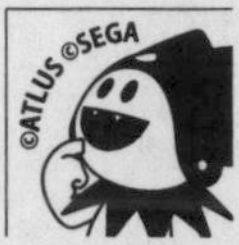
©ATLUS ©SEGA

Published in the United States by Kodansha Comics, an imprint of Kodansha USA Publishing, LLC, New York.

Publication rights for this English edition arranged through Kodansha Ltd., Tokyo.

First published in Japan in 2017 by Kodansha Ltd., Tokyo, as *Persona Q: Shadow of the Labyrinth, Side: P4* volume 4.

ISBN 978-1-63236-708-2

Printed in the United States of America.

www.kodanshacomics.com

9 8 7 6 5 4 3 2 1

Translation: Alethea Nibley & Athena Nibley
Lettering: James Dashiell
Editing: Lauren Scanlan
Kodansha Comics Edition Cover Design: Phil Balsman